THE CATHOLIC CHURCH IN MISSISSIPPI, 1837-65

JAMES J. PILLAR, O.M.I.

THE HAUSER PRESS
New Orleans, La.

Imprimi potest:

William P. Coovert, O.M.I.
Provincial

Nihil obstat:

Burchard Schneider, S.J.
Censor deputatus

Imprimatur:

Richard O. Gerow
Bishop of Natchez-Jackson
November 29, 1963

Library of Congress Catalog Card
No. 63-23197

To His Excellency

THE MOST REVEREND RICHARD O. GEROW, S.T.D.

Bishop of Natchez-Jackson

PREFACE

Purpose

This historical survey was undertaken for the purpose of presenting as complete a picture as possible of the Diocese of Natchez[1] from the time of its establishment until the end of the American Civil War. The first half of the work traces the efforts of the first three bishops to organize and stabilize the Diocese in the face of many obstacles and a number of reverses. The second half of the study follows the Church in Mississippi through the disruptive years of the Civil War, in other words, past its first major crisis. Although the survey is essentially an ecclesiastical history, a deliberate effort has been made to present secular events, both national and local, as they affected the interests of the Church in Mississippi. Attention has also been given to the general Catholic history of the United States, since a close-knit unity has characterized the Church in the United States, particularly evident in the reciprocal influences exercised by its leading personalities. Finally, the story has also been told in reference to other religious bodies, at least those in the state of Mississippi.

The present effort to portray the history of the Diocese of Natchez is not the first to have been made. Pioneer investigation of the available sources was made by the Most Reverend Richard O. Gerow, Bishop of Natchez-Jackson, and a few collaborators. The results of their labors appear in *Catholicity in Mississippi* (1939) and *Cradle Days of St. Mary's at Natchez* (1941). The first, for the most part, is a collection of sketches, written by the Bishop and various priests of the Diocese and appearing in the newspaper, *Catholic Action of the South,* on the occasion of the centennial of the Diocese in 1937. It is obvious from a number of inaccuracies and lacunae that the writers, working independently, did not always have the opportunity to correlate their findings. Furthermore, because of the need for brevity little effort was made to present the facts in the context of national history, whether ecclesiastical or secular. Because the book is fundamentally a collection of sketches, written by different men, it is somewhat difficult for the reader to form an over-all picture of the Diocese. Unfortunately, the collection of these articles in

[1] The see was re-designated in 1957, as the Diocese of Natchez-Jackson.

book-form has a number of printer's errors as well. The book's value, however, cannot be dismissed, for it is based on archival material in the diocesan chancery and, in many instances, the individual writers had opportunities for tracing and evaluating local traditions. The second work is a history of the Cathedral parish, but it also embraces many details on the extra-parochial activities of the first three bishops. The scientific value of the book is great, for the author, having personally organized and enriched the diocesan archives, utilized many hitherto unknown primary sources. Nevertheless, no comprehensive history of the Diocese has ever been written. The present writer has tried to fill this need up to a point. In doing so, he has made an effort not merely to rearrange facts already known, but also to uncover and present new information.

Sources

In producing this history, the writer has made use of archives in both Europe and the United States. The principal European archives consulted were those of the Sacred Congregation de Propaganda Fide in Rome. Here the series called *Scritture Riferite nei Congressi, America Centrale dal Canada all'Istmo di Panama,* Volumes XIII-XX, which are devoted to the years 1841-1865, was found to be the most useful collection. These volumes contained a few, but valuable, handwritten letters of the first three bishops of Natchez as well as other correspondence throwing light on the Diocese and its personnel. Except for a paragraph, these Roman documents have hitherto remained unpublished. Another European source was the archives of the Sisters of St. Joseph of Bourg, France. These yielded a number of unpublished letters on the Bay St. Louis foundation made by this community of Sisters. In Paris, the archives of the Eudist Fathers produced a number of original letters which removed some of the mystery connected with this community's short-lived foundation in Natchez. While the archives of L'Oeuvre de la Propagation de la foi in Lyon, France, were consulted, they yielded only two letters of limited value.

The American source which was most valuable for the writer was the expertly organized archives of the Diocese of Natchez-Jackson. Here are preserved authentic copies of many letters written by the first three bishops of the Diocese. Many original letters received by these bishops and their clergy are also on file. In addition, many miscellaneous documents, such as financial statements, parochial statistics, necrologies, etc., all dating back to the period covered by this history, are available. Second in importance for the writer were the archives of the University of Notre Dame where he was able to consult the Natchez Papers, the New Orleans Papers and the Cincinnati Papers. These contain many original letters received by ordinaries whose activities were associated with the Diocese of Natchez. Among the Kenrick and Spalding Papers in the archives of the Archdiocese of Baltimore a good number of Bishop Elder's letters were found. Especially valuable for producing an accurate account of Bishop Elder's dealings with the Federal military authorities during the War were letters found among the Brayman Papers in the archives of the Chicago Historical Society, in the archives of Georgetown University and in the archives of the Archdiocese of Cincinnati. For information on the activities of the Sisters of Mercy during the Civil War the writer found very helpful the local annals of this religious community and the unpublished memoirs of Sister M. Ignatius Sumner, both of which are preserved in the archives of the Sisters of Mercy in Vicksburg.

A number of private interviews with members of families long-resident in the state of Mississippi proved helpful in tracing local traditions. One published source was used extensively in this work. It is the Civil War diary of Bishop Elder. It provided an almost daily account of the Bishop's activities from October 20, 1862, until March 27, 1865. This document furnished much detail and also served as an aid in establishing the chronology of certain events.

Acknowledgements

In the process of producing a work of this nature the writer has incurred an enormous debt of gratitude. He thanks one and all for the encouragement, guidance and material assistance given him over the past three years. Without intending to slight anyone, he wishes, however, to single out a number of persons who merit a special word of thanks. To his former provincial superior, the Reverend Stanley C. Sergot, O.M.I., and his present provincial, the Very Reverend William Coovert, O.M.I., he is grateful for the opportunity to pursue university studies and to carry out this project. Very important has been the personal assistance given the writer in the field of research by the Most Reverend Richard O. Gerow, S.T.D., Bishop of Natchez-Jackson; the Reverend Thomas T. Mc-

Avoy, C.S.C., archivist at the University of Notre Dame; and Mr. David Lautermilch, student archivist at Mt. St. Mary's Seminary of the West, Norwood, Ohio. In obtaining photostats and authentic type-written copies of documents the writer is also grateful for the cooperation given him by the Reverend Joseph Gallagher of the Archdiocese of Baltimore; Mr. William C. Repetti, S.J., archivist at Georgetown University; Mother M. Alice, Provincial Secretary of the Sisters of St. Joseph of Bourg, New Orleans, La.; and Sister Grace Aurelia, archivist of the Sisters of St. Joseph of Carondelet, St. Louis, Mo. Of great assistance in transcribing manuscript and other material were the services of the Oblate Fathers and seminarians of Pine Hills Seminary, Pass Christian, Miss., and the chancery staff of the Diocese of Natchez-Jackson. To his Oblate confreres in Rome the writer is indebted for the help they gave him in preparing the final copy of his dissertation.

To the Dean and the Faculty of Ecclesiastical History of the Pontifical Gregorian University the writer is grateful for the historical training which he has received from them. For the directing of this project he is especially indebted to Father Ludwig Hertling, S.J., and Father Burchard Schneider, S.J., both of whom have engendered in the writer a great respect for their sound canons of scholarship and consummate patience. It was a pleasure and a privilege to have worked under them.

James J. Pillar, O.M.I.

Rome, Italy
July 6, 1962

TABLE OF CONTENTS

CONTENTS—Continued

LIST OF ABBREVIATIONS

AAB	=	Archives of the Archdiocese of Baltimore
AADC	=	Archives of the Archdiocese of Cincinnati
ACHS	=	Archives of the Chicago Historical Society
ADC	=	Archives of the Diocese of Charleston
ADNJ	=	Archives of the Diocese of Natchez-Jackson
AE	=	Archives of the Eudist Fathers (Paris)
APF	=	Archives of the Sacred Congregation de Propaganda Fide (Rome)
ASCC	=	Archives of the Sisters of Charity of Cincinnati
ASMV	=	Archives of the Sisters of Mercy, Vicksburg
ASSJB	=	Archives of the Sisters of St. Joseph of Bourg (France)
ASSJC	=	Archives of the Sisters of St. Joseph of Carondelet (St. Louis)
AUND	=	Archives of the University of Notre Dame
CHR	=	Catholic Historical Review
JMH	=	Journal of Mississippi History
ICHR	=	Illinois Catholic Historical Review
NAW	=	National Archives, Washington, D. C.
NCHR	=	North Carolina Historical Review
PMHS	=	Publications of the Mississippi Historical Society
RACHS	=	Records of the American Catholic Historical Society

INTRODUCTION

Mississippi is predominantly non-Catholic. In the popular mind it is a Protestant state with strong Protestant traditions. What is more, much of the progress that has been made in the State can be credited to non-Catholic leadership. These developments, however, should not obscure the fact that Mississippi has also many Catholic traditions. Indeed, they represent the State's oldest uninterrupted heritage.

In all probability the Dominican chaplains of De Soto's expedition were the first Catholic missionaries to enter what is now the state of Mississippi. This occurred some time in 1540. While traversing the State, the missionaries made every effort to convert the natives with whom they came in contact. They succeeded in baptizing only a few, most of them children. After the death of De Soto and the failure of the expedition, however, these chaplains most probably did not remain with their converts. More than likely they accompanied the remainder of the expedition into Mexico.[1]

In 1682, La Salle took formal possession of the Mississippi Valley for France. As a result, this immense territory which embraced the present state of Mississippi fell within the spiritual jurisdiction of the Bishop of Quebec, John Baptist Saint Vallier. Except for a short-lived arrangement,[2] the ecclesiastical government of this area remained in the hands of the Bishop of Quebec and his successors until 1763. He exercised control over the missions in this area by the appointment of vicars-general. In providing for the spiritual welfare of this territory the Bishop was assisted in the beginning by the priests of the Seminary of Foreign Missions in Quebec. The first resident priest in Mississippi was one of these missionaries, Father Anthony Davion. He labored among the Tonicas Indians on the Yazoo River.[3]

---

[1] Claiborne, *Mississippi as a Province, Territory and State with Biographical Notices of Eminent Citizens*, (Jackson, 1880), 1-11. Baudier, *The Catholic Church in Louisiana* (New Orleans, 1939), 14.

[2] A prefecture was erected for "Louisiana in America" and confided to the French Recollects in 1685. Opposed by Saint Vallier, it was quickly suppressed by the Holy See.

[3] Shea, *History of the Catholic Missions Among the Indian Tribes of the United States* 1529-1854 (New York, 1885), 440.

For a very short time at the beginning of the 18th century three Jesuit Fathers did missionary work in what is now the state of Mississippi. They were Fathers Paul Du Ru, Joseph de Limoges and Peter Dongé. These priests labored among the Pascagoulas, Chicasaws, Pensacolas and Biloxis—Indian tribes along the Gulf Coast. However, in 1703, they were recalled to France by their provincial when Bishop Saint Vallier objected to a permanent division of Louisiana between the Jesuits and his seminary priests.[4]

To secure her rights to the vast territory called the Province of Louisiana, France established a number of posts in the area. The earliest of these settlements was Biloxi, founded in 1698. Another one in the present state of Mississippi was established in 1714, on the bluffs of Natchez and called Fort Rosalie. Both places were provided with the services of a priest.[5] With the organization of development companies, other settlements were made in what is today Mississippi—in the Tunica area, on Pascagoula Bay, on Bay St. Louis and in the Yazoo Valley. As stipulated by contract, every effort was made to provide these "concessions," as they were called, with a Catholic chaplain and a church building.[6] For all practical purposes, we may consider these Catholic settlements.

To help them meet their obligation to provide for the spiritual welfare of the settlers, the companies secured the services of the Discalced Carmelites (1720), the Capuchins (1722) and later the Jesuits (1725).[7] Unfortunately the Carmelites withdrew from the scene in 1723. As a result, the territory of Mississippi was entrusted to the Jesuits and the Capuchins with the consent of the Bishop of Quebec. While the Jesuits devoted themselves to the Indian missions, the friars concentrated on serving the settlements of the French along the Mississippi River and the Gulf Coast.

The Capuchins supplied a priest for the Natchez post until 1729, the time of the Indian massacre in that area. After this tragic event Natchez was practically abandoned and nothing is heard of a priest in that district until 1783.[8] Of the activities of

---

[4] Baudier, *op. cit.*, 25-32.

[5] *Ibid.*, 24, 25.

[6] *Ibid.*, 44-50.

[7] *Ibid.*, 51, 64.

[8] (Janssens), *Sketch of the Catholic Church in the City of Natchez, Mississippi, on the Occasion of the Consecration of its Cathedral, September 19, 1886* (Natchez, 1886), 9, 10.

the friars on the Gulf Coast almost nothing is known. An account of the mission, drawn up in 1723, speaks of a Father Dorez as pastor of Biloxi. He is the last mentioned resident priest of that area until the founding of the diocese.[9]

During the intervening years the Catholics of the Gulf Coast depended for spiritual administrations on the occasional visits of missionaries from New Orleans and Mobile.

As for the Jesuits, they continued to work among the Indians of Mississippi off and on until 1770. The fruits of their labors were negligible, stymied often enough by political vicissitudes. One of their men, Father Souel, was murdered by the Indians. These missions represent the last effort on the part of the Catholic Church to convert the Indians in Mississippi until after the establishment of the Diocese of Natchez.[10]

In 1763, Great Britain took possession of the greater part of Mississippi. Under British rule most of the new settlers were non-Catholics. In keeping with the conditions of the Treaty of Paris those Catholics who remained in Mississippi were left unmolested in the practice of their religion. There exists no record of Catholic activity during this period.

In 1779, Spain declared war on England while the latter was preoccupied with the American Revolution. Galvez, the Spanish Governor of Louisiana, captured the British fort at Natchez. Shortly afterward, the forts on the Gulf Coast also fell into Spanish hands. Thus ended British rule in Mississippi. Strong Spanish garrisons were stationed at Natchez and Nogales, the site of present-day Vicksburg.

To provide for the needs of the Catholics in the Natchez district and with the hope of converting the English-speaking Protestants of the area, the Spanish authorities obtained the services of four Irish priests who had been trained in Spain. They were Fathers William Savage, Gregory White, Constantine McKenna and Francis Lennan, O.M.Cap. Two parishes were established in the Natchez district—one in Natchez itself and another at Cole's Creek, about

---

[9] Mereness, *The Journal of Divon d'Artaguette 1722-1723 in Travels in the American Colonies* (London, 1916), 17.

[10] Shea, *op. cit.*, 450, 651. Delanglez, *The French Jesuits in Lower Louisiana 1700-1763* (Washington, 1935), 476, 477.

eighteen miles away. A church was built at each place. One of the priests, Father Lennan, was assigned to Nogales (Vicksburg), but there is no proof that a church was ever built there.[11]

The spiritual supervision of the territory of Mississippi underwent many vicissitudes during the Spanish regime. At first Mississippi came under the jurisdiction of the Bishop of Santiago, Cuba. In 1787, when this diocese was split, the spiritual authority over Mississippi's Catholics passed to the Bishop of Havana.[12] These bishops exercised their authority over the mainland by means of vicars, but the arrangement was far from satisfactory. As a consequence, the Diocese of Louisiana which also embraced the greater part of Mississippi was established in 1793.[13] Between April and June of 1796, the new bishop, Luis Peñalver y Cárdenas, visited the Natchez area. Most probably this was the first time that a Catholic bishop had ever set foot within the limits of the present state of Mississippi.[14] Bishop Peñalver's spiritual authority over Mississippi, however, was short-lived. By the secret Treaty of San Lorenzo (1795) Spain ceded to the United States all of Mississippi north of the 31° N. latitude.[15] In 1810, Spain relinquished her claim south to the Gulf of Mexico. Thus came to an end Spanish authority, political and spiritual, over Mississippi.

In 1798, with the withdrawal of the Spanish from Natchez and Nogales, Bishop John Carroll of Baltimore became the Ordinary of the greater part of Mississippi.[16] However, in 1815, when Bishop William Du Bourg, S.S., was appointed Bishop of Louisiana and the two Floridas, Carroll confided the jurisdiction of Mississippi to him as his vicar.[17] This situation remained unchanged until 1822. At this time, in an attempt to ease the spiritual burdens of

---

11 Curley, *Church and State in the Spanish Floridas 1783-1822* (Washington, 1940), 93-97, 244. Baudier, *op. cit.*, 206-207.

12 Baudier, *op. cit.*, 204.

13 *Ibid.*, 223.

14 Curley, *op. cit.*, 262-264.

15 This treaty was not ratified by the United States Senate until 1796, and it was not until March 30, 1798, that the Spanish withdrew. For a time after the Territory fell within the jurisdiction of Bishop Carroll, Bishop Penalver kindly volunteered to look after the spiritual interests of the Catholics at Natchez. Curley, *op. cit.*, 320.

16 Antonelli to Carroll, Rome, Jan. 29, 1791, in Shearer, *Pontificia Americana: Documentary History of the Catholic Church in the United States 1784-1884*, (Washington, 1933), 91.

17 Shearer, *op. cit.*, 125.

the Archbishop of Baltimore, the Holy See erected the two states of Alabama and Mississippi into an independent ecclesiastical unit called a vicariate apostolic.[18] This arrangement, however, did not succeed. Father Joseph Rosati, C.M., who had been chosen to head the new vicariate, refused the appointment.[19] And although Archbishop Ambrose Maréchal of Baltimore was more than eager to be relieved of his responsibility for Mississippi's Catholics, he pointed out to the Holy See that the Vicariate could not support a bishop. Of the same opinion was Bishop Du Bourg. As a result, the Vicariate was suppressed.[20] With this action Mississippi was again made subject to the Archbishop of Baltimore, who again requested Bishop Du Bourg to act as his vicar-general in that area.

Finally, in 1825, Propaganda took a definite stand in the matter of the districts east of the Mississippi and bordering on the Gulf Coast. It erected two vicariates apostolic. Alabama and Florida were joined to form one jurisdiction while Mississippi was established as the other. Du Bourg was designated as Vicar Apostolic for the latter.[21] When the Diocese of Louisiana was divided in 1826, and the Dioceses of New Orleans and St. Louis created, the Vicariate of Mississippi became the charge of the Bishop of New Orleans.[22] This arrangement for Mississippi continued until the erection of the Diocese of Natchez in 1837.

From the time that Mississippi became a part of the United States, Catholic activity declined considerably. The bishops responsible for the area found it extremely difficult to furnish priests. Whenever a priest did appear, seldom could the Catholics in the area support him. On the other hand, Protestant churches with resident pastors were multiplying rapidly. In Natchez alone, in 1820, there were two or three Presbyterian ministers and as many Methodists, while in the whole State there was only one resident Catholic priest.[23] Frequent appeals by Mississippi's Catholics to Baltimore or to New Orleans met with little or no success. Because

---

18 Pius VII to Rosati, Rome, Aug. 13, 1822, in Shearer, *op. cit.,* 125-127.

19 Easterly, *The Life of the Rt. Rev. Joseph Rosati, First Bishop of St. Louis, 1789-1843* (Washington, 1942), 64-69.

20 Pius VII to Rosati, Rome, July 14, 1823, in Shearer, *op. cit.,* 136-137.

21 Leo XII to Du Bourg, Rome, Aug. 19, 1825, in Shearer, *op. cit.,* 143-144.

22 Brief of Leo XII, July 18, 1826, in Shearer, *op. cit.,* 145-146.

23 Blanc to (?), Natchez, c. 1820, in the *Records of the American Catholic Historical Society,* XIV (1903), 212.

of this lack of opportunity for practicing their religion many of the original Catholic settlers left Mississippi.[24] Many others who remained behind became indifferent or lukewarm in the practice of their faith. Children grew up without any religious instruction. Marriages went unblessed. People died without the consoling Last Rites of the Church. In 1823, the Catholic congregation at Natchez numbered only about thirty families while Bay St. Louis, one of the typical settlements along the Gulf Coast, had only about twenty Catholic families.[25] The wonder of it all is that there were any Catholics, worthy of the name, left in the State when the Diocese of Natchez was finally established.

---

[24] Shea, *Life and Times of Archbishop John Carroll* (New York, 1888), 505.

[25] Rosati to Consalvi, April 2, 1823, in *St. Louis Catholic Historical Review,* III (1921), n. 313.

ILLUSTRATIONS

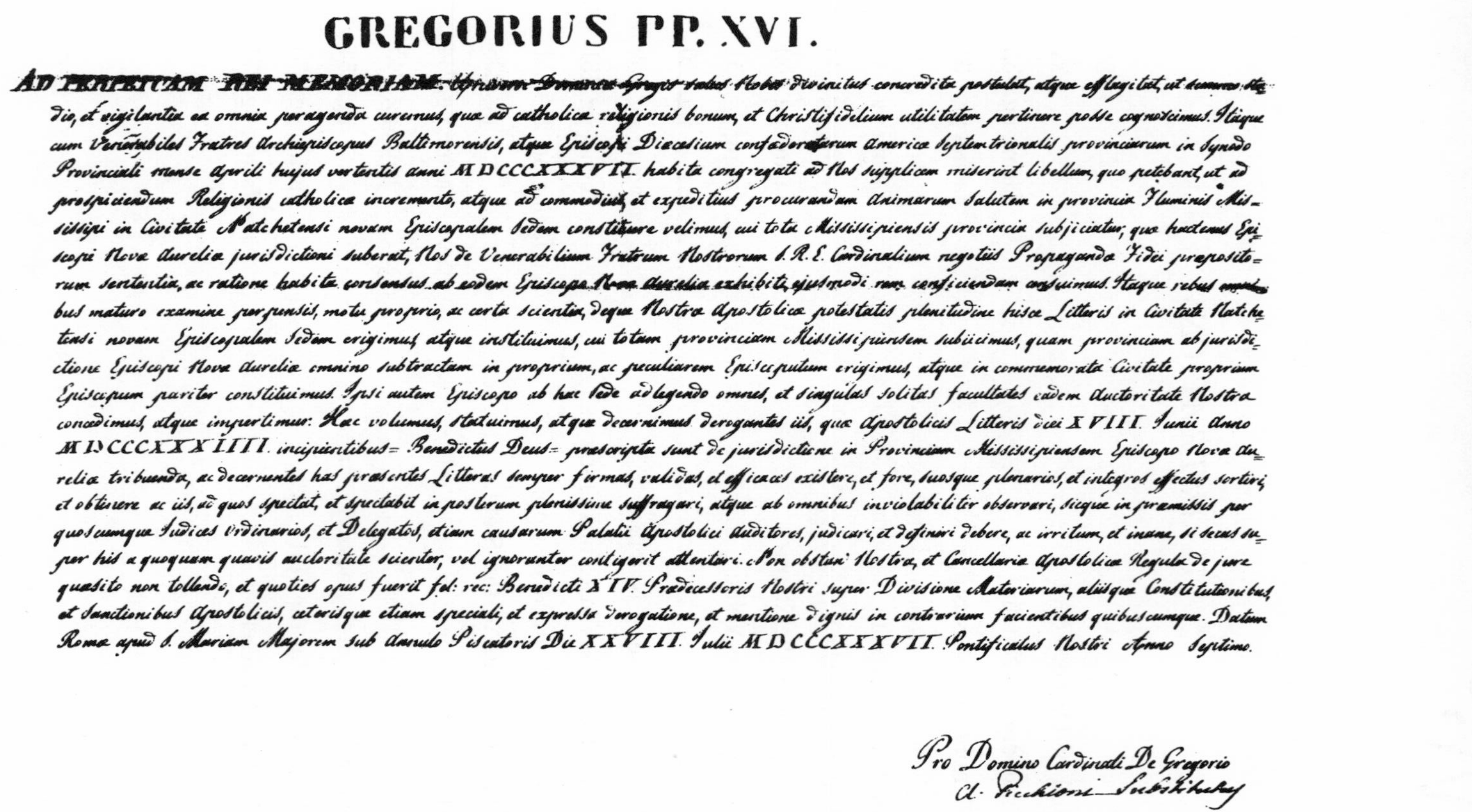

GREGORIUS PP. XVI.

AD PERPETUAM REI MEMORIAM. Supremi Dominici gregis cura Nobis divinitus concredita postulat, atque efflagitat, ut summo studio, et vigilantia ea omnia peragenda curemus, quæ ad catholicæ religionis bonum, et Christifidelium utilitatem pertinere posse cognoscimus. Itaque cum Venerabiles Fratres Archiepiscopus Baltimorensis, atque Episcopi Diœcesium confœderatarum Americæ Septemtrionalis provinciarum in Synodo Provinciali mense Aprili hujus vertentis anni MDCCCXXXVII. habita congregati ad Nos supplicem miserint libellum, quo petebant, ut ad prospiciendum Religionis catholicæ incremento, atque ad commodius, et expeditius procurandam Animarum salutem in provincia Fluminis Missisippi in Civitate Natchetensi novam Episcopalem Sedem constituere velimus, cui tota Missisipiensis provincia subjiciatur, quæ hactenus Episcopi Novæ Aureliæ jurisdictioni suberat, Nos de Venerabilium Fratrum Nostrorum S.R.E. Cardinalium negotiis Propagandæ Fidei præpositorum sententia, ac ratione habita consensus ab eodem Episcopo Novæ Aureliæ exhibiti, ejusmodi rem conficiendam censuimus. Itaque rebus omnibus maturo examine perpensis, motu proprio, ac certa scientia, deque Nostræ Apostolicæ potestatis plenitudine hisce Litteris in Civitate Natchetensi novam Episcopalem Sedem erigimus, atque instituimus, cui totam provinciam Missisipiensem subjicimus, quam provinciam ab jurisdictione Episcopi Novæ Aureliæ omnino subtractam in proprium, ac peculiarem Episcopatum erigimus, atque in commemorata Civitate proprium Episcopum pariter constituimus. Ipsi autem Episcopo ab hac Sede adlegendo omnes, et singulas solitas facultates eadem Auctoritate Nostra concedimus, atque impertimur. Hæc volumus, statuimus, atque decernimus derogantes iis, quæ Apostolicis Litteris diei XVIII. Junii Anno MDCCCXXXXIIII. incipientibus= Benedictus Deus= præscripta sunt de jurisdictione in Provinciam Missisipiensem Episcopo Novæ Aureliæ tribuenda, ac decernentes has præsentes Litteras semper firmas, validas, et efficaces existere, et fore, suosque plenarios, et integros effectus sortiri, et obtinere ac iis, ad quos spectat, et spectabit in posterum plenissime suffragari, atque ab omnibus inviolabiliter observari, sicque in præmissis per quoscumque Judices Ordinarios, et Delegatos, etiam causarum Palatii Apostolici Auditores, judicari, et definiri debere, ac irritum, et inane, si secus super his a quoquam quavis auctoritate scienter, vel ignoranter contigerit attentari. Non obstan: Nostra, et Cancellariæ Apostolicæ Regula de jure quæsito non tollendo, et quoties opus fuerit fel: rec: Benedicti XIV. Prædecessoris Nostri super Divisione Materiarum, aliisque Constitutionibus, et Sanctionibus Apostolicis, cæterisque etiam speciali, et expressa derogatione, et mentione dignis in contrarium facientibus quibuscumque. Datum Romæ apud S. Mariam Majorem sub Annulo Piscatoris Die XXVIII. Julii MDCCCXXXVII. Pontificatus Nostri Anno Septimo.

Pro Domino Cardinali De Gregorio
A. Picchioni Substitutus

Bull of Pope Gregory XVI, dated July 28, 1837, establishing the Diocese of Natchez in Mississippi.

Chapter I

A NEW DIOCESE

With striking optimism the American bishops, assembled in provincial council at Baltimore in April 1837, asked the Holy See to erect another ecclesiastical jurisdiction in the Deep South.[1] Acting upon their suggestion, after consulting the Bishop of New Orleans, Pope Gregory XVI, on July 28, 1837, established the Diocese of Natchez.[2]

The new diocese embraced the entire state of Mississippi, an area of more than 46,000 square miles (118.810 km^2) with a population of about 400,000. In the whole area there was not one Catholic church. There was not a single priest in permanent residence in the State. As one traveler passing through the State in 1835, observed:

> Contrary to the prevalent opinion at the north, Roman Catholic influence in this State is entirely unknown. Formerly there was a Romish church in Natchez, ill-endowed and seldom supplied with an officiating priest. This was accidently destroyed by fire a year or two since; and there is now no church of that denomination in the State, and hardly a sufficient number of Catholics to organize one.[3]

Natchez was designated as the the episcopal seat rather than Jackson, the state capital, for several reasons. In 1837, Natchez was still the economic center of the State. It had the largest population of any city or town in Mississippi. Situated on the bluffs overlooking the "Father of Waters," it was relatively easy to reach by steamboat or flatboat. And, finally, Natchez was reported to have the only known organized group of Catholics in Mississippi.

No one knew precisely how many Catholics lived within the new ecclesiastical division. There were groups at Vicksburg and

---

[1] The Acta et Decreta of the Council are given in *Concilia Provincialia Baltimori habita ab anno 1829 usque ad annum 1849* (Baltimore, 1851), 123-155. Guilday, *A History of the Council of Baltimore, 1791-1884* (New York, 1932), 114-115.

[2] Bull of Gregory XVI, dated July 28, 1837, in ADNJ.

[3] J. H. Ingraham, *The Southwest,* by a Yankee; quoted by Dunbar Rowland in *Mississippi,* I, 379.

Natchez on the Mississippi River and, along the Gulf Coast, at Pascagoula, Biloxi, Pass Christian and Bay St. Louis. In addition there was an undetermined number of Catholic families scattered throughout the entire State, some of whom had not seen a priest for many years. Only one scientifically calculated Catholic population statistic is available. It concerns the Catholic congregation at Natchez. Using the Book of Minutes of the "Roman Catholic Society of Christians in the City of Natchez and Its Vicinity" and the Baptismal Register of the community as a basis for his computation, Bishop Gerow estimated that there were at least five or six hundred Catholics in Natchez and its immediate vicinity between 1839 and 1841.[4] The individual congregations along the Gulf Coast must have been somewhat smaller, for twenty-three years after the Diocese had been established it was reported that the Catholic population at Bay St. Louis was about six hundred[5] while that at Biloxi, about four hundred.[6] For the most part, the Catholics in the newly erected diocese were poor. The congregation in Natchez, for instance, found it impossible not only to support a resident priest but even to maintain their church which, before it burned down in 1832, was leased to a dry-goods firm on condition that the lessee keep the building in good repair.[7] Along the Gulf Coast the Catholics were reportedly even poorer.

First Bishop

Understandably, then, when the Reverend Thomas Heyden, pastor of St. Paul's Church, Pittsburgh, Pennsylvania, was appointed to the new see of Natchez as its first bishop,[8] the man had many misgivings. Although many clerical friends and the Catholic congregation at Natchez urged Father Heyden to accept the office, Father John Hughes, the future archbishop of New York, styled

---

[4] Gerow, *Cradle Days of St. Mary's at Natchez* (Natchez, 1941), 51.

[5] Leduc to Elder, Bay St. Louis, Sept. 17, 1860; in ADNJ, File: Elder–L.

[6] Georget to Elder, Biloxi, Aug. 31, 1860; in ADNJ, File: Elder–G.

[7] Minutes of the Meetings of the Roman Catholic Society of Christians of Natchez (1821-1861), p. 4, in the Archives of St. Mary's Cathedral, Natchez.

[8] The bishops assembled at the Third Provincial Council of Baltimore recommended to the Holy Father three men as suitable for the See of Natchez. The names were presented in the following order: James Van de Velde, S.J., Thomas Heyden, and Richard P. Miles, O.P., (Cf. APF, in Acta della Sacra Congregazione de Propaganda Fide, Vol. 200 (1837), f. 184/184v.)

the appointment as being sent "to the Great Desert,"[9] while another priest-friend wrote: ". . . for my part I would rather you would not accept. The crown is full of thorns, the anxiety and solicitude in that far-distant place without church and without one to assist would occasion many sad moments."[10]

Not until the spring of 1838, did Father Heyden decide not to accept the appointment to Natchez. Honoring his refusal, the Holy See waited until December 15, 1840, before naming another man to the See of Natchez.[11] The extraordinary delay may be explained in terms of slow and uncertain facilities for communicating with Rome as well as difficulty involved in finding a man willing to accept the unattractive appointment to Natchez. The man selected this time was the Reverend John Joseph Chanche, a Sulpician, president of St. Mary's College in Baltimore.[12] Dr. Chanche, surprisingly enough, accepted the appointment. An eloquent preacher, a theologian of note, an able administrator and a gentleman of genial disposition, he had on three previous occasions blocked efforts to raise him to the episcopate. On these occasions the sees involved were the most important and well-established in the United States, viz., Baltimore, Boston and New York.[13]

Consecrated on March 14, 1841, in the Baltimore cathedral by Archbishop Eccleston, Bishop Chanche started for his See on April 27. After a visit with Bishop Purcell at Cincinnati, he boarded a river boat for New Orleans. It was his intention to confer with Bishop Blanc of that city before entering his own diocese. Until the establishment of the Diocese of Natchez, the Catholics of Mississippi had been under the jurisdiction of the bishop of New Orleans.[14]

---

[9] Hughes to Heyden, Pittsburgh, Sept. 28, 1837; in the Archives of the Diocese of Pittsburgh.

[10] Stillinger to Heyden, Blairsville, December 30, 1837; in the Archives of the Diocese of Pittsburgh.

[11] Gerow, *op. cit.*, 62.

[12] The Fourth Provincial Council of Baltimore (May 24, 1840) submitted, in the following order, three names of men suitable for the See of Natchez: John Joseph Chanche, S.S., John Ellet, S.J., and Peter R. Kenrick. Cf. APF: Acta della Sacra Congregazione de Propaganda Fide, Vol. 203 (1840), f. 383v/384. Herbermann, *The Sulpicians in the United States* (New York, 1916), 282-285.

[13] Clarke, *Lives of the Deceased Bishops of the Catholic Church in the United States* (New York, 1872), II, 167; Herbermann, *op. cit.*, 282-283.

[14] Bull of Gregory XVI, dated July 28, 1837; in ADNJ.

Arriving in New Orleans, the new bishop learned that Bishop Blanc was out of town. On hand to meet him, however, was Bishop Portier of Mobile. This bishop together with Bishop Blanc had been doing their best to take care of the spiritual needs of the Catholic congregations on the Gulf Coast. Nevertheless, visits of priests from New Orleans and Mobile were woefully infrequent and irregular. The condition of these Catholics was described by Bishop Chanche in his first diocesan report to the Society for the Propagation of the Faith:

> This (Gulf Coast) is an extremely interesting mission. There are about two thousand Catholics, descendants of the French, . . . who have lived up to the present almost without religion and in ignorance, although Biloxi is the first place where the French set foot in the new continent.[15]

Boarding a steamboat at New Orleans, Bishop Chanche traveled up the Mississippi to his cathedral city alone. It was night when he arrived. No one was at the landing to meet him. A Negro porter carried his trunk to the hotel. Here the new bishop spent the night. Such was the entrance of the first bishop of Natchez into his see city.[16] It was May 18, 1841.

Two days later, Ascension Thursday, the Catholics of Natchez gathered in Mechanics Hall on Main Street. For some time now they were accustomed to assemble in this rented hall for divine services.[17] Here Bishop Chanche celebrated Mass and announced to his little flock his intentions. His future movements, he told them quite frankly, would be guided by their degree of cooperation. If he received sufficient encouragement from them, he would remain in Natchez; if not, he would turn his attention to some other part of the State. He was bound to the state of Mississippi, he reminded them, but not to the city of Natchez.[18]

Anxious to have the Bishop remain in their midst, the Catholics of Natchez were quick to give some manifestation of their desire

---

[15] Chanche to Society of the Propagation of the Faith, 1844; quoted in *Catholic Action of the South* (Natchez Centennial Edition), Oct. 14, 1937, 23.

[16] Gerow, *op. cit.*, 62.

[17] A church dating back to Spanish times on Commerce Street had burned down on Dec. 28, 1832. It was replaced by a small chapel to which was attached a single room in which the priest resided. With the growth of Natchez and its Catholic population, the chapel soon proved too small and a public hall was rented for divine services.

[18] Clarke, *op. cit.*, 178.

to cooperate with him. At a general meeting held a few days later, the congregation, incorporated since 1818,[19] passed unanimously a resolution to transfer to Bishop Chanche by deed title to a lot of ground which had been set aside as a site for the future parish church.[20] A distinguished lady of the congregation, Madame Felicite Girodeau, turned over half of her beautiful home to the Bishop, until permanent living quarters could be acquired for the prelate. And there was talk of building a church at once.[21]

Such a demonstration of good-will did not blind the Bishop to several less encouraging facts. One of two priests temporarily residing in the State, and this at Natchez, was preparing to leave. Although the Catholics of Natchez were eager to build, there was not a penny on hand or even subscribed for the project. Before Chanche's consecration the trustees of the parish had promised Bishop Blanc that on the arrival of the new bishop he would want nothing; indeed, they would make a liberal allowance. Six months after his arrival Chanche confided to the bishop of New Orleans: "I have yet to see the first cent." [22] When an effort was made—by one man—to get subscriptions for the building of the church, he was unable to obtain even $5,000. People began to shy away from the Bishop for fear that the subject of money would be introduced into the conversation. With reason then did Chanche report to Blanc of New Orleans: "The people of Natchez are willing to do, but their means are very limited. A priest would have been sufficient for them for a long time." [23]

Nevertheless, Bishop Chanche went to work. He decided first of all to go ahead with plans to build a house of God in Natchez which would serve both as parish church and cathedral. It was to be a substantial building designed along Gothic lines. The project must have been considered a major operation in the minds of the citizens of Natchez, Catholic and non-Catholic alike, for on February 24, 1842 the cornerstone was laid in the presence of about two thousand persons.[24]

---

19 *The Revised Code of the Laws of Mississippi* (Natchez, 1824), 597-599.
20 Book of Minutes, 88; Cathedral Rectory, Natchez, Miss.
21 Gerow, *op. cit.*, 65.
22 Chanche to Blanc, Dec. 16, 1841; in AUND: New Orleans Papers.
23 Chanche to Blanc, May 27, 1841; in AUND: New Orleans Papers.
24 *The Mississippi Free Trader and Natchez Daily Gazette,* Friday, Feb. 25, 1842.

Problems to be Faced

Two problems that demanded the Bishop's immediate attention concerned the finances of the Diocese and personnel. The Catholics of Mississippi, for the most part, were poor. Worse still the new Bishop had been asked to establish a diocese at a most unfavorable time. The State was in the midst of a depression that followed the Panic of 1837.[25] Describing the events which led up to this business depression, the editor of the *Natchez Democrat* wrote many years later:

> It has already been said that during the decade from 1830 to 1840 Natchez had five banks of issue and deposit. During the same period some twenty-five were chartered and put in operation in other places in the State. These all discounted largely, while very few of them had any considerable line of deposits. A speculative mania had seized upon the people of Mississippi, in which those of Natchez largely shared. A personal endorsement, generally not of a gilt-edged character, was all that was necessary to secure loans at easy rates from the banks. A redundancy of currency naturally produced inflation in the value of real estate, and plantations and slaves were bought and sold at extravagant prices. This continued until the country was filled with irredeemable currency, and finally the bubble burst, bringing ruin upon those who bought at inflated prices. . . . the business of the city received a severe check from the reduction of values to one-tenth of what they had before been. Widespread ruin was the result, . . . a blow had been given to all kinds of business, from which, under the most favorable circumstances, it would have been hard to recover.[26]

To add to the business depression, in May, 1840, Natchez was visited by one of the most destructive tornadoes that had ever occurred in the country. Its business houses were leveled with the ground. For that matter, the whole city was a wreck. From this blow, under the depressed condition of financial matters, the city was very slow in recovering. Fortunately, Bishop Chanche was not dependent solely upon local financial resources. Since the

---

[25] The Panic of 1837 was not local in character but national. The stage had been set for it by the general prosperity of the country in the early 1830's, the removal of the deposits from the national bank to certain pet banks, and a laxity in banking which followed the withdrawal of the conservative influence of the national bank in Philadelphia.

[26] Major Thomas Grafton, "Natchez: Its Past, Present and Future," in *The Memento. Old and New Natchez, 1700-1897* (Natchez, 1897), 31.

establishment of the Diocese of Natchez in 1837, the Propagation of the Faith Society of Paris-Lyon had allocated 69.320 francs or about $7,864 to the diocese.[27] The first allocation had been made in 1839, and another the following year. These funds were held by Bishop Blanc until a bishop should be appointed to the see. Then in the fall of 1841, Bishop Chanche received letters from the Propagation of the Faith Society announcing the allocation of 24.600 francs, the equivalent of about $4,920.[28] Such allocations continued to be made by the Society each year during the administration of Bishop Chanche, thus providing some financial stability to the new and struggling diocese.

However, while this financial assistance was important, it was hardly adequate for organizing and building up a new diocese. Consequently, Chanche turned to his many friends in the East and North. In fact, some five or six weeks after his arrival in Natchez, before he had an opportunity to make a formal visitation of his diocese, he went off on a begging tour.[29] It was only the first of many which he made during the next eleven years, appearing in Cincinnati, Baltimore, Philadelphia and New York.

Another problem that called for immediate attention and which prompted him no doubt to visit the North so soon after his arrival in the Diocese was the lack of priests. When Bishop Chanche arrived in Mississippi, he discovered that only two priests were laboring in the whole State. And these two were not actually attached to the Diocese, they were on loan from the Diocese of New Orleans. One of them was Father M.D. O'Reily who was ministering to the needs of the Catholics of Vicksburg. The other, residing at Natchez, by name Father Joseph N. Brogard, was already making plans to leave the State. Although the Bishop's estimation of the man's abilities was not too high, he prevailed upon the priest to remain at his post until he returned from his trip up North. Chanche informed Bishop Blanc of the same.

---

[27] Cf. list of allocations made by the Society to the Diocese of Natchez from 1839 to 1910, sent by secretary general of Conseil Central de Lyon to Rev. H. A. Campo, June 13, 1932: in ADNJ. The Society for the Propagation of the Faith, a Catholic mission-aid society under lay control, was organized in 1822, at Lyon, France. During the next hundred years this French society sent more than $6,000,000 to the dioceses of the United States alone. Roemer, *Ten Decades of Alms* (St. Louis, 1942).

[28] Chanche to Blanc, Dec. 3, 1841; in AUND: New Orleans Papers.

[29] Gerow, *op. cit.*, 65.

From a letter that I saw while I was in New Orleans it seems that Father Brogard wishes to leave Natchez, although he has not yet told me this. He does not seem to be the proper one for the people here in Natchez and I therefore would make no objection to his leaving, but I hope he will remain until I return from the North.[30]

During the first week of January, 1842, Father Brogard left the Diocese.[31]

During the absence of Bishop Chanche on his first begging tour, a priest who had left the Diocese of Vincennes without the permission of his bishop appeared at Natchez.[32] He was Father Jean Claude Francois, originally from the Diocese of Verdun, France. Desperately short of priests, Chanche accepted the services of the clergyman. He explained his action to Bishop Blanc.

I received a letter this morning from the Bishop of Vincennes giving Mr. Francois his Exeat and allowing me to make use of his services. In my present situation I will do so. He is not qualified to attend this congregation. But I have a notion of trying to do something for the black people. Perhaps he might succeed in this mission. We will see.[33]

Before a month was up, Bishop Chanche felt more than justified in having accepted the services of the priest. The man seemed to be filling a real need. Writing somewhat enthusiastically to the Bishop of New Orleans, Chanche reported: "It is well that Mr. Francois is here; I thank God for it. I have opened through his means a mission amongst the blacks, which promises to be successful."[34] The following year, however, Chanche described the priest as having good will but as being inefficient. Indeed, for this reason the Bishop refused to leave the priest in charge at Natchez even temporarily while he himself should make a trip to New Orleans.[35] Nevertheless, Father Francois proved to be an apostolic man. To him apparently was confided the visiting of the various pockets of Catholics in the river counties north and south of Natchez, viz., Rodney, Port Gibson, Grand Gulf and Woodville. True to Bishop Chanche's original plans for him, the missionary

30 Chanche to Blanc, May 27, 1841; in AUND: New Orleans Papers.
31 Chanche to Blanc, Jan. 2, 1842; in AUND: New Orleans Papers.
32 Chanche to Blanc, Dec. 3, 1841; in AUND: New Orleans Papers.
33 Chanche to Blanc, Jan. 2, 1842; in AUND: New Orleans Papers.
34 Chanche to Blanc, Jan. 31, 1842; in AUND: New Orleans Papers.
35 Chanche to Blanc, Aug. 2, 1843; in AUND: New Orleans Papers.

made a point to instruct and baptize the Negro slaves of the Catholic masters and mistresses whom he visited. Less than four years after his arrival in Natchez, Father Francois left the Diocese to join the Congregation of the Mission.[36]

In February, 1842, another priest appeared at Natchez. It was Father Albino Desgaultiers. He had come from the Diocese of Dubuque, Iowa, but apparently was not a native-born American. Sent by Bishop Chanche to minister to a group of Catholic families near Paulding, he did not persevere very long. Admittedly the situation was not very heartening. The few Catholic families which were in the area lived miles apart from one another. There was no church and no rectory. No doubt the difficulty he experienced in trying to learn the English language also added to the priest's discouragement.[37] In any case, Father Desgaultiers left the Diocese less than a year after he had arrived.

In the fall of 1842, Bishop Chanche obtained the services of a Father Guillaume Labbé.[38] Assigned to the Gulf Coast, the priest established his headquarters at Pass Christian. Evidently a very capable man, before long he was superintending the erection of churches at Pass Christian and Biloxi. He laid the cornerstone of the Church of the Nativity of the Blessed Virgin Mary at Biloxi on Sunday, August 6, 1843, while the folowing year, on June 16, 1844, he held divine services for the first time in a newly-built church at Pass Christian. Unfortunately, later on in the year Father Labbé left the Diocese.[39]

On October 8, 1845, Chanche described his plight clergy-wise in a letter to Bishop Purcell of Cincinnati:

> So I am left with two priests in the Diocese—one in the east and one in the west. I must send Mr. Blenkinsop or go myself to Vicksburg, to Jackson and to several stations in that neighborhood and cannot leave Natchez without a priest.[40]

---

[36] Gerow, *op. cit.*, 99.

[37] Chanche to Blanc, Natchez, Sept. 26, 1842; in AUND: New Orleans Papers.

[38] Chanche to Blanc, Natchez, Sept. 12, 1842, Oct. 17, 1842; in AUND: New Orleans Papers. O'Connell, "Earliest Missionaries Served Historic Biloxi," in *Catholic Action of the South* (Natchez Centennial Edition), Oct. 14, 1937, 23.

[39] Chanche to Blanc, Natchez, Oct. 30, 1844; in AUND: New Orleans Papers.

[40] Chanche to Purcell, Natchez, Oct. 8, 1845; in AUND: Cincinnati Papers.

The two priests of whom Bishop Chanche speaks were Father Ghislain Joseph Boheme and Father William A. Blenkinsop. In the meanwhile, Father O'Reily had died at his post in Vicksburg. During his pastorate a frame church had been built in that city, on the east side of Walnut Street, between Second and Crawford Streets.[41] Thus, after four years of endeavor Bishop Chanche was still faced with the almost hopeless task of organizing a diocese and of ministering to the spiritual needs of a scattered flock with the aid of only two priests.

Ordained ten years before in Belgium, Father Boheme came to to New Orleans in 1842. That same year he joined the Diocese of Natchez and on January 6, 1843, was sent to Paulding to take charge of the Catholic congregation there. Although Paulding at this time seemed to be a good place to organize a parish,[42] few Catholics were actually residing in the town. Most of his parishioners were scattered over an area that embraced several counties. A practical man, Father Boheme first built a church[43] and then "went around over a large tract of country, and when he found a Catholic family at a distance from the church he advised them to move in the neighborhood of Paulding and there he established a little colony of Catholics."[44] The Belgian priest proved to be an indefatigable worker. For several years he had under his sole charge all of the eastern half of the state of Mississippi and the greater part of the western side of Alabama. His missionary travels on horseback extended from Biloxi on the Gulf of Mexico to the Tennessee line and beyond; and from the Pearl River and farther west to Tuscumbia and all the bordering counties of Alabama.[45] In numerous Catholic families scattered over that vast expanse it was this missionary on horseback who kept the faith alive and who made it known and respected by all who met him,

---

41 Mullin, "St. Paul's—Vicksburg," in *Catholic Action of the South* (Natchez Centennial Edition), Oct. 14, 1937, 19.

42 Paulding in Jasper County in 1842, was the only agglomeration of any significance in this part of Mississippi with roads in every direction and situated on the trade roads from Mobile and New Orleans.

43 Except for the Cathedral at Natchez, St. Michael's at Paulding was the first church to be built in the new diocese.

44 Elder to a friend, Sept. 1870; quoted in "St. Michael's—Paulding," by Rev. Joseph M. Dogny, in *Catholic Action of the South* (Natchez Centennial Edition), Oct. 14, 1937, 27.

45 Necrology Notes for 1862, drawn up by Bishop Elder in 1866; in ADNJ: Letter Book—#10, p. 410.

not a few of whom he had the happiness of receiving into the Church.

The other priest laboring with Bishop Chanche in the Diocese during the fall of 1845 was Father William A. Blenkinsop. An alumnus of St. Mary's College in Baltimore, Blenkinsop came to the Diocese as a newly ordained priest.[46] Much of his time was spent in traveling about the western half of the State, visiting Catholics at Vicksburg, Jackson, Yazoo City, Canton, Camden, Grand Gulf, Port Gibson and Woodville. Although he spent much time away from Natchez, Father Blenkinsop made a great impression on the people of that city. The secular press referred to him as "the eloquent and classic Blenkinsop," "a ripe scholar," "gentle and kind hearted."[47] Especially well-known was the priest's attendance on the sick and dying. The editor of one of Natchez's newspapers dared his readers to ask "Dr. Blackburn, the excellent physician of the State Hospital at Natchez, . . . who, of all the clergymen in Natchez, were oftenest within the walls of that institution, soothing bodily distress and ministering to 'the mind diseased.'"[48] So attached did the Catholic community of Natchez become to the priest that, when his transfer to the state capitol at Jackson was announced in 1848, a specially appointed committee waited upon the Bishop to beg him to reconsider.[49]

The shortage of priests in his diocese was a problem that weighed heavily upon the mind and heart of Bishop Chanche. Every effort he made to obtain workers for his portion of the Lord's Vineyard

---

[46] Chanche to Blanc, Natchez, Dec. 3, 1843; in AUND: New Orleans Papers. William A. Blenkinsop (1819-1892), born in Dublin, emigrated to the United States with his parents in 1826. He studied at St. Mary's College, Baltimore, from 1833-39, taught there (1839-1843), taking the A.M. degree, and was ordained by Archbishop Eccleston in 1843. That same year he went to the Diocese of Natchez where he remained about seven years. *Catholic Encyclopedia,* II, 597.

[47] *The Mississippi Free Trader,* April 25, 1848; quoted by Gerow, *op. cit.,* 100.

[48] *Ibid.,* 100.

[49] *Ibid.,* 100. Fr. Blenkinsop remained in Jackson until March, 1850, when he joined the Diocese of Boston. In 1854, he was nominated by Archbishops Kenrick of Baltimore, Hughes of New York and Blanc of New Orleans for the see of Portland, Maine. Hughes to Propaganda, Oct. 10, 1854, New York; in the Archives of the Sacred Congregation de Progaganda Fide, Rome, Scritture Riferite nei Congressi, XVI, ff. 1152rv-1154r. In 1864, he was appointed pastor of Sts. Peter and Paul Church in Boston at which post he remained until his death in 1892. *Catholic Encyclopedia,* II, 597.

came to naught. Manifesting his distress to Bishop Purcell, Chanche wrote on October 8, 1845:

> You see how dreadfully embarrassed I am for want of priests. I have knocked at every door but can get no favorable answer. My heart is rent almost every week by the reception of letters from different parts of the State calling earnestly for priests, and I have none to send them.[50]

The following year Chanche again wrote to the Bishop of Cincinnati on the subject of personnel for his struggling diocese. Although, since he wrote last to the Cincinnati prelate, two more priests had joined the Diocese,[51] the Bishop of Natchez did not hesitate to say: "I only take this opportunity to say that I am in more need of priests than ever and that I would be happy to employ anybody you would recommend." [52] Trying to understand his own failure to obtain priests for Mississippi, the prelate added: "It seems to me that everybody is afraid of the South." For anyone acquainted with the State and Diocese at this period in their history this might well have been the main reason for Chanche's difficulty in attracting priests to his diocese. Among other unfavorable features attached to working in his diocese were the fewness of Catholics, many of whom were scattered over a wide area; parochial life that involved frequent and difficult travel; often enough, inadequate financial support; oppressive summer heat that began early in the season; and a real and ever present danger of yellow fever epidemics.[53] All this added up to a need for a special type of priest, namely, one who would be zealous, self-sacrificing, and hardy.[54]

It is the task of any new bishop, but especially of the first occupant of a new diocese, to investigate and establish, if necesary, the validity of all church property titles. In the process of making this investigation with the trustees of the Cathedral parish, Bishop Chanche discovered that the King of Spain had purchased for the

---

[50] Chanche to Purcell, Oct. 8, 1845; in AUND: Cincinnati Papers.

[51] Rev. Stephen Montgomery, O.P. succeeded Fr. O'Reily as resident pastor at Vicksburg in 1845, while Rev. Symphorian Guinand took up residence at Biloxi on the Gulf Coast in the fall of 1846.

[52] Chanche to Purcell, Oct. 14, 1846; in AUND: Cincinnati Papers.

[53] Between 1853 and 1878, the Diocese lost nine priests who had succumbed to yellow fever.

[54] Chanche to Acton, Natchez, April 20, 1842; in APF: Scritture Riferite nei Congressi, XIII (1841-1844), f. 419rv.

Catholic Church in Natchez three hundred arpents of ground in 1788. Later in 1798, when Spain relinquished possession of the territory which embraced the present state of Mississippi [55] and the priests employed by the Spanish government withdrew as a result of this change in government, the Catholic congregation in Natchez remained without a representative competent to protect its civil rights until 1818.[56] In the meanwhile for want of such a representative, their claim to the above mentioned land was not made before the board of commissioners appointed to settle such claims. By default the property passed to the United States government who in turn sold most of it piecemeal.[57] Basing his claim on this old Spanish grant, Chanche instituted legal action to obtain possession of three lots, adjacent to the Cathedral property, all of which fell within the boundaries of the original grant. The Bishop was particularly interested in these three lots, now vacant and owned by the city, because he was looking for a future rectory and school site.[58]

As a result of the legal action instituted by Bishop Chanche for the recovery of the three lots, the church obtained possession of another plot of ground, 60 by 160 feet, also adjacent to the Cathedral property. Whether this was granted by way of compensation or compromise, is not known. In any case, the Bishop, feeling that even with this the church had not received justice, continued to press his claim for the three lots in question. Eventually he obtained a favorable judgment against the city, and the lots were turned over to Chanche's successor, Bishop Van de Velde.[59]

That Bishop Chanche obtained this property is surprising, but what is even more surprising is his attempt to gain compensation from the United States government for the entire Spanish grant made to the Catholic Church in 1788.[60] In hopes of being able to obtain documentary evidence upon which to base this larger claim,

[55] Bettersworth, *Mississippi: A History* (Austin, Texas, 1959), 114-117.

[56] The Catholics of Natchez were incorporated under Mississippi state law on February 6, 1818, under the title of "Catholic Society of Christians in the City of Natchez and Its Vicinity." Gerow, *op. cit.*, 16.

[57] Memorial of John Joseph Chanche, Catholic Bishop of Natchez, to the United States Congress; rough draft in *American Catholic Historical Researches* (1887-1888); quoted by Gerow, *op. cit.*, 88-89.

[58] Gerow, *op. cit.*, 86-87.

[59] Gerow, *op. cit.*, 89. As will be seen, this decision was reversed in a higher court.

[60] *Ibid.*, 87-89.

Chanche traveled to Havana, Cuba, at the end of January, 1844. During his stay in Havana, Chanche was the guest of Right Rev. Dr. Mando, Bishop-elect of Segovia, Spain, then Superior of the seminary in Havana. Here the Bishop from Mississippi consulted the old Spanish records and obtained authentic copies of the documents relating to the original Spanish grant. By the middle of March he was back in Natchez. Chanche subsequently submitted a memorial to the U. S. Congress in which he asked that the compensation be made to the Catholic congregation of Natchez to the sum of $2,000, the original purchase price paid by the Spanish Crown, or that lands of equal value be granted to the congregation. Although Chanche's petition was supported by Señor Calderón de la Bocca, Spanish minister at Washington, and other influential people, it met with no success. Unfortunately, while the land-grant had been made to the Catholic church at Natchez by the Spanish King, the legal title to it remained vested in the Spanish Crown. Accordingly, when the American government acquired sovereignty over the country, she claimed to have succeeded to all the rights and property of the former government.

Trip to Europe

Following the example of many fellow bishops in America, Chanche made a trip to Europe in May 1848,[61] hoping to obtain men and means. His appeals were not in vain. At the Grand Seminary at Nantes the Bishop of Natchez prevailed upon three seminarians to volunteer for his diocese.[62] Two of the young men, Messrs. John Baptist Babonneau and Julian M. Guillou, were deacons, while the third, Mr. John Andrew Fiérabras, was a sub-deacon.[63] On February 10, 1850, less than two months after their arrival in Natchez, Bishop Chanche was able to raise Guillou and Babonneau to the priesthood and before the end of March he had the added happiness of doing the same for Fiérabras.[64] During his stay in France the Bishop also had the good fortune to obtain the services of the Eudist Fathers. Chanche had in mind to open

---

[61] Chanche to Propaganda, Paris, Sept. 6, 1848; in APF: Scritture Riferite nei Congressi, XV (1849-1851), ff. 701 rv; also Clarke, *op. cit.*, 187; Gerow, *op. cit.*, 100.

[62] Guillou to Elder, Oct. 15, 1857; in ADNJ: Elder Letter Book—10, 178.

[63] *Annales de la Propagation de la foi*, Lyon, 1850, XXII, 72.

[64] Baptismal Register—#2, of St. Mary's Cathedral, Natchez, 107; a record of the ordinations is found in this Register.

a boys' college in Natchez and made arrangements to have these Fathers conduct the school.[65]

What Bishop Chanche failed to gain in numbers, he surely won in quality in his search for laborers for his diocese on the occasion of his trip to Europe. All of the recruits proved to be missionaries of very high caliber—examples of devotion to duty, zealous and self-sacrificing men. Three died of yellow fever while ministering to their flocks. Another served as rector of the Cathedral for thirty-five years and as vicar-general of the Diocese for thirty years. And another died as a result of exposure and privations endured at Corinth, Mississippi, while attending to the wounded and sick after the Battle of Shiloh.

Perhaps even more pressing than the need for priests at the time of Chanche's trip to Europe was the financial condition of the Diocese. Having inaugurated the building of a large and substantial cathedral in the midst of a depression with a guarantee of only limited financial assistance, Chanche soon found himself being pressed for payment of the enormous debt he had incurred. The construction of the cathedral had rested with a very simple building. On the day of its blessing, Christmas 1843, it consisted of rough, unplastered walls, a shingle roof, a rough floor and the most primitive furnishings. Serious pressure began to be applied by the creditors in 1847.[66] Harassed on every side, Chanche found himself accused of being a cheat, a swindler, a fraud. The situation became so bad that in July 1847, the cathedral was put up for auction. Fortunately the affair was compromised and the sale deferred. So matters stood when the Bishop left for Europe in the spring of 1848.

During the Bishop's absence the creditors again brought action against the Catholic congregation at Natchez. During the first week of May 1849, the cathedral and land upon which it stood were put up for auction. The vicar-general and only priest in Natchez, Father Blase Raho, C.M., had been doing his best during the Bishop's absence to save the cathedral. He took up special col-

[65] Chanche to Gaudaire, Paris, Aug. 17, 1848; in AE: dossier G.

[66] The following details were gathered from a letter sent by Chanche's successor, Bishop Van de Velde, to the Propagation of the Faith Society, on Jan. 1, 1854. A copy of the letter is in the ADNJ and is quoted by Gerow, *op. cit.*, 105-106.

lections in Natchez and in New Orleans.[67] The Catholic ladies of the congregation also did their best to help relieve the financial embarrassment of the Catholic community. Just prior to Christmas 1848, they held a five-day fair at the Natchez Court House.[68] Fortunately the sale of the cathedral was prevented. Acting for Bishop Chanche, Father Raho made a compromise with the creditors.[69] With the money that the Bishop had sent from France and that which he had collected in Louisiana, Raho was able to pay the creditors $7,000. In addition, he gave them promissory notes for the rest of the debt, payable each year on the seventh of May for the next ten years, with an interest at 6 per cent.

It is difficult to say how successful Bishop Chanche's trip to Europe was from the financial viewpoint. However, one is inclined to suspect that it was not up to his expectations. Although the Mississippi prelate was able to give a personal report to the Society for the Propagation of the Faith in Paris on the desperate state of his diocese, he met with disappointment at their hands. Instead of increasing his allocation for the year 1849, the Central Council reduced it.[70] Before the end of the year Chanche visited Rome. Here he had an interview with Cardinal Fransoni, Prefect of Propaganda.[71] The Cardinal received Chanche very cordially, and it was most probably through him that the Bishop of Natchez was introduced to Prince Alexander Torlonia of Rome. The latter proved to be a valuable contact, for he promised to provide a bell, newly cast, for the unfinished Cathedral of Natchez.[72] During his visit in the Eternal City Chanche discussed with his Roman agent, Canon Raphael Bertinelli, the possibility of obtaining marble al-

---

67 Van de Velde to the Propagation of the Faith Society, Natchez, Jan. 19, 1855: copy in ADNJ; quoted by Gerow, *op. cit.*, 106.

68 *Natchez Semi-Weekly Courier,* Dec. 15, 1848, 4.

69 Van de Velde to the Propagation of the Faith Society, Natchez, Jan. 19, 1855; copy in ADNJ; quoted by Gerow, *op. cit.*, 106.

70 Cf. list of allocations made by the Society to the Diocese of Natchez from 1839 to 1910, sent by secretary general of Conseil Central de Lyon to Rev. H. A. Campo, June 13, 1932; in ADNJ. Chanche found the directors of the Propagation of the Faith Society even harder to deal with a few years later. At the end of 1851, the President at Lyons demanded a detailed account of Chanche's financial situation and threatened to discontinue the annual allowance" . . . if Chanche did not consider it satisfactory. The Bishop of Natchez considered such a demand "humiliating" but met it nonetheless. Chanche to Blanc, Natchez, Jan. 17, 1852; in AUND: New Orleans Papers.

71 Chanche to Fransoni, Natchez, Aug. 12, 1850; in APF: Scritture Riferite nei Congressi, XIV (1845-1848), ff. 569r.

72 Gerow, *op. cit.*, 80-83.

tars and a tabernacle for his unfurnished cathedral. However, it would be necessary to find a benefactor who would be willing to donate these items. Chanche found no such benefactor before he left the city. And even though Bertinelli continued to correspond with the Bishop after his departure in an optimistic vein about the design of the altars and the types of marble to be employed,[73] nothing came of the project. Just before Chanche left the continent in the spring of 1849, he wrote a letter from Paris to the Leopoldinen-Stiftung in Vienna.[74] Reporting to the Austrian missionary-aid society on the state of his diocese, the Natchez prelate revealed his current financial distress. He had some hope of obtaining a favorable hearing, because the society had given financial assistance to the Diocese in the past. An appeal to the society in January, 1842, had brought 4,000 Florins or about $1,845,[75] and another in May, 1845, had produced 2,000 Florins or about $922.[76] Now, in response to Chanche's distress call from Paris, the directors of the society graciously sent 3,000 Florins which came to about $1,380.[77] On his way back to America in April, 1849, Bishop Chanche most probably stopped off in England. On a begging tour such as he was, the Bishop would hardly have overlooked close friends and benefactors there. These were the Duchess of Leeds and of Carmathan and the Marquise of Wellesley, both Americans and grandchildren of Charles Carroll of Carrollton.[78] When Chanche returned to Mississippi in July, 1849, he was able to do very little to improve the financial condition of the Diocese. At most his collections in Europe helped him save his Cathedral.

---

[73] Bertinelli to Chanche, Rome, Jan. 25, 1849; in ADNJ.

[74] Chanche to the Leopoldinen-Stiftung, Paris, March 8, 1849; in *Berichte der Leopoldinen-Stiftung im Kaiserthume Oesterreichs,* XXII (1850), 31. The Leopoldinen-Stiftung, an Austrian missionary-aid society modeled on the French Society for the Propagation of the Faith, was established under the auspices of Emperor Francis I on Dec. 8, 1828. Membership was confined strictly to the Austrian Empire, and the alms were to be distributed only for the needs of the Church in North America without thought of national preference. From its foundation to its final collapse during World War I, the society sent more than $700,000, to the Church in North America. Cf. Roemer, *Ten Decades of Alms,* St. Louis, 1942.

[75] Chanche to the Leopoldinen-Stiftung, Natchez, Jan. 6, 1842; in *Berichte der Leopoldinen-Stiftung,* XVI (1843), 23-24, 25-27.

[76] Report of the Leopoldinen-Stiftung, to Card. Fransoni, Vienna, May 2, 1845; in APF: Scritture Riferite nei Congressi, XIV (1845-1848), f. 100 rv.

[77] *Berichte der Leopoldinen-Stiftung,* XXII (1850), 34.

[78] Gerow, *op. cit.,* 117-118.

First Episcopal Visitation

When Bishop Chanche arrived in Mississippi, no one could give him even an approximate estimate of how many Catholics were living within his ecclesiastical jurisdiction. This much was known: there were Catholic communities at Vicksburg and Natchez on the Mississippi River, and along the Gulf Coast at Pascagoula, Biloxi, Pass Christian and Bay St. Louis. These communities enjoyed at least an occasional visit from missionary priests operating out of Mobile, New Orleans and St. Louis. But it was also rumored that there was a number of Catholic families living in the interior of the State. Scattered about and living off the main travel routes, they seldom, if ever, had any contact with the missionary priests operating in Mississippi.

It was not before the end of February 1842, that Bishop Chanche was able to investigate the matter. Even on this occasion the visitation was far from complete. However, it enabled the prelate to form a better picture of the condition of his diocese than he had before. Describing what he found in the course of his visitation in a letter to Cardinal Charles Acton of Propaganda, the Bishop wrote:

> The portion of the Vineyard which it has pleased Providence to place under my direction is large, and has hitherto been uncultivated. There are many families originally Catholic settled throughout the State, but never having had the opportunity of even seeing a Priest, the children have forgotten that their parents were Catholic. This is a very deplorable state of things, and it will require some time before this evil can be remedied. There is a vast deal of good to be done both among these Catholics and among the Protestants. But we want labourers and we want means.[79]

Most of the families about whom the Bishop speaks were either native-born Americans who had moved westward from the Atlantic seaboard or Irish immigrants who had left Ireland just prior to the Great Famine of 1845-1847. His report makes only more poignant John Tracy Ellis' judgment that the principal areas of loss to the Catholic Church in the United States in the nineteenth century were the rural districts, especially in the South and West, in

---

[79] Chanche to Acton,, Natchez,, April 20, 1842; in APF: Scritture Riferite nei Congressi, XIII (1841-1844), ff. 418 rv. Cardinal Aston was a member of the Sacred Congregation de Propaganda Fide and to some extent was considered the "protector" of the American bishops, because he knew English.

which many Catholics settled only to find that there were no churches or priests to serve them.[80]

Although the Bishop makes no mention of them on this occasion, there was a good number of Catholic families scattered throughout the State who did not abandon their faith. Some were discovered only on subsequent visitations or by such intrepid missionaries on horseback as Fathers Babonneau, Courjault, Guillou and Boheme, who literally combed the countryside looking for isolated Catholic families. Among those who kept the faith [81] when there were no priests on hand to nourish and enlighten that faith for years were Francis Keenan and his wife who, coming from Ireland in 1835, settled in Neshoba County. In 1840, Patrick Rush arrived from Ireland to become overseer on the Keenan plantation about three miles southeast of the town of Philadelphia. Three years later his brothers, Daniel and Peter, joined him, buying land adjacent to the Keenans. As early as 1836, John Hargon and his family, who came from Maryland, settled in Madison County near a settlement called Sulphur Springs. Originally from Georgia, Sylvester and Oliver Luckett also established themselves in the vicinity of Sulphur Springs in 1842. They were followed to Madison County by the O'Learys, Murrays, O'Rourkes, Brooks and Wards. The Donovans were in Lee County as early as 1834. They were from Ireland. Jeremiah was the first to arrive. He was followed by his father and his family. These settled in the Palmetto community. Bernard McGovern and his family were discovered living in Choctaw County, on the public road between Greensboro and Louisville. In Attala County two Irish families, the Welchs and the Kennedy's, drifted away from the Catholic faith and joined the Methodist Church.[82] However, when Father Guillou discovered them in 1851, they returned to the practice of their Catholic faith. At the end of the 1840's regular contact was being maintained with about a

---

[80] Ellis, *American Catholicism* (Chicago, 1956), 123.

[81] The following information was obtained from parish sketches drawn up by the respective pastors for the Natchez Centennial Edition of the *Catholic Action of the South,* Oct. 14, 1937, or for clergy conferences held within the Diocese of Natchez.

[82] Seldom did such conversions take place because the Catholic party felt that he had been living in religious error. In most cases the change-over took place because of a desire to participate in some form of public worship, anxiety over a lack of religious instruction for his children, mixed marriages or social pressure from various sources.

hundred Catholic families scattered through Lee, Madison, Yazoo, Neshoba, Attala, Jasper, Rankin and Hinds Counties.

Another part of his flock which Bishop Chanche came to know only gradually were the Catholic German immigrants who came to the State in the 1840's. In the early part of the decade the Bishop discovered very few,[83] but in 1845, he reported to the Leopoldinen-Stiftung: "We have several settlements of Germans, but, having seen no priest for some time, these have almost completely forgotten their religion." [84] A group settled near Jackson. However, when the Bishop sent them Father Müller,[85] a German priest, they were unable to support him. Consequently, it was left to Father Boheme, operating out of Paulding some ninety miles away, to minister to the spiritual needs of these German Catholics as best he could.[86] In the vicinity of Natchez there were also a number of German families. These were taken care of by a German-speaking priest attached to the Cathedral. Whenever this priest visited them, Chanche reported, they appeared delighted and provided the priest with everything he needed. In Natchez itself there were also about sixty German Catholic families. Most of them attended church regularly and even edified the rest of the English-speaking congregation. Gradually these German Catholics were integrated into existing congregations or served as nuclei for new ones.

Episcopal visitations in Mississippi in the 1840's were very informal affairs. In fact, they could hardly qualify as visitations in the canonical sense. There were no registers to check, no sacred vessels or altar linens to inspect, no financial books to examine. Traveling alone, Chanche's visits were like the usual visits of his missionary priests. On these occasions he would hear confessions and then say Mass in some one's parlor. Later on in the day he baptized and gave religious instructions to the children and prospective converts. His coming and going seldom caused any stir.

---

[83] Chanche to the Archbishop (Vincent Milde) of Vienna, Natchez, Jan. 6, 1842; in *Berichte der Leopoldinen-Stiftung*, XVI (1843), 23-24.

[84] Chanche to the Archbishop (Vincent Milde)of Vienna, Natchez, Oct. 21, 1845; in *Berichte der Leopoldinen-Stiftung*, XIX (1846), 33-35.

[85] Not until the spring of 1848, did Chanche make another attempt to provide this congregation with a resident pastor, viz., Fr. Blenkinsop. By this time the congregation had a church, newly-built.

[86] Father Müller came to the Diocese in 1843, and left it a year later. (Chanche to Propaganda, Natchez, June 19, 1844; in APF: Scritture Riferite nei Congressi, XIII (1841-1844), f. 1129 rv. Also *Metropolitan Catholic Almanac*, 1844, p. 115.)

An exception to the general reaction was Bishop Chanche's visit to Yazoo City on April 24, 1844. It created a good deal of excitement in the bustling town of a thousand souls, export center for the cotton crop of the area. It was the first time that a Roman Catholic priest, much less a bishop, had been seen in those parts. A contemporary magazine account of the visit gives some idea of the Bishop's labors and what effect his coming had on the townspeople, both Catholic and Protestant.

> The Catholics in this town (Yazoo City) are not very numerous but earnest and serious. As soon as it was known that the Bishop had arrived—Honorable E. C. Wilkinson invited him to his residence where he received the visits of the Protestant gentlemen as well as the Catholics of the City. He was invited to preach in the evening and the Methodist Meeting House was obtained for the purpose. (....) The Bishop complimented them on their zeal — dilated on the importance of religion and announced that the next day he would discuss the grounds upon which Christianity was founded. The next day the Methodists refused the use of their meeting house; so did the Presbyterians so that the gentlemen were obliged to have recourse to a large hall at the Phoenix House and on Friday the Bishop preached on *Transubstantiation*. It was an able argument and produced a great effect upon the people. On Saturday he preached on the *Sacrament of Penance* with equal effect. On all these days the rooms were very much crowded. (....) The Bishop celebrated Mass on Sunday morning at the residence of Judge Wilkinson in the presence of from 40 to 50 Catholics. He administered the Holy Eucharist to several persons and baptized several children. After Mass the Bishop started, accompanied by Judge Wilkinson, for the town of Benton where he expected to preach.[87]

As a result of the Bishop's visit, the Catholics of Yazoo City assisted by several Protestant gentlemen decided to build a church and school. Four thousand dollars were subscribed and a choice of four or five lots was offered to the Bishop.[88] Unfortunately, because of a lack of priests Chanche could not capitalize on this initial enthusiasm.

Protestant reaction in Yazoo City to Bishop Chanche's visit was not unique in the history of Catholic-Protestant relations in the

[87] *The Catholic Expositor*, Pise, N.Y., April-October, 1844, 242, quoted in Clarke, *op. cit.*, 184-185.
[88] *Ibid.*

South during the first half of the 19th century. Bishop John England of Charleston, at the invitation of some of the Protestants of that city, had preached in one of their churches. In North Carolina Judge William Gaston, a prominent Catholic layman, after serving in the state legislature almost continuously from 1800 to 1832, was elected by the Protestant majority of the General Assembly Chief Justice, an office he held until his death in 1844. When only seven years old, Jefferson Davis was sent by his Baptist father to the Catholic college of St. Thomas in Kentucky, nearly a thousand miles from his home in Mississippi. His niece, Mary Ann Davis, daughter of Joseph Emory Davis, was sent to the Ursuline convent school in New Orleans. For that matter, so highly esteemed was Catholic education among the Protestants of Mississippi that between 1814 and 1865, over a hundred of their daughters were educated at Nazareth Female Academy in Kentucky, a Catholic boarding school conducted by the Sisters of Charity of Nazareth.[89] Apparently the Nativist movement which brought on the violent "no-popery riots" in Philadelphia in May, 1844, had not yet penetrated among the people of Mississippi.[90] Even when it had a year later, a French-born Catholic, Colonel Felix Labauve of Hernando, could get himself elected as State senator from his district.[91] When the Know-Nothing Party took shape in Mississippi in the 1850's, it too lacked the spontaneity of feeling that was apparent elsewhere. The election of 1857, when they were swept down in defeat, was the last effort of the Know-Nothings in the State.[92] And thus the observation that the tolerance shown to Catholics in the ante-bellum South contrasts favorably with the treatment which they received in the North seems to be a valid one.[93]

Bishop Chanche did not confine his labors to the Catholics of his diocese. He was also interested in the many nominal Protestants who were living in the State, those who were not formally

[89] List of students enrolled at the Academy from Mississippi was obtained by the writer from the Office of the Dean, Nov. 22, 1961.

[90] Walmsley, "The Presidential Campaign of 1844 in Mississippi," in PMHS, IX (1906), 179.

[91] Saunders, "Col. Felix Labauve," in PMHS, VII (1903), 135.

[92] Overdyke, *The Know-Nothing Party in the South* (Baton Rouge, 1950), 278.

[93] Eaton, *Freedom of Thought in the Old South* (Durham, N.C., 1940), 302.

attached to any particular sect. Unlike one minister of the Gospel who felt "constrained to acknowledge that the Gospel seed was never sown upon a more ungracious and unproductive soil" [94] than in Mississippi and Louisiana of the 1830's and 1840's, the Bishop of Natchez felt that many people in Mississippi, fallen-away Catholics as well as nominal Protestants, were ripe for conversion. So the Bishop expressed himself when he wrote to Pope Gregory XVI on June 2, 1841:

> There are many Catholics scattered about far and wide, who have already nearly lost the faith. Nevertheless both these and the Protestants seem very much inclined to accept religious concepts and to listen to the preaching of the Catholic Faith.[95]

No doubt the interest of the Protestants at Yazoo City in the Catholic faith and their eagerness to help erect a Catholic church and school in their town confirmed the Bishop in his opinion. Further evidence of Protestant favor toward and interest in the Catholic Church may be gleaned from the following letter addressed to Bishop Chanche by Henry C. Ferris, a newspaper editor and a Catholic, residing at Macon, Noxubee County.

> Rt. Rev. Sir:
>
> I had the honor of receiving a letter from you last fall, in answer to one I wrote you in reference to the erection of a Catholic Church in this thriving town; and although it has been many months since I received your letter, it was a subject I had constantly at heart; and now I trust, by the mercy of God, it is about to be realized.
>
> An old gentleman by the name of Capt. Mathias Mahorner called on me a few days since, and said he understood I was a Catholic, and proposed to take steps to build a church, and said he would advance five hundred dollars towards it — he is a man of large family both blacks and white — and he said as he is an old man — he wishes to proceed at once to business, as he wishes to make all his family Catholics. He proposes that we shall erect a handsome church–house for a priest and a school house. He has the money and influence to carry through what he proposes. Since I saw him I spoke to Geo. H. Foote, Esq. of this town, a prominent law-

---

[94] Jones, *A Concise History of the Introduction of Protestantism into Mississippi and the Southwest* (St. Louis, 1866), 256.

[95] Chanche to Gregory XVI, Natchez, June 2, 1841; in APF: Scritture Riferite nei Congressi, XIII (1841-1844), ff. 130 rv. (Translation).

yer and late a member of the State Convention; and who was educated at Bardstown, Ky.; when I told him of Capt. Mahorner's proposition, and showed him your letter, he said at once he would *give* a *lot* – and pledged himself to raise several hundred dollars among his friends. I have spoke to several besides of smaller means who pledge themselves to cooperate. Now, dear Sir, I respectfully propose that you send a priest here at *once,* to secure the *lot,* and have it properly deeded to the church, to secure it against possible contingencies; and thus we can proceed to carry out Mr. Mahorner's plans.

(. . . .)

With very great respect, sir, I am
yours truly
Henry C. Ferris [96]

Neither Mahorner nor Foote were Catholic. Here again as at Yazoo City, Bishop Chanche was unable to take advantage of the attractive offer, for he had no priests to spare. Seven years later, Macon was still without a Catholic church, although, as one visiting priest reported to the Bishop, "they have the prittiest (sic) site in town for a Church." [97]

A tempered report made by Father Fiérabras from his post at Port Gibson must also have sounded very encouraging to the Bishop.

Last Sunday I said Mass for the first time in the new church at *Cedar Creek.* The crowd was immense, the church could not hold half the people. Everyone both inside and outside the church assisted at the ceremony in profound silence and perfect behavior. The Mass and sermon lasted a little more than two hours. It was the first time that most of them were present at our holy mysteries and heard our doctrine. Many of the most respected gentlemen of the area invited me to come see them; and they offered me their most generous hospitality. Some asked me for Catholic books. I am not deluding myself. I realize that no foundation should be laid on this momentary enthusiasm, and that it is a long way between reading a Catholic book and becoming a Catholic. But so what; some of it will always remain and the seed will one day bear its fruit. If we do not reap the harvest, our successors will.[98]

---

[96] Ferris to Chanche, Macon, June 17, 1852; in AUND: Natchez Papers.
[97] Grignon to Elder, Oct. 18, 1859; in ADNJ, File: Elder–G.
[98] Fiérabras to Monseigneur (Chanche), Port Gibson, June 25, 1852; in AUND: Natchez Papers. (Translation).

Nevertheless, it would seem that Bishop Chanche's optimism over the possibility of winning over to the Catholic Church large numbers of unchurched Protestants in Mississippi was not really well-founded. If some Protestants manifested an interest in the Catholic religion and even went so far as to attend Catholic services, in many instances it was simply a case of curiosity or politeness, the persons in question having no intention of pursuing the matter further. Moreover, many poorly instructed Protestants were known to be very fickle. A Catholic missionary writing in 1883 from Paulding made an observation which would seem to be valid even in the 1840's and 1850's.

> It is well known that Americans generally like variety and novelty; that is why they very often change opinions in religious matters. He who today calls himself a "Baptist" will after a meeting shake hands with a Methodist minister as a sign of agreement; from then on he will loudly proclaim himself a member of this new sect. Some try to do the same thing after having heard a Catholic instruction, but when we ask them to study our doctrine, very few persevere.[99]

Even when the number of the clergy in the Diocese had increased, the number of conversions from Protestantism was insignificant. "It is true," one Protestant observer noted in 1835, "that many planters and citizens of Mississippi send their sons to the Catholic seminary at St. Louis, or Bardstown in Kentucky, and their daughters to the French convents in Louisiana;" but this fact cannot be advanced as any proof of a prevalence of or preference for the "religion of Rome." [100] Furthermore, he went on to point out, "the same thing is done in New England, where stand the very pillars of the orthodox faith," namely, Protestantism. Indeed, it was this man's opinion that "such is the peculiar turn of mind of Mississippians, that they never can be catholicised." [101] Be that as it may, the going would have been difficult for any minister of the Gospel laboring in Mississippi during the first half of the nineteenth century. Among the obstacles to be faced were the people themselves, many of whom were refugees from civil justice; the lack of religious instruction and public means of grace; widespread breaking of the

---

[99] Baur to the Directors of the Propagation of the Faith Society, Paulding, Nov. 1883; in *Annales de la Propagation de la Foi,* XXXIII (1884), 118. (Translation).

[100] Ingraham, *The Southwest by a Yankee* (New York, 1835), 70.

[101] *Ibid.*

Sabbath; want of Bibles and religious literature; preoccupation with the idea of amassing wealth; and the easy vice available at Natchez, the commerce center for a large part of the State.[102]

Education and Charity

From earliest times in the United States no Catholic diocese was said to be fully organized until some provision had been made for the religious and secular education of its young people[103] and the care of its orphans and abandoned children. By 1840, at least two hundred Catholic parochial schools had been established with about half of these west of the Alleghenies.[104] At first Chanche had to be content with a privately run girls' academy, conducted at Natchez by his nieces, Rose, Eugenia and Emma Marcilly.[105] Originally from Maryland, the young ladies had returned with their uncle from his first begging trip up North. Because of the emphasis placed upon the French language, the academy came to be known as the "French-speaking school." Although operating under the auspices of the Bishop, the school was never distinctively Catholic. It was located on Union and B Streets. The school property, at first rented by the Marcilly sisters, was purchased by them in 1850. Covering over twelve acres, it ran as far back as Pine Ridge road and came to be called "Rose Hill" after the eldest of the Marcilly sisters.[106] The school was in operation from 1842 until March 1855, when Eugenia, the youngest of the sisters, died.[107] At this time the sisters closed the academy and returned to Maryland.[108]

As professor and later as president of St. Mary's College in Baltimore, Bishop Chanche had been well acquainted with the Sisters of Charity at Emmitsburg, Maryland. Indeed, the relationship must have been close, because when arrangements were being

[102] Jones, *op. cit.*, 252-256.

[103] The curriculum of the early Catholic parochial schools was in large measure that of the standard curriculum of the private Protestant and early public schools, with the exception that they taught classes in the Catholic religion rather than the classes in the Bible and Protestant beliefs, and that they tried to use textbooks which were not hostile to the Church.

[104] Ellis, *op. cit.*, 55.

[105] Gerow, *op. cit.*, 67-68.

[106] A fourth sister, Zulma, known also as Jane, was deaf and dumb. She acted as housekeeper for the trio who taught.

[107] *Natchez Daily Courier*, March 29, 1855.

[108] The Marcilly sisters must have retained the ownership of the Rose Hill property even after their departure, because in 1855, Bishop Van de Velde purchased the property from them for $16,000.

made by the American Sisters to affiliate with the French Daughters of Charity Chanche acted as their agent in Paris.[109] It is not surprising then that he was able to prevail upon the Sisters to extend their charity to his struggling diocese. On January 28, 1847, three Sisters, Martha, Philomena and Scholastica, arrived in Natchez with the intention of opening an orphan asylum and a girls' day school.[110] For the first two days the Sisters were the guests of the Marcilly sisters. Then, on January 30, the building known as Mechanics Hall on Main Street was assigned to them. On that same day the Sisters received their first charges, Margaret and Mary Ann Power, of Natchez; the following day another little girl, three years old, was brought to the Sisters from Grand Gulf. By March 2, the Sisters were also operating a day school for girls.[111] Both operations were conducted in the same building.

The next fifteen months must have been hectic ones for the Sisters. During that space of time they were obliged to change residences four times. Finally, in April 1848, they purchased the home of Mr. Joseph C. Ferriday on Jefferson and Rankin Streets. Aided by the subscriptions of the citizens of Natchez, together with the proceeds of a fair held the previous fall, the Sisters were able to pay more than half of the purchase price which was $5,567.[112] Three notes, payable in one, two and three years, covered the balance of $2,340. Endorsement of these notes and payment of them at the time of their maturity by a Protestant gentleman, Col. Rice C. Ballard,[113] is further indication of the good will shown to the Sisters by the non-Catholics in the Natchez area.[114] The property acquired included, besides the main house with eleven rooms, a brick kitchen, servants' rooms, a washhouse, ironing rooms, a cistern house and cellars.

---

109 Clarke, *op. cit.*, 187-188; Moreau, *Les Pretres Francais Emigres Aux Etats-Unis* (Paris, 1856), 512.

110 Gerow, *op. cit.*, 199-200.

111 *Natchez Semi-Weekly Courier,* March 12, 1847; quoted by Gerow, *op. cit.*, 201.

112 The *Mississippi Free Trader,* Natchez, April 20, 1848; quoted by Gerow, *op. cit.*, 203.

113 Colonel Ballard, who died in Louisville, Ky., on August 31, 1860, became a Catholic a short time before he died.

114 In the beginning (Feb. 1847) the Sisters may have encountered some Protestant opposition, for Bishop Chanche reported to Bishop Blanc of New Orleans that no sooner had the Sisters' school begun operating than "Presbyterian opposition began to make itself felt." Chanche to Blanc, Natchez, Feb. 11, 1847; in AUND: New Orleans Papers.

Before the Bishop's death in 1852, St. Mary's Orphan Asylum and School had become a solidly established institution in the Diocese. Operated by six Sisters, it served as a home for thirty orphans and as a school for seventy day scholars.[115] At this time there was even a plan afoot to establish a similar asylum and school in Vicksburg with some of the Sisters from Natchez.[116]

Having been an educator of young men for all of his priestly life, Bishop Chanche was determined to establish a college for boys at Natchez. This he planned to do when private academies still distinguished the educational life of Mississippi, when the State was just beginning to make its first serious move toward a public school system.[117] Three years before Natchez opened its first public school, Chanche tried to purchase Jefferson College, a private boys school about five miles from Natchez.[118] The institution had been failing financially for some time.[119] At the first meeting of the college's trustees the majority indicated that they were in favor of accepting the Bishop's proposal. However, before a definite decision could be made, news of Chanche's efforts to purchase the college spread abroad and stirred up "all the fanatical spirit of the neighborhood." Significantly at the next meeting of the trustees, a number of stipulations to which the Bishop found it impossible to submit were laid down. He accordingly withdrew his offer.[120]

Two years later the Bishop of Natchez made another attempt to open a college. Although nothing definite had been arranged, the Bishop thought prospects looked quite bright when on August 4, 1844, he wrote to Mr. Pierce Connelly, a distinguished convert of Natchez, who was studying for the priesthood in Rome.

> You will learn with pleasure that I have very flattering prospects for opening a college near Natchez. Almost all the gentlemen in the neighborhood urge me to it and will be liberal. I have begged the Jesuits of St. Louis to take charge

115 *Metropolitan Catholic Almanac*, 1852, 164.

116 Clarke, *op. cit.*, 188.

117 Bettersworth, *op. cit.*, 252, 256.

118 Chanche to Blanc, Natchez, July 12, 1842; in AUND: New Orleans Papers.

119 Bettersworth, *op. cit.*, 257.

120 Chanche to Blanc, Natchez, Aug. 22, 1842; in AUND: New Orleans Papers. Chanche felt that the "respectable portion of the community" had been in favor of his proposal, noting also that many Protestants had openly espoused his cause.

> of it. They know the importance of the place and are willing, if they had the subjects and the permission from their Superiors. I wrote to Father Rosario on the subject. May I ask you to take this matter also in hand and urge upon the Superior the great advantage which an establishment in Natchez would promise to religion? If the fathers in St. Louis had not the kind of persons who would suit Natchez, perhaps those in Maryland or Kentucky would. Please talk of it with the Superiors. It is important. The subject should be acted upon soon.[121]

Enjoying the status of a vice-province since 1840, the Missouri Jesuits had been recruited from various nationalities. Among its members the dominant element was Belgian. Of the eighty-seven fathers and scholastics in 1846, only thirteen were American.[122] The Jesuits in Kentucky were Frenchmen, members of the Lyons province. The Missouri Jesuits were operating the University of St. Louis; those in Kentucky were conducting St. Mary's College, near Lebannon, in Marion County.[123] Neither group felt free to accept Bishop Chanche's offer. No doubt the straitened condition of the finances of the Missouri vice-province as well as a lack of suitable personnel kept the St. Louis Jesuits from assuming the direction of the proposed college.[124] As for the French Jesuits, they were already, at the time of Chanche's invitation, encountering difficulties in making a go of their college near Lebannon. In fact, two years later they closed the institution and withdrew to New York.[125] Unable to secure the services of the Jesuit Fathers, Bishop Chanche had to let the matter rest for the time being.

A third attempt to open a young men's college at Natchez a few years later shows how fixed was the Bishop's resolve to provide the young men of his diocese with an opportunity of receiving a Catholic education locally. This time he turned to the Eudist Fathers in France. As early as August, 1848, Chanche proposed to the Eudist superiors that they open a college in Natchez.[126] The offer was accepted some time in 1849, most probably while Chanche

---

121 Chanche to Connelly, Natchez, August 4, 1844; copy in ADNJ; quoted by Gerow, *op. cit.*, 92.

122 Garraghan, *The Jesuits of the Middle United States* (N.Y., 1938), I, 506.

123 *Ibid.*, III, 294.

124 *Ibid.*, I, 507.

125 *Ibid.*, III, 294.

126 Chanche to Eudist superior, Paris, August 17, 1848; in AE.

was in Europe. On October 30, 1849, three Eudists sailed for New Orleans from Le Havre. Two were priests, Fathers Mathurin Grignon and Jean-Marie Moricet, and the third was an acolyte, Clement Ardois. Accompanying them were the three seminarians whom Chanche had recruited for his diocese while visiting the major seminary at Nantes. These were Guillou, Fiérabras and Babonneau. The group landed at New Orleans on Christmas eve, 1849. Two days later they arrived at Natchez. Here the Bishop received them very cordially but with evident disappointment: he felt the Eudist superiors had sent too few.[127] This reaction would very soon prove embarrassing for the Bishop.

From the start the Bishop's project was beset with difficulties. First of all, he could not find a suitable building to house both teachers and students. As late as April 1850, the Bishop was still searching for a place in which to set up his school.[128] In the meantime the two Eudist priests, Fathers Grignon and Moricet, lived with the Bishop. Although Chanche admitted that "it was necessary to make the start," the presence of the two priests was "a great strain upon his scanty purse."[129] After several disappointments a building was found at the corner of Commerce and Sycamore Streets which suited their purpose and in the fall of 1850, St. Mary's Collegiate Institute opened its doors.[130] Both day students and boarders were accepted. The facilities of the school must have been very limited, because all of the students had to provide themselves with their own desk and chair, while the boarding students were also expected to bring their own beds. The two Eudists were assisted by a Mr. Peter Holton, an Irishman and a student for the priesthood.[131] The following year they were joined by the third Eudist, Clement Ardois, who during the first year of the school's operation completed his seminary studies at St. Mary's in Baltimore and was ordained to the priesthood by Bishop Chanche on August 30, 1851.[132] The fourth man to join the staff at the beginning

[127] *Annales des Eudistes,* ms. 29, p. 520; in AE.

[128] Chanche to Blanc, Natchez, April 3, 1850; copy in ADNJ.

[129] Chanche to Blanc, Natchez, March 20, 1850; copy in ADNJ; quoted by Gerow, *op. cit.,* 93.

[130] *Natchez Courier,* Friday, August 9, 1850; quoted by Gerow, *op. cit.,* 93-94.

[131] *Ibid.*

[132] *Annales des Eudistes,* ms. 29, pp. 520, 539; in AE; Chanche to Blanc, Natchez, August 30, 1851; copy in ADNJ.

of the second school year was Mr. Francis Xavier Leray, a former student of the Eudists at Rennes.[133] He had come to America with some members of the Society and had remained with them until he entered St. Mary's Seminary in Baltimore, May 13, 1847. He was accepted as a student for the Diocese of Natchez in September 1850. Having completed his studies to the Bishop's satisfaction, Leray traveled to Natchez in the company of a fellow student, the Eudist Ardois.[134]

Evidently the college did not fare well from the very start. After being in operation only one year rumors spread abroad that the school was about to close.[135] Although the rumors were squelched publicly, there was some substance to them or to the suspicion that the school would close. There were several causes.[136] One was poor administration on the part of the Eudists, a fact admitted by their own historian. Secondly, the staff was insufficient and thus overworked; reinforcements were promised but they never arrived. Finally, there was the language barrier which these French teachers never really overcame much to the distess of the students and their parents. This being the case, it is no wonder that the student enrollment began to drop and that a prejudice built up against the institution. In view of the situation Chanche at the end of the year gave orders to close the school by April 1, 1852.[137] It was not his intention to abandon the college, but rather to reorganize it.

In the meanwhile things at the college went from bad to worse. The student enrollment had dropped so low that there were only a handful left. With an accompanying drop in income, the Fathers soon found themselves with hardly anything to eat.[138] Nor was the Bishop in a position to help them, for he himself did not even have enough money for bread and salt.[139] Once informed of the situation at Natchez and of the Bishop's intention to close the college temporarily, the superior general of the Eudists, Father Louis Gaudaire, acted quickly. On January 10, 1852, he ordered his

---

133 Registers of St. Mary's Seminary, Baltimore, Vol. I, p. 47.

134 *Ibid.;* also *Annales des Eudistes,* ms. 29, 539; in AE.

135 *The Mississippi Free Trader,* Natchez, Nov. 12, 1851; quoted by Gerow, *op. cit.,* 94.

136 *Annales des Eudistes,* ms. 29, p. 539; in AE.

137 *Ibid.*

138 *Ibid.* Father Haudebourg writes: ". . . et comme ils mouraient de faim, M. le Supérieur général les avait rappelés en France."

139 Chanche to Blanc, Natchez, Jan. 24, 1852; copy in ADNJ.

Fathers to return to France immediately.[140] When the news reached Natchez, Chanche reacted somewhat bitterly. Writing to his metropolitan, Archbishop Blanc of New Orleans, he complained:

> The supervisor of the Eudists has written to his priests here that as there is no prospect of succeeding with a school in Natchez he recalls them to France . . . He sent me two men last year entirely unfit for the purpose for which they were sent. They let the school fail through their incapacity . . . To reorganize this school was difficult and just at the time when patience and perseverance are getting the better of prejudice he calls all off without one day's notice. Add to this all the expense, all the trouble, and all the privations which I have undergone to establish this school. The conduct is highly unjust, and not to say iniquitous.[141]

In departing when they did, the Eudists could hardly be called unjust. So real was their destitution that, when Fathers Moricet and Ardois left for France, they had to obtain boat passage on credit.[142] Chanche's reaction to the superior general's order is equally strange on another score. The Eudists sent to Natchez were evidently not qualified for the work expected of them. This being the case one wonders why the Bishop should wish to retain them.

On March 15, 1850, Fathers Moricet and Ardois sailed from New Orleans for France.[143] Two days before their departure Bishop Chanche closed the college officially. Although an incorporated member of the Eudists, Father Grignon obtained leave to remain in America. He eventually was incardinated into the Diocese.[144]

There must have been many "practical" men who questioned the wisdom of the American bishops in calling for the erection of the Diocese of Natchez in 1837. After surveying the situation, even its first bishop wondered whether the step had not been premature. However, having accepted the task of organizing the Catholic Church in Mississippi, John Joseph Chanche set himself to it manfully.

---

140 *Annales des Eudistes,* ms. 29, p. 539; in AE.

141 Chanche to Blanc, Natchez, Feb. 21, 1852; copy in ADNJ.

142 *Annales des Eudistes,* ms. 29, p. 539; in AE.

143 *Ibid.*

144 Father Grignon was appointed rector of the Cathedral in 1852 and vicar-general of the Diocese in 1857. He held both offices until his death at Natchez in 1887.

St. Mary's Cathedral, Natchez, Mississippi, from an old lithograph print. Begun in 1842, the gothic church was not completed until 1859.

St. Joseph's Church, Port Gibson, Mississippi. This church was begun by Father Fiérabras in 1850.

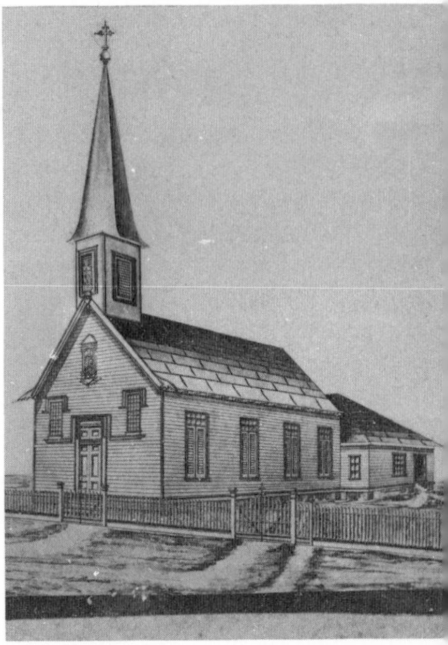

St. Paul's Church, Pass Christian, Missis sippi. Replacing an older one put up b Father Labbe, this church on the Gulf Coas was built in 1851. It was destroyed by fir in 1876.

Holy Cross Church, Philadelphia, Mississippi. Built before the Civil War, this church burned in 1925.

St Paul's Church, Vicksburg, Mississipp built in 1849.

Chapter II

EARLY ORGANIZATION

Parishes

Under Chanche's administration the Diocese grew, but this growth was somewhat anemic. As we have seen, one of the major problems was the lack of finances. Although the Propagation of the Faith Society continued to send an annual donation to the Diocese, it was far from adequate in view of the crying need for churches and the poverty of Mississippi's Catholics. For that matter, much of the money sent by the Society was used to satisfy the Cathedral's creditors, although the allocations were intended for the Diocese at large. Consequently, what growth did take place did so without much assistance from the Bishop. Thus, the erection of churches at Paulding, Biloxi, Pass Christian and Vicksburg in the early 1840's was achieved through the energies of the local pastors and the generosity of the Catholics in the respective areas. The same must be said of the churches built between 1847 and 1852, namely those at Camden, Jackson, Bay St. Louis, Cedar Creek, Port Gibson, Yazoo City and again at Pass Christian. [1]

Few of these houses of worship could be described as works of art. Only two of the churches were built with brick. The others were frame buildings. The church at Cedar Creek in Copiah County was nothing more than a rough log-cabin.[2] None of the churches erected were very large, except the one in Bay St. Louis which measured 165 feet long and 46 feet wide, making it perhaps the largest church in the Diocese at the time.[3] The interior of some of these churches was very simple; some lacked even the ordinary appointments such as a decent altar, pews and Stations of the Cross. Such a state of affairs, however, is not to be wondered at.

[1] A new church at Pass Christian was erected in 1851 by Father Anthony Paul Guerard to replace the one put up by Father Labbe.

[2] Fiérabras to Monseigneur (Chanche), Port Gibson, June 29, 1852; in AUND: Natchez Papers. The priest serving this church in 1852, states that Cedar Creek is in Copiah County but the *Catholic Almanac* lists it as being in the neighboring county of Claiborne. The writer could not find the place on the maps he consulted.

[3] Fahey, "Our Lady of the Gulf," in *Catholic Action of the South* (Natchez Centennial Edition), Oct. 14, 1937, 39.

It must be borne in mind that for more than twelve years even the Cathedral in Natchez was not much more than a shell. The interior walls for the most part were unplastered. The windows were boarded up, except for a small pane of clear glass in each to allow at least some light to enter. The furniture was the very simplest since it was meant to be only temporary. Indeed, in the eyes of Chanche's successor the Cathedral had "the appearance of a great barn." [4]

Catholic Life

Growth of membership in the Church during Chanche's administration is difficult to determine, because few records were kept during this period. However, from the few annual parish reports that have been discovered, one is inclined to believe few adults embraced the Catholic faith during Chanche's and his successor's administrations. For example, at Natchez where parish life was stable and a priest always on hand only nineteen adults embraced the Catholic faith between 1850 and 1855.[5]

Apparently Bishop Chanche and his priests concentrated on bringing back to the practice of their faith those Catholics who had drifted away and on strengthening the faith of those who had perservered. The first thing the Bishop did was to provide as many of his flock as possible with regular priestly ministrations. In some places he was able to furnish a priest as a resident pastor. Here stable parish life could be inaugurated and maintained. At the end of Chanche's administration there were eight such parishes, namely at Vicksburg, Port Gibson, Yazoo City, Jackson, Paulding, Biloxi, Pass Christian and Bay St. Louis. Catholics living in other settlements, in number about thirty-two, were visited regularly by one of these pastors on the average of once a month. In either case, the Catholics in Mississippi by the middle of the century were being given the opportunity to assist at Mass and receive the Sacraments as well as some religious instruction regularly, and one might say even frequently.

Other means were also employed to intensify the spiritual life of the Catholics in Mississippi and to make the Catholic

[4] Van de Velde to Propagation of the Faith Society in Paris, Jan. 2, 1854; (copy) quoted in Gerow, *op. cit.*, 117.

[5] List of Diocesan Statistics (1850-1867), undated but drawn up most probably in May 1867; in ADNJ, File: Elder—D.

religion more intelligible to them and their non-Catholic neighbors. Methods varied. Apparently missions and retreats as well as open-lectures were popular. One recalls Chanche's tour of the Diocese in 1844, when he lectured to mixed audiences in Yazoo City and Benton. While visiting the city Bishop Ignatius Reynolds of Charleston delivered a lecture in the Cathedral of Natchez to which the general public was invited.[6] Father John Timon, C.M., future bishop of Buffalo, conducted a retreat for the Catholic community in Natchez in March, 1844.[7] In the fall of 1846, Father Guinand, pastor of Biloxi, gave a series of missions to the Catholic communities along the Gulf Coast. Both Father Fiérabras and Father Babonneau saw the advantage of putting Catholic books and tracts within reach of Catholics and non-Catholics, especially in the interior of the State where there was a high incidence of ignorance about things Catholic and religion in general. In 1851, Father Babonneau established a Catholic circulating library at Sulphur Springs.[8] Father Fiérabras, convinced that libraries were a most efficacious way of spreading the Catholic faith, proposed to establish a small library with every church he erected. On June 29, 1852, he wrote to Bishop Chanche explaining his plan:

> Books being extremely rare in the interior some distance from the towns, the people should find little difficulty in accepting our books which are both instructive and interesting. I would like to have a little library or should I say a few volumes, attached to each church. But for the moment I lack absolutely the necessary resources. Nevertheless I hope to realize this plan before long if your Excellency sees no difficulty (involved) or (has) no objection (to it).[9]

Protestants in Mississippi at this time were more fortunate than the Catholics of the State in being supplied with religious literature. National organizations were at work on behalf of the Protestants. The American Bible Society, founded in 1816, was attempting to place Bibles in every family and in all public places. The American Tract Society was set up in 1825, to supplement the work of the Bible Society. As a result of the former's activity, a great

---

6 *The Mississippi Free Trader,* Natchez, March 7, 1848.

7 Gerow, *Cradle Days of St. Mary's at Natchez,* 90.

8 Meador, "Sulphur Springs Parish" in *Catholic Action of the South* (Natchez Centennial Edition), Oct. 14, 1937, 48.

9 Fiérabras to Monseigneur (Chanche), Port Gibson, June 29, 1852; in AUND: Natchez Papers. (Translation).

amount of imported Protestant "tractarian" literature was in circulation in Mississippi during the thirty years which preceded the outbreak of the Civil War.[10] Another plan aimed at reaching Protestants who were suspicious of the Catholic Church called for a multiplicity of small, plain churches to be scattered through the State. The man who devised the plan was Father Fiérabras, who explained the reason behind it in this way:

> My idea in trying to erect as many little churches as I can (my small resources do not permit me to build the most beautiful churches), is to familiarize our separated brethren with the word *Catholic*, constrain them to look upon us as resembling other men, and finally to agree that fundamentally we are not as absurd or unreasonable as they first supposed.[11]

Apart from the general plan of establishing as many parishes as possible with a number of mission stations attached to each, Bishop Chanche did not propose to his priests any detailed program of action to be followed by one and all. His priests enjoyed a good deal of freedom. Much was left to the ingenuity of the individual missionary. For that matter, to have imposed a uniform and detailed plan of action would have been very impractical. Conditions, economic, social and cultural, varied from community to community, from one section to another. A method which might be very effective among the newly arrived Irish and German immigrants along the River could very well be useless among the Creoles along the Gulf Coast. An approach which might appear attractive to the people of Natchez and Vicksburg, fast growing cultural centers of the State, might leave totally unimpressed the backwoodsmen of southwestern Mississippi who lived in log-cabins, who often enough could neither read nor write and whose sole form of recreation was hunting and fishing. Chanche was quite wise in allowing this freedom of action to his priests.

Negro Apostolate

A class of people whose spiritual welfare gave concern to Bishop Chanche from the first years of his administration were the Negroes living within his Diocese. This concern only increased

---

[10] Bettersworth, *Mississippi: A History,* 262.

[11] Fiérabras to Monseigneur (Chanche), Port Gibson, June 29, 1852; in AUND: Natchez Papers. (Translation).

as he watched the rapid growth of this segment of the population in Mississippi. In 1820, there were 32,814 Negroes in the State. Increasing at a phenomenal rate through the 1840's and 1850's, by 1860 their number had skyrocketed to 436,631.[12] Few of these were Catholic, for it was customary for the slaves, if they "got religion" at all, to take the religion of their masters, most of whom in Mississippi were Protestant. At the time of Chanche's arrival in Natchez there were only two Negroes who called themselves Catholic.[13] Undoubtedly there were many others living out in the country on plantations owned and operated by Catholics.[14] Altogether they most probably did not number more than four or five hundred, if we allow fifty or more slaves for each plantation and bear in mind that not every slave on these plantations was necessarily a Catholic.[15]

Chanche had every reason to be concerned about the spiritual welfare of the Negroes in Mississippi. The history of these times presents a very sad picture of the religious condition of the Negro slaves throughout the South. The facts which go to make up the general picture can, in almost every instance, be applied to the situation which prevailed in the state of Mississippi during the ante-bellum period.

During the early part of the nineteenth century the religious and moral development of the American Negro was slow and attended with difficulties. After being brought from his native Africa, the slave in time relinquished his former paganism and absorbed the religion, or irreligion, of his master. Often enough those masters who felt any obligation for the spiritual welfare of their slaves were incapable of giving a religious training. In many cases,

---

12 Randall, *The Civil War and Reconstruction* (Boston, 1937), 24.

13 Chanche to the Archbishop of Vienna (Milde), Natchez, June 7, 1842; in *Berichte der Leopoldinen-Stiftung*, XVI (1843), 25-27.

14 Most of these plantations belonging to Catholics were in the river counties: Fairfield Plantation eleven miles southeast of Vicksburg; Hardtimes and Beechgrove near Vicksburg; Fair View and Woodland near Port Gibson; the Dohan plantation near Rodney; Fair Oaks nine miles below Natchez; Ben Wade's plantation eleven miles from Natchez; Ben Roach's plantation near Greenville; Mrs. Norton's plantation between Kingston and Woodville in Wilkinson County, and Mrs. Hazlip's plantation between Washington and Natchez in Adams County.

15 Missionary priests were reluctant to baptize adult Negroes who had not gone through a period of instruction. Hence the appearance of a priest at a plantation did not mean that all un-baptized slaves would automatically receive the Sacrament.

slave-owners were opposed to anyone imparting a knowledge of Christian precepts to their slaves. The notion had gained ground that the Negro would become discontented and rebellious, and thus, less useful as a laborer, if his mind were enlightened by profane or even religious truths. Consequently, missionaries working among Negroes were considered a hazard to the public order; highly emotional preachers were viewed as possible incendiaries.

As a result of the above mentioned conditions most of the slaves in the South were woefully ignorant about religious matters and gross immorality among them was rampant.[16] Marriages among slaves, as well as divorces and rematings, required merely the approval of the master; they were not matters of legal record. Concubinage with Negro women on the part of planters and their sons and overseers is evidenced by the census enumeration of mulattoes and other data. Phillips maintains that concubinage was flagrantly prevalent in the Creole section of Louisiana and was at least sporadic from New England to Texas.[17] Children born of such unions legally had the status of their mother. Most of them were treated as any other slave. Some few were manumitted and vested with property. Many owners, according to Maynard, did not interfere with promiscuity among the slaves, because it was economically to their advantage.[18] He goes on to make the startling statement that "in some places breeding farms . . . were established."[19] A view of Negro morals which was not unique was expressed by one planter in this way: "We don't care what they do when their tasks are over — we lose sight of them till next day. Their morals and manners are in their own keeping."[20]

Often enough the moral caliber of the slaves attached to plantations owned by Catholics was not much higher than that of other slaves. As early as 1785, John Carroll, Prefect Apostolic of the United States, reported to Cardinal Antonelli on the sad plight of the Catholic Negroes in the new republic. He stated that the Negroes for the most part were of very low morals and ill instructed; however, this was a thing to be expected if they

---

16 Cf. Phillips, *Life and Labor in the Old South* (Boston, 1930), 203-205.

17 *Ibid.*, 205.

18 Maynard, *The Story of American Catholicism* (New York, 1941), 170.

19 *Ibid.*

20 Reported by an English traveler, Basil Hall, and cited in Phillips, *op. cit.*, 204.

were to be worked, as he said, continuously and rarely given an opportunity to hear any instructions from the priest.[21] In his report to Propaganda of October 16, 1818, Archbishop Maréchal referred to the morality of the colored women in his diocese. Many of them, he said, were faithful to God, but unfortunately a very large number lived and died in their vices.[22] In southern Louisiana, as late as the 1840's and 1850's, where there were thousands of baptized Negroes, a great many of them were only nominal Catholics, baptized solely because their masters had them baptized and poorly instructed in their religion.[23] With honorable exceptions, the slaves of Catholic masters were not, religiously speaking, better provided for than others.

A slight improvement in the Negro's religious and moral condition took place after the 1830's. It can be explained by the fact that the sentiment among a large proportion of slave holders concerning the need of instruction or education for slaves underwent a change. What stimulated this change of sentiment among Southern slave holders was the rise of the abolition movement in the North. The abolitionists called slaveholding sinful. Such an attitude only spurred Southern religious forces on to greater efforts for the salvation of Negro souls. Religious instruction of the Negro slaves would be one of the most effective ways to counteract the "calumnies" of the abolitionists.[24] Another factor which promoted interest in the spiritual welfare of the slaves was the realization of the value of religious training in preserving submissiveness and loyalty. As the danger of war between North and South grew, this value took on added meaning.[25] Admittedly this increased activity among the Negroes was also an expression of Christian ideals; it was an honest effort to win souls through the process of conversion common to all men.

The presence of so many uninstructed Negroes within his diocese was a problem which Bishop Chanche faced squarely at the very beginning of his administration. Less than nine months after

---

[21] Carroll to Antonelli, Baltimore, March 1, 1785; cited by Theobald in "Catholic Missionary Work among the Colored People of the United States" in RACHS, XXXV (1924), 327.

[22] Maréchal to Propaganda, Oct. 16, 1818; in Theobald, *op. cit.*, 330.

[23] Gillard, *Colored Catholics in the United States* (Baltimore, 1941), 58.

[24] Jackson, "Religious Instruction of Negroes, 1830-1860, with special Reference to South Carolina," in *Journal of Negro History,* XV (1930), 78-79.

[25] Wiley, *Southern Negroes 1861-1865* (New York, 1953), 98-99.

his arrival in the Diocese, the Bishop designated one of his three priests for work among the Negroes.[26] The man chosen was Father Francois, who apparently took his assignment quite seriously. During the absence of the Bishop he preferred to leave the Cathedral parish in the hands of a newly arrived priest rather than neglect the mission among the Negroes.[27] He began his apostolate by preaching a special Mission for the Negroes of the area. At first only two or three people attended the exercises. Undaunted Father Francois went on with the Mission. Before long his audience grew to sixty, and, as a result of his work, fifteen adult Negroes were converted and baptized.[28] The work inaugurated by him was well under way by the following year according to a letter sent by Chanche to the Archbishop of Vienna.

> I have begun a mission amongst the Negroes. On my arrival here there were only two who called themselves Catholic; at present many frequent the Sacraments. They are given instruction twice a week and from 150 to 200 are present and are preparing themselves for baptism.[29]

The mission of which he speaks was near Natchez.[30] Most probably it was on some plantation.

As a unit of religious activity, the plantation mission was a meeting house on the plantation grounds for the special benefit of the rural slaves.[31] For more than a generation prior to 1830, the Negroes had shared in the religious activities of the whites. These contacts, however, were confined largely to those Negroes near at hand, such as house servants and those who lived in cities and towns. On these occasions the whites and Negroes attended morning services together, the latter taking seats in the rear of the church or in the balcony.[32] In some churches, special meetings for the slaves were held in the afternoon. These meetings for the Catholic Negroes of Natchez took the form of instructions which

[26] Chanche to Blanc, Natchez, Jan. 31, 1842; in ADNJ; quoted by Gerow, *op. cit.*, 98.

[27] Francois to Chanche, Natchez, 1843; in ADNJ; quoted by Gerow, *op. cit.*, 265-266.

[28] Clarke, *Lives of the Deceased Bishops of the Catholic Church in the United States*, II, 182.

[29] Chanche to Archbishop (Milde) of Vienna, Natchez, June 7, 1842; in *Berichte der Leopoldinen-Stiftung*, XVI (1843), 26. (Translation).

[30] Chanche to the Propagation of the Faith Society, Natchez, 1844; copy in ADNJ; quoted by Gerow, *op. cit.*, 266.

[31] Jackson, *op. cit.*, 73.

[32] Wiley, *op. cit.*, 98.

were intended to prepare them for Baptism or the other Sacraments. The plantation mission, then, represents an effort on the part of all the churches to make contact with the colored majority, slaves who were not allowed to leave the plantation property.

It is interesting to note that, as the value of religious instruction for the Negro became recognized, more and more planters took it upon themselves to employ missionaries to work among their slaves. Such a master himself may or may not have been a Christian. Furthermore, under such an arrangement, it made no difference to the plantation owner what might be the particular religious affiliation of the missionary. Such an arrangement was made between Father Fiérabras of Port Gibson and a non-Catholic planter, Colonel Ballard. In a letter to Bishop Chanche, dated June 29, 1852, Father Fiérabras describes one of his visits to the Ballard plantation.

> Lastly I visited the negroes of Colonel Ballard. The brave Colonel gave me a perfect reception, with all possible politeness. I arrived on Saturday evening. The Colonel immediately sent out an order to his negroes who live on one of his plantations a slight distance from his magnificent plantation, *Magnolia,* for all to come the next day, tots and adults. All came the next day which was a Sunday. I preached and said Mass. In my sermon I insisted on the necesssity of Baptism. After Mass, as I was taking off the vestments, the Colonel on his own accord came to ask me if I would baptize the children; on my response to the affirmative, he told the negroes publicly that he was leaving them perfectly free to do as they pleased; that if anyone desired to have his children baptized, he could come, I would baptize them. Immediately they brought me all the children under the age of three. All the others above this age had been baptized three years ago by a Methodist minister who introduced himself without the Colonel's knowledge. I hope to re-baptize them later; the time has not yet come, they would not understand me, and an indiscreet zeal could spoil everything. The Colonel assisted at all the ceremonies from the beginning to end. He invited me to come whenever I want and remain as long as I may desire.[33]

Apparently another non-Catholic planter was happy to have the priest care for the spiritual welfare of his slaves, too, for in

[33] Fiérabas to Monseigneur (Chanche), Port Gibson, June 29, 1852; in AUND: Natchez Papers. (Translation).

the same letter Fiérabras goes on to say: "Finally, I baptized 22 negroes on a plantation between Rodney and Port-Gibson. All the others (adults) are preparing themselves for baptism. They have given me every permission to go and instruct them." [34]

None of the denominations in Mississippi was able to develop any extensive system of special missionaries working exclusively among the Negroes. Most of the ministers of the Gospel in Mississippi pursued operations among the slaves only in connection with their regular churches. Nevertheless, Bishop Chanche saw the need for developing such a system to cope with the prevailing situation. So he expressed himself in a letter to the Propagation of the Faith Society in 1844.

> It would be very important for religion in the country here that we could have zealous Priests who would be willing to give themselves entirely to the instruction of the Negroes. These poor people live in an entire ignorance of religion and they have not permission to go outside of the limits of the plantation. The good which would be done would be a permanent good.[35]

The Bishop saw an added advantage to be derived from such an apostolate.

> Besides, the good (evident among the Negroes) would reflect upon their masters. When these would see the change that would be produced in their slaves they could not but esteem a religion which could produce such . . . effects, and esteem would lead them to embrace it.

Unfortunately, because of a shortage of priests, neither Chanche nor his two immediate successors was able to develop a system of missionaries devoted exclusively to the Negro apostolate.[36]

---

[34] *Ibid.*

[35] Chanche to the Propagation of the Faith Society, Natchez, 1844; copy in ADNJ; quoted by Gerow, *op. cit.*, 266.

[36] Father Francois continued to devote himself to the Negroes until September, 1845, when he left the Diocese to join the Congregation of the Mission,

Bishop Chanche's residence, 1841-1846.

St. Mary's Orphan Asylum in Natchez, Mississippi. Purchased in April, 1848.

Bishop John Joseph Chanche, S.S., first Bishop of the Diocese of Natchez. He came to Mississippi to organize the Catholic Church in 1841. He died in 1852.

Chapter III

EPISCOPAL PORTRAIT

At the time of his appointment to the see of Natchez, Chanche was one of the few native-born priests to have been raised to the American episcopate.[1] Unlike some of his American-born predecessors, namely, Carroll, Neale, Fenwick, O.P., and Whelan, Bishop Chanche received all of his seminary training in the United States. He can, therefore, be judged as a genuine product of the young Church in America.

Preacher

It has been said that John Joseph Chanche was an eloquent preacher, a profound theologian and a man of fine administrative abilities.[2] The first claim seems to be valid, for his services were frequently requested when the occasion called for an especially eloquent speaker.

Among his most polished and powerful sermons were two which he preached in the Cathedral of New Orleans to celebrate the anniversary of the Battle of New Orleans. Another famous one, preached at the blessing of St. Paul's Church at Vicksburg in 1849, dealt with the subject of infallibility. On his return from Europe, Chanche delivered a sermon in his own Cathedral which created a profound sensation in the South. For it he was bitterly denounced by the sectarian press.[3] Nevertheless, the grace of his style and the logic of his arguments had a strong appeal for many Protestants. In Natchez alone, a town of about 7,000 inhabitants in 1849, Chanche could draw between 1,000 and 1,200 Protestants to some of his sermons or speeches.[4] As he himself reported in a

---

[1] Chanche's American predecessors in the episcopate were: John Carroll, 1789; Leonard Neale, 1815; Edward D. Fenwick, O.P., 1821; Benedict J. Fenwick, S.J., 1825; Samuel Eccleston, S.S., 1834; Richard P. Miles, O.P., 1837; Richard V. Whelan, 1840.

[2] Clarke, *Lives of the Deceased Bishops of the Catholic Church in the United States*, II, 168.

[3] *Ibid.*, 169.

[4] Report written by Chanche to the Leopoldinen-Stiftung, Paris, March 8, 1849; German translation of French letter in *Berichte der Leopoldinen-Stiftung*, XXII (1849), 31-34. (Translation).

rather impersonal way to the Archbishop of Vienna in 1845: "Although there are still many prejudices against Catholicism, people like to come and listen to our sermons, and it rarely happens that they don't receive a favorable impression from them." [5]

Theologian

As a theologian Chanche undoubtedly was a capable man. He was one of the promoters at the Provincial Councils of Baltimore held in 1843, 1846 and 1849.[6] At the first Plenary Council of Baltimore he was chosen to fill the office of chief promoter.[7] Nevertheless, there is evidence to the effect that some of his colleagues in the American hierarchy questioned his orthodoxy. Three of them, Hughes of New York, O'Connor of Pittsburgh and Purcell of Cincinnati, are reported to have denounced him as a Gallican to the Apostolic Nuncio in Paris. On this score efforts were made to block his possible appointment as coadjutor to Archbishop Eccleston of Baltimore. The charge of Gallicanism, on this occasion, was leveled not only against Chanche but against the Society of St. Sulpice in the United States. So seriously did the Nuncio in Paris view the charges that he took it upon himself to interfere in the affairs of the American Church and report the matter to Rome. Writing to Propaganda from Paris on April 27, 1843, Monseigneur Garibaldi [8] reported:

> Both the Bishop of New York and Monseigneur O'Connor, Bishop of Pittsburgh, recommended to me before their departure from Paris to beg your Eminence not to allow this archdiocese (Baltimore) to remain administered by the vicars general of the Archbishop (Eccleston), because, being Sulpicians, they are imbued with Gallican maxims; maxims which, because of the college which the congregation has in Baltimore, are already beginning to insinuate themselves, not only among the clergy of Baltimore, but also one can discern them in other dioceses of the United States.

---

[5] Chanche to Archbishop (Milde) of Vienna, Natchez, Oct. 21, 1845; German translation of French letter in *Berichte der Leopoldinen-Stiftung*, XIX (1846), 33-35. (Translation).

[6] Guilday, *History of the Council of Baltimore, 1791-1884* (N.Y., 1932), 136, 148, 156.

[7] *Ibid.*, 173.

[8] Although Msgr. Raphael Fornari is said to have taken possession of the Nunciature in Paris on April 22, 1843, he did not actually arrive until some time in May. His predecessor, Msgr. Antonio Garibaldi, remained until May 23, 1843.

> Knowing that I have nothing to do with the United States of America, I excused myself before those bishops from taking the task upon myself. But now that Monseigneur Purcell, Bishop of Cincinnati, has returned to Paris, he has (also) come to see me before departing for America, and urged on by the above mentioned bishops has made the same request, begging strongly even on behalf of the other American bishops who cannot tolerate Gallicanism insinuating itself into those areas which must remain heart and soul attached to the Holy Apostolic See and must follow and teach her doctrines in all their extension and in all their purity. (. . . .) . . . and considering how much more serious that disease is in a country so far distant from the center of Unity, I have decided to comply with their requests and beseech your Eminence . . . not to choose him (i.e., the proposed coadjutor for Baltimore) either from the priests of the Congregation of St. Sulpice or from among the alumni of that Congregation.
>
> I am told that a certain M. Abbé Chanche will be proposed who though he is an ecclesiastic of irreproachable conduct as all the Sulpicians are nevertheless lacks the necessary knowledge and who is a very strong Gallican in his principles.[9]

The accusation of Gallicanism leveled against the Sulpicians in the United States should not be viewed as an impossible one. It has been definitely established that their confreres at the seminary of St. Sulpice in Paris, namely, M. de Montaigne, M. Labrunie and M. Boyer, in their course on the Church taught a moderate form of Gallicanism, this during the days of the First Empire.[10] The Superior General of the Sulpicians himself, M. Emery, was a semi-Gallican.[11]

It would only stand to reason that these men would have had an influence upon the Sulpician professors at St. Mary's Seminary in Baltimore, most of whom had been educated in France. On the other hand, the bishops who had denounced the Sulpicians to

---

[9] Nuncio of Paris (Garibaldi) to Propaganda, Paris, April 27, 1843; in APF: Scritture Riferite nei Congressi, XIII (1841-1844), ff. 787 rv, 788 r. (Translation).

[10] J. Audinet, "L'Enseignement 'De Ecclesia' A St. Sulpice Sous Le Premier Empire, Et les Debuts Du Gallicanisme Modere," *Unam Sanctam,* XXXIV (1960), 115-139.

[11] "Entre les tendances des ecclésiastiques du second ordre, et les prétentions de l'Empereur, sa (M. Emery) position s'établit donc en 1807 dans un moyen terme, celui du gallicanisme modéré qu'il regarde comme le seul authentique." Leflon, *Monsieur Emery* (Paris, 1944), II, 306-307.

the Nuncio in Paris may not have been completely unbiased. All three were Irish-born. And at this late date the Church in the United States was still afflicted with French-Irish tensions. In any case, no evidence, except that mentioned above, has been uncovered to support the accusation that Bishop Chanche was even a moderate Gallican, much less a "Gallicano fortissimo."

Administrator

Before coming to Natchez, Chanche had already established a name for himself as a good administrator. First Vice-President, then, at the age of thirty-nine, President of St. Mary's College in Baltimore, he displayed such administrative talents that on three different occasions, as we have pointed out, attempts were made to raise him to the episcopate. Indeed, to one personally acquainted with Chanche and the College in the 1830's, it seemed: "At no period did the institution over which he presided enjoy a better name or move on more prosperously than under his administration."[12] At Natchez he again displayed a fine talent for administration. However, his achievements, remarkable in view of the circumstances, as we shall soon see, are overshadowed by one initial mistake. This was the attempt to build a grand cathedral, grand in terms of American churches, in the face of the most adverse circumstances. Unfortunately his zeal for God's honor and glory in executing liturgical functions blinded him to certain facts which should have given him pause before initiating a venture of such proportions.

What were these facts? The times in which Chanche chose to build was a period of national economic depression. The Catholics in Mississippi, including those in the Natchez area, were poor. Even as late as 1852, when economic prosperity had returned, Chanche reported to Blanc of New Orleans: "The congregation (at Natchez) is poor and not able to support a bishop and a priest without assistance." [13]

And a few days later: "I do not know what I shall do. I have not means of getting money here, not even enough for bread and salt." [14] When the first subscription was taken up among the

[12] *The Metropolitan Catholic Almanac,* 1853, 52.
[13] Chanche to Blanc, Natchez, Jan. 17, 1852; in AUND: New Orleans Papers.
[14] Chanche to Blanc, Natchez, Jan. 24, 1852; *Ibid.*

people of Natchez, both Catholic and Protestant, not even $5,000 could be realized. And even such subscriptions as were made should have been viewed with reservation, for six months after his arrival in the Diocese Chanche had yet to see the first penny of the "liberal allowance" which had been promised for his subsistence by the trustees of the parish. It is true that the Bishop had on hand $4,920 from the Propagation of the Faith Society and the promise of $7,864 more from the same organization when he decided to go ahead with his plans for building a cathedral. But, as the Bishop well knew, this money was meant to meet the needs of the whole Diocese, not only those of one community. It would seem, therefore, that Chanche should have postponed the project or at least executed it along more modest lines. It proved to be a mistake which would harass him for the rest of his life and which would hang like a millstone around the neck of the next two bishops of Natchez.

Character

In appearance Bishop Chanche was "tall, commanding and hand-some." [15] At the altar, in performing his sacred duties, he was a peculiarly imposing and distinguished figure. He was "urbane and cultivated in his manners, always accessible, courteous and kind." In his zeal for souls Chanche resembles another intrepid Sulpician bishop of the same period, Benedict Flaget.[16] We need only consider the former's begging tours throughout the country, his trip to Europe to obtain funds and man-power, his trip to Havana in an attempt to obtain compensation for the Spanish land-grants made to the Church at Natchez in the 18th century, and his many visitations of the diocese made alone and on horseback like any other missionary. Chanche had his share of courage, too. Only a courageous man would have accepted so unpopular an appointment as that to Natchez, a diocese whose Catholic population was undetermined, whose assets were practically nil, whose clergy consisted of two priests on loan from another diocese and whose institutions were limited to a small one-room chapel. His

---

[15] Clarke, *op. cit.*, 168.

[16] Benedict J. Flaget was one of the first Sulpicians to come to the United States from France. He was appointed Bishop of Bardstown in 1808, and ruled that diocese until 1850, except for one year (1832-1833), when, having resigned, he was re-appointed. The seat of the diocese was transferred to Louisville, Ky., in 1841.

courage takes on added luster when we recall that he was no backswoodsman, accustomed to frontier life. On the contrary, Chanche was born into a well-to-do family,[17] was accustomed to move in the best of social circles, and came from a city which, at the time, was one of the cultural centers of the United States, a city where he had numerous friends and admirers both among the clergy and laity.[18]

Only one note appears which mars the sketch of this almost ideal man. In 1846, the Holy See was intent upon giving Archbishop Eccleston a coadjutor. When a rumor began to circulate that the Bishop of Natchez was to receive the appointment, Bishop Francis Patrick Kenrick of Philadelphia, Propaganda's agent in the affair, wrote to Rome to forestall any such eventuality. The grounds for his objecting are somewhat surprising.

> I think it should be said that he (Chanche) should not be appointed; for although he is of upright character and outstanding piety, at one time he had a serious brain condition, with obvious danger of insanity.[19]

Why this fact should constitute an obstacle now, whereas five years previously it did not prevent Chanche from being nominated and consecrated for Natchez, is a little bewildering. That all, except Kenrick, should have been ignorant of the previous "serious brain condition" is most unlikely. In view of his actual appointment to Natchez and the previous efforts to obtain him for other dioceses, it would seem that the other American bishops did not consider the danger involved as being proximate or even real. Furthermore, nothing has come to light in his administration of St. Mary's College or of the Diocese of Natchez which would indicate that Chanche was laboring under any mental disability.

Death

On November 21, 1851, Archbishop Francis Kenrick of Baltimore announced that the first plenary council to be held in the United States would assemble in Baltimore on May 9, 1852.[20] To this historic ecclesiastical gathering Chanche went in the very best of health. In its deliberations he took a conspicuous and

[17] Clarke, *op. cit.*, 166.
[18] *Ibid.*, 168.
[19] Kenrick to Propaganda, Philadelphia, Dec. 7, 1846; in APF: Scritture Riferite nei Congressi, XIV (1845-1848), ff. 392 rv. (Translation).
[20] Guilday, *op. cit.*, 173.

active part. At a preliminary meeting of the prelates, held on Saturday evening, May 8th, in the Archbishop's house, Chanche was chosen to fill the delicate role of chief promoter at the Council. On the same occasion the prelate from Natchez was selected to serve on the Committee on the Catholic Education of Youth and Allied Matters and also on the Committee on Contentious Cases.[21] During the course of the Council, at its second Solemn Sesssion in the Cathedral, Bishop Chanche celebrated a Pontifical Mass of Requiem for the repose of the souls of the bishops who had died since the Provincial Council of 1849.[22] It was a privilege to which attention would soon be drawn, for within seventy days he himself would have joined them in death.

After the close of the Council on May 20th, Bishop Chanche visited Emmitsburg and, returning, stopped in Frederick City, Maryland. It was his intention to spend a few days with his nieces, the Marcilly sisters, who had conducted a school for girls in Natchez under his auspices. During this visit he suddenly contracted a violent form of cholera. Medical aid proved futile. After a severe illness of two weeks, the Bishop of Natchez died on July 22, 1852, at the age of 56, and in the twelfth year of his episcopate. His death, distinguished by patience and resignation, was as exemplary as his whole life had been. His remains were interred in the Cathedral cemetery at Baltimore at his own request after obsequies had been conducted by Archbishop Kenrick in St. Mary's College chapel.[23] Thus, the city near the upper end of the Chesapeake Bay which had given him birth, which had witnessed his baptism, his ordination and his consecration, also became the final resting place of John Joseph Chanche, one of the most esteemed bishops of the early Church in the United States.

Evaluation

Greatness is a difficult quality to measure; its factors are variable and often intangible. Nevertheless, we hazard the judgment that John Joseph Chanche was a great bishop. In itself the condition of his diocese at the time of his death hardly provides conclusive proof of his greatness. In the whole State there were eleven

---

[21] *Ibid.*, 173-174.
[22] *Ibid.*, 176.
[23] Clarke, *op. cit.*, 190; also Gerow, *Cradle Days of St. Mary's at Natchez*, 108.

churches, only eight of which had resident pastors. Four were situated in the river counties, three on the Gulf Coast and four in the central part of the State. Thirty-two mission stations were also being attended with some sort of regularity. To the Diocese were attached eleven priests. Nine were French-born; one was a Belgian; and another was most probably an Irishman. Most of them were young, having been ordained for only two or three years. A cathedral had been erected, but much remained to be done, both within and without, before it would be completed. The only other institution in the Diocese was a girls' orphanage to which was attached a day school. This institution was in charge of the Daughters of Charity, the first Sisters to settle in the State. All of this was accomplished in a period of a little less than twelve years.

These facts, however, begin to take on added meaning when the circumstances prevailing at the time of Chanche's arrival and during his administration are taken into account. For all practical purposes Chanche had absolutely nothing to work with when he first arrived in the State. The Catholic people were scattered and unorganized, except for the community in Natchez. He had no churches. There was not even a residence set aside for him when he first arrived in the episcopal city. He had no clergy of his own. When he did obtain the services of priests, they were for the most part foreigners who had difficulty in learning to speak English. Many of them were young and inexperienced. Some were drifters upon whom he could not depend to stay at their post. His people were of mixed national origin: French, Irish and German, and often enough very dependent in their religious life upon a priest who could speak their native tongue. For the most part, they were poor. Many were ignorant of the basic truths of their Faith; some were half-Protestant. And finally there were the times which were unfavorable for any material undertaking. A national economic depression had occurred from which at least the Catholics in Mississippi were slow to recover.

That Bishop Chanche was able to collect the Catholics of the State, to reclaim, with the help of his priests, so many fallen-aways and to organize a diocese in the face of such odds, this bespeaks extraordinary courage, zeal and foresight. His mistake in building the cathedral we do not overlook. It may detract from but it certainly does not rob John Joseph Chanche of his greatness.

Photographed by Dan Leyrer, Courtesy Albert Lietand

Natchez – A sketch by James Tooley, c. 1835.

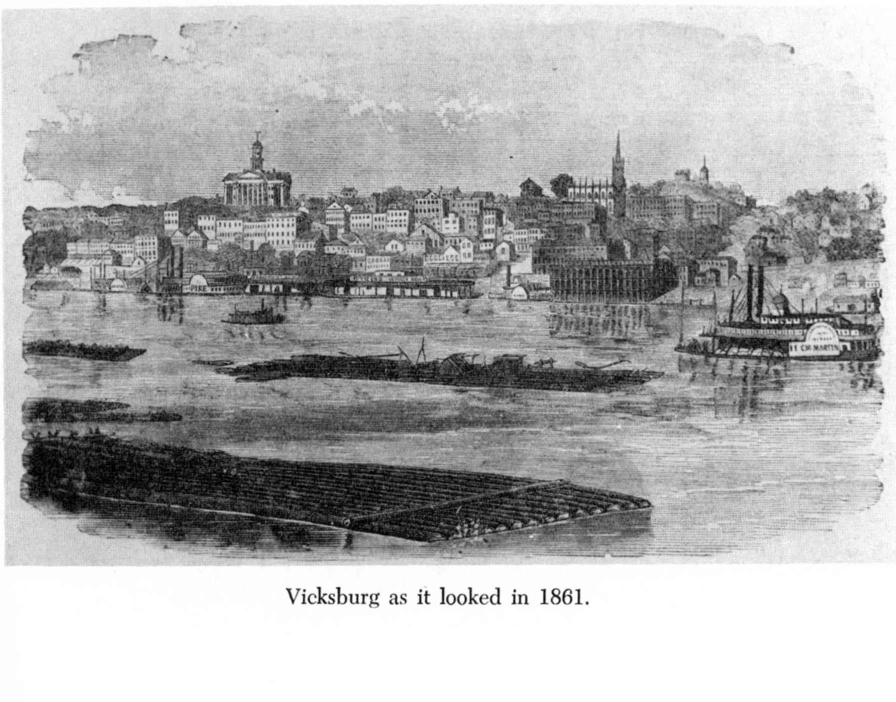

Vicksburg as it looked in 1861.

Bishop James O. Van de Velde, S.J., second Bishop of Natchez, was born in Belgium. Transferred from the Diocese of Chicago, Van de Velde ruled the Catholic Church in Mississippi from 1853 to 1855.

Chapter IV

ADMINISTRATION OF BISHOP VAN DE VELDE, S. J.

After the death of Bishop Chanche the Diocese of Natchez remained vacant for a little more than a year. During this time Archbishop Blanc of New Orleans acted as administrator. Father Grignon at Natchez represented him in managing the affairs of the Diocese.[1]

Transfer

On July 29, 1853, Pope Pius IX appointed a successor to Bishop Chanche. The man chosen, James Oliver Van de Velde, S.J., was already a bishop, having been the ordinary of the Diocese of Chicago since 1848. The transfer had been made by the Holy See at Bishop Van de Velde's own request.[2]

This appointment was not the first time that the name of Van de Velde had been linked with the Diocese of Natchez. In 1837, when arrangements were being made to erect the Diocese of Natchez, Father James Van de Velde had been among those nominated for the proposed bishopric.[3] And in January, 1838, when the newly established Diocese was still without a shepherd, Father Van de Velde had stopped off at Natchez, most probably at the suggestion of Bishop Blanc. The Catholic community there, having been without the services of a priest for some time, was thus given the opportunity of assisting at Mass and of receiving the Sacraments. Father Van de Velde remained for about two weeks. At this time it was supposed that Father Thomas Heyden of Pittsburgh would accept his newly announced appointment as the first bishop of Natchez. Little did the Jesuit priest or the community he served for those two weeks dream that he would return to Natchez as its second bishop fifteen years later.

---

[1] Gerow, *Cradle Days of St. Mary's at Natchez,* 109.

[2] Autobiographical Sketch of Rt. Rev. James Oliver Van de Velde; in the Archives of St. Louis University; published in ICHR, IX (July 1926), 56-70.

[3] Kenrick to Dr. Cullen, Philadelphia, May 22, 1837; text published in RACHS, VII (1896), 295.

During Bishop Van de Velde's lifetime and for some time afterward the impression had prevailed that he had obtained his transfer to Natchez in order to escape the unpleasant relations which had developed between himself and certain members of his clergy in the Diocese of Chicago. That a steady opposition to him among some of his clergy had been neutralizing his efforts for the good of the Diocese is true.[4] However, this fact was never advanced by him as the main reason for wanting to withdraw from his episcopal responsibilities in Chicago. Indeed, his difficulties with certain members of the Chicago clergy arose only after his initial attempt to resign. Originally, when he wrote in strong terms to beg the Holy Father to accept his resignation and to permit him to retire among his former brethren of the Vice-Province of Missouri, the reasons alleged, as he himself reports, were "the manner in which he had been compelled to accept (the appointment) at a time when Rome was in the power of the rebels, his advanced age, and the severity of the climate which undermined his constitution."[5] For several years before his appointment to Chicago, Van de Velde had been afflicted with rheumatism, which fact prompted him to spend the severest winter months of each year in the more genial climate of Louisiana. When appointed to Chicago the climatic conditions there only aggravated his poor health. Nevertheless, on this occasion Cardinal Fransoni of Propaganda did not hesitate to deny his request, encouraging the Bishop instead to bear the burdens associated with his office with patience and resignation. It was only on the occasion of his second attempt to resign that Van de Velde set forth as an accessory reason his difficulties with the clergy of his diocese.[6] This time the case was referred to the Fathers of the first Plenary Council of Baltimore. Unfortunately they viewed his annoyance with a few refractory clergymen as the principal reason for wanting to resign. Almost unanimous in refusing to accept his resignation, the Fathers of the Council urged him to exert his authority and to have recourse to ecclesiastical censures to bring the clergymen into line.[7]

---

[4] Shea, *History of the Catholic Church in the United States,* IV, 614. Garraghan, *The Catholic Church in Chicago* (Chicago, 1921), 161-163, 210-211.

[5] Autobiographical Sketch, in ICHR, IX (July 1926), 67.

[6] *Ibid.*

[7] *Ibid.,* 67. Archbishop Gaetano Bedini, a member of the papal diplomatic corps, after a visit to the United States (June, 1853-February, 1854) filed a report on the state of the Catholic Church in the U. S. at the Sacred Con-

But Bishop Van de Velde was not discouraged. He determined to lay his case before the Holy Father in person. This he did in the early summer of 1852, when he brought the Decrees of the Baltimore Council to Rome. Describing in his autobiographical memoirs the second of his two audiences with Pius IX, Van de Velde reveals another reason for wanting to resign his office. He reports the Holy Father as saying:

> You belong to the regular army of the Church, and I do not wish to give you up. You must continue to fight the battles of Christ. As, however, your principal reasons for wishing to resign are your desire to be a member of the Society of Jesus and the state of your health, which suffers from the cold and damp climate of Chicago, I will make arrangements with the good Father General to have you restored to the Society, and I may transfer you to another See in a more genial climate. Next Sunday night I will give my final answer to Monsignor Barnabo.[8]

On the following Monday Monsignor Barnabò, Secretary of Propoganda, informed the Bishop of the Pope's decision. His Holiness had decided not to accept Van de Velde's resignation. On the other hand, the Pope would insist that he be recognized as a member of the Society of Jesus even as a residential bishop[9] and would transfer him to another See. The Secretary assured Van de Velde that the Pope's decision was final and might be depended upon. Barnabò further advised the Bishop to take his choice of any of the new dioceses which would soon be erected at the suggestion of the Fathers of the recently held Plenary Council.[10] Greatly relieved, Bishop Van de Velde returned to the United States.

Several months passed and no action was taken for the Bishop's transfer. In the meanwhile Van de Velde learned that strong op-

---

gregation de Propaganda Fide. In the report, dated June 12, 1854, he makes an indirect reference to Van de Velde's difficulties with the Chicago clergy by suggesting that the trouble stemmed from a lack of prudence on Van de Velde's part which in turn may have been occasioned by a mental disorder. Connelly, *The Visit of Archbishop Gaetano Bedini to the United States, June, 1853-February, 1854* (Rome, 1960), 210-211.

[8] Autobiographical Sketch, in ICHR, IX (July 1926), 68.

[9] Van de Velde believed that members of the Society of Jesus on becoming residential bishops automatically ceased to be Jesuits. Even the Superior General Roothaan had been under the impression that such was the existing discipline in the Church. Garraghan, *The Jesuits in the Middle United States,* II, 134-135, fn. 58.

[10] These new dioceses were: Newark, Brooklyn, Burlington, Portland, Erie, Covington, Quincy and Natchitoches.

position on the part of the American bishops would be made to any suggestion that he be transferred. Before such opposition could organize, Van de Velde wrote to the Holy Father to remind him of his promise. Reluctant to wait any longer he cleverly dismissed the idea of accepting any one of the new dioceses to be erected, lest his nomination to one of them "become a cause of dissatisfaction," and suggested that he be transferred to the See of Natchez which had become vacant by the death of its first bishop, John Joseph Chanche.[11] This petition was granted.

Thus, Van de Velde's principal reasons for wanting to resign the See of Chicago were his strong attachment to the Society of Jesus and the poor state of his health in that place. When he was assured that as a residential bishop he did not cease to belong to the Society, he agreed to preside over the affairs of another diocese in a more favorable climate. The difficulties which he experienced with some of his clergy was never rated nor advanced by him as more than an accessory reason for resigning the See of Chicago or for seeking a transfer.

On November 3, 1853, Bishop Van de Velde left Chicago. After conducting some business at Quincy, Illinois, he set out for Natchez, arriving there by steamboat from St. Louis on November 23rd. No attempt was made to tender the new ordinary of the Diocese a formal reception, for he left two days later to assist at the consecration of Right Rev. Auguste Martin, first Bishop of Natchitoches, Louisiana, in the Cathedral of New Orleans. After this function Van de Velde repaired to the Jesuit college of Spring Hill at Mobile, Alabama. Here he made a spiritual retreat before returning to Mississippi to enter upon his new duties. After visiting some of the Catholic congregations along the Gulf Coast, he arrived in Natchez in the middle of December. On Sunday, December 18, 1853, James Oliver Van de Velde took formal possession of his See.[12]

Condition of the Diocese

During its vacancy no significant progress had been made in the Diocese of Natchez. Perhaps, it had become even a little worse off than it had been at the time of Bishop Chanche's death. Two

[11] Autobiographical Sketch, in ICHR, IX (July 1926), 69.
[12] *Ibid.,* 70.

of the younger priests, Fathers Fiérabras and Babonneau, had contracted yellow fever and died. The debt of the Diocese had increased with the building of a church at Port Gibson. And the half-finished cathedral had begun to deteriorate. Statistics-wise the Diocese had about 6,000 Catholics, nine priests, eleven churches and one orphanage to which was attached a girls' day school.

Figures balancing off one another, the overall pattern was much the same for three of the surrounding dioceses. Erected in 1843, the Diocese of Little Rock in Arkansas ten years later had only about 1,000 Catholics, ten priests, eight churches and two chapels.[13] Broken off from the Diocese of New Orleans, the newly established See of Natchitoches in northern Louisiana had a large number of Catholics, about 25,000, but it had only five priests, seven churches and one convent-school.[14] Established the same year as the See of Natchez, the Diocese of Nashville, embracing the whole state of Tennessee, in 1852 could count only eight churches and chapels for 5,000 Catholics served by nine priests, but it was relatively fortunate in having a boys' school, two girls' academies and a hospital.[15]

Bounding the See of Natchez on the east and on the south were the Diocese of Mobile and the Archdiocese of New Orleans. Both were in much better condition than the other dioceses bordering on the state of Mississippi. The Diocese of Mobile in 1853, had a Catholic population of not much over 6,000, but it was served by about a dozen diocesan priests assisted by the same number of Jesuit Fathers. Furthermore, the Diocese could boast a beautiful debt-free cathedral, a college for young men, a girls' academy, a boys' school, a hospital and two orphan asylums.[16] In a report to the Sacred Congregation of Propaganda in 1854, Archbishop Blanc of New Orleans described his diocese as containing forty-four churches, each of which was served by one or two priests.[17] Each church had a residence for the clergy attached to it. Assisting the diocesan clergy were the Jesuit Fathers, the Vincentians and the Redemptorists. The Archdiocese had its own seminary. There were at least four highly respected convent-schools which attracted

---

[13] Shea, *History of the Catholic Church in the United States,* IV, 287.
[14] *Ibid.,* 675.
[15] *Ibid.,* 241-242.
[16] *Ibid.,* 280-281.
[17] *Ibid.,* 668-669.

Catholics and non-Catholics alike from all over the Deep South. And the Catholic population of the city of New Orleans alone was estimated at 65,000.

Finances

One of the first problems which Bishop Van de Velde had to face upon his arrival in the Diocese concerned the debt-ridden, half-finished cathedral of Natchez which had already begun to deteriorate. His reaction, once he had sized up the situation, was one of distress. Writing to the Propagation of the Faith Society on January 2, 1854, the Bishop revealed the difficult straits in which he found himself.

> As for me I do not know on what side to turn. I will have what is necessary to pay the notes that are to fall due on the 7th of May of this year, but I am absolutely unable to do anything to furnish the church. (. . . .) Monseigneur Blanc has still about $2,000.00 for me. With that I can have the roof renewed, and then the church will be in the same state as in 1843.[18]

However, after becoming better acquainted with the Catholic community of Natchez, Van de Velde felt that prospects were not as bleak as he had first judged them to be. So he expressed himself to Archbishop Blanc in a letter written on April 25, 1854.

> It will give you much pleasure to learn that I have the hope, not to say the assurance of meeting with no difficulty whatever in finding here the sum necessary for its (the cathedral's) completion without having recourse abroad. Mr. Elliot, (the brave man with his one foot in the grave came to see me last week), Fr. (ancis) Surget, Jr., Henry Chotard, father and son, (the former abjured Protestantism and was baptised with General Long and several others during Easter week), are all very well disposed and will come to my aid. All our Catholics will make an effort to contribute their mite. They have never been in better disposition.[19]

The gentlemen whom the Bishop mentions in his letter were some of the more wealthy and distinguished citizens of the com-

---

[18] Van de Velde to the Propagation of the Faith Society, Natchez, Jan. 2, 1854; copy in ADNJ.

[19] Van de Velde to Blanc, Natchez, April 25, 1854 (translation); quoted in Garraghan, *The Jesuits in the Middle United States,* II, 135-136.

munity.[20] With their support and influence he was understandably optimistic about the future of the cathedral. That spring Van de Velde paid the notes on the cathedral amounting to $1,313.14, when they became due. He went on to have a new slate roof put on the building and had a great part of the exterior repainted. For the first time since it was built, the church was insured, but only against fire. There still remained, however, a debt of $6,646.53. To complete the cathedral, Van de Velde estimated that at least $14,000 was also needed.[21]

To obtain this sum the Bishop inaugurated a subscription drive in June of 1854. Pledges were to be obtained from the Catholics of Natchez and the surrounding area. On this occasion $4,200 was subscribed. It was agreed that one half of the sum pledged was to be paid by the fifteenth of October 1854, and the other half by the fifteenth of January 1855. But at the expiration of the latter date the Bishop had not received even two dollars of the total figure subscribed. In a letter to the Propagation of the Faith Society he explained the reason for the subscribers being unable to meet their pledges.

> A crisis arose in business. Many houses became bankrupt at New York, Philadelphia, Cincinnati, St. Louis, New Orleans, etc. Money was retired from circulation. All the world fears, and there is nothing to be had. The debts of justice come before those of charity.[22]

It is difficult to identify the financial crisis about which Van de Velde speaks, for both the national and the local historian de-

---

[20] Major Henry E. Chotard had served in the U.S. army, taking an active part in the Creek War and the War of 1812. While serving on General Jackson's staff at the Battle of New Orleans, he was, for gallant conduct, promoted to the rank of major. In 1819, he married Miss Frances Minor, daughter of Don Esteban Minor, last Spanish governor of Natchez. Resigning from the army in 1821, he settled permanently at Natchez. Here he purchased several thousand acres which became the magnificent plantation, Somerset. He also owned much valuable property in other parts of the State and in Louisiana. He died in 1870. His son married the granddaughter of Don Esteban Minor and settled on a plantation in Concordia parish, Louisiana.—Francis Surget, a wealthy planter, owned Clifton, the famous mansion which once stood on the edge of the park, facing Rosalie. For a time he served as one of the parish trustees.—Mr. William St. John Elliot, owner of D'Evereux Hall, served as one of the trustees of the parish even before the arrival of Bp. Chanche. He died in 1855.

[21] Van de Velde to the Propagation of the Faith Society, Natchez, Jan. 19, 1855; copy in ADNJ.

[22] *Ibid.*

scribe the fifties as "an era of unusual prosperity."[23] Perhaps, Van de Velde refers to the earlier depression which followed the Panic of 1837. If this be the case, then it would seem that the Catholics of Natchez were extraordinarily slow in recovering from this business setback. But again, if this were true, it seems strange that so many planters and small businessmen who belonged to the congregation would pledge sums ranging from $500 to $1,000.[24]

In spite of this reversal, regardless of how one explains it, the Bishop felt confident that he would be able to collect about $2,000 during the course of the year. Besides making collections among the people of the area, the prelate went on a begging tour outside of his diocese. In April, for instance, we find him in New Orleans, trying to collect funds.[25] At the same time he gave orders for the repairs on the outside of the cathedral to continue. These went on as long as the Bishop felt he was in a position to pay for them. At the end of the summer he called a halt to these repairs.

By September 1855, Van de Velde had been able to collect $2,000. With an equal amount in the bank left over from the previous year's allocation from the Propagation of the Faith Society, the total revenue-in-hand of the Diocese came to $4,000.[26] Not until May of 1856, would the next notes on the cathedral be due. On the other hand, there remained $1,200 worth of repairs to be done on the outside of the cathedral. The interior with its unplastered walls and rough floor had yet to be furnished for the first time. Nevertheless, when taken into consideration, these facts still left the Bishop unconvinced that anything more should be done on the cathedral at this time. He was apparently too alive to the un-

---

[23] Abell, *A History of the United States of America* (N.Y., 1951), 259. This historian writes: "From 1850 to 1857, the country enjoyed an era of unusual prosperity. . . . In the South, the tobacco crop increased from less than 200,000,000 pounds in 1849 to 430,000,000 pounds in 1859. Cotton prices rose from six cents a pound in 1845 to fourteen cents in 1857, and the cotton crop, which had totaled 2,500,000 bales in 1850, reached the enormous figure of 5,300,000 bales in 1860. Cotton was king! American cotton was supplying seven-eights of the world's requirements. Despite a brief depression in some parts of the country after 1857, the decade as a whole was a period of great prosperity." Cf. also Bettersworth, *Mississippi: A History*, 245; Moore, "Economic Conditions in Mississippi on the Eve of the Civil War," in JMH, XXII (July 1960), 167-178.

[24] Subscription Book, dated June 6, 1854, Natchez; in ADNJ; also Gerow, *op. cit.*, 118-119.

[25] Van de Velde to Grignon, New Orleans, April 29, 1855; in ADNJ.

[26] Van de Velde to Propagation of the Faith Society, Natchez, September 3, 1855; copy in ADNJ.

stable character of the American economy during the previous two decades and too well acquainted with the poverty of his flock to make any further expenditures on the building. Furthermore, as his letters indicate, he was slow to forget the financial embarrassment and agony of his predecessor,[27] and, thus, was quite unwilling to adopt a less cautious policy in financial affairs.

Further Difficulties

Two other experiences undoubtedly also contributed to this course of action. During the short time that Van de Velde was bishop of Natchez, he found himself faced with two law suits, one civil, the other ecclesiastical, involving property. In November 1854, the Bishop, as a result of his predecessor's efforts, was put in possession of some property which had originally been part of the land grant made to the Catholic Church at Natchez by the Spanish authorities.[28] Since 1817, the property had been used by the city as a cemetery. After some years the city ceased to provide for the upkeep of the property. The fences surrounding the area broke down and were left unrepaired. Children, taking pleasure in defacing the tombs and in rolling the headstones, soon made a playground of the place. It also became in time a thoroughfare for persons wishing to take a short-cut from Union to Rankin Street. And then, somewhat callously, the city leveled part of the area and used the earth obtained, mixed with human bones, to grade the city streets. The first thing Van de Velde did was to put up a high fence on Union Street to prevent it from being used any longer as a thoroughfare and repaired the fences on Rankin and Main Streets. All the bones scattered on the surface of the ground, which filled nearly two boxes, he had deposited in the crypt under the cathedral sanctuary. The upper part of the graveyard he enclosed with a fence. Here he had several skeletons of unknown persons buried. To this site he also transferred all the tombstones. Finally, the Bishop saw to it that all the holes and gullies were filled up and trees and shrubs planted on the property. Six months after the Bishop received title to the property, the City of Natchez

---

[27] Van de Velde to the Society for the Propagation of the Faith, Natchez, Jan. 2, 1854, Jan. 19, 1855; copies in ADNJ; quoted by Gerow, *op. cit.*, 117, 119.

[28] Memorandum of Van de Velde for his attorneys, in *American Catholic Historical Researches* (Philadelphia, 1887), 141-142; quoted by Gerow, *op. cit.*, 124-125.

instituted a suit against the trustees of the Roman Catholic Church of Natchez to recover possession of lots which made up the graveyard. The case was decided in favor of the City. Van de Velde contested the decision. Litigation dragged on even into the administration of the next bishop at which time the case was settled definitely in favor of the City of Natchez.[29] Neither Van de Velde nor his successor was ever able to obtain compensation for the $200 spent on property improvements. There was also the added loss of lawyer fees which during Van de Velde's administration alone exceeded $500.[30]

The other suit in which Van de Velde was more personally involved brought him into conflict with Bishop Anthony O'Regan, his successor in the See of Chicago.[31] While Van de Velde was still Bishop of Chicago, a Mrs. Anne L. Hunt of St. Louis made a donation of three estates to him. Shortly before his departure for Natchez, Van de Velde returned the property deeds to Mrs. Hunt. She in turn modified her original settlement with the result that two of the estates were left to the newly erected Diocese of Quincy in Illinois and the third was given to the Diocese of Natchez.[32] The new Bishop of Chicago challenged the legality of the transfer. He did so on two counts. According to the original grant, O'Regan contended, Mrs. Hunt had made the donation "to James O. Vandevelde *as Bishop of Chicago* and to his *successors in office* for the *exclusive* purpose of erecting & maintaining charitable & religious Institutions *within the said Diocese of Chicago.*"[33] O'Regan, in this instance, claims to be quoting from the original document. It would seem therefore that the gift was not personal, but intended rather for the benefit of the Diocese. O'Regan further contended that Van de Velde had no authority to return the property to Mrs. Hunt. He explains why in a letter to the Cardinal Prefect of Propaganda.

> . . . . it is also evident that Bishop Vandevelde could not dispose of this gift, after he ceased to be *Bishop & Adminis-*

---

[29] (Janssens), *Sketch of the Catholic Church in the City of Natchez,* 16.

[30] Minutes of the Meetings of the Roman Catholic Society of Christians of Natchez and Its Vicinity, 1821-1861, 1865, p. 128; original minutes book in Cathedral rectory, Natchez.

[31] Van de Velde himself had proposed O'Regan for the See of Chicago; Van de Velde to Blanc, March 5, 1854, in AUND.

[32] Van de Velde to Propaganda, Natchez, Feb. 18, 1855; in APF: Scritture Riferite nei Congressi, XVII (1855-1857), ff. 165 rv.

[33] O'Regan to Propaganda, Chicago (no date); in APF: Scritture Riferite nei Congressi, XVII (1855-1857), ff. 337 r, 340 r.

> *trator of Chicago,* yet his deed conveying it back to Mrs. Hunt, was made and signed full 21 days after he had lost all authority of every kind in the Chicago Diocese.[34]

Van de Velde expressed surprise that the legality of his action should be challenged by his successor in the See of Chicago. Without ever making any direct reference to the fact that his authority in Chicago had expired at the time of the property transfer, Van de Velde, in explaining himself to Propaganda, insisted that the original gift of property had been a personal one.[35] When questioned on the matter, Van de Velde reports, Mrs. Hunt confirmed his opinion. It was implied, therefore, that the time element had no bearing on the case.

Since the case had been submitted to Rome, Propaganda confided the matter to Archbishop Blanc of New Orleans, on April 26, 1855.[36] It was suggested by Rome that the two bishops submit the case to Blanc for arbitration. Blanc accepted the task. Van de Velde, though agreeing to make use of the Archbishop's services, was not too keen on the Holy See's choice. The Bishop of Natchez felt that Blanc knew nothing about the case and, being so far removed from St. Louis and Chicago, would not be in a very favorable position to get the facts.[37] Rejecting the services of Blanc outright, the Bishop of Chicago stated as his objection that, though the Archbishop of New Orleans was "meek & pious," he would "most assuredly confuse & embarrass the whole business" and "lose sight of all the principles by which it is to be determined." [38] O'Regan suggested that an American-born prelate be appointed as arbitrator instead.

When Propaganda first began to show signs of taking O'Regan's claims seriously, Van de Velde grew apprehensive and expressed the reason for his alarm to the Cardinal Prefect of Propaganda.

> . . . . since it never entered my mind that my future successor in the See of Chicago would reclaim or could reclaim that donation, I have made certain absolutely necessary

---

[34] *Ibid.*

[35] Van de Velde to Propaganda, Natchez, Feb. 18, 1855; in APF: Scritture Riferite nei Congressi, XVII (1855-1857), ff. 165 rv.

[36] Van de Velde to Propaganda, Natchez, June 12, 1855; in APF: Scritture Riferite nei Congressi, XVII (1855-1857), ff. 355 r.

[37] *Ibid.*

[38] O'Regan to Propaganda, Chicago (no date); in APF: Scritture Riferite nei Congressi, XVII (1855-1857), ff. 337 r.

> repairs on my Cathedral which was almost in ruin, repairs which had to be made before one could begin the task of completing it, and thus the debts with which it is already weighed down I have increased even more, expecting as I did to pay off the debts recently contracted by the sale of the estate, for those contracted previously are being reduced gradually by the annual allocation from the Soc. for the Prop. of the Faith in Paris. If, may God forbid, the decision . . . should go against me, not only will the church not be finished in my life time, but neither can the debts contracted be paid, and again in a short time, perhaps next year, it will be up for public sale. Nevertheless, may the will of God be done.[39]

As the case dragged on and Van de Velde saw no hope of being able to sell the property in St. Louis in the near future, he called a halt to the repairs on his Cathedral before the end of the summer of 1855.

Since O'Regan had rejected the services of the Archbishop of New Orleans, Propaganda sought the help of Peter Richard Kenrick, Archbishop of St. Louis. Kenrick was O'Regan's metropolitan; the property in question was located in St. Louis; furthermore, the Archbishop knew personally the three people involved in the case. It would seem that he would be in a very favorable position for undertaking the task. However, the Archbishop refused to be drawn into the controversy, because he could hardly be considered an unbiased third party since it was at his own instigation that Van de Velde returned the property to Mrs. Hunt. Kenrick did so, because, after consulting a lawyer, he was convinced that "the very instrument whereby this donation had been made to him (Van de Velde) was invalid, since it was contrary to the laws of the State of Missouri."[40] He justified Van de Velde's action, however, by saying that he was certain that "she (Mrs. Hunt) had for her motive of giving the *industry of the person* in Bp. Vandevelde."[41]

It is somewhat difficult to determine just what Mrs. Hunt's intentions were, for, after Bishop O'Regan had explained his side of the case to her, Mrs. Hunt returned to him the property being held

---

39 Van de Velde to Propaganda, Natchez, June 12, 1855; in APF: Scritture Riferite nei Congressi, XVII (1855-1857), ff. 355 r. (Translation).

40 Kenrick to Propaganda, St. Louis, July 2, 1855; in APF: Scritture Riferite nei Congressi, XVII (1855-1857), ff. 362 rv. (Translation).

41 *Ibid.*

for the still vacant See of Quincy.[42] Mrs. Hunt had been holding it "nominally" until a bishop should be appointed to the See. The title to the third piece of property Van de Velde had taken with him to Natchez. It was for this third part of the original donation that Bishop O'Regan continued to press.

No decision was handed down by the Holy See during the lifetime of Van de Velde. During the vacancy of the Diocese of Natchez Blanc as testamentary executor of the late Van de Velde had to veto by legal injunction O'Regan's attempt to sell the property in St. Louis.[43]

Handicaps

At Natchez, unlike at Chicago, Van de Velde was happy. He found himself in harmony with clergy and laity alike. On the other hand, there was little room for complacence. He found his people suffering both physically and spiritually. "Our Catholics are almost all very poor," he wrote in January 1855, "and with the best of the intentions in the world they can hardly help me."[44] Twice during his short administration a yellow fever epidemic hit the State. Especially hard hit were the Catholic communities at Vicksburg, Sulphur Springs and Yazoo City. In 1853, at Yazoo City, an epidemic destroyed almost the entire Catholic congregation.[45] Misfortune of this sort impoverished the Catholics of the State still further. The double evil of poverty and sickness afflicting the laity affected in turn the clergy of the Diocese. In the autumn of 1853, two of Van de Velde's young priests, Babonneau and Fiérabras, attending the victims of yellow fever, contracted the disease and died. Four or five others suffered an attack but all, except Father Guillou, recovered without any ill effects. Four months after his

---

42 O'Regan to Propaganda, Chicago (no date); in APF: Scritture Riferite nei Congressi, XVII (1855-1857), ff. 337 r.

43 Blanc to Propaganda, New Orleans, July 14, 1856; in APF: Scritture Riferite nei Congressi, XVII (1855-1857), ff. 639 rv. As late as December, 1859, no settlement had been reached between Bishop O'Regan and Bishop Van de Velde's successor, William Elder, over the property in St. Louis. At that time there was a danger that the property might even revert to the state. Elder to Juncker, Natchez, Dec. 22, 1859; in ADNJ, Elder Letter Book—#5, 6.

44 Van de Velde to the Propagation of the Faith Society, Natchez, Jan. 19, 1855; copy in ADNJ; quoted by Gerow, *op. cit.*, 119 ff.

45 Doyle, "St. Mary's of Yazoo City," in *Catholic Action of the South* (Natchez Centennial Edition), Oct. 14, 1937, 47.

initial attack, it appeared that Guillou's health was completely ruined.[46] When the second epidemic hit the State in 1855, it carried off Father Courjault, pastor of Canton.[47]

Hardly able to support themselves, the laity found it difficult to provide for their priests. Describing their plight, Van de Velde wrote in a letter to the Propagation of the Faith Society in Paris: "All the revenue of the Cathedral does not suffice to keep up the house. I have only one priest with me (Fr. Grignon), who receives no salary."[48] And later in a letter to the same society he said: ". . . the diocese . . . is so poor . . . that I myself must bear all my traveling expenses."[49] Some of the missionaries received financial support from their families and friends back home. However, up to and especially through the Civil War years the Catholic congregations in Mississippi provided for their priests only with great difficulty.

At the beginning of 1854, Van de Velde was reduced to seven priests.[50] Shortly after his arrival in the Diocese he had to suspend one of his priests, Father Stephen Montgomery, O.P. The Dominican had repeatedly refused to resign his Vicksburg pastorate in the face of charges made by his congregation that he had defrauded the parish of some property.[51] The priest, after defending himself in the secular press, withdrew to New Orleans where he died in 1855.[52] Of the remaining clergy, Father Hardey, who took charge

---

46 Van de Velde to the Propagation of the Faith Society, Natchez, Jan. 2, 1854; copy in ADNJ; quoted by Gerow, *op. cit.*, 117-118.

47 Notes taken during an interview with one of the Sisters of St. Joseph stationed in Sulphur Springs at the outbreak of the Civil War; no name; dated 1890; in ASSJC.

48 Van de Velde to Propagation of the Faith Society, Natchez, Jan. 2, 1854; copy in ADNJ; quoted by Gerow, *op. cit.*, 117-118.

49 Van de Velde to Propagation of the Faith Society, Natchez, Sept. 3, 1855; copy in ADNJ; quoted by Gerow, *op. cit.*, 121.

50 Van de Velde to Propagation of the Faith Society, Natchez, Jan. 2, 1854; copy in ADNJ; quoted by Gerow, *op. cit.*, 117-118.

51 Index notes on Rev. S. H. Montgomery in ADNJ.

52 *Ibid.* Also O'Daniel, *Dominican Province of St. Joseph* (New York, 1942), 101. Although Fr. Montgomery came to Mississippi in bad health, he did yeoman's service in the Diocese. He replaced the old frame church in Vicksburg with a beautiful brick structure which Bishop Chanche dedicated on Oct. 14, 1849. He also directed the building of the first Catholic church in Jackson which was given episcopal blessing on Aug. 23, 1846. As pastor of Vicksburg Fr. Montgomery also found time to visit Catholics at Camden, Brandon and Yazoo City. Mullin, "St. Paul's—Vicksburg," and Henne, "Capital Parish Among Pioneers in Diocese," in *Catholic Action of the South* (Natchez Centennial Edition), Oct. 14, 1937, 19, 29.

of the congregation at Vicksburg, was sickly; at the beginning of 1855, he almost died. On the Gulf Coast there was old Father Guinand, pastor of Biloxi, who was ready for retirement. At the same time the Catholic population of Mississippi was on the increase. As a result there was a crying need for priests from all sides. With so much sickness in the State this need was all the more pressing. The Bishop reported to the Propagation of the Faith Society at this time: "Many places are asking for priests. Impossible to have any here—lack of resources—nor can we have a seminary or seminarians." [53] A year later, in January 1855, conditions appeared to be just as bad: ". . . all the diocese suffers. Thousands of Catholics are abandoned for lack of priests—no seminary—no means even to pay for the upkeep of seminarians." [54]

With the present need so great and with prospects for the future so dim, Van de Velde made repeated efforts to obtain the services of the Jesuit Fathers of the Missouri vice-province.[55] Thousands of his flock, he pleaded, were being deprived of all religious succor and dying without the Sacraments. It was his suggestion that the Fathers open a residence in Natchez, of which he himself would be the superior. At St. Louis, however, the Jesuit authorities showed no disposition to take on this additional burden. As Garraghan points out, the vice-province still groaned under an excessive load of petty residences and parochial stations and Father Murphy, the vice-provincial, following out instructions from headquarters in Rome, was pursuing a policy of retrenching rather than of extending the activities of his men.[56] For the same reason Van de Velde was unable to obtain the services of the Missouri Jesuits for a college which he had hoped to open in Natchez.[57]

---

[53] Van de Velde to the Propagation of the Faith Society, Natchez, Jan. 2, 1854; copy in ADNJ; quoted by Gerow, *op. cit.*, 117-118.

[54] Van de Velde to the Propagation of the Faith Society, Natchez, Jan. 19, 1855; copy in ADNJ; quoted by Gerow, *op. cit.*, 119-121.

[55] Garraghan, *The Jesuits in the Middle United States,* II, 136.

[56] *Ibid.*

[57] Sometime in 1855, Van de Velde purchased the Rose Hill property in Natchez from Bishop Chanche's nieces, the Marcilly sisters, for $16,000—$3,000 cash and the balance in promissory notes. Writing to the Jesuit authorities in Rome, he suggested that the Society take over the property for a college. The proposal was refused because of a lack of priests, especially those conversant with English. Van de Velde to Etheridge, Natchez, June 21, 1855; Etheridge to Van de Velde, Rome, Aug. 25, 1855; in ADNJ, File: Van de Velde—R.

Sisters of St. Joseph of Carondelet

Far more successful was the Bishop in attracting to his diocese a second community of Sisters. Early in 1855, the Mississippi prelate applied to Mother Celestine Pommerel, Superior of the Sisters of St. Joseph of Carondelet, Missouri, for Sisters to take charge of a school which Father Courjault was about to establish at Sulphur Springs.[58] The Bishop's request was granted. On the feast of St. Joseph, March 19, a band of five Sisters, headed by Mother Cecilia Renot, was sent to open the new mission.[59] Traveling by steamer down the Mississippi River from St. Louis, the Sisters landed at Vicksburg. Here Bishop Van de Velde was on hand to welcome them into the Diocese. Arrangements were made to have the Sisters rest over night in Vicksburg before continuing their journey. Their host and hostess were Mr. and Mrs. Antonio Genella, one of the wealthier Catholic couples of Vicksburg. The next day the Bishop and Sisters took a stage for Canton—a one day's ride.

The trip was an eventful one. As described by one of these pioneer Sisters, it reveals the emphasis of the Know-Nothing movement in Mississippi.[60] The owner of the stage proved to be a Know-Nothing. Partially intoxicated, the man decided to ride inside. As the coach jogged along, he eyed the Bishop carefully for some time. Finally, he blurted out: "You know what, I think you're a priest. So take that!" A stream of tobacco juice hit the Bishop in the face. The performance was repeated several times. Patiently Van de Velde tried to protect his face with his hat. Finally, when the stage stopped to change horses, the Bishop threw the man out of the coach. Without protest the latter then mounted and rode with the driver. At Canton the spectre of the Know-Nothing movement caused some alarm to the Sisters' host, Judge Oliver Luckett. While eager to extend his hospitality to the Sisters and the Bishop, he admitted his uneasiness with their presence. If the local people knew that he was entertaining a Catholic bishop and several nuns, he

---

58 Notes taken during an interview with one of the Sisters who had been stationed in Sulphur Springs at the outbreak of the Civil War; no name; dated 1890; in ASSJC.

59 *Ibid.* The other pioneer Sisters were: Sisters Leonie Martin, Gabriel Corbett, Chrysostom McCann & Alphonse Byrne, a novice.

60 Although the Know-Nothing party in Mississippi showed a certain lack of spontaneity of feeling that was apparent elsewhere, at times it attacked Catholicism in no uncertain terms. Cf. Overdyke, *The Know-Nothing Party in the South* (Baton Rouge, 1950), 225-226.

confided, they might well be mobbed. The night passed, however, without incident. The next morning, while the Bishop remained behind, the Sisters left in private carriages for Sulphur Springs. At Judge Semmes', a country place about a half day's ride from Canton, the Sisters were served dinner. From there they went on to Sulphur Springs, arriving before night fall. It was March 30, 1855.[61]

As early as March 1854, Van de Velde had visited Sulphur Springs and expressed a desire to establish a school there under the direction of Sisters.[62] The Catholic community responded enthusiastically and took up a collection of $1,595, to get the project under way. Under the guiding hand of the pastor, Father Courjault,[63] a frame two-storied convent was begun well in advance of the Sisters' arrival. Measuring fifty-two feet by thirty-two, the building was surrounded by a ten acre grove.[64] On April 9, the convent-school opened with an enrollment of eight: one boarder and seven day students. All were girls. A few days later six or seven more students were enrolled.[65]

On May 20, Van de Velde handed over to the Sisters the deed to the property.[66] According to the agreement entered into by the Bishop and the Sisters of St. Joseph, the Sisters would hold title to the property as long as they conducted the school; if they should ever have to give it up, the property would revert to the Bishop, who would repay the Sisters for any improvements made upon it. At the time of the purchase from Mr. Francis Luckett the ground was worth $300. Some time later the Sisters purchased in their own name ten additional acres for the sum of $150. During the first few years of the school's existence the Sisters failed to attract many students. As late as October 1857, the academy or girls' school had

---

61 Notes, 1890, in ASSJC; also Parochial Record, Church of the Immaculate Conception, Sulphur Springs, Madison Co., Miss., (1841-1926); original in parish archives at Camden, Miss.; typed copy in ADNJ, 12.

62 Meador, "Sulphur Springs Parish," in *Catholic Action of the South* (Natchez Centennial Edition), Oct. 14, 1937, 48.

63 The day after the Sisters' arrival Father Courjault was transferred to Canton, where he died a few weeks later of yellow fever. At his own request he was laid to rest at Sulphur Springs at a point between the convent and the church. Mother Cecilia, superior of the group, also died of the fever before the end of the summer and was buried at the Springs. Cf. Notes, 1890, ASSJC.

64 Parochial Records, Sulphur Springs, (1841-1926), in parish archives, Camden; copy in ADNJ, 8.

65 *Ibid.,* 9.

66 *Ibid.,* 9.

only twenty boarders and ten day scholars.[67] To increase their usefulness the Sisters decided to open a school for small boys. For this purpose they had a small frame house built a short distance from the convent. It opened in September 1857 with nine boys.[68] The Sisters also took on a Sunday school for colored children.[69]

Brothers of Christian Instruction

The cause of Catholic education in the diocese was advanced still further during Van de Velde's administration through the efforts of the zealous pastor of Bay St. Louis, Father Louis Stanislaus Buteux.[70] During the vacancy of the Diocese after the death of Bishop Chanche, Buteux had built an unpretentious frame school house in the rear of his church. It opened its doors on September 1, 1852.[71] In charge were the Christian Brothers. Although intended primarily for boys from Bay St. Louis, the school accepted a few boarders from New Orleans. The latter were lodged in the rectory. Hardly had this first boarding school for boys in the Diocese gotten under way when the yellow fever epidemic of 1853, swept New Orleans and the Gulf Coast and forced the pastor to dismiss the boarders and close the school. Among the victims of the epidemic in Bay St. Louis was practically the entire teaching staff of Father Buteux's school.[72]

---

[67] Guillou to Elder, Sulphur Springs, Oct. 15, 1857; in ADNJ, Elder Letter Book—#1, 178.

[68] Parochial Record, Sulphur Springs, (1841-1926); in parish archives, Camden; copy in ADNJ, 14.

[69] Notes on Sulphur Springs, 1890, in ASSJC.

[70] Father Louis Stanislaus Marie Buteux was the first pastor of Bay St. Louis, conducting the affairs of that parish from July 31, 1847 to November 17, 1859. He was born in Paris on July 2, 1808, and received his education at the Seminary of St. Sulpice. He volunteered for the mission of Indiana and was ordained by Bishop Bruté in Paris in 1836. He was the first chaplain of the Sisters of Providence when they came to found St. Mary-of-the-Woods College near Terre Haute, Ind. In the construction of the first academy he worked as a day laborer. With the offerings of Irishmen employed on the railroads and canals, he personally helped build a brick chapel for the Catholics of the town. The northern climate proving too severe for the priest, he was forced to seek a mission in the South. Bishop Chanche gladly welcomed him into the diocese, assigning him immediately to Bay St. Louis.

[71] Fahey, "Our Lady of the Gulf," in *Catholic Action of the South* (Natchez Centennial Edition), Oct. 14, 1937, 39.

[72] Angelus Gabriel, Brother, F.S.C., *The Christian Brothers in the United States, 1848-1948: A Century of Catholic Education* (New York, 1948), 216. Thompson, "St. Stanislaus School for Boys," in *The Daily Herald,* Biloxi and Gulfport, July 29, 1958, 17 A.

Undaunted the next year Father Buteux approached the Brothers of Christian Instruction[73] in Mobile, Alabama.[74] One of the Brothers was sent to survey the possibilities locally. After receiving a favorable report, Brother Alphonse, the acting provincial superior of the Brothers at Mobile, accepted, apparently on a temporary basis, the direction of the school in Bay St. Louis. The pioneers were Brothers Basile Venable, Joseph Diemer and Leo Maligne. They opened the school behind the church in June 1854.[75] Again the few boarders from New Orleans were housed in the rectory.

Eager to secure the Brothers on a permanent basis, Buteux in the fall of 1854 traveled to Europe to present his case to the Superior General of the Brothers at Le Puy, France. Buteux explained that it was his intention to expand the small parochial school into a genuine boys' boarding school which would serve not only the town of Bay St. Louis but the whole state of Mississippi and southern Louisiana. Fortunately the reports from the Brothers in America supported the project, thus prompting the Superior General to accept Buteux's offer on a permanent basis. As a result, five additional Brothers returned to the United States with the priest. Joined by Brother Athanasius from Mobile, who became the Director of the Brothers at Bay St. Louis, Buteux set to work to teach the newcomers English. In the meanwhile Brothers Leo and Lucius and a few laborers from the Bay set to work, putting up a building in keeping with their expansion program.[76]

With the help of a loan of $2,000 from Father Buteux,[77] the Brothers purchased a piece of property just one hundred yards south of the parish church – a beautiful site that faced the Gulf of Mexico with one hundred and forty feet of beach frontage. The price was $4,000.[78] The building erected was a wooden one, eighty feet long

---

[73] One of the earlier names of the community now known as the Brothers of the Sacred Heart.

[74] This congregation of teaching Brothers was founded in France by Pere Andre Coindre in 1821. Their first foundation outside of France was made at Mobile in 1847.

[75] Macarius, *A Century of Service for the Sacred Heart in the United States*, 1946, 122-123. (Bro. Edmund) "St. Stanislaus College," in *Catholic Action of the South* (Natchez Centennial Edition), Oct. 14, 1937, 38.

[76] (Bro. Edmund), "St. Stanislaus College," in *Catholic Action of the South* (Natchez Centennial Edition), Oct. 14, 1937, 38.

[77] Buteux to Elder, Bay St. Louis, Feb. 25, 1859; in ADNJ, File: Elder-B.–This sum was to be returned to Buteux only in the event that the school were abandoned within 20 or 25 years.

[78] Macarius, *op. cit.*, 123.

by thirty feet wide with two and one-half stories. On the first floor were three class rooms and a parlor; on the second floor were dormitories and an infirmary, and in the attic there was expansion space for another dormitory. On the front and on the back were galleries. Costing $3,800,[79] the new boarding school was named St. Stanislaus Academy, in honor of Father Buteux's patron saint. Classes began in the autumn of 1855. From the start the institution prospered. Boarders flocked to the school from New Orleans and from the rich sugar plantations of Louisiana.[80]

Sisters of St. Joseph of Bourg

During his visit to France in the autumn of 1854, Father Buteux made efforts to engage the services of two communities of Sisters. One group, according to Bishop Van de Velde's plan, would be assigned the task of establishing a distinctively American religious community, independent of the congregation to which the founding Sisters would belong. The other group of Sisters would be expected to conduct a school for girls in Buteux's own parish in Bay St. Louis. For this latter task the priest obtained a commitment from the Sisters of St. Joseph of Cluny. In a letter dated October 27, the matter seemed to have been settled. Buteux wrote:

> The Congregation of the Sisters of St. Joseph of Cluny, gathered in a Chapter last Saturday, has decided to establish a house in my parish; I shall have four Sisters, three of whom will be for teaching; their Superior has been already named and will be in Paris tomorrow; the other Sisters will soon follow, and we shall leave France some time between now and the 6th of November.[81]

These Sisters, it was agreed, would remain attached to their motherhouse. At the Bay, it was understood, they would fulfill their ordinary functions of teaching girls and taking care of the sick. The four Sisters chosen to make the foundation were Sisters Ildephonse Robert, Florentine Gougeat, Leon Toler, and Valentine Loubierer.[82]

For the important task of forming the members of a future American community of Sisters, Buteux sought the services of the

---

[79] Thompson, "St. Stanislaus School for Boys," in *The Daily Herald*, Biloxi and Gulfport, July 29, 1958, 17A.

[80] Macarius, *op. cit.*, 124.

[81] Buteux to Rev. Mother (St. Claude), Bouloire (Paris), Oct. 27, 1854; in ASSJB. (Translation).

[82] Note in longhand, dated November 17, 1854, signed by Sr. Rosalie Javouhey, Superior General; in ADNJ, File: Van de Velde-S.

Sisters of St. Joseph of Bourg. His efforts were supported by a close friend and benefactor, Monseigneur Chalandon, Bishop of Belley.[83] The pastor of Bay St. Louis requested four Sisters and expressed the hope that they would be sent to the United States within ten months after his own departure from France.[84] Much to Buteux's surprise, Mother St. Claude, the Superior General of the community, offered four Sisters immediately.[85] In her letter announcing this good news and in a subsequent letter she nevertheless expressed a number of concerns. First of all, she insisted that her Sisters' spiritual welfare not be neglected; secondly, that they do not depart from the work proper to the institute; thirdly, that they be given adequate financial support; and, finally, that no attempt be made to remove the Sisters in America from her administration.[86] Buteux was quick to give Mother St. Claude the assurances she sought. In a letter from Orleans, dated November 7, the priest wrote:

> In the first place, Mother, you must have confidence in our Bishop. He is a member of the Society of Jesus—a religious since 1817. This is a guarantee in itself, I believe. (. . . .) I repeat: I will send the Nuns directly to Natchez, the episcopal see of our diocese. They will remain with his Excellency; he will employ them in conformity with the goals of your Institute, but especially with a view to founding a religious Community.
>
> All the Nuns in the United States receive financial support, unless their boarding school should provide a revenue sufficient for their needs. His Excellency himself will pay their salary until the boarding school has progressed enough to support the Sisters.
>
> In the Bishop's name, I assure you he will accept your request, namely: that the Nuns should always remain dependant upon your administration. It is not only preferable for them, but also for us—under all possible circumstances.[87]

The three Sisters destined for Natchez were Mother Eulalie, the superior, a strong, energetic woman, fifty-seven years old; Sister

---

83 Buteux to Rev. Mother (St. Claude), Bouloire, Oct. 27, 1854; in ASSJB.

84 *Ibid.*

85 Buteux to Rev. Mother (St. Claude), Paris, Oct. 29, 1854; in ASSJB.

86 Buteux to Rev. Mother Superior (Mother St. Claude), Orleans, Nov. 7, 1854; in ASSJB.

87 *Ibid.* (Translation).

Anatolie, thirty-two years old; and Sister Gonzaga, a young girl of about twenty.[88]

Final departure arrangements were made quickly once the Sisters from Bourg agreed to serve in the Diocese of Natchez. Writing to Mother St. Claude on November 7, Buteux presented his plan of travel.

> It will be much better for your Sisters if they leave with us. They will be accompanied by the 4 Sisters of Cluny whom I am bringing, by 5 Brothers and 4 good Clergymen. (. . . .) We will all leave Paris on the 13th of this month—in the evening.[89]

A few days later the priest changed his plans. In order to be back in his parish for the Christmas season, Father Buteux decided to take an earlier and faster ship, leaving his newly recruited missionaries to follow him in about a week or so.[90] At the last moment the five teaching Brothers destined for the boys' school at the Bay joined the pastor of Bay St. Louis on this trip.

Holding to the original plan, the four clergymen and seven Sisters sailed from Le Havre on November 19, aboard the American clipper, the *John Hancock*.[91] The trip across proved to be a miserable experience for the French missionaries. Mother Eulalie described the voyage in a letter to Mother St. Claude.

> When we left port Sunday, November 19, a favorable wind was blowing. Such was the speed with which we sailed that we crossed the English channel in two days, while very often it takes three weeks for that same journey.
>
> A half hour had barely passed when we became depressed and nauseated. You, Reverend Mother, who have been on the ocean, understand that terrible feeling, but what you have not experienced is its continuance for a whole month (and) heightened by reason of being among strangers whose language one does not understand. If you have never seen the sleeping quarters on a ship, picture to yourself the

---

[88] Centennial book of the Sisters of St. Joseph of Bourg, New Orleans Province, 1955.

[89] Buteux to Rev. Mother Superior (Mother St. Claude), Orleans, Nov. 7, 1854; in ASSJB. (Translation).

[90] Mother Eulalie to Mother (St. Claude), New Orleans, Jan. 5, 1855; copy in ASSJB in New Orleans. (Translation).

[91] Centennial book of the Sisters of St. Joseph of Bourg, New Orleans Province, 1955.

> shelves of a fruit pantry and you will have some idea of what are called berths on board a ship. That is where we were perched, one on top of the other, unable in our state of suffering and weakness to be of any mutual service. Did you say nourishment, the upset stomach could not bear it; a little broth was all we could take and even when we felt better, it was with difficulty that we added something substantial to our liquid diet. Such was our life for the greater part of the crossing and for once we experienced the lack of the devoted attention which a solicitous mother and sisters lavish on those who suffer.[92]

After a voyage of forty-one days, the weary band landed at New Orleans. As pre-arranged by Father Buteux, the Ursuline Sisters of the Crescent City welcomed the Sisters of St. Joseph of Bourg into their community, while the Cluny group became the guests of the Sisters of the Holy Cross. The clergymen who had crossed the Atlantic with them left immediately for Natchez by steamer.

Three days later, on January 2, Father Buteux arrived in the city, eager to escort his band of Sisters to Bay St. Louis. What high hopes the priest had, however, for the future of Catholic education in his parish were suddenly and mysteriously shattered. The superior of the Sisters of St. Joseph of Cluny who were destined for the Bay refused to see him. No explanation was offered. It was rumored, however, that the four Sisters did not want to settle at the Bay.

The following day the Bishop of Natchez arrived. When he was granted an interview by the Cluny Sisters, the superior announced haughtily that they had no intention of going to Bay St. Louis. Father Buteux, they claimed, had deceived them. Explaining the situation to the Sisters' Superior General in Paris a short time later, Van de Velde reported:

> The greatest objection that I could get from them was that at the Bay they would have a secondary school and a small boarding school, whereas they were intended for a large boarding school, and that they could not live on $50 (250 fr.) a month.[93]

---

[92] Mother Eulalie to Rev. Mother (St. Claude), New Orleans, Jan. 5, 1855, copy in ASSJB in New Orleans. (Translation).

[93] Van de Velde to Madame la Superieure (Mother Rosalie Javouhey), Natchez, Jan. 25, 1855; copy in ADNJ, File: Van de Velde-S. (Translation).

Commenting on the objection, the Bishop pointed out:

> No religious order in the U.S. except the Ursulines in New Orleans have begun with one quarter of what is offered at the Bay, and yet they have all prospered now.[94]

When Bishop Van de Velde asked the rebellious Sisters what they planned to do, they replied that they would go to Martinique or return to France. In desperation the Bishop asked them to go and see the establishment at the Bay where, he assured them, there was more than the contract called for. They still refused. When the prelate offered them Biloxi as an alternate site for a foundation, they would not listen. Instead they repeated the charge, almost to the point of monotony, that they had been deceived by Father Buteux.[95]

On a second visit to the Cluny Sisters about a week later Van de Velde found them more intractable than ever. At this meeting they even had the audacity to ask the Bishop to pay for their return fare to France. He refused. A short time later, after he had returned to Natchez, it was reported to Van de Velde that the rebel Sisters were preparing to sail for Martinique.[96]

How sincere these Sisters were in raising their objections is a very questionable matter. The clergymen who accompanied the nuns on their trip across the Atlantic informed the Bishop that on the very first day out of Le Havre they heard the women remark that they were going to the Bay against their will and that in reality their destination was Martinique. It was further reported to the Bishop by a priest who had known one and perhaps another of the women in question that they had been a source of trouble within their own community back in France.[97] Finally, when Bishop Van de Velde requested the Superior General of the Sisters in Paris to refund the travel money which he had paid for these Sisters on the grounds that they had broken their contract, she did so and apologized for the inconvenience and embarrassment which he had experienced in the whole affair.[98]

---

[94] *Ibid.*

[95] A list of the conditions for the establishment of the Sisters at the Bay, signed by Fr. Buteux and dated Paris, Nov. 12, 1854, is to be found in ADNJ, File: Van de Velde-S. If this be an authentic copy of the contract, then the Sisters' charge of deception is without substance.

[96] Van de Velde to Madame la Superieure (Mother Rosalie Javouhey), Natchez, Jan. 25, 1855; copy in ADNJ, File: Van de Velde-S.

[97] *Ibid.*

[98] Choiselat to Van de Velde, Paris, Aug. 3, 1855; in ADNJ, File: Van de Velde-S.

Feeling that Father Buteux should not be deprived of the services of Sisters after all of his labors, the Bishop prevailed upon the Sisters of St. Joseph of Bourg to establish themselves at Bay St. Louis. Before he was able to do so, however, Van de Velde had to answer to the Sisters' satisfaction many objections, "mostly lies that had been reported to them by the Sisters of Cluny." [99] As a result of this change in plans, the project of founding an American religious community had to be postponed. Accompanying the Sisters to the Bay, Van de Velde formally installed them in a small four-room house on Sunday, January 7, 1855.[100]

From the start there was much to test the missionary spirit of the French Sisters. Their residence was a modest frame cottage furnished only with beds and a few linens. The kitchen had the barest necessities. Until a school building was ready at the Bay, the Sisters conducted classes at Waveland, a small community about four miles distant.[101] Every day, in all kind of weather, the three women walked there and back. A narrow lane running through the woods was the only road. Often snakes dropped from the branches of overhanging trees limp with Spanish moss or crawled across their path which ran through the swamp. In rainy weather they had to ford a small torrent barefoot. Classes at Waveland were held in a cabin ordinarily used for Mass when the community was fortunate enough to be visited by a priest. After the long walk home each day the Sisters all too frequently found little to eat. Sometimes, however, a kind neighbor, Mrs. Combel, would bring over a dish of hot food. Before the year was out, the youngest of the trio, Sister Gonzaga, succumbed to discouragement and returned to France.

In April the school at Waveland was closed.[102] Since the Brothers would be moving into new quarters in September, it was decided that the Sisters would open up a day school in the house behind the church. However, even before the school opened, Mother Eulalie had her doubts about their chances for succeeding

---

[99] Van de Velde to Madame la Superieure (Mother Rosalie Javouhey), Natchez, Jan. 25, 1855; copy in ADNJ, File: Van de Velde–S. (Translation).

[100] (Sisters of St. Joseph), "St. Joseph Academy," in *Catholic Action of the South* (Natchez Centennial Edition), Oct. 14, 1937, 36.

[101] Centennial book of the Sisters of St. Joseph of Bourg, New Orleans, 1955; also notes drawn up by Sr. Sacred Heart, 1919, in ADNJ, File: Historic Notes–Bay St. Louis.

[102] *Ibid.*

in Bay St. Louis. That summer she expressed the opinion that "the Bay is too poor to feed a community" of Sisters.[103] On the other hand, both Bishop Van de Velde and Father Buteux were optimistic. Planning for a future boarding school, they purchased a large tract of land. To attract as many students as possible in a community where the art of music was greatly appreciated,[104] Father Buteux hired a special music teacher. Not sharing his manifest optimism, Mother Eulalie questioned the wisdom of this move. To her Superior General at Bourg, she wrote: "He is really undertaking too much—he has engaged a music teacher to whom we must pay $90.00 a month, and yet we have only three music pupils!" [105] Nevertheless, preparations continued to be made, and in September 1855, the day school opened with an enrollment of thirty-three pupils. By December the number had risen to forty. All the classes were conducted in a single room which also served as a kitchen and dining room for the students. Besides teaching in this school, the Sisters gave religious instructions to adults, many of whom had never made their first Holy Communion, to slaves and, for a while, to the Indians of the outlying districts.[106]

For the next few years the lot of the pioneer Sisters at Bay St. Louis was one of hard work and dire poverty. The mission survived only because of the indomitable will of Father Buteux, his financial support of the project at the cost of great personal sacrifice and the "patience," "self-denial," "zeal," and "gaiety" of the Sisters.[107]

Limited Progress

During Bishop Van de Velde's short administration [108] no new parishes were erected in the diocese. With a drop in the number of clergy it was a big enough problem finding priests for the already

[103] Mother Eulalie to Rev. Mother (St. Claude), Bay St. Louis, July 15, 1855; copy in ASSJB in New Orleans.

[104] "I think I have already told you that music here (Bay St. Louis) is not as in France—a rare art. A simple laborer who can hardly feed his family wants his children to know music that they may one day earn their living more honorably. And it is the same everywhere. As soon as a locality is civilized, they ask at once for music."—Mother Esperance to Rev. Mother St. Claude, Bay St. Louis, Dec. 6, 1856; in ASSJB. (Translation).

[105] Mother Eulalie to Rev. Mother (St. Claude), Bay St. Louis, July 15, 1855; copy in ASSJB in New Orleans, (Translation).

[106] Centennial book of the Sisters of St. Joseph of Bourg, New Orleans, 1955; also Leduc to Rev. Mother (?), Bay St. Louis, May 7, 1867; in ASSJB.

[107] Elder to Rev. Mother (St. Claude), Bay St. Louis, Sept. 13, 1857; in ASSJB.

[108] Dec. 1853-Nov. 1855.

established congregations. Failing this, the Bishop had to ask some pastors to accept responsibility for additional mission stations. At Port Gibson a church begun by Father Fiérabras stood unfinished, saddled with a debt of $1,500. After his death the Catholics of this town and the neighboring Fairview plantation were cared for by a priest operating out of Natchez. At the bustling river town of Vicksburg the growing Catholic community remained without a resident pastor during the epidemic year of 1853 and part of 1854. When Father Richard Hardey arrived as resident pastor in 1854, he apparently was not in the best of health. On New Year's day 1855, he was so ill that Father Leray of Jackson was sent for.[109] To provide the newly arrived Sisters of St. Joseph at Sulphur Springs with a chaplain, the Bishop had to deprive Yazoo City of its resident pastor, Father Guillou.

In spite of the handicaps of poverty, sickness and a shortage of priests, things were not entirely at a standstill in the diocese. Significant progress was made in a number of parishes. At Jackson, the fast growing capital of the State, Father Leray completed the rectory begun by his predecessor, Father Babonneau. A bell and organ were obtained for the church.[110] And a parochial school under the direction of Mr. John Kelly was initiated with forty children in attendance.[111] At Biloxi the church was enlarged and a parochial residence erected.[112] With the arrival of three religious communities in the Diocese a boarding school for boys and a day school for girls were established at Bay St. Louis while a girls' boarding school and a small boys' day school were inaugurated at Sulphur Springs. At Natchez the Bishop, in order to secure a legacy as well as an appropriation from the state government, had St. Mary's Orphan Asylum incorporated.[113]

---

[109] Journal of Mrs. I. R. Cook (Jan. 1, 1855-June 27, 1858); copy in Old Court House Museum, Vicksburg, 3.

[110] This church stood on South President Street immediately south of the Alabama and Vicksburg Railroad on a lot later occupied by the Granberry home.

[111] Henne, "Capital Parish Among Pioneers in Diocese," in *Catholic Action of the South* (Natchez Centennial Edition), Oct. 14, 1937, 29.

[112] O'Connell, "Earliest Missionaries Served Historic Biloxi," *ibid.*, 23.

[113] March 11, 1854; Gerow, *op. cit.*, 204. No evidence has been uncovered which would indicate that any grant was made to St. Mary's Orphan Asylum from state funds.

Death of Bishop Van de Velde

As has been intimated, Bishop Van de Velde's apostolic labors in the See of Natchez were of short duration. On October 23, 1855, as he was descending the front steps of the rectory at Natchez, breviary in hand, he slipped and fell, fracturing his right leg in two places. In the house all were sick and he lay there until some passers-by, attracted by his moaning, kindly carried him to his room. Although his sufferings were intense, up until November 9, no one considered him in immediate danger. On that day, however, the slight fever which he had took a malignant form and soon developed into the dread yellow fever.[114] About this time a fellow Jesuit, Father Peter Tschieder, arrived in Natchez. Unable to further Van de Velde's plans for a Jesuit residence and college in Natchez, Father Beckx, the Superior General, had insisted with St. Louis that it accede to his request for a Jesuit priest to reside with him as a member of his household. Accordingly, Father Tschieder, for whose services Bishop Van de Velde had expressly asked, was sent.[115] He described the circumstances of the Bishop's last moments in a letter to the Vice-Provincial in St. Louis:

> November 13, 1855. Bishop Van de Velde is dead. He expired this morning at 7. Two gentlemen watched and attended on him. At 2 o'clock in the night I was called—I said some prayers with the Bishop which he repeated—but his mind was wandering—he perceived it himself. At 2½ violent spasms took him, probably the effect of a very strong medicine which he had taken. Immediately he lost his senses and I gave him the last absolution and plenary indulgence. I began the recommendation of the soul. He was enabled to receive the viaticum which I could not give him yesterday. It was evidently a favor obtained through the intercession of St. Stanislaus. He had made a novena to the Saint—had several times expressed the wish to die on his feast. Whilst I was saying Mass at 5 for him, all the Sisters and orphan girls, who had also made a Novena for him, received communion. Father Grignon gave him the Viaticum. He remained suffering till 7 when he expired.[116]

From the time he recovered consciousness to receive Viaticum until he died, the Catholics of Natchez passed through the sick

[114] Gerow, "History of the Catholic Diocese of Natchez," in *Catholic Action of the South* (Natchez Centennial Edition), Oct. 14, 1937, 17.

[115] Garraghan, *The Jesuits in the Middle United States,* II, 137.

[116] Tschieder to Murphy, Natchez, Nov. 13, 1855; in Missouri Province Archives, S.J., St. Louis; quoted by Garraghan, *op. cit.,* II, 137.

room to receive the Bishop's last blessing. The dying prelate gave it fully conscious; he even spoke to each visitor, though very indistinctly. In fact, it was in the very act of raising his hand to bless someone that he died.

After the funeral rites conducted by Archbishop Blanc the body of Bishop Van de Velde was interred in a brick vault under the main altar of the Cathedral. Here it rested until 1874, when, at the request of the Jesuit Fathers of St. Louis acting in conformity with the expressed desire of Bishop Van de Velde,[117] the body was transferred to St. Stanislaus Novitiate, Florissant, Missouri, and laid to rest among the brethren of the Society he loved so well.[118]

Bishop Van de Velde was of an ardent and exuberant temper. His manner was vivacious. Hence, he appeared to be somewhat impetuous in his speech. To some of his Jesuit brethren he seemed to fail at times in that tactful prudence which the skillful executive must bring to his dealings with men and things.[119] Bishop Kenrick of Philadelphia expressed the opinion that as Bishop of Chicago Van de Velde lacked good judgment.[120] This is especially true in his handling of the rebellious Chicago clergy. However, during Van de Velde's administration of the Diocese of Natchez no such impression was created. He got along well with his clergy. The laity were very attached to him. And his care of the temporalities of the Diocese was practical. Furthermore, his efforts to increase the opportunities for receiving a Catholic education within the State bespeak an apostolic zeal that showed vision. All in all, Bishop Van de Velde's services to the Church in Mississippi were of a high order.

---

[117] The request of the Jesuit Fathers was evidently based upon a clause in Bishop Van de Velde's will in which he expressed a desire to have his body interred at Florissant.

[118] Even as Bishop of Chicago Van de Velde remained so attached to the Society that he often returned to the Jesuit community at St. Louis University where by his own wish he enjoyed almost no distinction, wearing the habit of the Society, following the daily order and performing the penances in the refectory like the rest of the community.—Elet to Roothaan March 4, 1849, in General Archives of the Society of Jesus, Rome; quoted by Garraghan, *The Jesuits in the Middle United States,* I, 518.

[119] Murphy to Beckx, St. Louis, Dec. 8, 1853; in General Archives of the Society of Jesus, Rome; quoted by Garraghan, *The Jesuits in the Middle United States,* II, 138.

[120] Kenrick to Frenaye, Nov. 18, 1852; in *Kenrick-Frenaye Correspondence* (Lancaster, 1920), 340, edited by Tourscher.

Bishop William Henry Elder, Third Bishop of the Diocese of Natchez. A native of Maryland, Elder governed the Diocese from 1857 to 1880.

Chapter V

SURVEY AFTER TWENTY YEARS

For a little more than a year after the death of Bishop Van de Velde the Diocese of Natchez remained vacant. As early as January 1856, three men were proposed for the vacant see. They were Rev. William Starr of New York, Rev. Isaac T. Hecker, C.SS.R.,[1] and Rev. William H. Elder of Emmitsburg, Md. This list of candidates was presented to Propaganda by Archbishop Blanc of New Orleans and countersigned by his suffragans.[2] However, it was not until about a year later that in a brief, dated January 9, 1857, Pope Pius IX named William Henry Elder as the third Bishop of Natchez.[3]

The New Bishop

To wear the mitre of Natchez the Holy See had chosen a professor of theology on the staff of Mount St. Mary's College, Emmitsburg, Maryland. In addition to his teaching duties at the seminary, he had been engaged in parochial work in the vicinity of the Mount, especially among the poor and the Negroes to whom he had endeared himself.[4] In this quiet field of labor Father Elder, nevertheless, had impressed many bishops with his abilities. On three successive occasions he had been proposed for the see of Philadelphia, first as ordinary of that diocese and then as coadjutor to Bishop Neumann.[5] At the time of his appointment to Natchez Elder was thirty-seven years old, having been a priest for ten. News of the appointment did not reach Elder until some time in

---

[1] Father Isaac Hecker at this time was still a member of the Congregation of the Most Holy Redeemer. In 1859, together with four other former American Redemptorists Hecker founded the Missionary Society of St. Paul the Apostle, known more popularly as the Paulist Fathers. Elliott, *The Life of Father Hecker* (New York, 1891); Holden, *The Yankee Paul* (Milwaukee, 1958).

[2] Blanc to Propaganda, New Orleans, Jan. 27, 1856; in APF: Scritture Riferite nei Congressi, XVII (1855-1857), ff. 534 rv. On the New Orleans terna Elder was listed in third place or merely as "dignus."

[3] Brief of appointment in ADNJ.

[4] (Susan Blanchard Elder), *Character Glimpses of Most Reverend William Henry Elder, D.D.* (Cincinnati, 1910), 36.

[5] Curley, *Venerable John Neumann, C.SS.R.* (Washington, 1952), 169, 274, 302.

April. The brief of appointment was forwarded to him by Archbishop Blanc on April 4, 1857. In a letter which accompanied the papal document, Blanc urged the young priest:

> I firmly hope, my Right Rev. Dear Sir, you will recognize the will of God in this appointment, and yield to the will of the Holy Father, who owing to the already too long vacancy of the See, desires that no time should be lost for your consecration.[6]

In the same letter the Archbishop spoke encouragingly:

> Be of good heart—The number of Priests through the Diocese of Natchez is not considerable, for the present, but they are all of an Apostolical spirit.—I love them much.—As you probably know, I have been, so far, the Administrator of the Diocese Sede Vacante. I am also the testamentary executor of the last will of your venerable Predecessor; in the last capacity your presence in Natchez is needed within as short a period as possible—things are all in a fair way.—The Episcopal wardrobe is well supplied—you need not trouble yourself for it—Pectoral Crosses, Rings, Mitres, &c. Crosier, Copes &c. there is plenty of them.—The House is well furnished with everything necessary and comfortable.[7]

With a sense of duty that was typical Father Elder accepted the appointment. Following out the advice of Archbishop Blanc, he had himself consecrated a few weeks after being informed of his appointment. The ceremony took place in the historic Cathedral of Baltimore on May 3, 1857, in the presence of his mother and father.[8] The consecrator was Archbishop Kenrick of Baltimore, assisted by Bishop McGill of Richmond and Bishop Wood, coadjutor of Philadelphia. Present in the sanctuary was the saintly Bishop John Nepomucene Neumann, C.SS.R. of Philadelphia. The sermon for the occasion was preached by Elder's close friend, Dr. McCaffery of Mount St. Mary's.[9] Nor did the new Bishop linger

[6] Blanc to Elder, New Orleans, April 4, 1857; in ADNJ, Elder Letter Book—#1, 1; quoted by Gerow, *Cradle Days of St. Marys*, 135. The Elder Letter Books contain letter press copies of almost all of the letters which Bishop Elder wrote.

[7] *Ibid.*

[8] Shea, *History of the Catholic Church, in the United States*, IV, 681; Gerow, "History of the Catholic Diocese of Natchez," in *Catholic Action of the South* (Natchez Centennial Edition), Oct. 14, 1937, 17; Gerow, *Cradle Days of St. Mary's at Natchez*, 137.

[9] Meline & McSweeney, *The Story of the Mountain* (Emmitsburg, 1911), I, 522.

long in the East after his consecration. Before the month was out he appeared in Natchez and was solemnly installed in his Cathedral the day after his arrival, May 31, 1857.[10]

The new Bishop was immediately confronted with a number of problems besetting his diocese, more particularly his Cathedral. Writing to Dr. John McCaffery back at Emmitsburg, Elder reported "I have not got fairly into business yet—for I have not been outside of Natchez," but he confessed that already:

> I am . . . beginning to appreciate Rev. Mr. McCloskey's (treasurer at Mt. St. Mary's) enjoyment for the last twenty years of the daily bread of bills due, and notes maturing and insurances expiring, and repairs urging, etc. etc. (. . . .) I have not seen the Archbishop, I learn from his letters that he has been saving us from bankruptcy, by paying some of our notes—I do not know how many with his own funds—I am beginning to penetrate the text, "Qui episcopatum desiderat." [11]

Although confronted with such hard realities within a week of his arrival in the Diocese, Elder displayed a healthy optimism. In the same letter to Dr. McCaffery he is quick to correct any false impression which his honest reporting might have created:

> But do not think now that I am in bad spirits. I am as lively as ever; indeed, to own the truth—though perhaps the contrary would be more creditable to my feelings—I have not yet felt homesick. Between the novelty of traveling and the engrossment of business—though my thoughts many and many a time run back to the Mountain and St. Joseph's, yet they are soon brought back by something that demands my attention. Indeed with all the labor and perplexity that lies before me, I find so many things to please and give comfort beyond what I expected, that it seems to me it would be ungrateful to indulge in regrets as long as I can resist them. Everywhere on the road I met the greatest kindness. Here I have been received with the warmest welcome. Though the Cathedral looks indeed sadly desolate with its unplastered walls—yet I like the building very much—and the people express their willingness to do all that they can towards finishing it. Then my personal comfort is well provided for by

[10] (Janssens), *Sketch of the Catholic Church in the City of Natchez, Miss.* (Natchez, 1886), 29.

[11] Elder to McCaffrey, Natchez, June 8, 1857; quoted in Meline & McSweeney, *op. cit.*, I, 515; also in Gerow, *Cradle Days of St. Mary's at Natchez,* 137.

> a large and well arranged new brick house—with wide porticoes in the rear; and a large yard around it, set with fruit-trees and shrubbery, very tastefully arranged. Above all I find the rector of the Cathedral, Rev. Mr. Grignon to be a young and zealous priest, with excellent judgment, great simplicity and a good acquaintance with all the affairs of the Church. Just such a friend as I need.
>
> . . . . Natchez is a very beautiful town—so far we have breezes almost continually. I will expect you here this fall when you go out on your begging tour. If you do not get much here, you can have a rest. Indeed I would be very happy if my friends from the Mountain would come down and just see what a fine place it is.[12]

Optimism such as Bishop Elder displayed did not spring from a complacency with the state of his diocese. He soon became even more aware of the pressing needs of the Church in the state of Mississippi and set to work with characteristic vigor to meet them.

One of his first moves was to have himself elected president of the parish corporation at Natchez.[13] It was a wise step in view of the difficulties which the American Church had experienced in the past, especially in the East, with the trustee system. However, it must be said in all fairness that at no time during the previous administrations had there been any conflict between bishop and trustees. Most probably Elder was only conforming to a general policy which was being adopted throughout the Catholic Church in the United States at this time.[14]

About the same time Bishop Elder appointed Father Grignon, rector of the Cathedral, as Vicar-General of the Diocese.[15] Not only was the man well acquainted with the affairs of the Diocese, but, in Elder's estimation, he was also a man of good judgment. When consulted previous to the appointment, Archbishop Blanc confessed that "Revd. Mr. Grignon is the only one in the Diocese who could be appointed.—Partly crippled as he is of one of his legs—

---

[12] Meline & McSweeney, *op. cit.,* I, 515-516; also Gerow, *Cradle Days of St. Mary's at Natchez,* 137-138.

[13] Minute Book of the Roman Catholic Society of Christians of Natchez etc., 140; in Cathedral archives, Natchez, Miss.

[14] Guilday, *A History of the Council of Baltimore 1791-1884,* (New York, 1932), 180.

[15] Blanc to Elder, New Orleans, July 28, 1857; in ADNJ, Elder Letter Book—#1, 95.

he cannot well be sent out on (the) Missions.—He is a well-deserving clergyman, besides."[16] Of the choice Father Guillou had this to say: "Father Grignon . . . is probably the worthiest priest in the whole diocese."[17] The appointment, in any case, was especially necessary in view of the Bishop's intention to begin a visitation of his vast Diocese in the near future, a visitation which would keep him away from his episcopal city for many weeks.

Episcopal Visitation

Before beginning an official visitation of his diocese, the Bishop made a short trip to Sulphur Springs to preside at the exhibition of the Academy conducted by the Sisters of St. Joseph.[18] Although he arrived a day too late, Elder made use of the visit to spark the congregation to action; at least so he thought. At a meeting of the trustees held in the pastor's residence, Elder stressed the need for enlarging the church without delay. The church building then in use was too small to accommodate both the white and colored members of the congregation. And, as the Bishop was quick to point out, the colored people were as entitled to church accommodations as any of the other members of the parish.[19] The Bishop and the pastor, Father Guillou, expressed themselves as being in favor of having a new church. All seemed to agree. However, no definite plans were drawn up on this occasion. This was left to be done by the pastor and the trustees. After spending a few days with the Catholic community in Sulphur Springs, the Bishop returned to Natchez via Canton where he interrupted his trip to deliver three sermons to a mixed audience in the Methodist meeting house.[20] At the time the Catholics of Canton had no church of their own. Mass was said for them by a priest operating out of Jackson or Vicksburg in one of the Catholic homes in the area, usually that of Colonel O. Luckett or of T. Semmes.[21]

---

[16] Blanc to Elder, New Orleans, May 26, 1857; in ADNJ, Elder Letter Book—#1, 14.

[17] Guillou to Elder, Sulphur Springs, June 17, 1857; in ADNJ, Elder Letter Book—#1, 40.

[18] Parish Record, Sulphur Springs, (1841-1926); in parish archives, Camden; copy in ADNJ, 14.

[19] *Ibid.*, 14-15.

[20] *Ibid.*, 14.

[21] Milot, "Sacred Heart—Canton," in *Catholic Action of the South* (Natchez Centennial Edition), Oct. 14, 1937, 52.

In the fall of 1857, before the warm weather was over, Bishop Elder proceeded to the Gulf Coast to begin his first official visitation of the Diocese.

Gulf Coast

In the 1850's southeastern Mississippi, that is, the area east of the Pearl River and south of the thirty-first parallel, was described as "a dreary and thinly inhabited pine forest." [22] The humble homes of the few settlers, most of whom were small farmers, were often as much as fifteen miles apart. Generally the forest was unbroken. There was little undergrowth and there was almost no wild life; even birds were scarce. Most of the soil was sandy. The meager economic activity of this area was chiefly connected with its vast long-leaf pine forests. There were numerous kilns that produced large quantities of tar, and, as a by-product, charcoal. A good deal of timber was exported to France for naval purposes; however, some was worked at sawmills on the coast, having been floated out of the forest during the rainy season partly by natural waterways as well as by long straight ditches. Large herds of scrub cattle grazed under the pine trees, and small patches of crops, especially rice, sweet potatoes and sugar cane, were raised for home consumption. Very little cotton was planted south of the thirty-first parallel. During the railway boom of this decade no line penetrated southeastern Mississippi. At Handsboro was the only other industry in the area, namely, two or three small foundries and machine shops.[23] As a result, few people living in this section of the State shared in the prosperity that Mississippi as a whole enjoyed in the late fifties.

The above statement might well have been challenged by a stranger visiting the Gulf Coast of Mississippi at this time. For, from the Pearl River as far east as Biloxi an almost continuous succession of "elegant residences and tasteful villas" faced the Gulf of Mexico. However, the people residing in such fashionable homes had made their fortunes outside of the area. Those of Biloxi and Bay St. Louis belonged to French-Catholics of New Orleans, while Pass Christian [24] and Mississippi City were resort centers for Protestant-

---

[22] Sydnor, *A Gentleman of the Old Natchez Region* (Durham, N.C., 1938), 189-190.

[23] Lang, *History of Harrison County, Mississippi* (Gulfport, 1936), 76.

[24] The first yacht club in the South was organized at Pass Christian in 1849.

American planters from the river counties and northern part of the State and Louisiana. Some of the owners spent only a third of the year on the Coast, while others, their fortunes assured, were in permanent residence.

The starting point for Bishop Elder's visitation which began on September 13 was Bay St. Louis.[25] Here the Bishop found the pastor, Father Buteux, struggling with all his might and main to keep the Sisters' school from closing down. After the arrival of reinforcements from the motherhouse in France in 1856, it was decided to expand the services of the Sisters by taking in boarders.[26] One of the reasons for doing so was the impossibility of being able to support themselves with their day school. Even this venture did not have the expected results. As late as 1860, the school had only ten boarders. No doubt the physical aspects of the makeshift boarding school discouraged parents of New Orleans from enrolling their daughters at the Bay school. One of the pioneer Sisters in a letter to her Superior in France speaks of another reason for the school's lack of popularity: ". . . students from New Orleans do not come because they fear contacts with the creoles." [27] Convinced from the start that the school in Bay St. Louis had no future as far as being able to support a community of Sisters, Mother Eulalie prevailed upon her higher superiors to accept an offer of Archbishop Blanc to open a house in New Orleans.[28] In a city of 65,000 Catholics there would be a greater chance for making the new foundation a functional as well as a financial success. Because her health had not been the best at the Bay, Mother Eulalie was transferred to New Orleans. Accompanying her to the Crescent City was Sister Anatolie. Before long, Mother Eulalie asked for and obtained a third Sister from the Bay community.[29] This left only two Sisters, Mother Esperance and Sister Esdras, to carry on at Bay St. Louis. In addition to teaching in the school the two

---

25 Elder to Rev. Mother (St. Claude), Bay St. Louis, Sept. 13, 1857; in ASSJB.

26 (Sisters of St. Joseph), "St. Joseph Academy," in *Catholic Action of the South* (Natchez Centennial Edition), Oct. 14, 1937, 36.

27 Sister Esperance to Rev. Mother (St. Claude), Bay St. Louis, Dec. 6, 1856; in ASSJB.

28 Provincial Centennial book of the Sisters of St. Joseph of Bourg, New Orleans province, (New Orleans, 1955).

29 Sister Esperance to Rev. Mother (St. Claude), Bay St. Louis, Dec. 6, 1856; in ASSJB.

Sisters had to keep house, cook, run their own errands and give religious instructions to adults, both whites and colored. Sometimes there were as many as five instructions a day.[30] The situation was more than the two Sisters could cope with. As early as December 1856, after just giving up a third Sister to the New Orleans foundation, Mother Esperance wrote to the Superior General at Bourg, pleading for reinforcements.[31] At the time of Bishop Elder's visitation, almost a year later, none as yet had arrived.

Fully confident that the school would yet prove a success because of its "advantageous location" and fully aware of the "great services rendered to so many souls" by the Sisters, Elder appealed to Mother St. Claude, the Superior General of the Sisters in France, directly from Bay St. Louis:

> I have just begun my episcopal visitation; Bay St. Louis was the starting point. I have experienced here a mixture of sorrow and edification: sorrow, in finding in this establishment only two Sisters who are operating a school which does not even supply their needs; edification, in seeing the courage, the resignation, the joy even of these two heroic women.
>
> Though their school is small, they have accomplished much through it. They have also rendered service by the religious instruction they give to adults and domestics. And they have radiated even more by the example of their zeal and devotion; their merciful acts, their sufferings for the glory of God have certainly drawn numerous blessings on the whole area.
>
> I am writing you today in order to thank you and your community for the service toward religion your Sisters have rendered in this country. I also pray that you will send two or three other Sisters so that they may establish themselves more solidly and radiate still more widely.[32]

As an added argument for sustaining the foundation in Bay St. Louis, Elder made it clear to the Superior General that the pastor was sharing the Sisters' life of sacrifice in order to maintain the school:

---

[30] Mother Esperance to Rev. Mother (St. Claude), Bay St. Louis, April 23, 1861; in ASSJB.

[31] Sister Esperance to Rev. Mother (St. Claude), Bay St. Louis, Dec. 6, 1856; in ASSJB.

[32] Elder to Rev. Mother (St. Claude), Bay St. Louis, Sept. 13, 1857; in ASSJB. (Translation).

> Reverend Father Buteux, pastor of the community, has continuously consecrated almost all of his personal resources to the maintenance of this house. For this enterprise, he has sacrificed not only luxuries, but also—too often—the very necessities of life.[33]

Another reason for sending reinforcements to the Bay community would be the increased opportunity for living a normal religious life. The Bishop is quick to point this out:

> I assure you, they really deserve all the help and encouragement you can possibly give them. In spite of so many hardships capable of tiring and discouraging them, they have faithfully kept the practices and spirit of their holy rule. Their small number renders it impossible to keep all the common observances and to accomplish among the poor souls surrounding them all the good they would like. This is their greatest trial.[34]

The Bishop concludes with one final appeal:

> Reverend Mother, please do not refuse to console your spiritual daughters by sending them two or three devoted Sisters, animated with the same zeal and perseverance as they. You will be rewarded by their own prayers and by those of the Guardian Angels of everyone in the vicinity. I myself will continue to remember you and your community at the Holy Sacrifice of the Mass.[35]

Not until August 14, 1858, after Father Buteux had traveled to France to plead the case of the Sisters before the authorities at Bourg, were reinforcements sent.[36] On this occasion of his second visit to France, Father Buteux stopped off at Ars. From this little town in southeastern France, made famous by its saintly curé, M. Jean Marie Vianney,[37] the pastor of Bay St. Louis addressed a letter to Mother St. Claude, informing her of his presence in France and of his intentions. With the cleverness of an apostle he had the Curé of Ars countersign the letter with its plea for more Sisters.[38] As a result, Mother des Anges and Sister Rolandine were

---

[33] *Ibid.*

[34] *Ibid.*

[35] *Ibid.*

[36] Provincial Centennial book of the Sisters of St. Joseph of Bourg, New Orleans province, 1955.

[37] Jean Marie Vianney died in 1859, two years after Fr. Buteux's visit, and was canonized by Pope Pius XI in 1925.

[38] (Sisters of St. Joseph), "St. Joseph's Academy," in *Catholic Action of the South* (Natchez Centennial Edition), Oct. 14, 1937, 36.

sent to join the two overworked Sisters at the Bay.[39] Shortly after their arrival in the summer of 1858, Father Buteux, urged on by Bishop Elder, began to formulate plans for erecting a permanent boarding school for girls at Bay St. Louis.

Besides the responsibilities associated with his office as pastor of the Catholic community at Bay St. Louis, Father Buteux at the time of Bishop Elder's visitation was also caring for the spiritual needs of several other semi-isolated Catholic communities in the area.[40] West of Bay St. Louis, down the coast, he ministered to the Catholics of Waveland and Point Clear. Bayou Cadet and Bayou La Croix were also attended by him. He also made periodic visits to the Jourdan River Settlement[41] and the Wolf River community,[42] both on the north shore of Bay St. Louis. Most of the people in the latter two communities were descendants of the early French settlers of the Gulf Coast. They spoke for the most part a French patois similar to the Cajun dialect of southern Louisiana. During the 18th and the early part of the 19th century these Catholics were ministered to by priests operating out of New Orleans and Biloxi.[43] Unfortunately these visits were rare. Even with the arrival at Bay St. Louis in 1847 of a resident pastor in the person of Father Buteux, visits to these communities were all too infrequent. As late as 1860, Point Clear was being visited only every six weeks while Wolf River saw a priest only every three months.[44] Understandably then the degree of religious ignorance among these people was high. Nevertheless, for the most part they maintained their allegiance to the Catholic Church, Protestantism making few inroads among them.[45]

As Bishop Elder moved east along the Coast from Bay St. Louis, the conditions he discovered were disturbing. Forewarned

[39] Provincial Centennial book of the Sisters of St. Joseph of Bourg, New Orleans province, 1955.

[40] Denis, "Annunciation Parish–Kiln," in *Catholic Action of the South* (Natchez Centennial Edition), Oct. 14, 1937, 61.

[41] Known today as Kiln.

[42] Also called Wolftown; today known as Delisle.

[43] The baptismal records of the older Catholics in these settlements were found in the registers of the Cathedral in New Orleans and of the Nativity of the BVM parish in Biloxi.

[44] Annual report of Fr. Leduc to Elder, Bay St. Louis, Sept. 17, 1860; in ADNJ, File: Elder–L.

[45] Boyd, *A Popular History of the Baptists in Mississippi* (Jackson, 1930), 145; Cain, *Methodism in the Mississippi Conference, 1846-1870* (Jackson, 1939), 375-377.

by Father Grignon, who had visited the Coast less than three weeks before,[46] the Bishop found a good deal of apathy and indifference among the Catholics of the area. Here too religious ignorance was quite general. Particularly distressing was the situation at Ocean Springs where there were about a hundred Catholics. Here the children were growing up ignorant of their Catholic faith. Some were attending Protestant Sunday schools. Still, both parents and children insisted they were Catholic and whenever a Catholic priest put in an appearance they welcomed him warmly. Not having a church, some members of the congregation refused to assist at Mass whenever it was celebrated in a private home for whose host they had a personal dislike.[47] At Biloxi, the largest town on the Mississippi Gulf Coast at the time, conditions were perhaps the worst. Here Father Grignon reported a few weeks before Bishop Elder's arrival that he found "a great deal of apathy and indifference." [48] A few years later the Reverend Thomas S. Savage, first rector of Trinity Episcopal church in Pass Christian, reported:

> All unite, Papists, Methodists and Baptists and others in admitting that the population of Biloxi is the most demoralized of any on the Coast. You would not know that any notice is taken of Sunday if you were not to visit the houses of worship. Protestants as well as Papists are regardless of that holy day.[49]

Pass Christian also came under fire in Father Grignon's report to Bishop Elder. After speaking about the apathy and indifference at Biloxi and vicinity, the Vicar-General added: "It would seem to be pretty much the same at Pass Christian." [50]

For this situation one could hardly blame the two priests in charge of this section of the Coast. Father Holton, besides being in charge of the Catholic community in Pass Christian, also visited Handsboro and Mississippi City regularly and Ocean Springs occasionally. At the time of the Bishop's visitation none of these stations had a church. Father Guinand, pastor of Biloxi, was already

---

[46] Grignon to Elder, Pass Christian, Aug. 31, 1857; in ADNJ, Elder Letter Book—#1, 132.

[47] *Ibid.*

[48] *Ibid.*

[49] *Journal of the (Episcopal) Diocese of Mississippi*, 1861, p. 137; quoted by Carter and Ragusin, *Gulf Coast Country* (New York, 1951), 106-107.

[50] Grignon to Elder, Pass Christian, Aug. 31, 1857; in ADNJ, Elder Letter Book—#1, 132.

an old man when Bishop Elder visited his parish toward the end of September 1857. In fact, on this occasion Guinand urged the Bishop to make arrangements for his retirement at the earliest date possible.[51] When the priest had been first assigned to Biloxi in 1846, he found himself in charge of the whole Mississippi Gulf Coast.[52] After the appointment of resident pastors to Bay St. Louis and Pass Christian he continued to serve Pascagoula regularly until 1854, in addition to his duties at Biloxi.[53]

While not lacking in zeal, the two priests nevertheless were faced with a language problem which militated against their being completely effective in the ministry. Father Guinand could speak only poor English while Father Holton spoke little or no French. Yet both priests found in their congregations people who were either exclusively French-speaking or English-speaking. For example, because of his inability to understand the French patois of the Catholics at Wolf River, Father Holton rarely visited this community.[54] Eventually the priest at Bay St. Louis re-assumed responsibility for this mission station. As a remedy for the apathy and indifference found at Biloxi Father Grignon in his report to Bishop Elder stressed the need for giving religious instructions there both in English and French.[55] Apparently Father Guinand had been neglecting to do so. A few years after his first visit to the Gulf Coast Bishop Elder had to remind Father Holton not to neglect the French-speaking

---

[51] Guinand remained in Biloxi for some time after his retirement in March, 1858. His relations, however, with the Bishop and the newly appointed pastor, Father Richard B. Hardey, were quite strained. The old priest had failed to keep separate account books for parish and personal property. It took some time before a satisfactory financial settlement could be made. Furthermore, Guinand repeatedly refused to give up a young housekeeper whose presence in his house occasioned some scandal. Eventually the Bishop had to administer a canonical warning to the priest. The unpleasantness of the whole situation may account for Father Hardey's short term of office—about four months—as pastor in Biloxi. Elder to Hardey, Natchez, March 23, 1858; in ADNJ, File: Elder—H. Elder to Guinand, Natchez, April 20, 1858; in ADNJ, File: Elder—G. Elder to Buteux, Natchez, July 27, 1858; in ADNJ, Elder Letter Book—#2, 137.

[52] O'Connell, "Earliest Missionaries Served Historic Biloxi," in *Catholic Action of the South* (Natchez Centennial Edition), Oct. 14, 1937, 23.

[53] Hunter, "Our Lady of Victories—Pascagoula," *ibid.*, 49.

[54] Annual report of Leduc to Elder, Sept. 17, 1860, Bay St. Louis; in ADNJ, File: Elder—L. It should also be noted that Fr. Holton's health was not the best at this time. It eventually forced him to retire to New Orleans.

[55] Grignon to Elder, Pass Christian, Aug. 31, 1857; in ADNJ, Elder Letter Book—#1, 132.

members of his congregation. It was suggested on this occasion that Holton have a Mission in French for his parish.[56]

There is no evidence that Bishop Elder visited Pascagoula at this time. However, information, passed on undoubtedly to him by Father Guinand, prompted the Bishop to make plans for establishing a parish there and providing it with a resident priest. Early in 1858, he sent Father Pont[57] to Pascagoula.[58] On a piece of property donated by Mr. John Baptiste,[59] apparently one of the pillars of the Catholic community there, Father Pont erected a small, but well-built chapel-house. The building was literally the work of his own hands, Pont having even cut the timber and rafted it down the river himself. While he was building, the priest cooked for himself in the open air and lodged in a shed, proof neither against the summer's sun nor the winter's cold. At length, he had the pleasure of opening his modest "Cathedral in the Pines." Unfortunately, the Bishop was able to leave the priest there for only a year. Early in 1859, the Bishop, transferring Father Leray to Vicksburg, had Father Pont take his place at Jackson.[60] For the next year and a half Father Benausse, S.J. of Spring Hill College, Mobile, Alabama, took charge of visiting the parish occasionally.[61] During this time the Catholics at Pascagoula gave every evidence of a good spirit, frequenting the Sacraments whenever possible and reiterating their desire to have a resident pastor.[62]

Paulding

Leaving the Gulf Coast at the end of September, Bishop Elder traveled north to Paulding in Jasper County. At this time Paulding was the county seat. In spite of the sterility of the soil the settlers before the Civil War achieved sporadic wealth and a culture unusual in the Piney Woods. Much of this could be accounted for by

---

56 Elder to Holton, Natchez, Feb. 27, 1861; in ADNJ, Elder Letter Book —#6, 78.

57 Fr. Francis René Pont had come to America from France in 1855, as a seminarian. He finished his studies at Spring Hill College, Mobile, Ala., and was ordained in Natchez by Archbishop Blanc on Nov. 25, 1855, the Diocese being vacant at the time. Cf. ADNJ, File: Chanche—P.

58 Hunter, *op. cit.*

59 Mr. John Baptist was one of the early settlers of Pascagoula. Cf. Lowry and McCardle: *A History of Mississippi*, Jackson, 1891, 497.

60 Hunter, *op. cit.*

61 *Ibid.*

62 Elder to Benausse, Natchez, Aug. 25, 1859; in ADNJ, Elder Letter Book—#4, 242.

the fact that Paulding was situated on the trade roads from Mobile and New Orleans. The steady flow of traffic meant business and contact with two of the largest cities in the South. During court week especially the small town came alive with color and excitement. Every other activity was suspended. Aristocratic family carriages, stylish buggies, light sulkies and battered farm wagons crowded the long shady main street that ran through a double row of immense live oaks. Women wore their richest gowns and gayest plumes, planters their fanciest waistcoats. But the lawyers held the center of the stage. Driving into Paulding in elegant carriages with Negro attendants, they attracted all eyes. The girls coquetted with them, and the young men imitated their mannerisms, noting at the same time the color of ties and the cut of waistcoats. Among these was Joseph Heyfren, an Irish-born lawyer. Accurate and articulate he was instrumental in developing the colony which was, for the most part, made up of Irish Catholics.[63] Among other prominent Catholics of Paulding was Colonel Oliver C. Dease. One of the early settlers in Jasper County, the Colonel entered into state politics, serving in both branches of the legislature.[64] Another outstanding Catholic of the Paulding community at the time of Bishop Elder's visit was Mr. James J. Shannon, editor of the Paulding *Eastern Clarion,* the largest newspaper of any town in the State up to and including the Civil War period.[65]

When Bishop Elder arrived in town, he found a substantial white frame church with a peaked roof and spire. It stood on the main street, already flanked with store buildings and white frame mansions. Except for the two-storied red-brick courthouse, the church, dedicated to St. Michael, was probably the largest building in Paulding.[66] The Catholic congregation at the time numbered about two hundred.[67] Father Boheme, the pastor, lived with the Shannon

---

[63] Lowry and McCardle, *op. cit.*, 501; also notes on the history of Paulding, in Bishop Gunn's handwriting (no date), in the ADNJ, File: History Notes—P.

[64] Lowry and McCardle, *op. cit.*, 500.

[65] Hayes, *A Historical Sketch of the Catholic Church in Laurel and Jones County, Miss.* (Ellisville, Miss., 1937), 40; also notes on the history of Paulding, in ADNJ, File: History Notes—P.

[66] One long red clay street, forming an aisle between immense live oaks, an ante-bellum home or two, the 100-year-old Catholic church and a jail are all that remain today of the town once called the "Queen City of the East."

[67] Dogny, "St. Michael's—Paulding," in *Catholic Action of the South* (Natchez Centennial Edition), Oct. 14, 1937, 27.

family nearly four or five miles outside of town.[68] Most of the time the priest was on the road, ministering to little groups of Catholics along the Mobile and Ohio Railroad between Quitman and Aberdeen as well as to other pockets of Catholics, living some miles distant from the railroad, such as at DeKalb in Kemper County and Houston in Chickasaw County. West of Paulding at Raleigh in Smith County there was also a group of Catholics whom the missionary visited regularly. Making the complete circuit involved a trip of over 350 miles, most of which was made on horseback.

Eastern Mississippi

Following Father Grignon's suggestion, Bishop Elder most probably arranged his travel-time so as to be at Paulding over a weekend.[69] It is hardly likely that he stayed more than a day or so, for by October 6, the Bishop had traveled as far north as Macon.[70] It would appear from correspondence of a later date that Elder on this occasion made a point to visit the various stations attended by Father Boheme.[71] Most of the Catholics at these stations were Irish immigrants and of these a good number were railroad workers. Such a population was not very stable. At Enterprise, a little town just below the junction of the two streams that form the Chickasawhay River, there were only two or three Catholic families. Further up the railroad line at Macon there were about five Catholics.[72] Here the Bishop baptized Henry Stone Connolly and Mary Rebecca Cahill.[73] This entry in the parish baptismal register at Columbus is the only evidence on hand of the Bishop's visit to Macon in 1857. The Catholics here had secured a beautiful church site as early as 1852. At that time prospects looked so bright that there was serious talk of building not only a church and priest's house but a school as well.[74] Unfortunately, neither Bishop

---

[68] *Ibid.*

[69] Grignon to Elder, Pass Christian, Aug. 31, 1857; in ADNJ, Elder Letter Book—#1, 132.

[70] Baptismal register of the Church of the Annunciation, Columbus, Miss., 1857; in parish archives.

[71] Elder to Boheme, Natchez, Sept. 6, 1858; in ADNJ, Elder Letter Book —#3, 53.

[72] Pont to Elder, Jackson, July 10, 1857; in ADNJ, Elder Letter Book —#1, 54.

[73] Baptismal register of the Church of the Annunciation, Columbus, Miss., 1857; in parish archives.

[74] Ferris to Chanche, Macon, June 17, 1852; in AUND: Natchez Papers.

Chanche nor Bishop Van de Velde was able to provide a resident priest to launch and sustain the project. When Bishop Elder could not satisfy the request of these people, enthusiasm began to die out. Two years later, during a second visit to Macon, the Bishop found the congregation, now numbering about thirty, considering quite seriously an offer made to them by the Masons of the town to sell the church site for a sizeable profit.[75] On this occasion Elder was able to convince them that the sale would be a mistake.[76]

The next point in the Bishop's visitation was Columbus, in Lowndes County. At the time Columbus was at the end of a branch line of the Mobile and Ohio Railroad. It was one of the few urban centers in the State. Some of the major attractions in the town were the Gilmore Hotel, the Odd Fellows building, the Franklin Academy, the Columbus Female Institute and a great amphitheatre at the fair grounds. Elder was impressed by the town. On a subsequent visit he wrote to his vicar-general: "Columbus is a large & beautiful city, larger than Natchez in its extent of ground—& they say also in its population. The streets are broad —most of the houses of brick—& many elegant residences like those of Natchez."[77] At the time of his visit the Bishop learned that Mass was customarily celebrated for the Catholics of the town in one of their own homes. Sharing this privilege while extending their hospitality to the Catholic community were the Monroe, Galvin and Hury families.[78] It is difficult to calculate the exact number of Catholics at Columbus in 1857. Eight to ten families can establish the fact of their residence in the town at this time.[79] Most probably there were not many more.[80] Although convinced that there was a clear need for a resident priest in the Columbus area, Elder was unable to supply one. As a result, he became anxious about the spirit of these Catholics. Neglected as they were by force of circumstances, they might not understand and might easily become discouraged. In a letter to Father Boheme the

---

75 Elder to Grignon, Columbus, Oct. 18, 1859; in ADNJ, File: Elder—G.

76 Today (1962) Macon is still without a resident priest. It is a mission served by the pastor of Columbus, Miss.

77 Elder to Grignon, Columbus, Oct. 18, 1859; in ADNJ, File: Elder—G.

78 Lawrence, "Church of Annunciation—Columbus," in *Catholic Action of the South* (Natchez Centennial Edition), Oct. 14, 1937, 55.

79 *Ibid.*

80 After a visit to Columbus in 1859, Boheme reported to Elder that nine people had received Holy Communion. In 1866, Elder spoke of the Catholics being few in number.

Bishop urged the missionary to dispel any notion among these people that he was indifferent to their situation:

> When you see or write to the Catholics of Columbus express to them the warm interest I feel in them, my earnest desire to have them supplied with all the helps of religion, and my hope to be able to visit them, as well as all those places where I had so much consolation last year.[81]

Fortunately the Catholics of Columbus did not lose heart. As a matter of fact, they exhibited a broadness of outlook that was properly Catholic. In the spring of 1860, Elder received from the Catholics of that place a collection they had taken up among themselves for the Holy Father.[82]

From Columbus Bishop Elder moved on to Aberdeen, the seat of Monroe County. Aberdeen, near the head of navigation of the Tombigbee River and with the almost ideal cotton growing area to the west, was one of the most prosperous of the Mississippi ante-bellum plantation towns. Steamboats on the Tombigbee carried cotton grown in the area down to Mobile in the fall and carried back supplies in the spring. Negroes, brought from Virginia to work on the newly-created prairie plantations, made possible a swift transition from pioneer conditions to plantation comfort. Aberdeen fast became a social center with attractive town houses built by the planters for their "women-folk." Here the Bishop found a good number of Catholics. No precise figure is available, but, after a second visit in 1859, the Bishop reported to his Vicar-General that "Aberdeen has more Catholics than any other point" in the northeastern part of the State.[83] Thus, comparatively speaking, Aberdeen's Catholic community would have numbered somewhere between fifty and a hundred people. There was no church.

Holly Springs

From Aberdeen the Bishop traveled west to Houston in Chickasaw County. After visiting a handful of Catholics there, he went north to Holly Springs. Unlike other Mississippi towns, Holly Springs scarcely knew a frontier life. One year after it was in-

---

[81] Elder to Boheme, Natchez, Sept. 6, 1858; in ADNJ, Elder Letter Book —#3, 53.

[82] Elder to Boheme, Natchez, May 15, 1860; in ADNJ, Elder Letter Book —#5, 229.

[83] Elder to Grignon, Columbus, Oct. 18, 1859; in ADNJ, File: Elder—G.

corporated in 1839, the town had fourteen law offices, six doctor's offices, two banks, nine dry good stores, five grocery stores, five churches, three hotels and several private schools. In place of log cabins the town's pioneers built mansions that rivaled one another in elaborate treatment and grand proportions. Although land and cotton remained the backbone of the town, other industries were established. Most notable of these was the iron foundry that furnished iron for the Mississippi Central Railroad (which ran from Holly Springs to Canton) and later cannon for the Confederacy.

By request of Elder's predecessors the Dominican Fathers of Sts. Peter and Paul's Church in Memphis, Tennessee were ministering to the Catholics in northern Mississippi. Before setting out on his visitation, Elder had received a report on conditions in this part of his diocese from Father Thomas Grace, O.P.[84] of Memphis:

> I deem it my duty to communicate with you in regard to the Catholics in the northern portions of the state of Mississippi, whom we have been accustomed to visit occasionally by request of your predecessors. There are some three or four Catholic families in Holly Springs with some few others in the vicinity, fifty miles from Memphis. Along the line of the rail road & scattered over two or three communities some few more are found.
>
> We have urged some of the Catholics in Holly Springs to make an effort to get up a Church no matter how small in demension in which Divine Service may be had, and through the assistance of Rev. Father Daly they have succeeded in procuring a lot and have purchased a very neat Episcopal Church 30 feet by 45 feet which they will remove to the lot immediately. They hold only a title bond to the property and are ready to make a deed in favor of you so soon as you will be pleased to signify your acceptance, and your approval of what has been done. The Church will have to undergo refitting, but can be got ready for your blessing in the course of two or three months.[85]

---

[84] Father Thomas L. Grace, O.P. was pastor of Sts. Peter and Paul's Church in Memphis and also vicar-general for the western part of Tennessee (Diocese of Nashville). In 1859, he was appointed second bishop of St. Paul, Minnesota.

[85] Grace to Elder, Memphis, Aug. 2, 1857; in ADNJ, Elder Letter Book —#1, 110.

The railroad about which Father Grace speaks was undoubtedly the Mississippi Central which connected with the Memphis and Charleston Railroad at Grand Junction, Tennessee. Along this line Catholics were to be found at Oxford, Coffeeville and Grenada—communities south of Holly Springs. If Father Grace used the term "rail road" in a generic way, then the labors of the Dominican Fathers in northern Mississippi might well have extended also to Hernando, Pope's Station, Oakland, Gardner Station and Hardy Station on the Mississippi and Tennessee Railroad which had been built southward from Memphis to within a short distance of Grenada, and to Corinth on the Memphis and Charleston Railroad which cut across the northeastern corner of the State. This latter interpretation seems quite probable for two reasons. Both railroads in question went on into Memphis, headquarters for the Dominican Fathers. And, when Father Basilio Elia succeeded the Dominican Fathers in northern Mississippi in 1861, he reported soon afterward that he was visiting Catholics at these points regularly.[86] At the time of Bishop Elder's visitation the area was being covered by Father James V. Daly, O.P. Early in 1858, he was succeeded in the field by Father Stephen Byrne, O.P.[87]

When the Bishop arrived in Holly Springs, the church building which had been purchased from the Episcopalians was hardly ready for his official blessing. As late as November 15, 1857, after Elder's departure, the "refitting" of the church was far from completed. In a letter of explanation Father Grace wrote:

> . . . . owing to the hard times little progress has been made towards the completion of the Church in Holly Springs. In moving the church edifice to the lot, it was found necessary to take off the roof; the whole of the plastering, the gallery & other wood work had also to be removed. The roof has been reshingled, but besides this little has been done. There is a prospect of better times now, and no efforts shall be spared to bring the church to an early completion—of which you will be advised.[88]

---

[86] Report from St. Joseph's Church, Holly Springs, dated Jan. 12, 1862, submitted by Fr. Elia; in ADNJ, File: Elder—E.

[87] O'Daniel, *The Father of the Church in Tennessee* (New York, 1926), 548; Elder to Grignon, Biloxi, Sept. 29, 1858; in ADNJ, File: Elder—G.

[88] Grace to Elder, Memphis, Nov. 15, 1857; in ADNJ, Elder Letter Book —#1, 222.

In the summer of 1857, the Catholic congregation of Holly Springs was made up of three or four families residing in the town itself plus a few others in the immediate vicinity. Yet, less than three years later, in proportion to the phenomenal growth of the general population of Holly Springs, the Catholic community had increased to more than three hundred people.[89] Most of them were workers and their families, the menfolk being employed in the foundry and railroad shops.[90] At the time of the Bishop's visit there was no residence for a priest. The congregation was being visited once a month from Memphis.

Sulphur Springs

In the middle of November Bishop Elder reached Sulphur Springs.[91] Located in the eastern part of Madison County, eighteen miles northeast of Canton, the Springs was only a hamlet. As yet no public conveyance ran to or through the place.[92] Father Guillou was the resident pastor. From a material standpoint the parish was well-organized and functioning smoothly.[93] There was a wooden church, a priest's house, and a graveyard occupying four acres of ground to which the Bishop held title. The pastor received an annual salary of $400 raised by subscription. Mr. Hugh Ward was the official collector. In addition to his salary the pastor was given $50 for such church expenses as candles, wine, altar linen, etc. The parish also furnished the pastor with a horse and feed. Although Father Guillou had his own living quarters, he took his meals with the Ward family who also took care of his laundry. For these services the priest paid the Wards $100 a year. Except for twelve dollars which it owed on the newly erected priest's house, the parish was financially solvent. Since the Bishop's last visit to the Springs in August, the project of enlarging the church had been at a standstill. During this official visit it was agreed definitely that an addition of thirty feet would be built on to the church.

89 Elder to Mother Leonie, Natchez, Feb. 27, 1861; in ADNJ, Elder Letter Book—#6, 80.

90 Elder to Superior of Seminary College of Brignole-Sale, at Genoa, Natchez, Jan. 20, 1864; in ADNJ, Elder Letter Book—#9, 114.

91 Parish Record, Sulphur Springs, (1841-1926); in parish archives, Camden; copy in ADNJ, 15.

92 In September 1858, arrangements were made with a Mr. Warren of Carthage to run his hack through the Springs three times a week, the people of the Springs agreeing to subsidize the service.

93 Notes on Sulphur Springs, dated Nov. 15, 1857, probably made by Elder; in ADNJ, File: Elder—S.

To realize this project a subscription was inaugurated immediately.[94] Taking into account several factors,[95] one might hazard a guess that the number of Catholics, white and colored, who made up the Sulphur Springs congregation in 1857, was in the neighborhood of two hundred.

On the occasion of this visit Elder had to face a more personal problem. In October, during the course of his visitation, he received a letter from Father Guillou.[96] The young pastor of the Springs expressed a strong desire, of some years standing, to embrace the religious life.[97] This desire had increased all the more when Guillou found himself out on the missions alone:

> After my ordination, I was sent to Yazoo City, where I remained four years. I felt then, for the first time, how dangerous it is for a young priest to be thus cast away by himself, deprived of all spiritual assistance and advice, and (I) became more and more anxious to follow my vocation; but (I) was prevented from doing so by the death of the Bishops and various circumstances. Since I took the charge of the good Sisters here, the desire of embracing that mode of life which I knew to be suited to my taste & wants of my soul has increased more and more.[98]

To add weight to his petition for release from the Diocese, Guillou asserted that his spiritual director at the Grand Seminary of Nantes had suggested that he join a religious community and just recently Father Alexander, C.SS.R.,[99] the Sisters' retreat master, with whom Guillou discussed the matter, supported the young

[94] Parish Record, Sulphur Springs, (1841-1926); in parish archives, Camden; copy in ADNJ, 15.

[95] These factors are the number of names of parishioners which appear in the parish record and other letters; the fact that the church had to be enlarged from a building 30' by 40' to one 30' by 70'; and the number of parishioners known to have slaves in large numbers.

[96] Guillou to Elder, Sulphur Springs, Oct. 15, 1857; in ADNJ, Elder Letter Book—#1, 178.

[97] It was Guillou's initial resolve to join "the Oblate Fathers, who have the charge of the Oceania Missions." Guillou is in error. The Marist Fathers were in charge of those missions.

[98] Guillou to Elder, Sulphur Springs, Oct. 15, 1857; in ADNJ, Elder Letter Book—#1, 178.

[99] Fr. Alexander Cvitkovicz (Czvitkovicz), C.SS.R. was born in Hungary in 1806. Ordained in 1830, he served in Holland and Austria before coming to the United States in 1841. When he preached and also worked among the German-speaking Catholics in Mississippi, he was attached to the Redemptorist house in New Orleans where he died in 1883. Archives of the Congregation of the Most Holy Redeemer, Rome.

priest's decision. Delicate as the matter might be, Elder was able to prevail upon Guillou to remain at his post. It is not known whether Guillou gave up the idea or simply postponed the step. To lose the priest at this time would have been particularly distressing to Elder who, as a result of his visitation, was all too conscious of the need for priests in his Diocese. Besides, the young man was doing a yeoman's service in this part of the State. In addition to being pastor and chaplain at the Springs, Guillou traveled a circuit which embraced stations and plantations in Madison, Neshoba, Kemper, Rankin and Leake Counties, as well as various other stations and railroad camps in Attala, Holmes and Choctaw Counties. Where would Elder find a replacement for such a man? Perhaps, it was in keeping with a promise made to Guillou at this time that the Bishop sent a young priest to Sulphur Springs in 1859, to serve as his assistant.[100]

Yazoo City

Several weeks after his arrival in the Diocese, in response to a letter announcing this fact, Bishop Elder received a report from Father Le Corre of Yazoo City.[101] In the letter the young pastor urged the Bishop to visit the Catholic congregation there as soon as possible. The people would surely be consoled by such a visit, for they had come to believe that they had been "abandoned and completely neglected." As an added incentive for making the trip, Le Corre relayed the information that one of his parishioners, a Mrs. Hogan, formerly Miss Miles, claimed that she was related to the Bishop.[102] Although there is no evidence on hand, it would seem that, if Elder did not travel to Yazoo City during the summer, he most probably did stop there during the course of his official visitation in the autumn of 1857. Most likely this would have been after his visit to Sulphur Springs.

At the time of the Bishop's supposed visit, Yazoo City had grown to the point where it offered a contrast of delta with

---

[100] Namely, Fr. Mouton. Cf. Parish Record, Sulphur Springs, Part I (1841-1859); in parish archives, Camden.

[101] Le Corre to Elder, Yazoo City, June 20, 1857; in ADNJ, Elder Letter Book—#1, 34. Paul Marie Le Corre had come to the Diocese as a sub-deacon from France. He was ordained to the priesthood on June 29, 1855 by Bishop Van de Velde and appointed pastor of Yazoo City on July 4, 1856 by Archbishop Blanc, administrator of the then vacant Diocese of Natchez.

[102] Bishop Elder's maternal grandmother was a Miles.

bluffs, since part of the city was built on a low flat bordering the Yazoo River and the other part perched on the steep hills above. Cotton export-center for the area, the bustling community had a population well over two thousand. A frame church, not very large, had been erected during the pastorate of Father Guillou (1851-1855). At the time, the outside of the church had been painted but little was done on the inside. Since Father Le Corre's arrival in July of 1856, the interior of the church had been painted and decorated; an altar, hand-carved by one of the parishioners, had been installed; a baptistery and a large religious picture had been donated; and a Way of the Cross, also a gift, had been erected. Before long the pastor hoped to have a bell for the church as well.[103] At the time of the Bishop's visit, the pastor was boarding with the Hogan family. In 1844, there were about forty or fifty Catholics at Yazoo City. During the next decade many Irish Catholics arrived. They were followed by a number of Germans.[104] Although they were only a minority in the congregation, they were numerous enough to warrant a special visit by a German-speaking priest to enable them to fulfill their Easter duty.[105] Apart from these facts, no further information is available on the size of the Catholic congregation at Yazoo City prior to the Civil War.[106]

Jackson

Traveling south again into Hinds County, Bishop Elder arrived in Jackson. Capital of the State since 1822, the city lacked nevertheless the venerable character of Natchez as well as the vigorous commercial atmosphere of Vicksburg. Before all else it was the seat of government, and in 1857, its advantageous location at the junction of the main cross-state railroad lines was only beginning to affect its commercial life. Its five thousand inhabitants, especially those engaged in mechanical and commercial trades, contained many German, Irish, Italian and French immigrants, who lent a cosmopolitan air to the capital. At the time of the Bishop's visit

---

103 Le Corre to Elder, Yazoo City, June 20, 1857; in ADNJ, Elder Letter Book—#1, 34.

104 Doyle, "St. Mary's of Yazoo City," in *Catholic Action of the South* (Natchez Centennial Edition), Oct. 14, 1937, 47.

105 Elder to Le Corre, Natchez, March 14, 1861; in ADNJ, Elder Letter Book—#6, 128.

106 Most of the early parish records—baptismal and marriage registers—are missing.

Father Pont was acting-pastor of the Catholic community in Jackson.[107] He was replacing Father Leray who, sometime in June, had left for his native France to visit his dying mother. The young pastor had left behind a parish which was well-organized and which gave every hope of developing into one of the largest in the Diocese.[108] On a quarter of an acre in the center of town stood a frame church and rectory. There was no debt on either. Recently a bell and an organ, each worth about $600, had been purchased. Both items had been paid off in full. The Catholic community did not have a graveyard of its own. Instead almost all of the families owned lots in different parts of a common graveyard. A Catholic gentleman, Mr. John Kelly, conducted a Catholic elementary school under the auspices of the pastor. In 1857, there was an enrollment of forty, only twenty-five of whom were Catholic. Apparently Mr. Kelly had been bearing the expense of running the school personally, collecting as much as he could from the students' parents. Most probably this arrangement did not work out too well. Consequently, the whole revenue of the parish for the current year was going to be turned over to Mr. Kelly. The income of the parish for one year amounted to about $750: $600 from pew rent and about $150 from Sunday collections. In addition, the pastor received about $150 in perquisites and $150 from the missions he attended. In 1846, the Catholic congregation of Jackson numbered about four hundred.[109] Taking into consideration the rapid growth of the city's general population during the following decade with its high proportion of Irish, Italian, German and French immigrants, one might set the Catholic figure in 1857, at well over five hundred. Running down a roster of parishioners at the end of the decade, one is immediately struck by the immigrant character of the Catholic community in Jackson at that time: Miazza, Rietti, and D'Ambrogio from Italy; Kelly, McLaughlin, Farrell and Quinn from Ireland; Terry, Julienne and Olivier from France; Nahrgang and Muller from Germany; Spengler from Alsace; and Fraggiacomo from Austria. However, as

[107] Pont to Elder, Jackson, July 10, 1857; in ADNJ, Elder Letter Book —#1, 54.

[108] Notes on Jackson's Catholic congregation, found among other notes dated 1857, in Bp. Elder's handwriting; in ADNJ, File: Elder—J.

[109] *Catholic Advocate*, Louisville, Ky., 1846; quoted by Henne, "Capital Parish Among Pioneers In Diocese," in *Catholic Action of the South* (Natchez Centennial Edition), Oct. 14, 1937, 29.

we shall see, this character was not peculiar to the Catholic congregation at Jackson.

Vicksburg

Directly west of Jackson, beyond the Big Black, on the bluffs overlooking the Mississippi River was Vicksburg. Advantageously located at the point where the Yazoo River reached the "Father of Waters" and at the terminus of the Southern Railroad, Vicksburg was by 1857 a growing cotton port and a booming industrial community. Its prosperity and stability were reflected in the costly new courthouse being constructed on a high spot that dominated the town, in the numerous Greek Revival homes which dotted the hillside, in the bustling stores and shops which lined Washington Street, in its five churches and synagogue, in its private academies and its large public school serving alone five hundred students, and in its two hospitals. Steamboats from New Orleans, Memphis, St. Louis and Louisville arrived daily. Three times a week boats left Vicksburg for New Orleans and Memphis, while the Yazoo boat, which went deep into the delta to Greenwood, made its run four times a week. And every half hour a ferry crossed the river to De Soto City, Louisiana, the eastern terminal for the Vicksburg, Shreveport and Texas Railroad.[110] The population of the city in 1857, was in the neighborhood of four thousand, making it the third largest city in the State.[111] Although the majority of Vicksburg's citizens were either native Mississippians or had come to the city laterally across the South from Alabama, Georgia or the Carolinas, a good portion of the population was made up of immigrants. By 1861, they constituted a third of Vicksburg's population.[112]

Shortly after his arrival in the Diocese, Bishop Elder following the advice of Archbishop Blanc, replaced Father Pont at Vicksburg with Father Jeremiah O'Connor. Apparently word had reached the Archbishop even before Elder's installation that the congregation at Vicksburg was very much dissatisfied with the young French priest. On the other hand, Pont was unaware of his low popularity

---

[110] *General Directory for the City of Vicksburg* (Vicksburg, 1860), 55-56.

[111] *United States Census Population of the United States in 1860* (Washington, D.C., 1864), 271. The total population of Vicksburg in 1860 was 4,591.

[112] Walker, *Vicksburg, A People at War, 1860-1865* (Chapel Hill, 1960), 15.

rating.[113] His difficulty stemmed from his lack of experience in the ministry and his inability to speak English fluently. Realizing what a difficult time Elder would have in finding a replacement for Pont, Blanc decided to furnish the Bishop of Natchez with one of his own priests who had the assets Pont lacked so conspiciously. Announcing the new priest's arrival, Blanc made a point of reminding Elder of the purpose for which Father O'Connor was being sent:

> I send you Rev. Jeremiah O'Connor. I would willingly keep him with us if I thought he might not be placed to greater advantage in Vicksburg, where a priest more conversant with English and more experienced in the ministry is needed. The young priest who is now there is well qualified for any other station which needs zeal and exertions. He is active and of good spirit. Should as yet no other station be prepared to receive a stationary priest, two would be well occupied in Vicksburg, indeed, under all circumstances, two priests would do much good there and be well supported.[114]

It is well to note that the Archbishop of New Orleans in no way questions the personal integrity of Father Pont. Fortunately, Elder had no difficulty in finding another post for Father Pont who, as we have seen, was sent to Jackson to act as pastor while Father Leray was in Europe.

In 1857, the most salient feature of Vicksburg's skyline was the spire of St. Paul's Catholic Church. The building stood at the intersection of Crawford and Walnut Streets, opposite Sky Parlor hill. Built of brick in gothic style, the church had been dedicated by Bishop Chanche on October 14, 1849.[115] Apparently at the time of its dedication the church was not completed. Improvements were being made gradually. After his appointment, during the summer of 1857, Father O'Connor arranged to have the inside of the

---

[113] Only after having been transferred, did Pont learn the real reason behind the move. He wrote to Elder on this occasion: "When at Vicksburg, I flattered myself of having done my duty: but, afterward, I found out that such was not the opinion of all: a Priest spoke to me, a few weeks ago, of my having *plaid* (sic) *comedy* in the church, three or four Sundays successively, and of many other things, concerning which my conscience reproaches me nothing with (sic)." Pont to Elder, Jackson, July 10, 1857; Elder Letter Book —#1, 54.

[114] Blanc to Elder, New Orleans, May 26, 1857; in ADNJ, Elder Letter Book—#1, 14.

[115] *In and About Vicksburg* (Vicksburg, 1890), 148; Mullin, "St. Paul's —Vicksburg," in *Catholic Action of the South* (Natchez Centennial Edition), Oct. 14, 1937, 19.

church plastered.[116] Beside the church stood a modest priest's house.

As in Jackson, a large proportion of the Catholic congregation in Vicksburg was made up of immigrants, especially from Ireland and Germany. From O'Connor's own remark that the congregation was a large one, from Blanc's report that two priests could be effectively employed at the post and from the amount of annual revenue taken in at the end of the decade, one is led to conjecture that the Catholic community in Vicksburg in 1857 was close to seven hundred, exceeded in size only by the congregation at Natchez. In the opinion of the pastor the spiritual level of the parish left much to be desired. Announcing his intention of having the Redemptorist Fathers preach a mission in his parish, O'Connor reported to Bishop Elder:

> Their (the Redemptorists) services are much needed here. Communions are very few for so large a congregation and attendance at Mass on Sundays though considerable is not perhaps half as large as it should be.[117]

If Father O'Connor was not completely satisfied with the religious life of his parishioners, they were quite pleased with their new pastor. They manifested their pleasure by cooperating with him in improving the parish temporalities and in making a special donation to him from church funds. On the first point the Bishop was quite gratified. Writing to the pastor of Vicksburg after he had sent in a financial report, Elder said:

> I have not been able to look into the details (of the report) as yet: but I see there is good reason for congratulation to you & to the congregation:—& for thanks to all whose labours & liberality have effected so much for the temporalities—to Mr. Genella especially, & Mr. Donovan, & the other trustees.[118]

But when the Bishop learned that the trustees were seriously

---

[116] O'Connor to Elder, Vicksburg, July 20, 1857; in ADNJ, Elder Letter Book—#1, 74.

[117] *Ibid.*

[118] Elder to O'Connor, Natchez, Aug. 30, 1858; in ADNJ, Elder Letter Book—#3, 28.—Mr. Antonio Genella who came from Switzerland had one of the largest mercantile houses in Vicksburg. Mr. Michael Donovan had come from Ireland to Vicksburg via Boston. He may have run a saloon in Vicksburg.

intending to make a donation to the pastor over and above his stipulated salary, Elder objected:

> I heard in Vicksburg an intimation of an intention to make you a donation of a sum of money from the Church funds. I may tell you frankly that I objected to it; & if perhaps the Trustees, thinking my objection not very positive, should still make you such an offer, I beg you not to accept of it, at least not without first writing to me & receiving my approbation.—I was much pleased with the evidence of their esteem for your zealous labours.—But considering the debts of Vicksburg, & the many urgent wants of religion & charity there I feel an obligation to see its resources carefully husbanded. So far as I can judge, I think your temporal position is quite comfortable, & rather better than that of other zealous & hardworking Priests of the diocese—so that such a donation is rather a compliment, than a supplying of wants. If I am mistaken, & you really have want of such a sum, you have only to write & explain to me the condition of things. I believe you know me well enough to have confidence, that I will not suffer narrowminded economy to deprive a deserving Priest of anything reasonable.[119]

It would seem that the Bishop's letter did not reach the pastor of Vicksburg in time. The donation to O'Connor had been made perhaps even before the Bishop wrote. When O'Connor made mention of this fact in his next financial report, Elder replied:

> With regard to your own finances,—after the statement you have given, I do not ask you to return what has been presented to you.—But I beg you in future cases to let me know before it is done—if they speak of either a donation or an increase of salary.[120]

Perhaps, in an attempt to mollify the Bishop's reaction the pastor and trustees sent along a sizeable collection which had been taken up among the Catholics of Vicksburg for the Catholic orphan asylum at Natchez.[121] So attached had the congregation become to their pastor that, when rumors of Father O'Connor's impending removal spread abroad in 1859, certain members of the congregation went so far as to express their feelings of deep regret in a let-

---

119 Elder to O'Connor, Natchez, Dec. 27, 1858; in ADNJ, Elder Letter Book—#3, 131.

120 Elder to O'Connor, Natchez, Jan. 12, 1859; in ADNJ, Elder Letter Book—#3, 169.

121 *Ibid.*

ter addressed to the pastor. Apparently the language employed or sentiments expressed implied a lack of docility, for Bishop Elder referred to this communication in a letter to one of the members of the congregation, excusing the signers, however, because of their ordinarily excellent religious spirit.[122] In any case, it must have been very gratifying for Elder when he visited Vicksburg in 1857, to discover an altogether different spirit there than had prevailed under Father Pont. It must have been equally encouraging to learn that the parish, though still in debt, was financially stable, even capable of making improvements gradually.

In 1857, there were a number of missions attached to Natchez. To the north in Claiborne County were Grand Gulf, Port Gibson and Cedar Creek; in Jefferson County were Rodney and Fayette; to the east in Franklin County was Meadville; and to the south in Wilkinson County was the town of Woodville.[123] The two missions which enter most into the history of the Diocese in its first two decades were Port Gibson and Woodville.

Port Gibson

Resting tranquilly in the curve of Bayou Pierre, Port Gibson was a small cotton-growing town. Its quiet oak-lined streets and well proportioned white frame homes prompted General Grant to say, when he passed through on his march to Vicksburg in 1863, "Port Gibson is too beautiful to burn." Linked to Grand Gulf on the river by the diminutive Grand Gulf and Port Gibson Railroad, the town served as an outlet for the cotton grown in the area. As early as 1844, Catholics were in residence in the Port Gibson area.[124] Among the pioneer members of the Catholic community were the Holdens, the Shannons, the O'Kellys, the Richardsons and the Moores. During the 1840's they were visited periodically by Fathers Francois, Blenkinsop and Raho, operating out of Natchez.[125] Late in 1850, Bishop Chanche sent Father Fiérabras to Port Gibson as its first resident pastor.[126] Besides taking care of the

[122] Mullin, *op. cit.*, 20.

[123] A few years later (1860) Port Adams, also in Wilkinson Co., was added to the Natchez circuit.

[124] Baptismal Register of St. Mary's Cathedral, Natchez, #1; in Cathedral archives.

[125] *Ibid.*

[126] Parochial Record, Sulphur Springs, (1841-1926); in parish archives, Camden; a copy in ADNJ. *Metropolitan Catholic Almanac*, 1851, 1852, 1853 (Baltimore, 1851, 1852, 1853).

Catholics of Port Gibson, the young French priest traveled a circuit which included Grand Gulf, Fayette and Cedar Creek as well as several plantations for the benefit of the Negroes on them.[127] At Port Gibson Fiérabras, expecting financial backing from his relatives in France, purchased a lot and began to build a brick church. Unfortunately, he died before the church was completed, leaving a debt of more than $1,500.[128] For a short time in 1854 a Reverend Patrick Duffy was in residence at Port Gibson. From 1855 to 1858 the congregation was visited occasionally by a priest from Natchez. In the meanwhile [129] Mr. John Taylor Moore, one of the wealthiest Catholic planters in the area, assumed the debt on the church, completed the exterior and added a very comfortable parsonage.[130] About the same time a Catholic woman, Miss Louise Barbaroux, opened a ladies' school in Port Gibson.[131]

In response to a letter of introduction written to him several days after his consecration in Baltimore by a Jesuit friend of Mr. Moore,[132] Elder made a point to visit the planter and investigate the situation at Port Gibson in 1857. On this occasion the Bishop was very impressed by the zeal of Mr. Moore who pressed him to provide the congregation with a resident pastor and to interest some religious community in establishing a Catholic school at Port Gibson. Not until the following year was Elder able to send a priest to the Catholic community at Port Gibson. The priest, Father Frederick Muller,[133] was assigned only on a temporary basis and this for two reasons. First of all, the Bishop had other more important plans for Muller and, secondly, no details as yet had been worked out for the support of a priest at Port Gibson. Nevertheless, Elder sent a priest as soon as possible in order to

---

[127] *Ibid.*

[128] Van de Velde to Propagation of the Faith Society, Natchez, Jan. 2, 1854; copy in ADNJ, quoted in Gerow, *Cradle Days of St. Mary's at Natchez,* 118.

[129] Most probably some time in 1857, for the *Catholic Almanac* lists St. Joseph's Church at Port Gibson as still unfinished in 1856.

[130] Stonestreet to Elder, Georgetown, May 5, 1857; in ADNJ, Elder Letter Book—#1, 8. Mr. Moore was the wealthiest of the old Port Gibson planters, the "Marse John" of Irwin Russell's verse and the son-in-law of Resin P. Bowie.

[131] Elder to Barbaroux, Natchez, June 21, 1858; in ADNJ, Elder Letter Book—#2, 76.

[132] Stonestreet to Elder, Georgetown, May 5, 1857; in ADNJ, Elder Letter Book—#1, 8.

[133] Elder to Muller, Natchez, Jan. 2, 1859; in ADNJ, Elder Letter Book —#3, 139. Fr. Muller signed his name with the German umlaut, but he came to be known as Father Muller or Miller.

sustain the good spirit he found there. Thus, he instructed Father Muller:

> I wish that while you are at Port Gibson you would see what arrangements can be made for a resident priest there at once.—I promised Mr. Moore that I would endeavor to supply the place as early as possible, and since my visit there I have been still more desirous to cooperate with the zeal exhibited there, especially by him. I am quicker about it than I would have been, because I have heard of Mrs. Moore's return home, and the great interest she has taken in the work of religion entitles her to all the opportunities of religious practice that it is in my power to afford her.[134]

Not only was Elder intent upon assigning a permanent resident pastor to Port Gibson, but he was also determined to secure the services of some teaching order for a proposed Catholic school in that town. The one aim Elder realized when he was able to assign a newly ordained priest, Father Philip Huber, to Port Gibson in early January 1859.[135] The latter plan, however, never materialized although an invitation was extended to the Sisters of St. Joseph of Carondelet through Mother Leonie, the Superior at Sulphur Springs.[136]

At Port Gibson the Catholic community must not have been very large in 1857. There was very little to attract the Irish, German or Italian immigrant to this town. Consequently, the Catholic congregation in Port Gibson did not grow as did those at Natchez, Vicksburg and Jackson or even Holly Springs. In 1862, before the enemy had appeared in the area, the congregation in Port Gibson itself numbered scarcely more than a half dozen persons.[137] At Mr. Moore's plantation,[138] a little north of town, the same source reports, the congregation was much more numerous. Most probably, then, there were no more than about

---

[134] Elder to Muller, Natchez, Sept. 8, 1858; in ADNJ, Elder Letter Book —#3, 65.

[135] Elder to Boheme, Natchez, Jan. 30, 1859; in ADNJ, Elder Letter Book—#3, 187. Huber was ordained at Sulphur Springs on December 14, 1858, and left for Port Gibson on Jan. 15, 1859.

[136] Elder to Mother Leonie, Natchez, Sept. 1, 1858; in ADNJ, Elder Letter Book—#3, 40.

[137] *Diary of Bishop William Henry Elder (1862-1865);* original in Archives of Woodstock College, Woodstock, Md.; photostat copy in ADNJ; published by Bishop Gerow, Jackson, 1961; hereinafter cited as Elder Diary, 1.

[138] This plantation was called Fair View. Moore owned another plantation called Woodland whose location is not known.

thirty white persons who belonged to the Catholic congregation of Port Gibson in 1857, even if we take into account that in 1862, some of the menfolk were in the army. It must be kept in mind, too, that the "much more numerous congregation" at Mr. Moore's plantation was made up of slaves for the most part. Two facts lend credibility to this estimate. Well before the pinch of war-time economy was felt in the State, Father Huber experienced difficulty in obtaining sufficient means from his congregation for his own support.[139] Secondly, Bishop Elder in 1862, did not hesitate to ask Father Huber to leave his congregation at Port Gibson and Mr. Moore's plantation over Holy Week and Easter to help out with the solemn services in the Cathedral.[140]

Woodville

The second mission on the Natchez circuit about which we have more ample record was Woodville. Situated about thirty-five miles south of Natchez and about seven miles north of the Louisiana state line, Woodville was the official seat of Wilkinson County. During the 1850's it was a well-built and pleasant court-town, with a small but pretentious hotel, a bank, a newspaper, a steam cotton mill and a railroad station, terminal of the West Feliciana Railroad which ran from Woodville to St. Francisville, Louisiana.[141] The early settlers at Woodville were predominantly Protestant. However, three Catholic families, the Poseys, the Gordons [142] and the Elders,[143] were among the pioneers. They were all native-born.

During the administration of Bishop Chanche the Catholics of Woodville received an occasional visit from a priest operating out of Natchez. Writing to Bishop Purcell of Cincinnati in 1845, Chanche confessed that the prospects for the development of the Church in Woodville were not very bright: "I send a priest oc-

---

139 Elder to Huber, Natchez, April 26, 1861; in ADNJ, Elder Letter Book—#6, 196.

140 Elder to Huber, Natchez, March 15, 1862; in ADNJ, Elder Letter Book—#7, 379.

141 This was the first railroad built in Mississippi. Its rails were made of cypress, cedar and heart of pine hewn by slaves. It was financed by the wealthy planter and mill owner, Edward McGehee of Woodville, and chartered in 1831.

142 George H. Gordon, state senator from 1859 to 1862, was converted to the Catholic faith shortly after his marriage to Miss Helen Posey.

143 Mr. and Mrs. Edward Elder came from Massachusetts. Mr. Elder was a cousin of Bishop Elder.

casionally to Woodville. But the Catholics in that neighborhood are very few in number. It will be a long time, I fear, before the cross shall glitter on the steeple of a Catholic church in that place."[144] During Bishop Van de Velde's short administration the visits of priests to Woodville became even more rare. Hoping to remedy the situation, the Catholics there appealed to the Archbishop of New Orleans early in 1857. With the approval of Bishop Elder arrangements were made to have the priest stationed in Jackson, Louisiana visit the Woodville congregation regularly.[145] In 1858, Father G. McMahon of Jackson was attempting to provide the Catholics at Woodville with Sunday Mass at least once a month.[146] However, through press of duties in his own parish Father McMahon had to neglect Woodville at times. Appraised of the situation, Elder sent a priest to visit these Catholics whenever an extra one was on hand at Natchez. At this same time the Catholics of Woodville promised to give $2,000 toward the construction of a church.[147] Because no priest could be provided nothing came of the offer. Instead, a house was rented by the congregation for $75 a year. Here Mass was celebrated on the average of once every two months. Here also the ladies of the congregation taught catechism every Sunday.[148] In 1861, Woodville became a mission attached to Port Gibson.[149] It was hoped that Father Huber would be able to serve these Catholics more frequently and more regularly.

Levee Workers

Besides the Catholics who had taken up permanent residence in the State, Bishop Elder soon discovered another group of Catholics for whose spiritual welfare he became greatly concerned. These were the workers on the levees. Although there had been levee construction going on since as early as 1819, the great age of levee building in Mississippi was the fifties.[150] In 1849-50, the United

---

144 Chanche to Purcell, Natchez, July 29, 1845; in AUND: Purcell Papers; photostat copy in ADNJ.

145 Woodville–History Notes, drawn up by Bishop Gerow from archival sources; in ADNJ, File: History Notes–W.

146 *Ibid.*

147 *Ibid.*

148 Elder to Mouton, Natchez, April 30, 1861; in ADNJ, Elder Letter Book–#6, 203.

149 Woodville–History Notes, in ADNJ, File: History Notes–W.

150 Bettersworth, *Mississippi: A History,* 248-249.

States Congress passed an act transferring title to more than three million acres of unsold swamp and overflow land in Mississippi to the state government for use in flood control and drainage work. From this point on, work of levee building began in earnest. In the Delta area [151] a total of 310 miles of levees was constructed during the fifties, and by 1860, Mississippi's Board of Levee Commissioners had let contracts for more than one hundred miles of new construction.

Numbering in the thousands, most of the workers on the levees were transients. The majority of them, furthermore, were Irish immigrants, and, consequently, the percentage of Catholics among them was high. Unfortunately, however, the spiritual assistance given these men was woefully inadequate and unorganized. One could hardly blame the bishops on either side of the river; [152] they were having a difficult time providing spiritual assistance for people who had a permanent domicile in their respective dioceses. As a result, it was only at intervals that a priest could be spared to go among the workers on the levees.[153] Sometimes it was one priest; sometimes another. Some places were visited often; some not at all. Ordinarily only a few men were able to get to confession, because the priest appeared at unannounced times and through press of duties at home could not remain for long. Seldom was he able to spend a Sunday with them. Often the little good achieved was undone by unscrupulous priests who appeared along the river from time to time, giving scandal by their personal conduct and taking up unauthorized collections among the workers.[154]

[151] The Yazoo-Mississippi Delta is a fertile wedge of land in northwestern Mississippi 200 miles long, sometimes as much as 85 miles wide, reaching down through 35 feet of alluvial soil deposits. Through it runs the Yazoo River and its tributaries. Before the levees were built, floods in this area were frequent and devastating.

[152] The other bishops faced with the problem of giving spiritual assistance to the levee workers were Bishop Andrew Byrne of Little Rock, Arkansas, and Bishop Augustus Martin of Natchitoches, Louisiana.

[153] Elder to Martin, Natchez, Sept. 6, 1860; in ADNJ, Elder Letter Book —#5, 327-328.

[154] Bishop Martin of Natchitoches reported to Elder on Sept. 20, 1860: "I wish, Rt. Rev. sir, you would and could oppose any collection from other dioceses: last fall two were made along the river, one bringing $600, the other $400, this by the admission of the collecting Clergymen themselves." (Elder Letter Book—#1, 158.) On Feb. 8, 1861, Fr. Leray of Vicksburg reported to Archbishop Odin of New Orleans that a Fr. Murphy of Illinois had arrived at Vicksburg. He was "brought out of a steamboat drunk as a beaut," "a scoundrel," "a thief," "taking collections along the river without authorization." (AUND: New Orleans Papers).

Painfully aware of the situation for some time, Bishop Elder finally hit upon a plan which he proposed to Bishop Martin of Natchitoches, Louisiana in early September, 1860:

> There is a totally different subject on which I have to communicate with you:—the care of labourers on our levees during the winter.—
>
> I propose that some one, two or three Priests—according to the extent of the works & the number of men—be appointed to take entire charge of all those men during the whole working season.—If more than one—that each have his district—each to devote himself exclusively to that office—caring for his district as for a Parish—visiting the different works over and over again—staying at each one as long as may be required for hearing Confessions—correcting misconduct, etc.
>
> The primary end to be gained by this will be that the poor men will receive better religious assistance than they receive now. They will know their Pastor—he will know them—he will see all—& not skip over some:—he will know their faults:—& those who are not prepared for the sacraments when he first comes—will be ready before he leaves, or when he returns—He can keep off those wretched Priests who often give scandal. Because being always in the line—the men can enquire of him whether such person has authority or not.
>
> The secondary end—and a very important one, would be the regulation of the collections. This Priest would take them up at such times as he would find best—& the Bishop would apply them to such purposes as he judged best— [155]

Unfortunately, the proposal was never put into effect. When war broke out eight months later, levee construction came to a standstill. Left without jobs, many of the levee workers joined the army.[156]

Negroes

Finally, there was a third class of people in the Diocese who in some respects represented Elder's chief anxiety. These were the plantation slaves.[157] Writing to the Society for the Propagation of the Faith in Paris, the Bishop confessed:

155 Elder to Martin, Natchez, Sept. 6, 1860; in ADNJ, Elder Letter Book —#5, 327-328.

156 William L. Nugent to Pettus, April 18, 1861, Gov. Corr., File E—51; in Mississippi State Archives, Jackson.

157 It is interesting to note that Elder never made a distinction between the slaves belonging to Catholic planters and those of Protestant plantation owners. He was equally concerned about all 400,000 (1860).

> These poor negroes form in some respects my chief anxiety. I believe they are generally well cared for, so far as health & the necessaries of life are concerned. But for learning & practicing religion, they have at present very little opportunity indeed.[158]

In this same report of 1858, Bishop Elder described the problems associated with trying to improve the religious life of the Negro slaves.[159] First of all, "some masters . . . object to having a Minister come to preach to their slaves," and "they rather encourage some one of the blacks themselves to become a preacher for the rest." Commenting on this arrangement, Elder remarked: "You can imagine what kind of religious instruction the poor creatures get." However, this attitude was not general. As Elder pointed out: "Commonly their Masters are well disposed to allow them religious instruction, & sometimes they pay Ministers to come & preach on the plantation." This arrangement worked a great hardship on the Catholic Church, since most dioceses in the South were critically short of priests. Going from plantation to plantation would have been a full time job in itself with little or no time left for ministering to the congregations attached to the churches in town. Another difficulty stemmed from the master's refusal to allow his slaves to leave the plantation for worship or instruction. Though this policy admittedly militated against the spiritual improvement of the Negro, the rule had some merit which could not be absolutely ignored. Elder seemed to consider it a circumstance beyond anyone's control. He wrote:

> They (the planters) do not like to let negroes go to a public church, because there is danger of their misbehaving when they are away from home, & out of sight of the Overseer; & because various inconveniences result from the servants of one plantation mingling with those of another. Each master has something particular in his regulation & his method of management, & if the servants have free intercourse together, they are apt to make each other jealous & dissatisfied.[160]

---

[158] Elder to the Society for the Propagation of the Faith in Paris, Natchez, 1858; in ADNJ; also in Ellis, *Documents of American Catholic History* (Milwaukee, 1956), 334-337.

[159] *Ibid.*

[160] *Ibid.*

Even if the masters were to allow their slaves to attend the public church in the area, Elder foresaw difficulties:

> The negroes must be attended in a great measure on the plantation, both for the reasons given above, & because in our case there are so few churches; & even where there is a church, the negroes of four or five plantations would fill it up, & leave no room for the whites, nor for the other negroes (town domestics and free negroes) of the neighborhood.

Although the Negroes, as Elder saw them, were not ill disposed, indeed they often manifested "a craving for its (religion's) ministrations," he discovered certain qualities in the Negro which made his conversion difficult. Among these qualities was an inclination to sensuality: ". . . often again they are so entirely animal in their inclinations, so engrossed with the senses, that they have no regard for anything above the gratification of the body." However, the Bishop was quick to excuse them, remarking that "their sensuality arises not so much from malice, as from the want of religious instruction—the want of knowing that there is anything better than this world within their reach." Elder also saw in the Negro a natural weakness of mind and will. "This weakness of mind," he pointed out, "makes it hard for him to understand an argument; his weakness of will makes it hard to resist temptation, & still harder to break bad habits."[161] This two fold weakness, according to the Bishop, also made the Negro "liable to great fickleness." Elder confessed:

> This is one of the hard trials of a missionary among them. It is not uncommon for a negro to attend religious instruction for a considerable time with great fidelity & a lively interest, & yet drop off before receiving the Sacraments. Sometimes there is no apparent cause, but just fickleness of character, or perhaps temptation. But more generally it may be traced to some irregularity in the instruction, or some little neglect which begets an indifference on their part. They are very much creatures of feeling.

On the other hand, the prelate recognized certain dispositions in the Negro, arising from his place in society, of which the missionary could take advantage. First of all, Elder pointed out: ". . . the negro is naturally inclined to be dependent on others; therefore he is disposed to listen & believe what he is told by his

[161] *Ibid.*

superiors." Secondly, "having few comforts & no expectations in this world," the Negro's "thoughts & desires are the more easily drawn to the good things of the world to come." [162]

The Negro apostolate, as Elder saw it in 1858, was fret with many difficulties, some connected with the Negro's character, some stemming from his environment; but the prelate of Natchez was optimistic. Admittedly the Negro, even when better instructed, was not always ready to abandon his habits of sin, but Elder contended that "patient & persevering instruction & exhortation, together with the use of the Sacraments will commonly succeed at last in bringing them to a better life." [163] What is more, a priest devoting himself to this apostolate, "may have the unspeakable consolation of finding among them vocations to a high degree of sanctity." This possibility was not altogether unlikely as Elder, drawing from his personal experience, went on to explain in his report.

> The humility of their condition & the docility of their character take away many of the ordinary obstacles to the workings of grace; & where other circumstances are favourable, these lowly ones in the eyes of the world sometimes rise very high in the favour of God. I have known a case of a servant girl's being really revered as a saint by the family in which she had been reared, & where she was working with all simplicity & fidelity in the lowest offices.

There is no doubt that Bishop Elder was painfully aware of the Negroes' plight in his Diocese, of his personal responsibility for their salvation and of his inability to improve their lot spiritually. What grieved Elder in particular was the fact that "Catholic masters . . . are taught that it is their duty to furnish their slaves with opportunities for being well instructed, & for practising their religion, and yet he was in no position to "enable those masters to do their duty because there are not Priests enough." Here is how Elder viewed the problem. In order to reach the Negro, the priests of the Diocese had to go to the plantations. These plantations were scattered about the country, separated from one another by great distances. All the priests whom Elder had were residing in congregations from which they could not be absent for any great length of time. The remedy, as he saw it, consisted in forming a

[162] *Ibid.*
[163] *Ibid.*

band of traveling missionaries who would attend these plantations almost exclusively. As early as 1844, Bishop Chanche had hit upon this plan, but Elder was no more successful in implementing it than his predecessor. Always it was a case of a shortage of priests.

As matters turned out, each priest was held responsible for the spiritual welfare of the Negroes in his area. Those Negroes who lived in town or who were able to come to town in the company of their owners on Sundays worshipped together with the white members of the congregation.[164] In sickness or in death they were prayed for publicly.[165] Generally, on Sunday afternoons catechism classes were conducted for them.[166] In one parish a church society was formed for them. Those Negroes who were plantation laborers were seldom able to assist at Mass on Sunday. Ordinarily, the local priest was able to visit the plantations only during the week. On these occasions he heard confessions, celebrated Mass for the whole plantation community and preached. In the afternoon he taught catechism to the colored people or, if the mistress of the plantation was in the habit of fulfilling this duty, he reviewed with them what they had been taught. Those who had been sufficiently prepared were baptized, if willing. Marriages were performed, church legislation being applied with equal force to them as to the whites. Thus, in the available parish registers one can read such entries as the following:

> 1860—October 23rd I granted a Dispensation in the Impediment of Disparitas Cultus between Navis not baptized, and Eleanor or Ellen, both colored Servants; and on the same day at Fairfield Plantation, the residence of Mr. John Hynes, near Vicksburg, I joined the same parties in lawful Matrimony: they having been married invalidly ten months previously.
>
> † *William Henry*
> Bishop of Natchez [167]

[164] The institution of the segregated church was first introduced in the Catholic Diocese of Natchez during the administration of Bishop Thomas Heslin (1889-1911). In some cases he encountered opposition from the colored people who were strongly attached to the local mother-church where they and their people before them had been baptized, given their first Communion, confirmed and married. ADNJ, File: History Notes—P; Pass Christian —St. Philomena.

[165] Announcement Books—#1 & #2, & #3, of the Natchez Cathedral; in the Cathedral archives, Natchez, Miss.

[166] *Ibid.*

[167] Marriage Register (1852-1886), St. Paul's Church, Vicksburg, 22a; in the parish archives, Vicksburg, Miss.

> On Aug. 15, 1858—I, Jeremiah O'Connor, Pastor of St. Paul's Vicksburg—joined in Holy Matrimony—permission of Masters being previously obtained—and dispensation granted—the slave *Harrison*—belonging to Sam R. Bolls of Hinds Co. and *Johanna* slave of A. B. Reading of this county of Warren.[168]

How well Catholic slaves were able to live up to their religious principles depended to a large extent on their owners. The owners in turn must have been faced with many moral problems in living up to their religious responsibilities toward their slaves. For instance, to what extent was an owner bound to provide future religious opportunities for a Catholic slave whom he was about to sell? Or how far had a Catholic slave-holder to go, when selling some of his slaves, to preserve marriage and family ties? Although there is no clear evidence on hand to prove that Catholic slave-holders in Mississippi were remiss in their duties on these points, one suspects that, through ignorance or social custom, they sometimes made it morally impossible for a Catholic slave, once he had been sold, to live up to the religious principles and duties he had been taught. Bishop Elder himself reported meeting a good number of slaves in Mississippi who had been torn loose from their Catholic moorings many years before. It is interesting to note the almost heroic perseverance of some of these slaves.

> I have frequently met (colored) men and women who had left Maryland, Virginia or Kentucky more than twenty years before the War, and had not seen a priest in all that time, and yet they had steadfastly preserved their faith. Some of them had yielded partially to the influences around them, either from weakness or from ignorance. Others, however, I have met who had been faithful to all their obligations—had said their own prayers on Sundays, had brought up their children Catholic as well as they knew how—and some even had abstained from meat on Fridays as much as they possibly could do with their rough plantation diet. I remember one old man whose fidelity was well known and esteemed by the White gentlemen of the neighborhood. As I was once visiting some Catholics in a village where I had not been before, a Protestant gentleman told me of this old colored man who lived six miles away, and he offered to send him word of my being in the village, be-

---

[168] *Ibid.*, 14.

cause he knew the poor man would be sadly grieved when he should learn of his having missed such an opportunity, and in fact the next morning at 5:30 A. M. the old man was in the village, after walking six miles fasting so that he might receive the Sacraments. He was one that had left Maryland twenty-five years before and had not seen a priest until about two years before this incident.[169]

From a letter written by Mrs. Eliza Wilkinson of Yazoo County one is led to suspect that some Catholic slaveholders made moral compromises involving the rights of their slaves. However, it is doubtful that these owners were all as conscientious as she was. Writing to Archbishop Odin of New Orleans in 1862, she asked the prelate to help her reunite a Negro man and wife for whose separation she was responsible.

> Rev. & dear Sir—I am compelled to call on you for an act of kindness & beg that you will forgive the liberty I take in doing so.—You will remember last year, in Galveston, my speaking to you about a servant girl whom I had been compelled to separate from her husband to whom she had been married here in the Church.—You advised me by all means, either to purchase him, or return her to him—The former was impossible & I have been trying ever since I have been here, to get her back—My father now writes me that he thinks he can get F. Chambodut to bring her along with him to N. Orleans—May I beg, dear Sir, that you will add to your many former kindnesses by permitting her to remain with you until she can be placed under the care of some one coming either here or to Vicksburg—I think there is not a day that some one does not leave N.O. for Vicksburg . . . .[170]

It is encouraging to note after examining synodal legislation, sermons and correspondence of the time that there is no evidence to indicate any widespread abuse in these matters.

General Picture

As Bishop Elder completed his official visitation, the following picture of his Diocese would have taken shape in his mind. There were about 10,000 Catholics residing within his jurisdiction[171]

---

169 Elder to Vaughan, Natchez, March 30, 1873; in ADNJ, Elder Letter Book—#14, 380.

170 Wilkinson to Odin, Yazoo City, April 8, 1862; in AUND: New Orleans Papers.

171 *Metropolitan Catholic Almanac* for 1859 (Baltimore, 1859), 129.

Numerically they were a religious minority, forming only 7 per cent of the total population of the State. Of these Catholics about a thousand were slaves.[172] The bulk of the Catholic population was concentrated along the Gulf Coast and in the river counties of Warren, Claiborne, Jefferson, Adams and Wilkinson. The rest were scattered through the State over twenty-five counties. Socially they were represented in almost ever stratum of society in the State. There were native-born Americans with such Anglo-Saxon names as Hazlip, Cook, Whittaker and Blake. Most of the Catholic plantation owners were from this group. Along the Gulf Coast most of the Catholics were native-born, but they were Creoles with such foreign-sounding names as Dedeaux, Ladnier, Niolet, Cuevas, Saucier and Necaise. In this class were to be found many small farmers, some barely eking out an existance from the poor soil. A few Catholic immigrants from Ireland, Italy, France and the German States came relatively early to Mississippi. The majority of them settled in the cities and towns and made names for themselves in the business world, operating general supply stores, saloons, grocery stores, a textile mill, a book bindery and a construction business. A few, however, became large plantation owners, for example, O'Reilly and O'Leary in Madison County, Dohan in Jefferson County and Roach in Washington County. The first great wave of immigration hit Mississippi only in the late 1850's. Most of the new arrivals were Irish Catholics, the majority of whom were of the laborer-artisan class, finding employment with the railroads and on the levees. A significant number of Catholics, both native-born and immigrant, were also to be found in the various professions: government, medicine, education, law and journalism. Oliver Luckett of Canton, Joseph Heyfren of Paulding and Felix Labauve of De Soto County were Catholic lawyers. Dr. Richard O'Leary of Madison County, Dr. O'Reilly of Canton, Dr. Carroll of Belle Prairie, Yazoo County, and Dr. Goldsmith of Claiborne County were physicians. Serving in the State legislature at various times were Oliver C. Dease of Paulding, George H. Gordon of Woodville, Francis C. Semmes of Lauderdale

172 This figure is based on several factors, viz., the number of known Catholic plantations, allowing an average of fifty slaves for each; figures obtained from the available baptismal registers; and the fact that many Catholic town and business people kept a few slaves as domestics.

County and Oliver Luckett of Canton. On the teaching staff of the University of Mississippi was Dr. Eugene W. Hilgard, who was also serving as the state geologist. Patrick H. McGraw was a druggist of Natchez. And James J. Shannon was part publisher of the *Eastern Clarion* of Paulding. From the viewpoint of financial status, Bishop Elder's flock spanned all three levels. About twenty-five families, owning one or more plantations, could be considered wealthy. There was a growing number of Catholics who fitted into the middle-income bracket, that is to say, small business men and self-employed artisans; these would have numbered well under a thousand. The majority of white Catholics in Mississippi in the late 1850's, therefore, were poor, being small farmers and common laborers, many of them transients.

From the viewpoint of structure, the Diocese was organized with eleven parishes, having a resident pastor, and twenty-eight mission stations. These were being served by twelve priests from the Diocese and two from outside the Diocese. Of the eleven churches, five were of brick, though one was still unfinished, and the rest were of wood. Furthering Catholic education in the Diocese were three groups of Sisters and one community of teaching Brothers. They were conducting one boarding school for boys, a boarding school and two day schools for girls, and one day school for small boys. Two small parochial schools were also in operation.

From the viewpoint of membership, the Catholic Church in Mississippi was one of the smaller religious bodies in the State. Three-fourths of the State's churchgoers belonged to the Methodist and Baptist denominations, with the Methodists holding on to a slight numerical lead.[173] The Presbyterians, while exercising an influence far out of proportion to their numbers, lagged far behind the two leading donominations in membership. Represented by small numbers in the population were the Episcopalians, Christians or Campbellites, Cumberland Presbyterians and Lutherans. Although most of these smaller groups had more churches than the Catholic body,[174] one is inclined to believe that the Catholic Church exceeded in membership anyone of them, at least by the end of the decade. But this is a moot point because of the different methods of determining membership in each body.

---

173 Moore, "Religion in Mississippi in 1860," in JMH, XXII (Oct. 1960), 225.

174 Bettersworth, *Mississippi: A History,* 261-262.

The Catholic Church's relations with other religious bodies in the State were apparently peaceful during the 1840's and 1850's. At least there is very little evidence of any organized opposition on the part of the Protestant churches in the State. Most probably this lack of opposition did not stem from any great respect for the Catholic Church. It was simply due to the fact that she was not regarded by Protestants in Mississippi as a real threat to their ascendancy in State.[175] It might also be explained by the fact that Protestants in Mississippi were too busy quarreling with one another in the press and from the pulpit.[176]

[175] Moore, *op. cit.*, 226.
[176] *Ibid.*, 229-232.

Chapter VI

STABILIZATION OF THE DIOCESE

In the spring of 1858, Bishop Elder, fully familiar with his diocese at last, set out to realize a number of projects geared to meet certain needs of the Diocese. During the next three years many of them he was able to carry out; a few never materialized. Some concerned the laity; others the clergy. Some had an eye to immediate needs of the Diocese; others looked to the future.

First Synod

In order to establish a set policy in a number of areas for the good of the whole Diocese Bishop Elder convened the first Synod of Natchez on the fifteenth of April 1858. In attendance were all twelve priests of the Diocese. The statutes, nine in number, promulgated the decrees of the Baltimore Councils, regulated the dress of the clergy, required annual financial statements from each church and stipulated that three collections be taken up among the laity each year: one for the education of clerics, one for the support of the Bishop, and another for the orphans of the Diocese. It was strongly urged that in each parish the Association for the Propagation of the Faith be established. Ecclesiastical conferences were to be held regularly. And a prayer for the increase of vocations to the priestly and religious life with an indulgence attached was earnestly recommended to all the members of the Diocese.[1] One thing the Synod did achieve: it made both clergy and laity more conscious of the needs of the Diocese as a whole at a time when some might have been completely absorbed by local needs.

Clerical Conferences

The regulation concerning the holding of clerical conferences regularly was an effort on the part of Elder to comply with the seventeenth decree of the First Provincial Council of New Orleans,

---

[1] Synodus Diocesana Natchetensis prima, habita ab illmo. et rmo. Gulielmo Henrico Elder, Episcopo Natchetensi, hebdomade secunda post Pascha anno 1858. New Orleans, 1858.

held in 1856, which had recommended them.[2] Furthermore, since their aim was the good of the priests themselves and of their people, it is understandable that Elder, as bishop and as former seminary professor, would have given orders that they be held. For the time being the Bishop established three conferences to be held at Natchez, Vicksburg and Biloxi.[3] The clergy in these areas would meet every second month. Among the rules governing the conference were the following: the evening before the conference they will recite night prayers in common, and the subject of meditation will be presented; all the Breviary will be recited in common; a half hour's meditation in the morning; the subjects to be discussed will be assigned by the Dean; and each treatise will be sent to the Bishop.[4] When one or the other priest tried to excuse himself from attending one of the conferences or from preparing a paper to be read at the clerical gathering, Elder was quite firm. To Father Jeremiah O'Connor he wrote:

> A week's collections on the Levees are not near as important as the faithful discharge of all the duties of the Conference. (. . . .) The soul of the Priest is his first care, & the Bishop's highest responsibility after his own soul.— And I know of no means for preserving the Priest's soul, equal to that of the Conferences if faithfully attended to.[5]

With equal firmness Elder insisted that the conferences be held on the Gulf Coast where apparently they had not been held at all or at least not regularly.[6] It is understandable why the Bishop should have felt so strongly about the value of these conferences. He had not been in the Diocese very long before he began to receive complaints from some of the young clergy about being "cast away" by themselves on the missions, "deprived of all spiritual assistance and advice" which their "inexperience" needed.[7] One of these young priests was of the opinion that "if piety is so feeble in

[2] Concilium Neo-Aurelianense Provinciale Primum. Habitum Anno 1856. N.O.: Le Propagateur catholique, 1857; in Archives of Notre Dame Seminary, New Orleans.

[3] Parish Record, Sulphur Springs, (1841-1926); in parish archives, Camden; copy in ADNJ, 15.

[4] These regulations were drawn up at the first Vicksburg conference held on July 7, 1858; in ADNJ, File: Elder—C; Conferences in general—1859.

[5] Elder to Jeremiah O'Connor, Natchez, March 29, 1859; in ADNJ, Elder Letter Book—#4, 25.

[6] Elder to Holton, Natchez, Feb. 27, 1861; in ADNJ, Elder Letter Book—#6, 78.

[7] Guillou to Elder, Sulphur Springs, Oct. 15, 1857; Le Corre to Elder, Yazoo City, June 20, 1857; in ADNJ, Elder Letter Book—#1, 178, 34.

this Diocese it is owing to the want of experienced confessors, the congregations having been given in charge to young clergy, even without experience, and very little versed in the direction of souls." [8] Another young priest complained about the embarrassment he suffered when it was reported to him that he had "plaid comedy in the church, three or four Sundays successively," all of which could have been avoided if there had been some priest on hand to correct him.[9] Thus, Elder viewed these conferences not only as valuable in themselves, but also as meeting a specific and a pressing need among his clergy. As Elder saw it, here was an opportunity especially for his young priests to seek advice concerning personal as well as pastoral problems.

Annual Retreat

The opportunity to make an annual retreat, it would seem, had not been within reach of every priest in the Natchez Diocese prior to Bishop Elder's arrival. Father Guillou in 1857 complained that since his ordination seven years previous he had not been able to make a retreat.[10] How soon this situation was corrected it is difficult to say. But one is inclined to believe that an annual retreat for the clergy was held regularly from 1858 onward. The retreat masters for 1860, 1861, and 1862 were successively Bishop Elder, Father Gautrelet, S.J. of Mobile, and Bishop Verot of Savannah.[11] On each occasion after a retreat of six days, before the clergy returned to their respective posts, a diocesan synod was held.[12] Once the State became a battleground and large sections of it became occupied territory, Bishop Elder found it impossible to hold such clerical gatherings.

Vocations

Another goal which Elder set out to realize early in 1858 was to increase the number of clergy in his Diocese. Writing to the

---

[8] Guillou to Elder, Sulphur Springs, Oct. 15, 1857; in ADNJ, Elder Letter Book—#1, 178.

[9] Pont to Elder, Jackson, July 10, 1857; in ADNJ, Elder Letter Book—#1, 54.

[10] Guillou to Elder, Sulphur Springs, Oct. 15, 1857; in ADNJ, Elder Letter Book—#1, 178.

[11] Parish Record, Sulphur Springs, (1841-1926); in parish archives, Camden; copy in ADNJ, 21, 24, 28. The parish record, when it makes mention of the 1860 retreat at Sulphur Springs, does not refer to it as the first in the diocese, something it was very apt to do had this been the case.

[12] *Ibid.;* copy in ADNJ, 21, 24, 28.

President of All Hallows College in Dublin, Ireland, Elder revealed how critical the situation was in 1858:

> We are sadly in want of priests. For more than half a million of souls, there are but twelve ministers of God's work and dispensers of his sacred mysteries. To be sure, only a small part of that half million are Catholics, but they are scattered over fifty thousand square miles. . . . In five places, now, they are ready to build churches, if only they had priests to push on the work. The first person of the diocese that I saw, after my consecration, was a Protestant gentleman, who traveled thirty miles on purpose to urge me to send a priest to the neighborhood of his residence.[13]

There was also Elder's "chief anxiety," namely, the Negro apostolate which was being neglected because of a priest shortage.

Of all the clergy in the Diocese in the spring of 1858, the Bishop was the only native-born American: seven were from France, one from Belgium, one from Saxony and three from Ireland. Half of them were young and inexperienced in the ministry. Many spoke the English language with difficulty; some never mastered its idioms. All of them had to face the problem of adapting themselves to a new way of life made more complicated by Southern race relations.

As so many other American bishops at this time, Elder had to look to Europe for recruits. American seminarians were still few in number and their bishops guarded them jealously. The European seminaries which provided Elder with new manpower were: the Grand Seminary of Nantes in France, the Brignole-Sale College of Genoa, Italy, Carlow Seminary and All Hallows College in Ireland, and the American College which had been established at the University of Louvain in Belgium. Generally speaking, young men at these seminaries volunteered for the Natchez missions two or three years before they were ordained. When Bishop Elder would discover a vocation to the priesthood in an American boy, he would send the young man to be trained at St. Thomas Seminary at Bardstown, Kentucky, or, if he were more advanced in his studies, to Mt. St. Mary's College at Emmitsburg, Maryland, St. Mary's

---

[13] Elder to the President of All Hallows College (Woodlock?), 1858; quoted in Shea, *History of the Catholic Church,* IV, 682.

Seminary in Baltimore, or Mt. St. Mary's Seminary of the West in Cincinnati. In 1859, Elder reported that he had nine young men preparing for the missions of the Diocese.[14] In 1860, there was an increase of three clerical students. The following year the figure had risen to fifteen.[15] One of the three collections which Elder had directed to be taken up among the Catholics of the Diocese each year was earmarked for the support of these students.

To provide his Diocese with a steady supply of clergy, especially native priests, Bishop Elder as early as 1859 began to consider the feasibility of establishing a preparatory seminary in Mississippi. As the Bishop saw it, there was "undoubtedly great need of a native clergy" in his Diocese.[16] This was so for a number of reasons. In conscience no bishop could go on indefinitely, relying upon European Catholics to supply the needs of the Church in the United States; provision must be made for the future. For that matter, the expanding needs of the Diocese were not being met by the European seminaries with which the Bishop was in contact. And, furthermore, relations in the Diocese between foreign-born priests and their people were often strained, because they did not understand each other. On the other hand, Elder had no doubt that he would find sufficient vocations among his flock. "We have no reason to believe," he wrote to the French mission society in Paris, "that God will not give to our own people the vocations and the graces necessary to form a clergy among ourselves." [17]

So seriously did Elder consider the project of establishing a preparatory seminary in his Diocese that during the Synod of 1860 he proposed it to his priests.[18] The response was one of unanimous approval. With a view to obtaining professors for the future seminary, Father Grignon traveled to Europe that same year. To everyone's regret the Vicar-General was able to recruit only one man, namely, Rev. Mr. Charles Heuzé, and he was only a sub-deacon

---

[14] Elder to the Society for the Propagation of the Faith, Natchez, 1859; quoted by Gerow, "History of the Catholic Diocese of Natchez," in *Catholic Action of the South*, (Natchez Centennial Edition), Oct. 14, 1937, 18.

[15] *Metropolitan Catholic Almanac* (Baltimore, 1861), 118.

[16] Elder to the Society for the Propagation of the Faith, Natchez, 1859; quoted by Gerow, *loc. cit.*

[17] *Ibid.*

[18] Parish Record, Sulphur Springs, Part II (1860-1870); in parish archives, Camden; copy in ADNJ, 21.

at the time.[19] Elder was further frustrated in his attempt to establish a seminary when a house on the Rose Hill property in Natchez which he intended to use for the pioneer seminary burned down in November, 1860.[20] Undeterred Elder next decided to locate the proposed seminary at Sulphur Springs, placing it under the direction of Father Guillou who would be assisted by a newly-ordained priest, Father John Finucane.[21] To insure its success, the Natchez prelate approached Bishop Quinlan of Mobile and Bishop Martin of Natchitoches, seeking their support. To Quinlan he wrote:

> I have now a house suitable for a Preparatory Semy.—far removed from Yellow Fever—up at Sulphur Springs, Madison County:—& if no accident happens to frustrate my almost certain expectations, I shall have one or two Priests suitable to begin it on a small scale—What I shall need is the *money*—or the assurance of students who could pay a full compensating pension—from $150 to $200.—May I expect any such from your Diocese?—I would like to begin either in Novr. or January.—[22]

Apparently Elder viewed the support of these prelates as not only advantageous but even necessary. Such at least was the implication in a letter he addressed to Father Finucane:

> It is my hope to establish a Preparatory Seminary at Sulphur Springs—under Fr. Guillou's direction & your immediate care. (. . . .) Whether it can be accomplished depends upon other persons from whom I hope to hear before long. As soon as it is decided, I will let you know—[23]

Bishop Martin's promise of support was half-hearted.[24] Even less enthusiastic must have been Bishop Quinlan's response, for

[19] *Ibid.;* also *Annals of the Propagation of the Faith,* XXI, London, 1860, 366. Heuzé was studying at the major seminary of Rennes when he volunteered for the Diocese of Natchez. He was ordained deacon by Bishop Elder in the middle of December, 1860, and about a week later raised to the priesthood.

[20] *Ibid.*

[21] Elder to Finucane, Natchez, Nov. 4, 1861; in ADNJ, Elder Letter Book—#7, 177. Finucane was born in Ireland. Orphaned at thirteen, he came to live with an uncle in Dayton, Ohio. He began his seminary studies at St. Thomas', near Bardstown and completed them at St. Mary's Seminary, Baltimore. He was ordained by Archbp. F. P. Kenrick on June 30, 1861, for Natchez.

[22] Elder to Quinlan, Natchez, July 31, 1861; original in ADMB; copy in ADNJ, File: Elder—Q.

[23] Elder to Finucane, Natchez, Nov. 4, 1861; in ADNJ, Elder Letter Book—#7, 177.

[24] Elder to Guillou, Natchez, Nov. 9, 1861; in ADNJ, Elder Letter Book—#7, 206.

early in December Elder informed the two priests at Sulphur Springs that he had been forced to postpone the project indefinitely.[25] No doubt the fact that war had broken out was an added deterrent. At the time one Mississippian—with some reservation we might say the first [26]—was studying for the priesthood. He was John Ryan of the Sulphur Springs congregation. Some time in June he had gone to France in the company of Father Rene Louis Mulot to pursue his studies.[27]

Society for the Propagation of the Faith

During the first Provincial Council of New Orleans in 1856, Archbishop Blanc and his suffragans wrote a joint letter to the Central Council of the Society for the Propagation of the Faith, thanking the French society for its financial support of their missions. They also informed the Council that each bishop had established in his diocese a branch of the same society.[28] Eager to go along with the policy of the other bishops in the province as well as to manifest his gratitude to the Society for its annual allocations to the Natchez Diocese, Elder urged each pastor to erect a branch of the mission society in his parish. The Catholics of Mississippi had every reason to be grateful. Between 1839 and 1858, the Society had given over $73,200 to the Diocese.[29] If the

---

[25] Elder to Guillou, Natchez, Dec. 4, 1861; Elder to Finucane, Natchez, Dec. 4, 1861; in ADNJ, Elder Letter Book—#7, 219, 221.

[26] An Episcopalian minister of Natchez, Rev. Mr. Pierce Connelly, joined the Catholic Church in 1836, was later ordained to the Catholic priesthood, but after a short time returned to Protestantism. Cf. Wadhams, *The Case of Cornelia Connelly* (New York, 1957).

[27] Parish Record, Sulphur Springs, (1841-1926); in parish archives, Camden; copy in ADNJ, 26. Rene Louis Mulot, a student at the major seminary of New Orleans, had been accepted for the Diocese in 1860. In June of that year he was ordained to the priesthood by Bishop Elder. Before a year had elapsed, Mulot asked to be released from the Diocese to return to France, apparently his native country. (Elder to Mulot, Natchez, July 24, 1861; in ADNJ, Elder Letter Book—#6, 282.)

[28] *Annals of the Propagation of the Faith,* XVIII, London, 1857, 190. Within a few years after the French society was founded, the Holy See granted generous indulgences to its members and permitted membership outside of France. One by one the other European countries established branches of the society. Gifts began to come from the United States in the early thirties, and a few branches were established, but final enthusiastic reception was made in our country only toward the end of the nineteenth century. Roemer, *Ten Decades of Alms.*

[29] List of allocations made by the Society to the Diocese of Natchez from 1839 to 1910, sent by the secretary general of the Conseil Central de Lyon to Rev. H. A. Campo, June 13, 1932; in ADNJ. The exact figure in francs is 366.192 Fr.

contributions from the Diocese would not be large at first, Elder was apparently convinced, nevertheless, that the establishment of the Society on the local level would have a good effect upon the people of his diocese. It would make them more conscious of the Church universal at a time when they enjoyed only a minority status among the religious bodies in Mississippi, and, secondly, it would make them more appreciative of the sums of money being directed to their own missions in the State. All things considered, the Catholics of Mississippi responded well to the idea of collecting money in their midst for the foreign missions. In 1859, they contributed about $458, the following year about $310, and again in 1864, when they were feeling the full impact of the Civil War, the sum of $576.[30] In the years ahead Bishop Elder would prove to be one of the staunchest supporters among the American bishops of the Society for the Propagation of the Faith.[31]

Cathedral Finished

Concerned from the time of his arrival in Natchez with the unfinished state of his cathedral, Elder did not feel that he was in a position to do anything about it until he had made a survey of the whole Diocese. Consequently, not until June of 1858 did he take steps to finish the church which he himself had described earlier as "sadly desolate." [32]

Under the direction of Mr. Peter Warner, who had finished St. Paul's Church in Vicksburg the previous year, the work on the cathedral began in September, 1858. It continued until August of the following year. During this time the present floor of the cathedral was laid, the entire interior plastering was done, beautifully carved woodwork was added throughout the church, pews were installed and new windows of colored glass were put in. While these improvements were being made, Mass was celebrated in the basement of the cathedral, part of which continued to be used as the parochial school for boys. On August 14, 1859, the church was reopened with solemn ceremonies. Present for the

---

[30] *Annals of the Propagation of the Faith,* XXI, XXII, XXVI, London, 1860, 1861, 1865; 162, 166, 155.

[31] L'Oeuvre de la Propagation de la Foi, Conseil Central, & Elder, Paris, Nov. 28, 1879; in ADNJ, File: Elder—P.

[32] Elder to McCaffrey, Natchez, June 8, 1857; quoted in Meline & McSweeney, *The Story of The Mountain,* I, 515. Elder to Warner, Natchez, June 30, 1858; in ADNJ, Elder Letter Book—#2, 99.

occasion was Archbishop Blanc of New Orleans who celebrated a pontifical high Mass.[33] The expenses for these improvements and others which continued to be made until 1863, amounted to a little over $21,000. Funds were collected not only in Natchez, but also in New Orleans, Baltimore, Emmitsburg and St. Louis. About $4,000 of the money allocated to the Diocese by the Society for the Propagation of the Faith were also used to meet these expenses.[34] By the sale of a lot in the city of Natchez, Elder was able to realize another $3,500.[35] In meeting his financial responsibilities Bishop Elder, in the early years of his administration, was more fortunate than his predecessors. The times were far more prosperous; he had many personal friends in the East; and his family, established as they were in the East, South and Midwest, provided valuable contacts for him in these areas.[36]

Further Parochial Organization

During the next few years, before the outbreak of the Civil War, progress in the Diocese was steady. Much of it was the result of the close personal contact which Elder maintained with all parts of his Diocese, even the most remote. These visits were not limited to organized congregations but extended even to individual Catholic families, living at a distance from population centers in thinly settled areas. So unlike formal episcopal visitations, they were a mixture of hazard, humor and hardship. Traveling alone on horseback, searching from house to house for scattered Catholic families, Elder was apt to appear unannounced at any time of the day or night. On one occasion, after visiting the Palmetto neighborhood in what is today Lee County, he traveled toward the Potato Hills, arriving after dark at the Joseph Kelly home. The country was thinly settled; visitors at night were few. The Bishop

---

[33] (Janssens), *Sketch of the Catholic Church in the City of Natchez, Miss., on the occasion of the consecration of its Cathedral, Sept. 19, 1886*, 36-38.

[34] Gerow, *Cradle Days of St. Mary's at Natchez*, 141. Realizing how much money from the French mission society had already been spent on the Cathedral to the inevitable neglect of other parts of the Diocese, Elder acted a little more scrupulously than his predecessors. Before making use of these funds, he consulted his metropolitan. It was agreed that the cathedral parish would return some of the money each year to the Diocese as its revenues increased.

[35] *Ibid.*, 143. This lot on Commerce Street, between Main and Franklin, was the site of the old church of Spanish times which had burned down in 1832.

[36] Of Bishop Elder's brothers, Basil and Joseph lived in St. Louis; Charles and Thomas in New Orleans; John in Baton Rouge; Frank in Baltimore.

rode his horse into the yard. As he did, Kelly came out, but the darkness prevented him from distinguishing the figure on horseback. Elder asked: "Does Joseph Kelly live here?" To an affirmative answer Elder replied: "How long has it been since you have seen a Catholic priest?" Thinking that someone was jesting at his expense, Kelly retorted: "Is it any business of yours?" By this time the Bishop had dismounted and strolled into the light shining through the open door. Recognizing his distinguished visitor, Kelly fell upon his knees in apology for his unintended rudeness.[37] On these visitations Elder experienced the same vicissitudes which his priests did when they rode their circuits: riding through driving rain storms; forced to make unexpected detours; crossing swollen creeks, the water coming up to and into his saddle bags; getting lost; sleeping on the floor or sharing a bed at the home of some poor, and now uncomfortable, host. Identifying himself as closely as possible with these people, Elder bound them to himself by the strong ties of affection and loyalty.

During the years immediately prior to the outbreak of the Civil War there were a number of encouraging developments all of which spelled progress and greater stability for the Diocese. At Pascagoula the congregation was given a resident pastor for the third time. He was Father Constantine Vandemoere, a Belgian priest who came to the Diocese late in 1859 with high recommendation from his own bishop.[38] At first there was some difficulty concerning arrangements made for his support. Vandemoere threatened to leave his post. Elder wrote to the priest to forestall his withdrawal. Pointing out the serious consequences of his intended action, the Bishop said:

> I do not like the thought of leaving abandoned any part of our flock.—I trust that the meeting called by Mr. Baptiste, may have devised some way of providing for their Pastor. —So far as boarding is concerned, I am sure Mr. Baptiste himself would be glad to show you his usual hospitality. Madame Renee would not be sorry to have the Pastor near her

---

[37] Elder recalled this incident himself on the occasion of a confirmation tour in northeastern Mississippi in December, 1871. Cf. Reitmeier, "St. James Church—Tupelo," in *Catholic Action of the South*, (Natchez Centennial Edition), Oct. 14, 1937, 76.

[38] Elder to Grignon, Biloxi, Sept. 29, 1859; in ADNJ, File: Elder—G; also Elder to Baptiste, Natchez, Aug. 25, 1860; in ADNJ, Elder Letter Book—#5, 304.

again: — & Madame Gurlic (?) would be happly to do any thing in her power. — Although it is desirable that the Priest live in his own house — yet in extraordinary circumstances — & for a temporary arrangement — it is well to bear the inconvenience of boarding with a family: rather than interrupt the progress of religion, in the whole congregation. — . . . .

It would also be a great discouragement to them. Twice before they have had Pastors, who were obliged to leave them. If you — with your zeal & endurance, & all your success, leave them now, they would think (it) useless for them to attempt it again & another Priest would be afraid to undertake it after you have given it up. (. . . .)

If it should become absolutely necessary for you to leave I would rather you keep as near to them as possible. Possibly you could make some arrangements with Fr. Georget to assist him at Biloxi or Ocean Springs, & still continue to attend Pascagoula on certain Sundays.

I much prefer however that if possible you remain at Pascagoula. Perhaps the meeting of the 19th has devised some means — . . . or else after what they have said, you can devise some means such as I have suggested — of living in a private family. And if you can stay first with one & and then with another. — I know this is not very agreeable — & I wish to see Priests provided for in a better manner — but you have always been ready to do what is unpleasant to yourself for the sake of saving souls, & I am sure you are ready still to do the same if it can be done — & if God's interests will be advanced by it.[39]

Apparently arrangements satisfactory to Father Vandemoere were made by the parishioners for the support of their new pastor. He remained at his post through the War until 1867.[40]

At Canton, the seat of Madison County, the building of a brick church was begun in August, 1859. Up until the appointment of Father Francis Orlandi as pastor late in 1859, Canton had been a mission dependent upon the priest at Jackson.[41] Located on the New Orleans, Jackson and Great Northern Railroad, it was easily

---

[39] Elder to Vandemoere, Natchez, Sept. 26, 1861; in ADNJ, Elder Letter book—#7, 93.

[40] Hunter, "Our Lady of Victories—Pascagoula," in *Catholic Action of the South* (Natchez Centennial Edition), Oct. 14, 1937, 49.

[41] Milot, "Sacred Heart—Canton," *ibid.*, 52. Educated in Italy at the Collegio di Brignole-Sale of Genoa, Father Francis Orlandi came to Natchez late in 1859, in the company of another young Italian missionary who died quite suddenly shortly after his arrival.

served by Father Leray and later by Father Pont. On June 15, 1860, the new church was blessed by Bishop Elder and dedicated to the Sacred Heart.[42]

At the very end of the decade before the Civil War three small wooden chapels were built in the thinly settled counties of Choctaw, Attala and Neshoba. At the time they were put up, none showed much prospect of developing into an established parish with a resident priest. They were simply intended to serve as fitting places for the celebration of Mass and other religious functions for the few Catholic families living in these counties. All three became missions attached to the parish of Sulphur Springs in Madison County, and came to be served with regularity. In 1859, at the suggestion of Father Guillou, a few Irish families decided to build a church near Attalaville in Attala County. One of the Catholics in the area, Mr. Patrick Welch, donated the property. The men of the congregation cut and split their own logs and then erected the church. The building must have been very modest, for it cost only $40. Mass was celebrated in this new chapel, dedicated to the Holy Angels, for the first time on November 13, 1859.[43] Henceforward, Mass would be offered here once a month.[44]

Sometime in 1857, Father Guillou, pastor of Sulphur Springs, received a letter from Mr. Bernard McGovern, a resident of Choctaw County. The gentleman asked the priest if it might be possible for him to pay an occasional visit to the McGovern family and a few of his Catholic neighbors. Guillou promised to do so but was unable to keep his promise until March of 1859. On the occasion of this visit the priest found three Catholic families; he baptized a child and received the renewed marriage consent of a couple. In November of the same year Guillou paid these Catholics a second visit. They admitted that they were dissatisfied with their location, because the opportunities for practicing their Catholic faith were so limited, but they were not disposed to leave their homes which they had labored so hard to improve. Guillou suggested that they build a small chapel which he promised to visit at least six times a year. They gladly consented to the proposal. A

---

42 *Ibid.*, 52.

43 Parish Record, Sulphur Springs, (1841-1926); in parish archives, Camden; copy in ADNJ, 18-19.

44 *Ibid.*, 21.

site for the proposed chapel was found on Mr. McGovern's land on a public road from Greensboro to Louisville.[45]

In Neshoba County a few Catholic families, most of whom had come from Ireland, became quite concerned about the religious life of their children and their own inability to assist at Sunday Mass and receive the Sacraments regularly. At a very great sacrifice some prepared to sell their homesteads and move to Paulding. In the midst of these preparations Father Guillou came to pay them a yearly visit. Appraised of their plans, the pastor of Sulphur Springs offered to extend his spiritual ministry to them on a regular basis if they would build a chapel at a central point. The suggestion was applauded by all, especially by those who were eager to avoid the sacrifices involved in abandoning their homes. A subscription was inaugurated immediately. Eventually $600 was collected. The church site was donated by Mr. Daniel Rush — an eight-acre plot located about four miles east of Philadelphia, the county seat. Built during the summer of 1860, the church was named Holy Cross. It was visited on the third Sunday of every month by the pastor of Sulphur Springs.[46]

With an eye to the future development of the Catholic community at Brookhaven in Lawrence County, Bishop Elder sent $155 to Father Pont to help buy several lots in the town as future building sites for a church, rectory and school.[47] Before 1851, when the New Orleans, Jackson and Great Northern Railroad was built into Brookhaven, the town was little more than a straggling group of plantations centered around the crossroads store of Samuel Jayne, who had settled there in 1818. With the advent of the railroad, the town began to grow. Among the early Catholic families were the Beckers, McGraths, Schnorrenbergs, Grants, Naltys and Connollys. They were visited for the first time by a priest in 1859. During 1860 and 1861, regular visits were made by a priest operating out of Jackson.[48] In November, 1861, Brookhaven received its first resi-

---

45 *Ibid.*, 20. Although Fr. Mouton, assistant to Fr. Guillou, reportedly served Choctaw County in 1860, there is no definite proof that a chapel was ever built there. It is not listed in the *Catholic Almanac* for 1861, 1864, or 1865.

46 *Ibid.*, 19, 22.

47 MacHale, "History of St. Francis of Assisi Church—Brookhaven," a paper read at a clergy conference, Natchez, May 16, 1934; in ADNJ, File: History Notes—B.

48 *Ibid.*

dent pastor in the person of Father Henry Picherit.[49] Until a church was built, the priest celebrated Mass for the small congregation in the front room of his two-room house.[50] Besides his duties at Brookhaven Father Picherit was asked by Elder to take charge of several missions along the railroad between Brookhaven and the Louisiana line, the Bishop adding: "And you need not scruple saving a few souls above or below those points."[51]

On the Gulf Coast, through the labors of Father Henry Georget,[52] the new pastor of Biloxi, church buildings were put up at Back Bay, a settlement behind Biloxi, and at Ocean Springs. Both buildings represented an effort to extend the influence of religion over about five hundred poorly educated Catholics whose allegiance to the Church and her teachings was largely nominal.

In April 1859, Bishop Elder asked the pastor of Biloxi to take charge of the Catholic congregation at Ocean Springs.[53] That summer, on a lot donated by Mr. Bellande of the same community, a church was begun. A year later Father Georget gave a progress report to the Bishop.[54] The church, begun the previous August, was still not finished. Among other things the priest was waiting for an altar which was being shipped in from New Orleans. It was reported to be worth about $200. Although Doctor Austin, the superintendent general of Charity Hospital in New Orleans, was guaranteeing payment for this item, he had asked Father Georget to raise as much money as possible among the Ocean Springs congregation. The Doctor, a Protestant, had already donated the door and windows for the church, a gift valued at $153. During the course of the year Father Georget had also purchased a lot with a house on it for the sum of $400. In due time it would serve as the

---

[49] Father Henry A. Picherit was born in France in 1831. He came to America as a missionary in 1854. Serving for several years on the Texas frontier and in the Indian Nation, he came to the Diocese of Natchez in 1861, where he worked until his retirement in 1900. He died in Rome in 1919.

[50] MacHale, *op. cit.*

[51] Elder to Picherit, Natchez, Oct. 4, 1861; Elder to Picherit, Natchez, Feb. 9, 1864; in ADNJ, Elder Letter Book—#7, 99, Elder Letter Book—#9, 191.

[52] Father Henry Georget, a young French priest, had resigned a comfortable curacy in his own country in 1858 to embrace missionary life in Mississippi. He succeeded Father Richard B. Hardey as pastor of Biloxi toward the end of 1858.

[53] Chauvin, "St. Alphonsus—Ocean Springs," in *Catholic Action of the South* (Natchez Centennial Edition), Oct. 14, 1937, 62.

[54] Georget to Elder, Biloxi, July 6, 1860; in ADNJ, File: Elder—G.

rectory. About a month later the French priest reported that, until a resident priest could be appointed to Ocean Springs, he planned to use the house for a parochial school which he had hopes of opening that fall.[55] Before the end of the summer of 1860, the congregation was worshipping in its new church. Father Georget, the pastor of Biloxi, was able to offer Mass for them every Sunday.[56] At this time the Catholics of Ocean Springs numbered about two hundred or half of the total population of the town.[57]

In the spring of 1859, when Bishop Elder asked Georget to take charge of the Catholics of Ocean Springs, he said in the same letter: "I would like you to attend to the people on Back Bay and also to go into the country and see how many Catholics are there."[58] Back Bay was a small settlement on the north shore of the Bay of Biloxi. Here, a little to the east, Pierre le Moyne, Sieur d'Iberville, and his colonists in 1699, had built Fort Maurepas, the first headquarters of a colonizing company sent to establish France's claim to the Gulf Coast and the lower Mississippi Valley. After a destructive fire in 1702, the administrative center of the colony was moved to Mobile Bay. In 1719, headquarters were moved from Mobile back to their original location. Two years later the administrative center was moved again, this time across the Bay to Fort Louis, around which the present town of Biloxi developed. Back Bay, from this time on, became a neglected area – politically, economically and even religiously.

Carrying out Bishop Elder's directive, Father Georget visited the Back Bay area. Here he discovered that nearly all of the people were Catholic. They numbered about three hundred.[59] Most of them were descendants of the early French and French-Canadian colonists.[60] A good many of them lived in the woods, four, five or six miles from the village. In March 1860, the pastor of Biloxi sparked the building of a church in the village. On the

[55] Georget to Elder, Biloxi, August 31, 1860; in ADNJ, File: Elder–G.

[56] Georget to Elder, Biloxi, Sept. 5, 1861; in ADNJ, File: Elder–G.

[57] Georget to Elder, Biloxi, Aug. 31, 1860; in ADNJ, File: Elder–G.

[58] Elder to Georget, Natchez, April 11, 1859; in ADNJ, Elder Letter Book –#4, 48.

[59] Georget to Elder, Biloxi, Aug. 31, 1860; in ADNJ, File: Elder–G.

[60] Among these colonists were many convicts and adventurers of both sexes who were shipped to the colony, usually against their will. Although a good number of poor but well reared French girls had been imported to the colony to become wives and establish homes, they were not sufficient. In many cases, therefore, the Frenchmen took Indian wives.

sixteenth of August Mass was celebrated in the new building for the first time. Because these people had been neglected for a long time, Georget decided to visit this mission every week.[61] Eventually, because of press of duties elsewhere he was forced to limit his visits to this congregation to once a month.[62]

Education

Other signs of progress in the Diocese of Natchez at the beginning of the new decade could be noted in the field of education. Encouraged by Elder, several pastors made efforts to establish parochial schools. At Paulding a parochial school, located near the church, went into operation in 1859.[63] At the beginning of 1860, Father Nealis, O.P. was making plans to open a parochial school at Holly Springs. Elder wrote encouragingly to him: "I am particularly glad that you are trying to establish a good school. Try hard that it be really a *good* one – no sham. Let it be humble if you please – & undertake but little – but let that little be *well* taught." [64] On March 1, 1860, Father Georget opened a parochial school at Biloxi. Attendance was up around forty or forty-five. The pastor, however, was not very optimistic about the venture; in August he wrote the Bishop: "I am afraid it cannot be sustained." [65] No doubt the fact that there were a great many poor among his flock made the school's continued operation doubtful. As we have seen, the pastor of Biloxi also planned to open a school in Ocean Springs in the autumn of 1860.[66] Not long after the Catholics of Neshoba County had built themselves a church, they decided to establish a parochial school. On November 18, 1860, Miss Mary Ann Rush, daughter of one of the parishioners accepted the teaching post.[67] In the spring of 1861, the pastor of Pascagoula, Father Vandemoere, informed the Bishop of his intention to inaugurate a parochial school.[68] However, not content with creating opportunities for a Catholic education, Vandemoere toyed with the idea of

[61] Georget to Elder, Biloxi, Aug. 31, 1860; in ADNJ, File: Elder–G.

[62] Georget to Elder, Biloxi, Sept. 5, 1861; in ADNJ, File: Elder–G.

[63] Dogny, "St. Michael's–Paulding," in *Catholic Action of the South* (Natchez Centennial Edition), Oct. 14, 1937, 27.

[64] Elder to Nealis, Natchez, Jan. 31, 1860; in ADNJ, Elder Letter Book–#6, 28. This school did get into operation. It remained open until 1862.

[65] Georget to Elder, Biloxi, Aug. 31, 1860; in ADNJ, File: Elder–G.

[66] *Ibid.*

[67] Parish Record, Sulphur Springs, (1841-1926); in parish archives, Camden; copy in ADNJ, 22.

[68] Elder to Vandemoere, Natchez, March 22, 1861; in ADNJ, Elder Letter Book–#6, 145.

publicly forbidding Catholic parents to send their children to the local public school. While encouraging the priest to establish a parochial school, Elder cautioned him:

> If the school you speak of is *positively* and *manifestly* injurious to the faith and morals of the children, you should endeavor to keep Catholic children from attending it — using however the most prudent means. I think it would be more prudent not to speak of it publicly in Church, but to speak to the individual parents.
>
> If however there is no positive injury to faith — only an absence of religious teachings; nor a *manifest* injury to morals — but only a fear that there is danger — then I do not see that you ought to hinder parents from sending their children.[69]

Making allowances for local conditions, one nevertheless suspects that Father Vandemoere had a mistaken notion about the nature of public schools in America. He had been in the country only a short time — less than a year. Furthermore, when he was sent to Pascagoula, Elder had asked that allowances be made for the priest's lack of familiarity with American ways.[70]

One Catholic family in the Diocese had the singular good fortune of having a priest as the tutor of their children. In the spring of 1861, when the congregation at Port Gibson found itself unable to support a resident pastor, Father Huber accepted Mr. Moore's invitation to live at his plantation, Fair View, a little north of town. At the suggestion of Mr. Moore, who had been concerned for some time about the lack of opportunities for providing his large family with a Catholic education, Father Huber took it upon himself to fill this need.[71] He apparently threw himself heart and soul into the work, teaching six days a week. So seriously did he view his new role that, when he was invited to attend a clerical conference at Natchez, he begged off because of his teaching duties.[72] At first the Bishop did not approve of the arrangements which Father Huber had made with Mr. Moore.[73] But later, after the

---

[69] Elder to Vandemoere, Natchez, March 11, 1861; in ADNJ, Elder Letter Book—#6, 106.

[70] Elder to Baptiste, Natchez, Aug. 25, 1860; in ADNJ, Elder Letter Book —#5, 304.

[71] Elder to Huber, Natchez, April 26, 1861; in ADNJ, Elder Letter Book —#6, 196.

[72] Elder to Huber, Natchez, July 31, 1861; in ADNJ, Elder Letter Book —#7, 11.

[73] Elder to Huber, Natchez, April 26, 1861; in ADNJ, Elder Letter Book —#6, 196.

priest assured the Bishop that his living at Fair View and teaching there would not interfere with his pastoral duties at Port Gibson, the arrangements were allowed to stand.

At Natchez a Catholic boys' school had been in operation off and on since the time of Bishop Chanche.[74] When Bishop Elder arrived in the spring of 1857, classes were being conducted by a layman in the basement of the Cathedral. Unfortunately, the people had no confidence in the teacher and, therefore, refused to patronize the school. At the beginning of the 1857-1858 school term, there was an enrollment of about eighteen students. But all of the fault did not lie with the teacher. Grignon ascribed some of the school's failure to "covetousness and pride" in some of the Catholic parents.[75] In other words, with some it was a case of being unwilling to pay school tuition when free public education was available; with others it was a case of being reluctant to send their children to such an unpretentious school. To remedy the situation partially the Bishop tried to obtain the services of the Christian Brothers, but his efforts met with failure.[76] Rather than close down the school, Elder continued to employ lay teachers. They came and went. Some had to be let go, because they were incompetent; others, though satisfactory, did not stay long, but moved on looking for better-paying positions. At the outbreak of the War classes were being conducted in the basement school by a young married man, Mr. Martin J. Corbett, assisted by newly ordained Father John Hearns.[77] Conditions were still far from satisfactory. Writing to Archbishop Kenrick of Baltimore, Elder described the odds which the school was up against.[78]

---

74 Gerow, *Cradle Days of St. Mary's at Natchez,* 251.

75 Grignon to Elder, Natchez, Oct. 1, 1857; in ADNJ, Elder Letter Book —#1, 166. Though drawing no salary, Grignon during the previous school term had himself paid for the school tuition of three or four boys.

76 *Ibid.*

77 Elder to Holton, Pass Christian, March 22, 1861; in ADNJ, Elder Letter Book—#6, 142. John Hearns, originally from the Diocese of St. Louis, came south to study for the priesthood at the seminary of New Orleans because of his health. While a sub-deacon in N.O., he had several lung hemorrhages. He recovered sufficiently to warrant Elder's ordaining him just before Christmas, 1860. The following Christmas he had a relapse and died at Natchez of consumption on April 23, 1862, at the age of twenty-four.

78 The girls' school conducted by the Daughters of Charity in Natchez was up against some of the same odds, for Elder remarked in the same letter that the girls' school "is regarded with more favor but it is far from being esteemed as I would wish."

> I have another great perplexity here, with regard to our schools. The public Institute has such advantages in means, & in popularity both with rich & poor, that we cannot get our school on an equality as to school house nor as to efficiency. Children prefer the public school because they have more companions, & they regard it as fashionable. Parents prefer it because they pay taxes for it. — Our teacher is good — really *very* good — considerably above the ordinary level of teachers in Parish schools: but a single teacher cannot do as well, as a number of teachers dividing labor. Parents send their children rather through an unwillingness to oppose us, than through hearty approval of the school. This deprives the school of the requisite *spirit* — & weakens even the enforcement of discipline. — I have sometimes thought that if I had foreseen the difficulties when I first came, I would have suffered the children to go to the Public School & said nothing about it. — I do not know whether it would have been wise. — The Pastor was desirous to keep our school & I thought I ought to cooperate with him & help him to improve it: & we have done so. It was a very miserable one then: it is now a good one — & if it had not such odds against it, it would be the best in the town. But still it is not in good estimation.[79]

In spite of these odds the Bishop refused to close down the school. "To give it up," he said, "would be — I think — a great injury — a confession of incompetency — a triumph to our enemies, & to the luke-warm Catholics who send their children to the Public School." [80]

Of the parochial schools inaugurated at the beginning of the new decade, only two survived; some did not even get off the ground. Thus, when the Civil War began, there were only five parish schools in operation in the Diocese, namely, at Natchez, Jackson, Holly Springs, Bay St. Louis and Paulding. Father Huber continued to conduct classes at Fair View until April 1862, when he was given a new assignment.[81]

At Bay St. Louis, the girls' academy, conducted by the Sisters of St. Joseph of Bourg, was still struggling along. During the school year of 1860, it had the modest enrollment of ten boarders and

---

79 Elder to Kenrick, Natchez, April 12, 1861; in AAB, 29-D-11.

80 *Ibid.*

81 Elder to Huber, Natchez, April 16, 1862; in ADNJ, Elder Letter Book—#7, 472.

thirty day scholars.[82] That year a fair was held for the benefit of the four Sisters, who were still not self-supporting. As a result the Sisters had hopes of being able to hire a lady who would teach in English.[83] In spite of the school's poor record, Bishop Elder was determined that the institution should succeed. He assured Mother Esperance, the superior, that he would enlarge the school, even if he had to beg and borrow.[84] Elaborate plans were drawn up to provide the academy with added facilities so it might function as a genuine boarding school.[85] However, in the month of January 1861, as the threat of war became more real, Elder advised Father Leduc, the pastor of the Bay, to modify the original plans "because of the disturbed state of Public Affairs."[86] The priest was directed to build at only a fraction of the original intended expenditure, that is, somewhere between $580 and $1,000. With this limited amount to work with Father Leduc was only able to put up a building which included a classroom, a dining room and a kitchen.[87] Before the building was finished, war broke out.

A big step forward in the field of Catholic education in Mississippi was taken in 1860, when the Sisters of Mercy arrived in the Diocese. Those to benefit immediately by their presence were the Catholics of Vicksburg. However, as the years rolled by and the Sisters multiplied their institutions of learning, the whole Diocese became indebted to them.[88]

In 1859, Father Leray replaced Father O'Connor as pastor of the Catholic congregation of Vicksburg.[89] One of his chief

---

[82] Annual parish report, Leduc to Elder, Bay St. Louis, Sept. 17, 1860; in ADNJ, File: Elder–L.

[83] *Ibid.*

[84] Elder to Leduc, Natchez, Jan. 18, 1860; in ADNJ, Elder Letter Book—#5, 57.

[85] Although a few boarders had been taken in by the Sisters before 1861, the academy was not listed in the Catholic Almanac as a boarding school.

[86] Elder to Leduc, Natchez, Jan. 25, 1861; in ADNJ, Elder Letter Book—#6, 5. Father Henry Leduc succeeded Father Buteux as pastor of the Bay on Nov. 17, 1859. He held that post until his death on Aug. 27, 1897. Born in Nantes, France in 1834, he was ordained in the same city on Jan. 30, 1859, and came to the Diocese three months later.

[87] Mother Esperance to Rev. Mother (St. Claude), Bay St. Louis, April 23, 1861; in ASSJB.

[88] In 1960, the Sisters of Mercy were conducting seventeen elementary and secondary schools in the Diocese of Natchez-Jackson.

[89] Mullin, "St. Paul's—Vicksburg," in *Catholic Action of the South* (Natchez Centennial Edition), Oct. 14, 1937, 20. O'Connor joined the Dubuque Diocese in 1860.

concerns was the great number of Catholic children growing up in the city without any formal Catholic training.

His concern only increased when he discovered how many of these children, sons and daughters of poor immigrant parents, were living in shanties on or close to the levee. Fortunately, Father Leray had no difficulty interesting the Catholics of the city in the establishment of a parochial school. Interest had been aroused earlier by Father O'Connor, who reported to the Bishop in 1858, that the people were not only ready but willing to support Catholic education.[90] By the middle of the summer of 1859, the Catholics of Vicksburg had secured a large two-story brick house, located in a very fashionable part of town, for their future school. Situated on Crawford Street between Cherry and Adams, the building, the old Cobb house, was only three blocks from the parish church.[91] There was another advantage: the property included a large garden, thus providing sufficient room for a playground.[92] While pleased with the progress being made at Vicksburg toward the establishment of a Catholic school, Bishop Elder became worried about the congregation's ability to finance the project. He reported to Bishop Spalding of Louisville in August, 1859:

> The Catholics of Vicksburg have made great exertions, & secured a large brick dwelling, with a large & handsome yard, in the most elegant & healthy part of the city – about three blocks from the Church.–It cost $8,000. One half they have yet to raise. They can do it, if encouraged by seeing a good school among them. – If they do not get a good school this fall, I am afraid they will not succeed in . . . making the payment due next January.[93]

Although the school did not open that fall, the Catholic congregation retained its initial optimism and met its financial responsibilities. Perhaps, the news that Bishop Elder was trying to obtain the services of the Sisters of Mercy in Baltimore kept the spirits of the Catholics of Vicksburg from flagging.

---

[90] *Ibid.*, 19.

[91] Bernard, *The Story of the Sisters of Mercy in Mississippi, 1860-1930* (New York, 1931), 8-9.

[92] *In and About Vicksburg* (Vicksburg, 1890), 112; also Elder to Spalding, Natchez, Aug. 8, 1859; in ADNJ, Elder Letter Book–#4, 218.

[93] Elder to Spalding, Natchez, Aug. 8, 1859; in ADNJ, Elder Letter Book–#4, 218.

Overtures were first made to the Sisters of Mercy by Bishop Elder through his friend, Archbishop Kenrick of Baltimore.[94] Father Grignon, on his way to Europe, was also asked to stop in Baltimore to press the Bishop's case. Although her community had been hard hit by sickness and death since its foundation in 1854, Mother M. Catherine Wynne, superior of the Baltimore Sisters, responded to Bishop Elder's plea magnanimously. On April 30, 1860, the final details of the contract were ironed out.[95]

On October 9, 1860, a band of four Sisters and two postulants, headed by Sister M. De Sales Browne left Baltimore in the company of Father Leray who had come from Vicksburg to chaperon them.[96] Traveling by rail, the party reached Vicksburg at nightfall on October 12th. At the station the group was met with carriages driven by Messrs. Antonio Genella and Clement Guidici. They were driven at once to the home of Mr. Genella. Here Mrs. Genella received them cordially. The reception surprised the Sisters, as did their surroundings. As one of the Sisters later reported:

> We were driven to Mr. Genella's house where at the head of the stairs, stood the bouyant little figure of his wife, who welcomed us warmly from a heart full of affectionate cordiality. The light, glow, comfort and warmth of the surroundings astonished some of the Sisters, who had an idea that they were coming to some half Indian place, which would call forth all their fortitude as Missionaries and (they) had been mentally resolving to offer all the imaginary deprivations patiently.[97]

The Sisters remained as guests of the Genellas until October 15, when they moved into the building on Crawford Street. Bishop Elder arrived on the 20th and two days later presided at the school's opening, delivering an eloquent address to the parents and children assembled. Classes began with a student enrollment of about sixty which soon increased to more than a hundred.[98]

The opening of the convent-school on Crawford Street was not greeted enthusiastically by all. As soon as the aristocratic house-

---

[94] Memoirs of Sister M. Ignatius; in ASMV, 2.

[95] *Annals* of the Sisters of Mercy, Vicksburg, Miss.; in ASMV, 1.

[96] The pioneers were: Sister M. De Sales Browne, Sister M. Ignatius Sumner, Sister M. Vincent Browne, Sister M. Stephanie Ward, Miss Mary Maddigan and Miss Kate Reynolds. Memoirs of Sr. Ignatius, 4-5.

[97] Memoirs of Sister M. Ignatius; in ASMV, 3.

[98] *Ibid.*, 3-4.

holders on the opposite side of the street discovered the use to which the "old Cobb house" was to be put, they became very indignant. They resented the coming invasion of their respectable precincts by hordes of immigrant children. Fortunately, Father Leray, the pastor, was able to lull to rest the fears of these agitated ladies. He assured them that the Sisters would conduct the school with order and decorum and, then, pointing to the high arbor vitae hedge which enclosed the playground, he expressed the hope that this would sufficiently screen from view anything disagreeable in dress and manner.[99]

It soon became evident that the one building could not serve as both convent and school, especially as the student body continued to increase. Before the end of the first school year Father Leray made plans to build an addition to the school. A subscription was raised. In May 1861, a Mrs. Ann Pitcher of New Orleans loaned a thousand dollars to the Sisters without interest.[100] Although Bishop Elder reported to the pastor of Vicksburg that he would be unable to help him financially in the building of the Sisters' school, a short time later he made a loan of $2,000, interest free, to the Sisters.[101] In spite of the precariousness of the times, for war had already broken out, Father Leray had apparently collected a sufficient amount of money to warrant the Bishop giving him official permission to build.[102] However, this permission was never acted upon, for before the end of the summer the first symptoms of an economic paralysis which would eventually grip the city could be detected.[103] As a result the pastor judged it more prudent to postpone the undertaking.

Boys' Orphanage

One final project which Bishop Elder was able to realize before the outbreak of the War was the establishment of a Catholic orphanage for boys. The problem of providing for Catholic orphan boys in the Diocese had been pressing for a solution for some years. The yellow fever epidemics of the 1850's had not helped

---

99 Bernard, *op. cit.*, 9.

100 Memoirs of Sister M. Ignatius, 5.

101 *Ibid.;* also Elder to Leray, Natchez, May 15, 1861; in AUND: New Orleans Papers. This Letter speaks of only $1,000.

102 Elder to Leray, Natchez, July 10, 1861; in ADNJ, Elder Letter Book—#6, 260.

103 Walker, *Vicksburg, A People at War, 1860-1865,* 60.

matters any. But then circumstances combined shortly after Elder's arrival in the Diocese to hasten the realization of this urgent need.

On June 6, 1855, a wealthy Catholic of Natchez, Mr. William St. John Elliot, nephew of the famous General D'Evereux, died, leaving his country estate to his widow. After her death the property was to pass on to a nephew of Mr. Elliott, Parker by name, with the proviso that the said Parker recover his health and legally take on Elliot's name. These conditions failing, the estate was to be converted to a male Catholic orphan asylum, styled D'Evereux Hall Orphan Asylum.[104] Mrs. Elliot, evidently moved by sentiments of affection for the old home, offered to purchase from the Bishop and his trustees the reversionary rights which they held against the estate for the sum of $25,000, an offer she later raised to $27,500. In 1859, the offer was accepted.[105]

This unexpected turn of events enabled the Bishop and the trustees to proceed immediately with the establishment of the orphanage. By deed dated June 23, 1860, D'Evereux Hall Orphan Asylum, incorporated since 1858, acquired the Alexander Turner property from Mr. John B. Quegles and wife for $6,500. While enjoying the advantages of a rural setting, the site was sufficiently near the city – about a half mile from the Courthouse – to make it a convenient location. The property consisted of about thirty-five acres fronting on Aldrich Street, beginning at Pine Street. On the grounds were a small frame house and a barn and stable.[106]

There was some delay in putting the orphanage into operation. A number of material improvements had to be made which included plastering, whitewashing, re-shingling, ploughing fields and mending fences.[107] There was also the problem of finding someone to take charge of the orphanage. After failing to secure the services of the Christian Brothers, Bishop Elder announced to the board of trustees on August 30, 1860 that Father Frederick Muller ex-

---

[104] Gerow, *Cradle Days of St. Mary's at Natchez,* 231.

[105] *Ibid.,* 232.

[106] *Ibid.;* Natchez *Courier,* Wednesday, May 23, 1860.

[107] Minutes of the Meetings of the Trustees of the D'Evereux Hall Orphan Asylum, Natchez, Miss., Jan. 25, 1858 to Dec. 19, 1865; original register in Cathedral rectory, Natchez, Miss., 25.

pressed a willingness to accept the post. The German priest's offer was accepted.[108]

Shortly after taking over the orphanage, Father Muller obtained permission to build an addition on to the existing small frame house. The extension, put up at the cost of $400, provided space for a dormitory and a dining room.[109] About a year later the Bishop reported to the board of trustees that nine boys were being taken care of at the orphanage. Two very small boys were being boarded out with Catholic families.[110] While there was still room for three or four more boys, it was hoped that during the course of next year the institution's capacity would be increased to twenty. Besides managing the temporalities of the orphanage, Father Muller taught school and was even supervising the boys' recreation.[111]

Just as the Catholic orphan boys of the Diocese had become the objects of the charity of Mr. and Mrs. Elliot, so too did the girls of St. Mary's Orphan Asylum become the beneficiaries of the largess of Mr. Frank Surget, Sr. of Natchez, who left $5,000 to that institution.[112] With the reception of this legacy it was decided in 1859 to build a brick addition on to the main building of the girls' orphanage. Plans materialized rapidly after Messrs. Nevitt, Frank Surget, Jr. and Ben Roach pledged $1,000 each toward the project. By the end of the summer of 1859, the work was completed.[113] At the time the Sisters were caring for seventy orphan girls who were joined each day by forty young misses from Natchez in the day school conducted on the premises.[114]

As the Storm Clouds Gathered

In the spring of 1861, before the "Irrepressible Conflict" broke out, the Catholic Church in Mississippi, though small in numbers and poor, presented a picture of sound organization which included

---

[108] *Ibid.*, 23

[109] *Ibid.*, 26.

[110] Among the Catholic families of Natchez who accepted Catholic orphan boys into their homes at this time were the Gleasons, Boyles, Burns, Ogdens and Perraults.

[111] Report of Bishop Elder to the Board of Trustees, Nov. 1861; quoted by Gerow, *Cradle Days of St. Mary's at Natchez,* 237.

[112] *Ibid.*, 205-206.

[113] O'Connell, "St. Mary's Orphanage," in *Catholic Action of the South* (Natchez Centennial Edition), Oct. 14, 1937, 10.

[114] Elder to the Society for the Propagation of the Faith, Natchez, 1859; quoted by Gerow, "History of the Catholic Diocese of Natchez," *ibid.*, 18.

wise provision for future development. Its 10,000 members were being served by one bishop and eighteen priests.[115] Assisting them on a temporary basis were a diocesan priest from Covington, La., and a Dominican friar from Memphis. Preparing for service in the Diocese were fifteen seminarians. The Diocese was organized into thirteen parishes with one or more resident priests and twenty-eight mission stations. At the time there were fifteen churches with several more in the process of being built. Catholic education was available in the State at five parochial schools, one boarding school for boys and two for girls, plus two other day schools. These institutions were being conducted by four communities of Sisters, one group of teaching Brothers and several lay men and women. In full operation were two orphanages, one for boys and another for girls. Efforts were also being made to foster a more intense and more intelligent Catholic life among the laity. The Redemptorist Fathers, operating out of New Orleans, were moving about the State, giving missions with very gratifying results.[116] Various parish societies had also been organized to care for the poor and to promote Catholic education, temperance, the foreign missions and devotion to the Blessed Virgin Mary.[117] Regularly held clerical conferences, annual retreats for the clergy, and annual synods made for unity and maturity of action on the part of the clergy as well as for a holier and more dedicated priesthood. To be sure, the Catholic Church in Mississippi was faced with a number of problems which could be reduced to poverty and a shortage of priests, but even in these areas, at the beginning of the new decade, there were signs of improvement. Furthermore, none of the problems posed a real threat to the stability of the existing institution. As the lowering clouds of war drifted in over the national scene, there was every reason to believe that the Catholic Church in Mississippi would weather the coming storm.

---

[115] These priests were: Fathers Grignon, Muller, Mulot, Hearns, Elia, Leray, Heuzé, Pont, Orlandi, Guillou, Mouton, Leduc, Holton, Vandemoere, Georget, Boheme, LeCorre, and Huber. Father Mulot left the Diocese shortly after war was declared. This loss was made up for by the ordination of Father Finucane in June 1861, and the arrival of Fr. Picherit, most probably in the summer of 1861.

[116] Krieger, *Seventy-Five Years of Service,* (New Orleans, 1923), 125-126.

[117] *The Metropolitan Catholic Almanac,* 1861, 118.

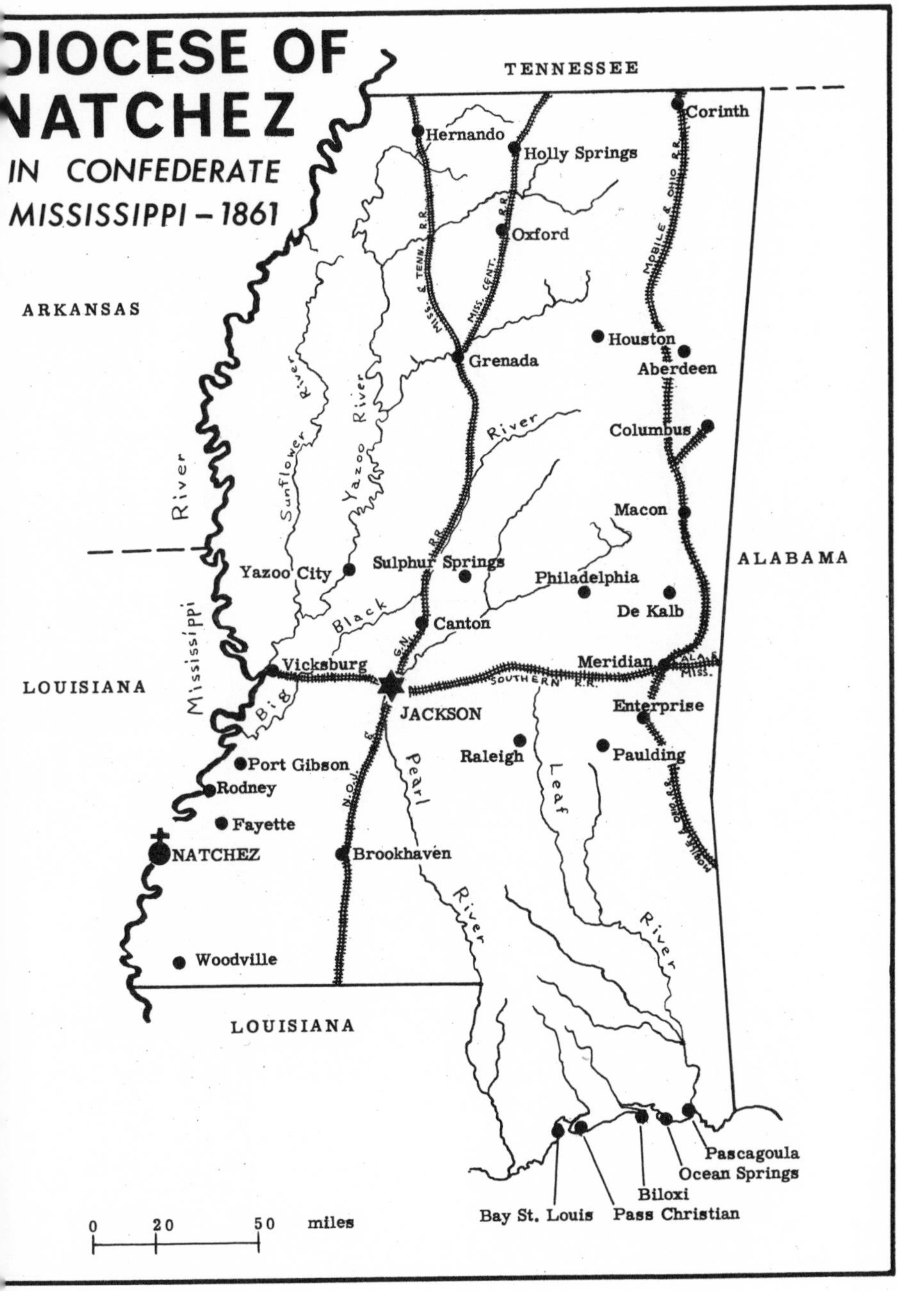
DIOCESE OF
NATCHEZ
IN CONFEDERATE
MISSISSIPPI – 1861
TENNESSEE
ARKANSAS
LOUISIANA
ALABAMA
LOUISIANA
Corinth
Hernando
Holly Springs
Oxford
Houston
Aberdeen
Grenada
Columbus
Macon
Yazoo City
Sulphur Springs
Philadelphia
De Kalb
Canton
Vicksburg
JACKSON
Meridian
Enterprise
Raleigh
Paulding
Port Gibson
Rodney
Fayette
NATCHEZ
Brookhaven
Woodville
Pascagoula
Ocean Springs
Biloxi
Bay St. Louis
Pass Christian
Mississippi River
Sunflower River
Yazoo River
Big Black River
Pearl River
Leaf River
MISS. & TENN. R.R.
MISS. CENT. R.R.
MOBILE & OHIO R.R.
SOUTHERN R.R.
N.O.J. & G.N. R.R.
ALA. & MISS.
0 20 50 miles

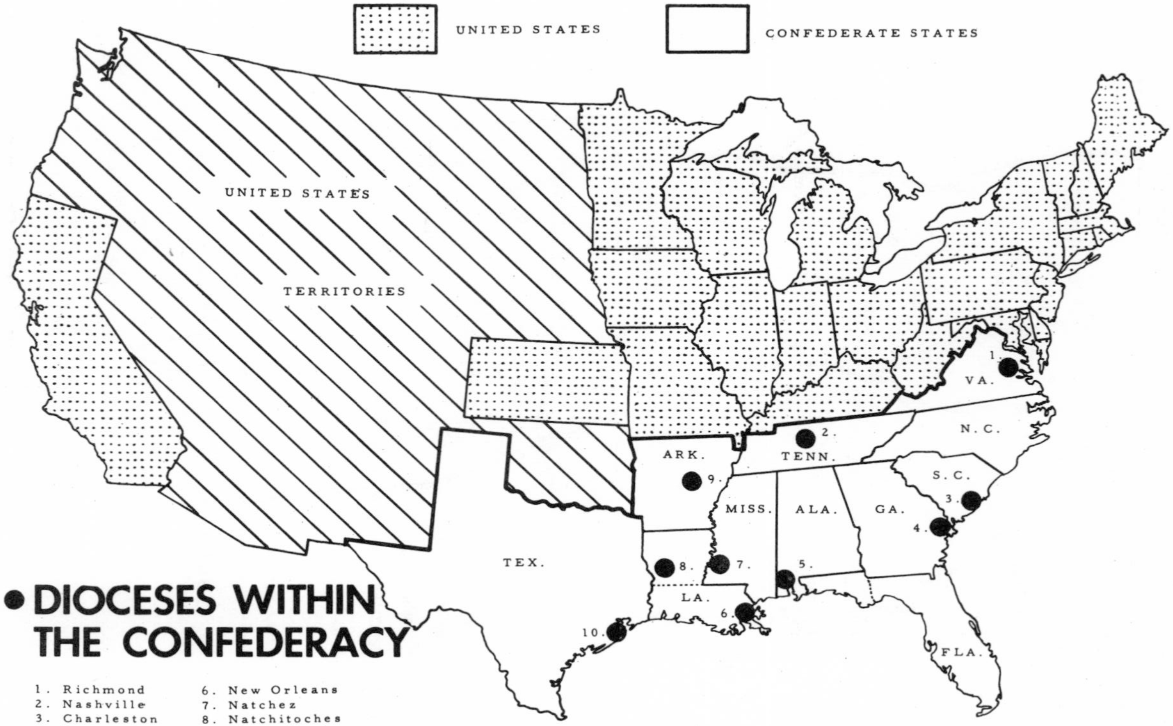

• DIOCESES WITHIN THE CONFEDERACY

1. Richmond
2. Nashville
3. Charleston
4. Savannah
5. Mobile
6. New Orleans
7. Natchez
8. Natchitoches
9. Little Rock
10. Galveston

Chapter VII

SLAVERY AND SECESSION: WAR ISSUES

The Civil War

At 4:30 in the morning, on April 12, 1861, the cannonading of Fort Sumter in Charleston harbor began. The Federal fort was soon under cross fire from a number of batteries in the harbor. After a bloodless bombardment of forty hours, during which the walls were impaired, the ammunition nearly exhausted and great damage done by fire, Major Robert Anderson, the commanding officer, surrendered the fort, his garrison being permitted to depart by boat unmolested. Two days later, President Lincoln issued a call to arms to "the militia of the several States of the Union," to suppress "combinations" in seven states "too powerful to be suppressed by the ordinary course of judicial proceedings."[1] So began the Civil War, one of the greatest wars in American history.[2]

After forty years of mounting bitterness and misunderstanding between the Northern and Southern sections of the United States, in 1860-1861, a large segment of Southerners broke away from the Union and set up a government of their own. The causes of secession were many, and their relative importance will always be disputed by historians.[3] We content ourselves with simply presenting these causes.

Economic Problem

On the economic level, Southerners were dissatisfied with the inequality which existed between the North and South resulting from the concentration of manufacturing, shipping, banking and international trade in the North. This concentration, in turn, gave rise to an unhealthy dependence of the South upon the North for

---

1 Nicolay and Hay (eds.), *Abraham Lincoln: Complete Works, Comprising His Speeches, Letters, State Papers, and Miscellaneous Writings* (N.Y., 1920), II, 165.

2 Participation of the United States in World War I, great as it was, fell short of the Civil War in duration, in the number who served in fighting sectors and more especially in casualties. Randall, *The Civil War and Reconstruction,* 685.

3 Pressly, *Americans Interpret Their Civil War* (Princeton, 1954).

the stability of its economy and the distribution of profits. In the eyes of the South it was the wealth-producing section of the country, and yet the North was enjoying the lion's share of the profits. When through unsound business maneuvers Northern centers produced a "panic," the South along with the North had to suffer, not for any fault of its own, but because of its economic vassalage. Redress in Congress was impossible, for the South lacked the necessary majority. Southerners were therefore saying: the only way to free ourselves from this economic subservience is to secede from the Union.[4]

Slavery

Another issue which prompted the South to secede was slavery.[5] This institution was intimately connected with the economy of the South. Furthermore, the three and a half million slaves living south of the Mason-Dixon line occupied a unique position in Southern society. They enjoyed no political rights and were judged to be, if not by nature, at least in fact, morally, intellectually and socially inferior to the white population. To give heed to the Abolitionists of the North and emancipate these black men would mean making sweeping changes not only in the domestic economy but also in the social order and in the political regime. These changes the South was unwilling to make.

States' Rights

Another reason why some Southerners voted for secession was not to defend slavery as such but to defend states' rights against the growing power of the federal government. It was this reason more than any other which prompted Virginia and three other slave states to secede after Lincoln called for volunteers to coerce their sister states. The states' rights thesis had been enunciated as early as 1837, by John C. Calhoun, senator from South Carolina and former vice-president under Jackson. According to his theory, the federal constitution was an instrument of union between sovereign states which did not agree to unlimited submission to the government created by the compact, but only delegated certain powers to it.

---

[4] Randall, *op. cit.*, 111-114.

[5] Cf. Dumond, *Antislavery Origins of the Civil War in the United States* (Ann Arbor, 1959).

The gradual acceptance of Calhoun's theories by the whole South was to furnish in 1860, the legalistic basis for the secession of eleven southern states when they became convinced that their rights had been or soon would be violated by the majority in control of the federal government. In the meanwhile, however, one big difficulty did arise. Because the states' rights theory was quite suited to the defense of slavery and was used as such, the two issues became confused in the minds of many people to the extent that for them the defense of states' rights meant unqualified endorsement of Southern slavery.

Political Reasons

Historians of the Civil War also speak of political reasons for secession. In the 1830's and 1840's the South had held a dominant position in all federal administrations. For a generation the Southern planters had controlled the Democratic organization and had also been very influential in the old Whig party. Now the Whig party, replaced by the Republican party in which the South had absolutely no voice, was no more. The 1860 convention had shown that Southern politicians could no longer hope to control even the Democratic party. For years, the South had been losing the economic fight; now it had lost its political supremacy. Under a Republican administration the South would be stripped of a rich federal patronage. For ambitious Southern politicians who saw only lean years ahead secession began to look more and more attractive.

Election of Lincoln

The pivotal point about which the events of 1860-1861 turned was the election of Abraham Lincoln. His election in November 1860 to the Presidency of the United States marked the elevation to power of a party whose announced policies were at direct variance with the South's: high protective tariffs vs. free trade; higher-law doctrine vs. strict interpretation of the Constitution; abolition or at least non-extension of slavery vs. protection of slavery or at least non-intervention by Congress; an indivisible Union of States vs. the compact theory. Even if the mildness of Lincoln's own purposes were to be admitted, Southerners could not forget that he was a Republican President: "they feared increasingly radical tendencies within his party, which would draw him inevitably beyond his own desires or judgment."[6] Thus, Southerners tended to regard Lincoln's election as a challenge to their social, economic and political system. With such a conviction in mind it was but natural to exercise the fundamental right of altering their government and throwing off an alien rule.[7]

The Confederate States of America

The first state to secede from the Union was South Carolina. She took the drastic step on December 20, 1860, a month and a half after Lincoln's election. In quick succession her action was imitated by six other Southern states: Mississippi, Florida, Alabama, Georgia, Louisiana and Texas.[8] Early in February, 1861, a convention of Southern states met in Montgomery, Alabama, to form a new government.

The framers of the Southern Confederacy went about their task leisurely. As yet there was no war. In their minds the right to alter their form of rule and to frame a government of their own choosing was undeniable; and the exercise of that right according to constitutional methods offered no just occasion for war. Three main functions were discharged by the Convention: it drew up a constitution for the Confederate States; it chose a provisional President and Vice-President; and it acted as a provisional legislature for the new government pending the holding of regular congressional elections. In its general pattern the constitution of the new nation greatly resembled that of the United States; for that matter at most points its wording was precisely the same. As was to be expected, the main differences were in those features which took care to guarantee states' rights and to safeguard slavery.

The Churches and Secession

During the period of debate and argument, before the Confederacy was an accomplished fact, religious discussions in Mississippi on the issue of secession was significant. The Churches had come to exercise considerable influence upon the lives of Mississippians. Whereas in 1817, when the State entered the Union, not more than one person in twenty was a church member, in 1860, it is probable that one white adult out of three belonged to some church. This was due in part to the passing of the frontier

[6] Randall, *op. cit.,* 228.
[7] *Ibid.,* 229.
[8] *Ibid.,* 183-192.

and the increasing urbanity of village life. The growing urbanity of Mississippians in turn had its affect upon the clergy of the State. From earliest times the Presbyterian and Episcopal ministers, who had excellent educations, were recognized as men of ability whose opinions were highly regarded. The influence of clergymen of other denominations also increased when these, no longer itinerants, settled in towns and showed great interest in community affairs. Religion also extended its influence in the State through church-sponsored educational institutions and church newspapers and periodicals.[9]

Although the fire-eaters in Mississippi in searching for reinforcements for the debate would have gladly welcomed the support of ministers of the gospel, they received as a matter of fact very little before the end of 1860. Conservative by tradition, they could hardly have been expected to act differently. Some even spoke out against secession. However, after Lincoln's election, almost overnight, many of the clergy became secessionists.[10] For instance, the Reverend Thomas W. Caskey, pastor of the Christian Church in Jackson, even took to the field during the week to campaign against the Hinds County Co-operationists for the Secession Convention. On the eve of the elections for the convention Bishop William Mercer Green of the Episcopal Church endorsed secession in a vigorous pastoral letter, because he was convinced that the differences between the North and South were irreconcilable. Once the state convention voted Mississippi out of the Union on January 9, 1861, the action of the clergy and the Churches was even more dramatic.

> The withdrawal of Mississippi from the Union found the clergy not only for the most part acquiescent but also in many cases preaching secessionist and even militaristic sermons, many of which were printed by the newspapers and circulated in pamphlet form. (. . . .) When state conventions and conferences met to decide their future policy, the church invariably endorsed the new order. Both the Baptists, who met in May, and the Methodists, who met in November, passed favorable resolutions. In October the Synod of Mississippi elected delegates to the General Assembly which was to form the Presbyterian Church in the Confeder-

---

[9] Moore, "Religion in Mississippi in 1860," in JMH, XXII (Oct. 1960), 224-229.

[10] *Ibid.*, 234-238.

ate States of America; and recognizing 'the cause of our Country as the Cause of God,' adopted a belligerent preamble to its resolutions, pledging support to the Confederacy.[11]

While the majority of the clergy in Mississippi came to the support of the Confederacy, there were a number of exceptions, most of whom were produced by the Presbyterian Church.

> The Presbyterian evangelist John Aughey . . . was hounded out of Choctaw and Attala counties and finally imprisoned at Tupelo for his militant opposition to the Confederacy. Another Presbyterian Unionist, E.Z. Feemster, had to resort to obtaining a doctor's certificate of bad health lest he be drafted in the army before he could escape to the Federal lines. A Reverend Mr. Galladet of Aberdeen and the Reverend James Phelan of Macon, both of whom were likewise Presbyterians, had to leave their charges because of their Unionism; the former escaping to the North, the latter fleeing to the country, where his enemies murdered him. At one time in 1862, the military prison at Columbus contained a Methodist minister, a United Brother, and a Presbyterian, all held on charges of Unionism. Also at Columbus but not incarcerated was the Presbyterian minister James A. Lyon, whose prominence enabled him to escape the severe persecution meted out to other Unionists.[12]

Bishop Elder and Secession

During the period of agitation over the subject of secession Bishop Elder made no public statement for or against the move. He was obviously being very careful to maintain the policy long advanced by the bishops of the country, namely, non-interference by the Catholic Church in the political arena.[13] When political tension mounted in the late 1850's this stand of the Catholic Church in America was re-affirmed. Assembled in Council in 1858, the Bishops of the ecclesiastical Province of Baltimore declared: "Our clergy have wisely abstained from all interference with the judgment of the faithful, which should be free on all questions of polity and social order, within the limits of the doctrine and law of Christ." [14] The same idea was expressed by the Bishops

[11] Bettersworth, *Confederate Mississippi,* 286.

[12] *Ibid.*

[13] Spalding, *Life of the Most Reverend Martin J. Spalding* (New York, 1873), 238.

[14] Pastoral Letter issued by the Ninth Provincial Council of Baltimore, 1858; quoted by Murphy, "The Catholic Church in the United States during the Civil War Period, (1852-1866)," in RACHS, XXXIX (Dec. 1928), 296.

of the border Province of Cincinnati two weeks after the firing on Fort Sumter: "While (the Church's) ministers rightfully feel a deep and abiding interest in all that concerns the welfare of the country, they do not think it their province to enter into the political arena." [15] In keeping with this policy, neither Bishop Elder nor his priests used the pulpit to agitate for or against secession. There were other reasons for Elder's apparent reluctance to endorse secession as a remedy for the South's ills before the State legislature acted. He would not have wanted to scandalize the many Catholic immigrants in his diocese who had not forgotten their naturalization oath to obey and defend the U.S. Constitution. This was not a far-fetched possibility, for many members of his flock came to the Bishop seeking moral advice on this point.[16] That the Federal government would allow the South to secede peacefully was a moot question in December, 1860. Thus, as he considered the South's chances for setting up an independent government, Elder would have had to take into account the possibility that secession would mean war. Yet he knew how important peace and public order are for the fruitful exercise of even a spiritual ministry and the construction and maintenance of churches, schools and charitable institutions. There was still another factor which would have given Elder pause before giving public support to the idea of secession, were he in favor of it. Two of his largest congregations were located in Union strongholds—Natchez and Vicksburg.[17] Most probably the Catholics there were as much in favor of remaining in the Union as the rest of their fellow-citizens.

Personally Bishop Elder would appear to have been a moderate on the question of secession. Although he was eager to have the South's grievances remedied, he was not sure that this should be done by a dissolution of the Union. Writing to his father on December 11, 1860, the Bishop expressed his fears and uncertainty:

> It is hard to tell what is to be the lot of the country. I fear nothing can keep us together unless some extraordinary

[15] Pastoral Letter issued by the Third Provincial Council of Cincinnati, May, 1861; quoted by Murphy, *op. cit.*, 303.

[16] Elder to Kenrick (?), undated fragment, found in a file after a letter dated April 12, 1861; in AAB, 29-D-12.

[17] Elder to Keogh, Natchez, March 14, 1861; in ADNJ, Elder Letter Book—#6, 132. Also Walker, *Vicksburg, A People at War, 1860-1865*, 27.

advances on the part of the North. Many persons here are persuaded that we can have no safety for lives & property—until we take measures as an independent government. I have not enough of political sagacity to see what will be the course of events—nor what would be the fruit of the remedies proposed.—We elect members of Convention the 20th.—The Convention meets, Jan. 7th.[18]

While the Reverend Thomas W. Caskey and other Protestant ministers in the State publicly urged the people of Mississippi to elect delegates to the Convention who would vote for secession, the Catholic bishop of Natchez, respecting the individual political convictions of his people, gave counsel of a different nature. Recognizing the seriousness of the forthcoming state convention, Elder addressed the following circular letter to his parish priests:

Rev. and Dear Sir:—The present condition of our political affairs calls urgently for the most fervent supplications to Almightly God.

It is not for us here to discuss the question connected with our situation. It is enough to know that it has been found necessary to summon the Legislature of our State, 'to take into consideration,' in the words of the Governor's Proclamation, 'the propriety and necessity of providing surer and better safeguards for the lives, liberties and property of her citizens:' and that every thinking man is solemnly impressed with the conviction that the present time demands the exercise of every virtue and the generous discharge of every duty.

Endeavor, then, that no one of your flock be guilty of neglecting the first duty of the Christian Patriot;—which is to beg for the light and protection of Him, in whose hands are the hearts of men and the destinies of nations;—that He may inspire both the Legislature and the people to determine wisely and effect happily whatever may be most for His glory and their own temporal and eternal happiness. Exhort them to offer up to God Prayers, Fasting and Alms Deeds, for His merciful guidance and protection.

Invite all to assist at the Holy Sacrifice of the Mass as often as possible, and to recite every day in addition to the usual prayers, at least once the *Our Father*, the *Hail Mary*, and the *Glory be to the Father*.

---

[18] Elder to his father, Natchez, Dec. 11, 1860; in ADNJ, Elder Letter Book—#5, 416.

We desire you to hold a public Triduum, or three days' devotion—in which we recommend you to recite the Psalm, *Have Mercy on me, O God,* and one part of the Rosary of the Blessed Virgin,—and to give the Benediction of the Blessed Sacrament.

But the most effectual means to obtain God's favor is to purify the soul from sin, and to receive worthily the Sacrament of the Blessed Eucharist: and no Catholic should imagine he has done his duty to himself and his fellow-citizens on this occasion, so long as these duties to God are left undone.

Urge all, therefore, to approach to those Sacraments as early as possible. We should be glad that where it is practicable, all unite in one general Communion, on Sunday, December 9th,—being within the Octave of the Immaculate Conception of the Blessed Virgin: for our Holy Mother is by excellence the Help of Christians.

While our Diocese is exempted from the obligation of fasting on the Fridays of Advent, We recommend that this year that fast be observed by all, whose health and occupation will permit: and We desire you to remind the people of this recommendation, each successive Sunday.

Finally, let every one, for this same intention, give some especial alms, according to his devotion and means—either to the Orphans, or to other subjects of charity.

For yourself, We direct you to insert in Mass the prayer —Pro Quacumque Necessitate, every day until December 23d inclusive, as pro re gravi:—and We beg you to offer the Holy Sacrifice at least once for this intention.

We exhort you that both by words and example, 'being made a pattern of the Flock from the soul,' you animate them to the practice of all those virtues which draw down God's blessing on individuals and nations.

May the Grace of our Lord Jesus Christ be with you and them. Pray for Us.

† William Henry, Bishop of Natchez
Bay St. Louis, Miss., Nov. 25th, 1860.[19]

Again five days before the Convention met to decide on the important question of secession, Bishop Elder in a circular letter urged the faithful who made up his flock to redouble their prayers for the successful outcome of the Convention:

---

[19] *New York Tablet,* Vol. IV, No. 30, Dec. 22, 1860, 11.

> With regard to our political affairs, we shall not speak now more than to remind you how entirely we depend on the favor of God to establish peace and prosperity. 'Unless the Lord build the house, they labor in vain that build it.' (Psalm cxxxvi) And that Lent is the time when our prayers are most powerful before the throne of grace, because at this season so many millions of our brethren throughout the world are joined with us in offering extraordinary supplications for God's mercy and protection. 'Now is the acceptable time; now is the day of salvation.' (2 Cor. vi, 3) Let us then continue with one heart and one soul to offer holy violence to Him Who calmed the winds and waves, that He give happiness to our country, animate us all with courage and fidelity to our duty, and at the same time pour out over the hearts of all His own sweet spirit of peace and brotherly love.[20]

Although the prospect of disunion was so painful to the Bishop of Natchez that he would have cheerfully made any personal sacrifice to prevent it,[21] he made no effort to influence his people even when they consulted him privately. In a letter to Archbishop Kenrick of Baltimore, Elder revealed the course he followed on these occasions:

> My course, & I believe the course of my clergy, has been not to recommend secession—but to explain to those who might enquire, that—if they were satisfied, dispassionately —that secession was the only practical remedy, the only means of safety—their religion did not forbid them to advocate it—on the contrary they were bound to do, what they believed the safety of the community required; & that the oath of naturalization did not hinder one who had taken it, from doing any thing that it was lawful for native citizens to do.[22]

Distasteful as the dissolution of the Union was to Bishop Elder, once Mississippi seceded[23] he gave and encouraged others to give to the new government their full support. His reaction was the same when the State Convention ratified the Confederate Constitution on March 29, 1861. In a letter to Bishop Duggan of Chicago, Elder announced his stand:

---

[20] *The Catholic Mirror,* Baltimore, Vol. XII, No. 6, Feb. 9, 1861, 2.

[21] Elder to Kenrick of Balt., Natchez, April 12, 1861; in AAB, 29-D-11. Also Elder to Keogh, Natchez, March 14, 1861; in ADNJ, Elder Letter Book—#6, 132.

[22] Elder to Kenrick (?), undated fragment, found in a file after a letter dated April 12, 1861; in AAB, 29-D-12.

[23] Jan. 9, 1861, by a vote of 84 to 14.

> I hold it is the duty of all Catholics in the seceeding (sic) states to adhere (?) to the actual government without reference to the right or the wisdom of making the separation—or to the grounds for it:—our State governments & our new Confederation are *de facto* our *only existing* government here, & it seems to me that as good Citizens we are bound not only—to acquiesce in it—but to support it, & contribute means & arms—[24]

Elder spelled out even more clearly in another letter, this time to Kenrick of Baltimore, what sort of support was to be given:

> . . . since secession has been accomplished—I have advised even those who thought it unwise—still to support our State Govt. & the new Confederacy—as being the only Govts. which exist here *de facto.* I have encouraged all to give a hearty support—to enrol (sic) as soldiers—to go forward with their taxes—to co-operate in any way they had occasion for.[25]

Elder's stand was not one of unqualified expediency. He felt that he was supported in his view by sound moral theology, at least so he intimated in a letter to Father Napoleon Perché, editor of the New Orleans' *Propagateur catholique.* After admitting that he had heard of three distinct grounds advanced by Southerners for their separation from the Union, Elder went on to declare:

> I may say that others . . .—without adopting any one of these theories—adhere cordially to the actions (?) of their State—& support it by every means in their power—because it *is* their State—the body politic to which they belong—which they are bound to obey in all that is not sin & which they must presume to act rightly—as long as she is not clearly wrong.[26]

This does not mean that Bishop Elder found any difficulty in justifying the action of the Southern people in seceding from the Union. On the contrary, he was quick to defend them. However, he was careful not to commit himself to any one of the theories advanced, writing cautiously, writing as a man would write who had little confidence in his own judgment of political

---

[24] Elder to Duggan, Natchez, Feb. 19, 1861; in ADNJ, Elder Letter Book—#6, 65.

[25] Elder to Kenrick (?), undated fragment, found in a file after another of Elder's letters dated April 12, 1861; in AAB, 29-D-12.

[26] Elder to Perché, Natchez, Feb. 4, 1861; in ADNJ, Elder Letter Book—#6, 37.

affairs and of human beings.[27] In a letter to the editor of *Le Propagateur catholique* of New Orleans, the Bishop of Natchez reviewed the various reasons advanced for getting out of the Union:

> I have heard three distinct grounds given for our separation from the Union.—Some say the Union was a kind of free association, which any state had a right to forsake whenever she judged it conducive to her interests—the right of secession.—Others say it was a perpetual compact in intention: but that other parties having unjustly broken it—we were no longer bound by it.—Others again—say that we were released not so much by the direct violation of the compact on the part of Northern States—but by the right of self preservation—because it was impossible for us to live in the Union: & we had a right to provide for our safety outside of it.[28]

The Bishop, then, added, without admitting that all or any of the conditions actually prevailed: "Now any of these positions is perfectly consistent with Catholic morality—& with the highest patriotism." In a letter to the Archbishop of Baltimore Elder was a little more committal:

> I am far from finding fault with the movement. While I deeply regret the destruction of the Union—yet I think our people as a body have proceeded calmly & dispassionately. —Whether there was another remedy or not—I think they were convinced that there was none. I have not seen any indications of that haste & passion, which many of our northern friends attribute to the people:—nor any of that intimidation, which some of them speak of.—[29]

Perhaps, the most revealing letter was one which Elder wrote to Bishop Duggan of Chicago on March 5, 1861:

> Above all I could not accept the term *disloyalty* as applicable to the course of our Southern People. Without discussing whether the grounds for our separation . . . . were (?) before God sufficient or not—they certainly were such

---

27 Elder to his father, Natchez, Dec. 11, 1860; in ADNJ, Elder Letter Book—#5, 416. Also Elder to Kenrick, Vicksburg, Oct. 21, 1860; in AAB, 29-D-10, and Elder to Barnabò, Natchez, Sept. 3, 1860; in APF, Scritture Riferite nei Congressi, XVIII (1858-1860), ff. 1504.

28 Elder to Perché, Natchez, Feb. 4, 1861; in ADNJ, Elder Letter Book —#6, 37.

29 Elder to Kenrick (?), undated fragment, found in a file after another of Elder's letters dated April 12, 1861; in AAB, 29-D-12.

> as honest men might easily accept (?) as sufficient. And from what I have seen & heard, I am satisfied that the great body of the people have acted conscientiously according to their sense of duty.—It is a great mistake in the north to imagine our people are rushing on in an excitement of passion.[30]

At the time Governor Pettus of Mississippi called the State Convention to decide on the all-important question of secession, Bishop Elder's political thought was in a state of ferment. He was neither an ardent secessionist nor a blind Unionist. Coming as he did from an old Maryland family, it is understandable that he would be strongly attached to the Union, but this did not blind him to the reality of the South's grievances against the North and the latter's growing fanaticism. In a letter to Rev. William G. McCloskey, Rector of the American College at Rome, Elder described his thinking on the subject of secession in 1860: "I thought at first . . . . that the movement was rash, & that the South ought rather to have relied on 'Constitutional remedies.'"[31] But, then, the progress of events in the north began to undermine this conviction. Among the events which Elder singled out were "the scornful treatment of all attempts at compromise in Congress," the North's "setting aside the whole power of the United States Courts," and, finally, "the contempt with which (the North) treated the old man we all venerated so much—Roger B. Taney."[32] During the five crucial weeks before the Convention met in Jackson, the Bishop became more and more convinced, as a result of his reading and private discussions with some of the better informed Catholics in Natchez, that the reasons being advanced for secession were valid and just. He was pleased to note that prior to the Convention the people were at complete liberty to express themselves. To the Archbishop of Baltimore he reported: "I have heard men express themselves in public very strongly against the movement—without their being molested."[33] And to the

[30] Elder to Duggan, Natchez, March 5, 1861; in ADNJ, Elder Letter Book—#6, 96.

[31] Elder to McCloskey, Natchez, June 23, 1863; in ADNJ, Elder Letter Book—#8, 435.

[32] *Ibid.* Roger B. Taney (1777-1864) was a prominent Catholic layman of Maryland and Chief Justice of the U.S. Supreme Court when the controversial Dred Scott Decision was rendered. *Catholic Encyclopedia,* Vol. XIV, 442-443.

[33] Elder to Kenrick (?), undated; in AAB, 29-D-12.

Bishop of Chicago: "Nor have I seen or heard anything of terrorism or intimidation."[34] Elder was equally impressed by the calm seriousness with which the people considered the move.

> All along I have seen nothing of what could be called excitement: no passionate appeals—no flaming announcements—feverish anxiety to hear the news & comment upon it:—& no bitter denunciations . . . . No doubt there have been such things to some degree—but so little that they have not fallen under my notice.[35]

To another correspondent he reported: "I must give our people credit of having proceeded—as far as I know—with coolness & conscientiousness."[36] That the actual decision to secede from the Union was arrived at by constitutional means was another factor which satisfied the scruples of the Bishop of Natchez. The enthusiastic support of the new government by all, even by those who had opposed secession, was the final development in the drama which helped Bishop Elder reach a personal decision in the matter.[37] Accordingly, having already satisfied himself that he was on solid moral ground, Bishop Elder publicly endorsed the new government and urged his flock to support it cordially and completely. However, to the end he regretted the dissolution of the Union, and it was only long after the outbreak of hostilities that he was able to rid himself of doubts about the wisdom of secession.

It is interesting to trace the feelings of the Bishop on this subject as the political and military events of the War unfolded. At the beginning of March, 1861, after the formation of the Confederacy, Elder confided to the Bishop of Chicago: "Although I deeply regret the (dissolution of the) old Union, . . . yet I am inclined to hope that Almighty God will bring much good out of the movement."[38] A few days later he wrote to a priest-friend even more optimistically: ". . . if peace prevails—I have not lost

---

[34] Elder to Duggan, Natchez, March 5, 1861; in ADNJ, Elder Letter Book —#6, 96.

[35] Elder to Kenrick (?), undated; in AAB, 29-D-12.

[36] Elder to Keogh, Natchez, March 14, 1861; in ADNJ, Elder Letter Book —#6, 132.

[37] *Ibid.*

[38] Elder to Duggan, Natchez, March 5, 1861; in ADNJ, Elder Letter Book—#6, 96.

hope of seeing a reconstruction (of the Union)—after a while."[39] The old nagging doubt, however, is very much in evidence in a letter which Elder wrote to Bishop Lynch of Charleston in early May, 1861, after word had been received of the Baltimore riot between Federal troops and angry citizens: "I must confess I have strong fears that we may not profit by the change of our affairs. Certainly 'the times are evil'—wherever may lie the fault."[40] Elder's reaction to news from Missouri about internecine war in that state, to reports of a "massacre" of defenseless women and children bordered on depression. To Dr. McCaffrey of Emmitsburg the Bishop wrote in July, 1861:

> Poor, unstable earth—I am losing interest in it. The breaking up of the Union was hard enough—but the deplorable conditions of Maryland & Missouri is harder still —& makes us all rejoice in our escape from such rulers and grieve over the insecurity of all liberty on earth.[41]

By the middle of 1863, after Mississippi itself had become a battleground, at the very time that Vicksburg was under seige,[42] Elder, himself living in an occupied city, had come to recognize the futilty of "Constitutional remedies" in the face of "fanaticism" and had become persuaded:

> . . . that there must have been a very deep seated & wide spread hatred against the South, before the election of 1860 & which wd. have brought on the despoliation of the Union in some other way, when the South wd. have been more entirely at the mercy of the Black Republicans, holding entire control of Army, Navy, Post Office & all Federal property.[43]

Thus, in two years time Bishop Elder had run the gamut of emotions with respect to the advisability of secession. Hope had given way to fear, fear to depression, and depression to disillusionment. But in the end gone were all his doubts.

---

39 Elder to Keogh, Natchez, March 14, 1861; in ADNJ, Elder Letter Book—#6, 132.

40 Elder to Lynch, Natchez, May 9, 1861; in ADC, Envelope 126.

41 Elder to McCaffrey, Natchez, July, 1861; quoted in Meline & McSweeney, *The Story of The Mountain,* II. 8-9.

42 The seige of Vicksburg lasted from May 19 to July 4, on which day General Pemberton, C.S.A. surrendered to General Grant.

43 Elder to McCloskey, Natchez, June 23, 1863; in ADNJ, Elder Letter Book—#8, 435.

Among the nine Catholic bishops [44] of the South Bishop Elder was not alone in his support of the Confederacy. With the exception of the Bishop of Nashville, the Catholic prelates within the Confederacy supported the new government wholeheartedly. No less sincere, the Bishop of Natchez, however, was far more moderate in expressing himself on the subject than many of his confreres. In January, 1861, in a letter to John Mullaly, editor of the New York *Metropolitan Record,* Bishop Lynch of Charleston betrayed an almost "devil-may-care" attitude toward the dissolution of the Union and the threat of war: "Let the Union be broken. —We at the South will suffer to some extent, but the North will have to drain the Cup, which they have but taken a sip of as yet." [45] In his enthusiasm for the new state of affairs the Bishop of Mobile, John Quinlan, advocated an even more radical separation than the one already achieved in the spring of 1861. Writing to the Bishop of Charleston a month after the firing on Fort Sumter, Quinlan urged: "We must cut adrift from the North in many things of intimate social conditions and interests—we of the South have been too long on 'leading strings'." [46] One of the most outspoken of the Southern bishops was August Martin, Bishop of Natchitoches, La. In a highly emotional pastoral letter dated the twenty-first of August, 1861, the French-born prelate minced no words. For him the Republicans were a "party without a conscience," whose war goal was "bondage or extermination" for the South. Sounding very much like a general addressing his troops before battle, the Bishop declared:

> After having blockaded our commercial ports and invaded our land, in the name of the federal pact which it

[44] Archbishop John M. Odin, C.M. of New Orleans, La.; and Bishops August M. Martin of Natchitoches, La.; William H. Elder of Natchez, Miss.; John Quinlan of Mobile, Ala.; Claude Dubuis, C.M., of Galveston, Tex.; Andrew Byrne of Little Rock, Ark.; James Whelan, O.P. of Nashville, Tenn.; James McGill of Richmond, Va.; Patrick N. Lynch of Charleston, S.C.; and Augustine Verot, S.S. of Savannah, Ga. At no time were there more than nine bishops in the Confederacy. Bishop Dubuis was consecrated in November, 1862, but by that time Bishop Byrne of Little Rock had been dead for several months and the see remained vacant until after the War. From 1863 on, when Bishop Whelan resigned his see and no appointment was made for two years, there were only eight bishops in the South.

[45] Lynch to Mullaly, Charleston, Jan. 6, 1861; edited by Wight, "Some Wartime Letters of Bishop Lynch," in CHR, XLIII (Oct. 1957), 21-25.

April

[46] Quinlan to Lynch, Mobile, May 19, 1861; in ADC, Lynch Papers, Envelope 126; quoted from Lipscomb, "The Administration of John Quinlan, Second Bishop of Mobile, 1859-1883," unpublished master's dissertation, Washington: Catholic University of America, 1959, 50.

> has violated and (in the name) of the Constitution for which it has substituted itself, it clearly announces today its determination to crush us under the weight of its legions, and to erase our name from the roster of free peoples. (. . . .) After having uselessly insisted upon our rights in the face of injustice, we must oppose force with force, legion with legion. Every man capable of bearing arms and free to dispose of himself must be a soldier and be ready to answer the call of his country. And let us note well that if we do our duty we shall possess a strength above every strength, that which a people derives from an awareness that they are right. And this moral strength, no matter what reverses are in store for it, will always be victorious in the end, because it rests on what is most invincible, justice and truth.[47]

How strikingly different must have been the language of the Bishop of Natchez when addressing his flock, especially those who were eligible for military service. In May, 1861, when enlistment in the Natchez area was going on at a rapid pace, Bishop Elder wrote to his brother Francis in Baltimore:

> We have been kept very busy for two weeks past preparing our Soldiers for their Confessions and Communions. We avoid all inflamatory harangues.—I preached at the Camp last Sunday, for most of the soldiers there just now are Irish Catholics. But I only exhorted them to fear God & live as good Christians.[48]

This policy of speaking or preaching with moderation was maintained throughout the War, not only by the Bishop, but also by all of the priests of the Natchez Diocese, even those who became military chaplains. As a result, Bishop Elder was spared much of the embarrassment which his metropolitan, Archbishop Odin of New Orleans, had to face during the War because of the 'improprieties' of such strong-willed priests as Father Claude P. Maistre, Napoleon Perché, James I. Mullin and Adrien-Emmanuel Rouquette.[49]

---

[47] (Martin) *Lettre Pastorale de Mgr. L'Evêque de Natchitoches a L'Occasion de la Guerre du Sud pour Son Independence,* 21 août 1861; in APF: Scritture Riferite nei Congressi, XIX (1861-1862), ff. 1207.

[48] Elder to his brother Francis, Natchez, May 15, 1861; in ADNJ, Elder Letter Book—#6, 235.

[49] Dabney, *One Hundred Years* (Baton Rouge, 1944), 159-160; Lebreton, *Chahta-Ima, The Life of Adrien-Emmanuel Rouquette* (Baton Rouge, 1947), 222-225.

The Churches and Slavery

As intimately tied up with the economic, social and political life of the South as slavery was, it is understandable that the ministers of religion in the South would be expected to pronounce themselves on the morality of this institution when, as early as 1832, anti-slavery agitation became a powerful religious crusade whose cardinal thesis was "slavery is a sin." [50] As a result, long before the Union was dissolved, the slavery controversy divided the Baptist and Methodist churches into northern and southern branches and prompted the formation of the United Synod for the New School Presbyterians. Furthermore, just as in the North, where Protestant churches were the forums and the preachers the most consistent and powerful denouncers of slavery, so in the decade before the war southern Protestant clergymen became the staunchest defenders of their region's 'peculiar institution.'

In Mississippi Protestant clergymen were far more unanimous in their defense of slavery than they were in their support of secession.[51] The Mississippi Methodist Conference may never have been pro-slavery, but it was surely anti-abolitionist. At the end of the ante-bellum period two of its more prominent ministers, Winans and Marshall, were agreeing that "Slavery is the most favorable state for Africans here." [52] On the eve of the Civil War the editors of the Mississippi *Baptist* declared themselves to be the "uncompromising friends" of slavery.[53] As for the Presbyterian Church, it provided some of the strongest support for the institution of slavery, not only in Mississippi, but throughout the South. As early as 1833, one of its more distinguished preachers in the State, Rev. James Smylie, argued that slavery was a positive good. His arguments, drawn from Scripture, are reported to have had a tremendous influence on subsequent slavery legislation in Mississippi.[54] However, the mildest and probably the more common position taken by Protestant clergymen in the State prior to the

---

[50] Dumond, *op. cit.*, 35, 37-41.

[51] Moore, *op. cit.*, 232-234.

[52] Winans to Marshall, Dec. 2, 1856; in Mississippi State Archives, Winans Correspondence; quoted by Moore, *op. cit.*, 233.

[53] Cf. Rainwater, *Mississippi, Storm Center of Secession, 1851-1861* (Baton Rouge, 1938), 175, quoting from *A Republication of the Minutes of the Mississippi Baptist Association . . . from 1806 to the Present Time* (New Orleans, 1849), 167-168.

[54] Moore, *op. cit.*, 233-234.

war was that slavery was a civil institution introduced into the country by previous generations and protected by law; that the the sole duty of the Church as such was to preach faithfully to both master and slave and to influence each to discharge their relative Christian obligations as plainly taught by the Bible.[55]

Unlike the great Protestant denominations, the Catholic Church in the United States experienced no organizational split over the slavery issue. This does not mean that there was a unanimity of opinion on the subject. Far from it. Its members fought on both sides during the War; there was a certain amount of controversial correspondence between northern and southern ecclesiastics; and there were brisk passages at arms between the religious journals of the respective sections.[56] It is obvious that the Catholic Church's position at the time must have allowed a good deal of freedom for discussion to have been able to absorb all the stress and strain which were part of the controversy. In the first half of the 19th century in the United States it was commonly taught by Catholics that human bondage was not morally wrong "per se" provided the conditions laid down for a "just servitude" were observed. Bishop England of Charleston who dominated Catholic thought in the United States during this half century publicly stated that the Church did not condemn the institution.[57] Bishop Kenrick of Philadelphia in his manual *Theologia Moralis* taught that slavery was not against the natural law.[58] When having to take into account Pope Gregory XVI's apostolic constitution, "In Supremo Apostolatus Fastigio," Bishop England distinguished between slave trade and domestic slavery which prevailed when a large section of society was in bondage since birth. In one of his famous *Letters to Forsyth,* the prelate of Charleston wrote: "The pope neither mentions nor alludes to this latter in his Apostolic Letter, which is directed, as were those of his predecessors, solely and exclusively against the former." [59] So forcefully did the Bishop present

[55] Cabaniss & Cabaniss, "Religion in Ante-Bellum Mississippi," in JMH, VI (Oct. 1944), 221.

[56] Cf. Rice, *American Catholic Opinion in the Slavery Controversy* (New York, 1944); Ellis, *American Catholicism,* 87-96.

[57] Guilday, *The Life and Times of John England, First Bishop of Charleston, 1786-1842* (New York, 1927), II, 295.

[58] Kenrick, *Theologia Moralis* (Baltimore, 1841), I, Tr. 5.; Brokhage, *Francis Patrick Kenrick's Opinion on Slavery* (Washington, 1955).

[59] Messmer (ed.), *Works of the Rt. Rev. John England* (Cleveland, 1908), V, 186.

his case that he was thought to be positively favoring slavery. To correct this impression he wrote to the editors of the *United States Miscellany* on Feb. 25, 1841:

> I have been asked by many, a question which I may as well answer at once, viz: Whether I am friendly to the existence or continuation of slavery? I am not—but I also see the impossibility of now abolishing it here. When it can and ought to be abolished, is a question for the legislature and not for me.[60]

It is safe to say that Bishop England's view can be taken as representing those of the majority of his fellow prelates. Even Archbishop Hughes and Archbishop Kenrick who had Northern interests and sympathies were at one with him in their attitude toward abolition and emancipation. The pastoral letter issued by the American bishops at the end of the Second Plenary Council of Baltimore held in 1866, seems to bear this out:

> We could have wished, that in accordance with the action of the Catholic Church in past ages, in regard to the serfs of Europe, a more gradual system of emancipation could have been adopted, so that they might have been in some measure prepared to make a better use of their freedom, than they are likely to do now.[61]

Such conservatism or lack of enthusiasm for the abolition movement on the part of the Catholic bishops in the United States[62] can be explained in terms of a dislike of the methods and agents of abolitionism.[63] In the Old World the Catholic Church at the time was on the defensive against Marxism, anti-clericalism, extreme liberalism and secularization.[64] The American hierarchy, predominantly European in origin and greatly dependent upon Europe for money and personnel, were inclined to view conditions here from a European vantage point. Thus, they were apt to link American reformers with the much disliked revolutionaries and radicals of the Old World. Many of the Catholic clergy anticipated social chaos as the inevitable accompaniment of any

---

[60] *Ibid.*, 311.

[61] Guilday, *A History of the Council of Baltimore* (New York, 1932), 220.

[62] Archbishop John Purcell and his auxiliary, Bishop Rosecrans, stood apart from their fellow bishops, being advocates of abolition.

[63] Rice, *op. cit.*, 86-109.

[64] Cf. Latourette, *Christianity in a Revolutionary Age* (London, 1959), I.

sudden emancipation of the Negroes.[65] Finally, the presence of active leaders of the "Protestant Crusade" in the councils of abolitionism together with Catholic mistrust of contemporary Utopianism tended to increase their dislike of abolitionists.

Another factor might explain to some extent the attitude of the American hierarchy with regard to the abolition issue. During his official visit to the United States (1853-1854)[66] Archbishop Gaetano Bedini, personal representative of Pope Pius IX, reported that he had given "some advice" to the American bishops concerning the Negro question. The tenor of this advice may be gathered from his subsequent report to Propaganda:

> . . . the problem of the negro slaves in the United States is so delicate that it might be considered dangerous. Even if one limits his interests to the religious aspect of the question, either he is forced to state to which party he belongs, or he is exposed to the consequences of their approval. (. . . .) As matters stand, we must admit that the Bishop, who uses too much zeal in defending one cause or the other is imprudent. Even though he might be able to restrict his work to religious matters, his actions would always be abused or interpreted in a political sense. Therefore, it might be better for the Bishops to show and profess a marked neutrality.[67]

How many American bishops were influenced by this advice of the papal diplomat is a moot question. Bedini admitted that he saw only half of the bishops and usually separately. Futhermore, it is unlikely that the Roman prelate handed out the above advice systematically to every bishop whom he met. After all, his was the delicate task of examining discreetly the deportment of the American bishops without appearing to do so.

---

[65] In an otherwise objective report to Propaganda about the Civil War in America, Bishop Spalding expressed the belief that Lincoln's "atrocious Proclamation" invited "more than three million Negroes . . . to begin servile insurrection, and to massacre the whites—men, women, and children—in the example of the horrible massacre of the whites by the Negroes which took place on the island of San Domingo." Dissertazione Sulla Guerra Civile Americana, 1862; in APF: Scritture Riferite nei Congressi, XX (1863-1865), f.1. (Translation).

[66] Connelly, *The Visit of Archbishop Gaetano Bedini to the United States, (June 1853-Feb. 1854),* 1-15.

[67] Relazione de Monsig. G. Bedini, Arcivescovo di Tebe a S.E. il Sig. Card. Fransoni al suo ritorno dagli Stati Uniti di America, Roma, 12 Luglio 1854; in APF: Scritture Originali Riferite nelle Congregazione Generale, Vol. 981 (1856), ff. 1172r–1208v. Translation in Connelly, *op. cit.,* 193-265.

The tenor of Catholic clerical opinion of abolitionism, according to one historian, was also influenced by the laity.[68] Factors which would have made the Catholic laity in the United States decidedly cool toward the movement were: the affiliation of so many Catholics with the Democratic Party, the nationalist predispositions of the Irish and German immigrant Catholics toward abolitionist activities,[69] and the economic challenge which a free Negro population would be to American Catholics, the bulk of whom belonged to the laboring class.

> Out of all this there had crystallized by 1860, a "Catholic position", unofficial in character, but which commanded, nevertheless, the adherence of the majority of the church membership. It rested first upon the theological argument which denied that slavery was intrinsically wrong. It recognized the existence of evils in the slave system which made eventual emancipation desirable, but it held that such emancipation should come gradually and with due regard for the welfare of society and the protection of the property rights of the owners. Finally, it condemned abolitionism absolutely, both for its methods and for its associations.[70]

Bishop Elder and Slavery

As important a part as slavery played in the events leading up to secession and as much as the institution itself had been under heavy fire as a moral evil for two decades or more before 1861, it may seem strange that the Bishop of Natchez made no public statement, before or during the War, on the moral aspects of domestic slavery. Elder's silence, however, should not be interpreted as an abdication of moral leadership. There simply was no need for such a statement. The South, and Mississippi in particular, was "almost hermetically sealed against abolitionists and abolition arguments."[71] Consequently, consciences of Catholic Mississippians were not being disturbed. For those few Catholic slaveholders in Mississippi whom the abolitionists reached and im-

---

68 Rice, *op. cit.*, 154-155.

69 Irishmen, obsessed with the idea that no nation had so suffered as had theirs at the hands of England, viewed with little favor the interest shown by British anti-slavery groups in the American domestic problem. In this instance it was sufficient to turn them against proposals emanating from a source tainted by contact with John Bull. Similarly the sympathies of German Catholics were alienated by the participation of rationalist and freethinking emigres in abolitionist activity.

70 Rice, *op. cit.*, 155.

71 Dumond, *op. cit.*, 83.

pressed, no statement from their Bishop would have resolved the dilemma which faced them. One of these Catholics, Catherine Minor, described her predicament in this way: "I was always an abolitionist at heart, but I am afraid not a philanthropist. I did not know how to set (my slaves) free without wretchedness to them, and utter ruin to myself." [72] For that matter, for any Catholics looking sincerely for practical moral guidance on the question of slavery, the American bishops at the First Plenary Council of Baltimore in 1852, had already provided a rule of conduct:

> Show your attachment to the institutions of our beloved country by prompt compliance with all their requirements, and by the cautious jealousy with which you guard against the least deviation from the rules which they prescribe for the maintenance of public order and private rights.[73]

In the absence of any public statement by Bishop Elder, it is somewhat difficult to know precisely what his views were on the subject of slavery as it existed in the United States. It would seem, however, that they coincided, more or less, with the views of Bishop Augustine Verot, S.S., Vicar Apostolic of Florida and later Bishop of Savannah, Ga. Early in the War Elder sent fifty copies of a pro-slavery sermon written by Verot to one of his priests serving as chaplain in the Confederate army for distribution among the Catholic soldiers.[74]

Delivered by Bishop Verot on January 4, 1861, in St. Augustine's Church, St. Augustine, Florida, the sermon was published shortly afterward under the title, *A Tract for the Times: Slavery and Abolitionism.*[75] In the beginning of his sermon Verot occupies himself with trying to prove that the assertion of the abolitionists, "who brand Slavery as a moral evil, and a crime against God, religion, humanity, and society," is "unjust, unscriptural, and un-

---

[72] Klingberg, *The Southern Claims Commission,* 108; quoted in Silver (ed.), *Mississippi in the Confederacy* (Baton Rouge, 1961), 299.

[73] Guilday, *National Pastorals of the American Hierarchy, 1792-1919* (Washington, 1923), 192.

[74] Elder to Pont, Natchez, Jan. 2, 1862; in ADNJ, Elder Letter Book—#7, 283.

[75] *A Tract for the Times: Slavery And Abolitionism,* being the substance of a Sermon preached by Rt. Rev. A. Verot, D.D., Vicar Apostolic of Florida in St. Augustine's Church, St. Augustine, Fla. on Jan. 4, 1861, 14 pp.; in APF: Scritture Riferite nei Congressi, XX (1863-1865), ff. 1262.

reasonable." He contends that domestic slavery[76] has received "the sanction of God, of the Church, and of Society at all times, and in all governments." And, when certain conditions are fulfilled, servitude, according to the Florida prelate, can be not only "legitimate, lawful, approved by all laws" but even "consistent with practical religion and true holiness of life in masters." The obligation to meet certain conditions for the legitimacy of domestic slavery stems from the fact that:

> A man, by being a slave, does not cease to be a man, retaining all the properties, qualities, attributes, duties, rights and responsibilities attached to human nature, or to a being endowed with reason and understanding, and made to the image and likeness of God. A master has not over a slave the same rights which he has over an animal, and whoever would view his slaves merely as beasts, would have virtually abjured human nature, and would deserve to be expelled from human society.

That Bishop Verot should have found it necessary to make this ordinarily obvious point is interesting. Evidently, he felt that some Southerners had to be reminded that there was a world of difference between a slave and, for instance, a beast of burden or a bale of cotton. No doubt the Dred Scott decision of 1857, contributed to the existing confusion on this point. However, Verot apparently had no intention of abdicating his right or duty to make moral pronouncements, even if it meant improving upon a judgment of the United States Supreme Court.[77]

In his sermon of 1861, Bishop Verot lists the various conditions which must be fulfilled for the legitimate possession of slaves. First of all, the "libertinism and licentiousness" of slaveowners who take advantage of their slave women must stop. Masters must see to it that the laws of marriage between slaves are respected. Families are not to be separated by sale. Adequate food, clothing and shelter are to be provided at all times. Slaves must be given religious in-

[76] Verot made a distinction between domestic slavery and the African slave trade. The latter he rejected outright as absolutely immoral, in keeping with the pronouncement of Gregory XVI in 1839. Bishop Elder endorsed this view, too, on one of the rare occasions when he committed himself in writing on the subject of slavery. Elder to Perché, Natchez, Feb. 4, 1861; in ADNJ, Elder Letter Book—#6, 37.

[77] Among other things, the Dred Scott decision ruled that in the eyes of the law a slave was just another species of property which the Federal government was bound to protect. Randall, *op. cit.*, 154.

struction. And finally, slaves should be given the opportunity to fulfill their religious obligations. Owners who fail to meet these conditions are declared to be guilty of "grievous sin," while those who live up to their responsibilities will find themselves better served in this world and at the same time assured of their well being in the next by acting as "instruments of the eternal happiness of many."

The need to meet these conditions scrupulously and promptly in 1861 was, as the Bishop saw it, of paramount importance. First of all, "if (the) Confederacy is meant to be solid, durable, stable, and permanent, it must rest upon justice and morality." Therefore, whatever in its domestic institutions offends "justice and morality" must be eliminated. Secondly, if the wrongs associated with the institution "be perserved in, . . . the Almighty, in his justice and wise severity, may sweep Slavery out of the land, not because Slavery is bad in itself, but because man will abuse it through wanton malice." Finally, by reforming the institution the South will be able to prove to the world "that (she) is on the side of justice, morality, reason and religion." [78]

Bishop Verot was not content to leave the reformation of the South's 'peculiar institution' to private initiative. Personal experience and that of his fellow bishops in the South told him how impractical this would have been.[79] Thus, at the end of his sermon he makes the following appeal:

> Let then the wise and the virtuous unite and combine their prudence, their patriotism, their humanity, and their religious integrity to divest Slavery of the features which would make it odious to God and man. Now is the time to make a salutary reform, and to enact judicious regulations. I propose as the means of setting the new Confederacy upon a solid basis, that a servile code be drawn up and adopted by the Confederacy defining clearly the rights and duties of masters, and the rights and duties of slaves.

Bishop Verot's proposal to reform the institution of domestic slavery by legislative action was not something new.[80] At various

---

[78] The existence of slavery along with the abuses connected with it in the South was one of the chief reasons why the Confederacy failed to gain diplomatic recognition from England, France and the Papal States.

[79] (Martin) *Lettre Pastorale de Mgr. L'Evêque de Natchitoches a L'Occasion de la Guerre du Sud pour Son Independence,* 21 août 1861; in APF: Scritture Riferite nei Congressi, XIX (1861-1862), ff. 1207.

[80] Wiley, *Southern Negroes,* 166-172.

times before 1861, attempts had been made by religious groups in the South to have legislation introduced which would humanize the institution, but the movement made little headway for fear that Northern abolitionists would use admission of abuses in slavery to the detriment of the institution. The severance of political ties with the enemies of slavery and the establishment of a government pledged to its protection gave rise to a renewal of the agitation for reform.[81] During the last two years of the War the movement was viewed with increasing favor by both clergymen and laymen,[82] but unfortunately very little was accomplished in the way of remedial legislation. Certainly no servile code, as suggested by Bishop Verot, was ever drawn up and adopted by the Confederacy.

No attempt has been made here to present and evaluate the arguments drawn up by Bishop Verot in support of his pro-slavery thesis, which we believe represents Bishop Elder's view, too. Nevertheless, it is interesting to note what was the reaction of the Sacred Congregation of Propaganda[83] in Rome to Bishop Verot's sermon of January, 1861. A printed copy of the sermon has been discovered in the archives of Propaganda. On the back side of the document is written this terse comment of the Secretary of the Congregation: "It would seem that one cannot accept everything which is affirmed in this argument."[84] Whether logic and the facts supported Verot's thesis or not, Rome's reaction to the sermon could well have been expected, for the sentiment in Europe at the time of the American Civil War was strongly anti-slavery. In fact, the impression had been created by the United States government that the War was being fought to abolish slavery. How well informed the Pope and the Roman Curia were as to the issues involved in the

[81] The program of reform as advocated in 1861 and 1862, was limited largely to the enactment of measures recognizing and protecting slaves' marriages and the repeal of laws which forbade teaching slaves to read. In 1863, it was extended to include: the passage of laws prohibiting the separation of mothers from their children by sales; the admission of the testimony of slaves in court as equivalent to circumstantial evidence; a restriction of the practice among absentee owners of entrusting the control of their slaves to overseers; and the repeal of laws prohibiting slaves from assembling and exhorting one another in religious meetings. Wiley, *op. cit.,* 167.

[82] Active supporters of the movement among Protestant religious leaders were: Bishop Elliott of Ga., Rev. W. B. W. Howe of S.C., Rev. James A. Lyon of Miss., Edward A. Pollard of Va., and Calvin H. Wiley of N.C.

[83] The Catholic Church in the United States was under the immediate jurisdiction of this Roman Congregation up until Nov., 1908.

[84] "Non sembra però poter ammettersi tutto ciò che in tale argomento si afferma."

American conflict it is difficult to say.[85] Of one thing, though, we can be sure: to Pius IX the future of slavery in the South was a vital issue. When the Confederate agent, Dudley A. Mann, came to Rome with the hope of obtaining diplomatic recognition for his government, Pius delicately suggested, as Mann later reported to the Confederate Secretary of State, "that it might perhaps be judicious in us to consent to gradual emancipation." [86] In any case, Verot's sermon, with its great emphasis on the acceptance of domestic slavery by scriptural and church authority and with its failure to mention emancipation even as a remote possibility, did not win the full approval of the Holy See.

Bishop Elder's Policy

One factor, more than any other, will explain Bishop Elder's cautious attitude whenever he was forced to approach the delicate issues of secession and slavery before or during the War. Ever present in his mind was the fear that any stand which he might publicly take on either of these issues would be construed as the official position of the Catholic Church with the consequent danger of alienating a portion of his flock or of stirring up prejudice and hatred for the Church. The outrages perpetrated against the Church by the Nativists and more recently by the Know-Nothings in the country made this danger very real. So genuine was this fear that the Bishop of Natchez even recommended that his people "speak & act with their fellow citizens as fellow citizens & not . . . bring forward their religion in arguing, as if it had pronounced on the questions, expression of fact or of human judgment, involved in the case." [87]

[85] Although Fr. Leo Stock in his article, "Catholic Participation in the Diplomacy of the Southern Confederacy," CHR, XVI (April, 1930), 17, suggests that Pius IX was not too well informed on the American Civil War, I am inclined to believe that Pius and the interested parties in the Roman Curia were well acquainted with the issues and developments. During the War the American bishops continued to correspond with the Holy See. Many did not hesitate on these occasions to discuss the War, sometimes at great length. Spalding's full length report, for the most part quite objective, should have been especially informative. Furthermore, through the War a U.S. minister was resident in Rome who had frequent access to Pius IX and Antonelli. And when Mr. Mann, the Confederate agent, arrived in the Eternal City, he too was cordially received by the Pope once and by the Cardinal Secretary of State twice.

[86] Mann to Benjamin, Rome, Nov. 14, 1863; in *Official Records: Navy*, Ser. II, Vol. III, 952-955.

[87] Elder to Duggan, Natchez, March 5, 1861; in ADNJ, Elder Letter Book —#6, 96.

Unfortunately, not all of the American bishops were as circumspect as the Bishop of Natchez. Apparently, some of them did not even see "the impropriety of giving the express sanction of religion" to one or the other of the various solutions being proposed for the settlement of political differences between the North and the South.[88] For instance, Bishop James Whelan, O.P. of Nashville openly expressed his northern sympathies and fraternized with Union officers. As a result, he completely alienated the members of his flock as well as local non-Catholics and was forced to resign his see and retire to a monastery of his Order in May, 1863.[89] Farther south in Louisiana, Bishop Martin did not hesitate to express his ideas on slavery through the official medium of a pastoral letter.[90] Although he made a number of extravagant claims for slavery on this occasion,[91] he was in no danger of alienating his flock, for the institution was too well entrenched in his diocese and, for that matter, operating lucratively. However, his public statements must have surely embarrassed his Northern colleagues. In the North some Catholic bishops, it was reported, were acting equally indiscreetly. To his metropolitan Bishop Elder complained that:

> Bishops—like Bp. Timon—(are) recommending that the war be vigorous so as to be speedily ended—It sounds very strange to my ears:—& coming from one who has so often appealed to the charity of the South.[92]

So critical was Elder of the Northern bishops and priests on this score that he asked the Archbishop of New Orleans:

> Would it not be well for you to write a letter of expostulation to some of our Northern Brethren—in reference to their fierce exhortations to war? (. . . .) I think if the clergy of the North would take a more moderate & charitable view of our affairs, they would greatly soothe the excitement that exists & allay the violence of public opinion.[93]

---

88 *Ibid.*

89 O'Daniel, *The Father of the Church in Tennessee,* 573-574.

90 (Martin) *Lettre Pastorale de Mgr. L'Evêque de Natchitoches a L'Occasion de la Guerre du Sud pour Son Independence,* 21 août 1861; in APF: Scritture Riferite nei Congressi, XIX (1861-1862), ff. 1207.

91 Among other things Martin referred to the Negro slaves as "children of the race of Chanaan, upon whom the curse of an outraged Father continues to weigh heavily" and described Southern slavery as "the manifest will of God," that "far from being an evil" it "could be an eminently Christian work."

92 Elder to Odin, Biloxi, June 15, 1861; in AUND: New Orleans Papers. Bishop John Timon, C.M. of Buffalo, N. Y. had done missionary work in Mississippi in 1839 and in 1844.

93 *Ibid.*

The Northern bishop who drew heavy criticism from Elder was Archbishop John Purcell of Cincinnati. This prelate prior to secession had been "judiciously conservative." [94] Even two weeks after the firing on Fort Sumter he agreed with his suffragans that it was best for them to pursue a policy of neutrality.[95] Living in the North as he did it is understandable that he would be loyal to the Union cause. However, as the months rolled by the Archbishop became quite vocal in his support of the Lincoln administration and its policies. Publicly he expressed his joy at the abolition of slavery and admitted that he found nothing objectionable in the way it was accomplished. Soon he began to denounce by name in public those who disagreed with the administration's policies. Thus, he rebuked not only the Catholic editors, James A. McMaster of the *Freeman's Journal* and John Mullaly of the *Metropolitan Record,* but even the Episcopal bishop of Vermont, John Henry Hopkins. Such activity annoyed and embarrassed Purcell's suffragans, especially Bishop Martin Spalding of Louisville.[96] In the end, Spalding felt obliged to report his metropolitan to the Holy See. This he did in January, 1864, and again in March of that year.[97] The Louisville prelate charged Purcell with abandoning the line of conduct agreed upon by the bishops of the Province at the beginning of the War, namely, to abstain from all political agitation; [98] with neglecting to publish the Pope's peace appeal as was customary whenever receiving a papal letter; with failing to communicate this same letter to his suffragans; and, finally, with allowing his diocesan journal, edited by his brother and vicar-general, to become a "most violent political newspaper." [99]

As early as 1863, Bishop Elder expressed annoyance with the

[94] Rice, *op. cit.,* 127.

[95] Pastoral Letter of the Third Provincial Council of Cincinnati to the Clergy and Laity, Cincinnati, 1861, 6; quoted by Murphy, "The Catholic Church in the United States During the Civil War Period (1852-1866)," in RACHS, XXXIX (Dec. 1928), 303.

[96] At least so Spalding reported to Propaganda in 1864. The other suffragans at this time were: Bishops Louis A. Rappe of Cleveland, Maurice de St. Palais of Vincennes, and Frederick Rese of Detroit. At this time Rese was in Europe and the Diocese of Detroit was being administered by his coadjutor, Peter Lefebvre.

[97] Spalding to Barnabò, Louisville, March 8, 1864 and March 30, 1864; in APF: Scritture Riferite nei Congressi, XX (1863-1865), ff. 725, 749.

[98] Pastoral Letter of the Third Provincial Council of Cincinnati to the Clergy and Laity, Cincinnati, 1861, 6; quoted by Murphy, *op. cit.,* 303.

[99] Editor Purcell's views are discussed by Rice, *op. cit.,* 127-129.

line of conduct being followed by the Archbishop of Cincinnati.[100] What irked the Natchez prelate was Purcell's very loud and unqualified endorsement of Lincoln's Emancipation Proclamation. Purcell seemed to be completely oblivious of the consequences of immediate and violent emancipation as envisioned by the Southern bishops, namely, social, economic and political chaos. Even after problems began to multiply for the North as it tried to provide for the thousands of slaves who flocked to the Union lines, there was no let-up from Cincinnati. Spalding advised the Bishop of Natchez to write to the Cardinal Prefect of Propaganda about the Archbishop and his diocesan newspaper, *The Catholic Telegraph,* but Elder felt loath to take such a step in regard to one "so venerable & so estimable." [101]

Elder finally had a personal clash with the Archbishop of Cincinnati in the spring of 1864. How the trouble started Elder explained in a letter to his own metropolitan, Archbishop Odin:

> Some months ago I wrote to the Arbp. Cincinnati that I cd. not ordain just now a Seminarian who is there, because by law he wd. be liable to conscription.—The Telegraph published that a Bishop in the rebel states *"warns us not to encourage clergymen to return South because all not in charge of congregations are conscripted."* I wrote to the Arbp. representing that if it was my letter that was alluded to the paragraph was incorrect, & it was liable to bring odium on us. I begged him to rectify it. He acknowledged that it is my letter—but he sees nothing to rectify.[102]

In January, 1864, one of Elder's priests, the newly ordained Father Patrick O'Connor, was ordered to report for active duty in the Confederate army, because, according to the conscription officer, the draft law exempted only those who were "licensed to preach" before the law's enactment in April of 1862.[103] In view of this interpretation Elder had written to Purcell, apparently advising him not to send south one of his students who was ready for ordination until the matter was cleared up. As a result of this private communication there appeared in the March 2 issue of *The Catholic Telegraph* the following article:

---

[100] Elder to Spalding, Natchez, Dec. 30, 1863; in ADNJ, Elder Letter Book #–9, 58.

[101] Elder to Odin, Fair Oaks near Natchez, June 9, 1864; in AUND: New Orleans Papers.

[102] *Ibid.*

[103] Elder to Odin, Natchez, Feb. 6, 1864; in ADNJ, Elder Letter Book –#9, 139.

> A Bishop, writing from one of the Rebel States, warns us against encouraging clergymen to return to the South while the Confederate Government is in power. All clergymen not in charge of congregations, he writes, have been conscripted; and even the pastors in charge, he says, will be forced, he fears, into the ranks of the army.[104]

Regardless of the exact content of Elder's letter to Purcell, one can easily imagine the embarrassment which such an article would have caused the Bishop of Natchez. Elder immediately recognized the "immense mischief" which the article was liable to cause, not only "because it is untrue," but also because "the circulation of a falsehood attributed to a Bishop will draw odium on the whole Church."[105] It could even bring on each bishop of the South "the suspicion of writing a falsehood to damage the Southern Confederacy."[106] Elder was particularly alarmed, because only he and the Archbishop of New Orleans could easily communicate with Cincinnati.[107] If the article in *The Catholic Telegraph* was not due to malice, it surely manifested a lack of propriety and good judgment on the part of both the Archbishop and his brother, for, as Elder pointed out to Odin, his communication to Archbishop Purcell was "a private letter in private business, with which the Editor of the paper had nothing to do."[108] Elder himself could explain the appearance of the article only in terms of "a fanaticism in the cause of abolition."[109]

When the article, supposedly based on Bishop Elder's letter, first appeared, the Mississippi prelate thought that it would be well for Archbishop Odin to register a protest with the Archbishop of Cincinnati for "allowing such mischievous articles" to appear in the diocesan paper.[110] There is no evidence, however, that Odin acted on this suggestion. When Purcell refused to correct the misrepresentation as requested by Elder, the Bishop of Natchez thought

104 *The Catholic Telegraph,* Cincinnati, March 2, 1864, 76.

105 Elder to Odin, Vicksburg, April 14, 1864; in AUND: New Orleans Papers.

106 Elder to Odin, Fair Oaks near Natchez, June 9, 1864; in AUND: New Orleans Papers.

107 Elder to Odin, Vicksburg, April 14, 1864; in AUND: New Orleans Papers.

108 Elder to Odin, Fair Oaks near Natchez, June 9, 1864; in AUND: New Orleans Papers.

109 *Ibid.*

110 Elder to Odin, Vicksburg, April 14, 1864; in AUND: New Orleans Papers.

of writing to Cardinal Barnabò, prefect of Propaganda. Before doing so he asked his metropolitan's advice.[111]

While waiting for a reply from Archbishop Odin, Elder sent a "little paragraph" to the *Catholic Mirror* of Baltimore with the hope that it might correct the mischief done.[112] In it Elder was careful to make no reference to the Archbishop of Cincinnati and dealt only with the newspaper.[113] He also wrote a letter to Purcell which apparently did more harm than good. When writing to Martin Spalding, the newly appointed archbishop of Baltimore, in late July, Elder described the response which his letter to Purcell drew:

> I have another letter from (Cincinnati). I never understood before the force of your remark about a great change from the person we used to admire & love.—It is short, but it shows a temper & unreasonableness which frightens me. —Instead of writing to the Palazzo del Col. Urbano—I had thought it wd. have as good an effect to tell him frankly I had been advised to do so "by a person of great prudence." I told him also that I had sent a moderate correction of that unhappy paragraph. (You have seen it in the Mirror of the 9th inst.) I wrote frankly, but as affectionately as I could. —He answers with indignation at my "threats"—& threatens to use my letters if he pleases.[114]

When Purcell's letter arrived, Elder, fearful that their quarrel might become public, wrote the Cincinnati prelate "a most humble & imploring letter—that there may be no division—& above all that there be no scandal before the public." Elder confided to his friend in Baltimore:

> I hope it will reach his heart.—If he shd. give a violent answer to the correction in the Mirror, it is my intention not to notice it—unless compelled. I shall consult the Archbp. N.O. —I wd. rather suffer a good deal—than have any appearance of division before the people.[115]

Fortunately, there the matter rested; neither prelate pursued the quarrel any further.[116]

---

111 Elder to Odin, Fair Oaks near Natchez, June 9, 1864; in AUND: New Orleans Papers.

112 Elder to Odin, Natchez, July 12, 1864; in AUND: New Orleans Papers.

113 *Catholic Mirror,* Baltimore, July 9, 1864.

114 Elder to Spalding, Natchez, July 22, 1864; in AAB, 33-T-5.

115 *Ibid.*

116 The quarrel must have been patched up, for in 1880, when the Archbishop found himself in financial straits, he successfully requested the appointment of Bishop Elder as his coadjutor.

The Catholic Telegraph, however, continued to exasperate the Bishop of Natchez until, finally, in August of 1865, four months after the cessation of hostilities, Elder suggested that Archbishop Spalding write to the Holy See and request that the editor, Father Edward Purcell, be officially rebuked. He urged the Archbishop to press for "an injunction—(no *advice* nor *remonstrance*—to be thrown away) but a positive injunction—& all the better if under pain of censure." [117]

The drastic action proposed by Bishop Elder was the result of a letter from a Philadelphia correspondent which the editor published in the June 28th issue of the *Telegraph.* In it the correspondent denounced by name Bishop Lynch of Charleston who in the spring of 1864 had gone to Europe as an officially appointed Confederate commissioner to the Papal States.[118] Writing to Archbishop Spalding, the Bishop of Natchez gave vent to his indignation over the letter's appearance in the *Telegraph:*

> I do not remember that I have ever seen nor heard of before—an open attack on a Bishop by name, in any paper published under ecclesiastical authority. It looks (to) me like an outrage on every Bishop whether of North or South. (. . . .) This is very different from all the other strange things that have appeared in that paper. The denouncing of all in general—as traitors, rebels, man-stealers, &c. &c.—may or may not include Bishops. He may pretend not to know what a Bishop's sentiments are:—but to name a Bishop & declare him guilty of political treason—& likewise of horrible crimes against God & society—is something unheard of—& incredible if it were not certain.[119]

Elder refused to excuse the editor of the *Telegraph* on the grounds that he was simply presenting the views of his correspondent, for as Elder pointed out to his friend in Baltimore:

> I examined three or four successive numbers to see if there was any excuse offered—or any rebuke to the writer. I have not seen any.—The last number that I did see, re-

---

[117] Elder to Spalding, Jackson, Aug. 17, 1865; in AAB, 33-U-9.

[118] Lynch's mission was a failure. He had frequent interviews in Rome with Antonelli and several audiences with the Pope, but his cause was given neither recognition nor encouragement. He was received at the Quirinal only in his episcopal position, never as an accredited representative of Davis or the Confederacy. Stock, "Catholic Participation in the Diplomacy of the Southern Confederacy," in CHR, XVI (April 1930), 17-18.

[119] Elder to Spalding, Jackson, Aug. 17, 1865; in AAB, 33-U-9.

jected another letter of the Philadelphia correspondent, as "unfit for the columns of the Telegraph"—because it censured President Johnson—who, the Editor thinks "is doing the best he can." [120]

Elder's loyalty to the South did not blind him to questionable policies pursued by Southern Catholic editors. Two papers in particular, both of New Orleans, drew his criticism. They were the *Catholic Standard* and *Le Propagateur catholique,* a French-language newspaper. Both papers, even before the outbreak of the War, seemed disposed to identify religion with the cause of the South and to assume the role of official spokesmen for the Catholics of the South.[121] For example, in 1861 in the January 26 issue of *Le Propagateur catholique,* the editor, Father Napoleon Perché, wrote an article entitled "Les Catholiques du Sud." Presuming to clarify for all interested parties the attitude of Catholics toward secession, Perché declared:

> that among the clergymen and Catholics in the South there exists a very definite opinion, one determined neither by passion nor by sectarianism, but by reasons of conscience. They agree on the following points: 1. Each State is sovereign. Upon joining the Union, the States had agreed to forfeit certain of their rights, but not their sovereignty. 2. Due to their sovereignty, the States maintained the right to secede from the Union whenever they judged that reasons of honor, liberty, or security were sufficient to warrant such a separation. 3. For the Southern States, these sufficient motives exist today. Therefore, the States which seceded (or are about to do so) have acted (or will act) legitimately, within the limits of their rights. 4. It is a duty for the residents of a State already separated to recognize no other sovereign authority but that of his State.
>
> Since these are questions of principle, one can rest assured that Catholics agree on these points and will act accordingly. They will show firmness and courage, unselfishness and devotion in their loyalty to the State, because patriotism is for them a religious duty.[122]

Elder was quick to object to the position and the way in which Perché had committed all the Catholics of the South. Writing "as

[120] *Ibid.*

[121] Elder to Duggan, Natchez, Feb. 19, 1861; in ADNJ, Elder Letter Book —#6, 65.

[122] *Le Propagateur catholique,* Nouvelle-Orleans, 26 jan. 1861. (Transtion).

a Southern Catholic" to the priest-editor a few days after the article appeared, the Bishop outlined four possible positions which Catholics could adopt to support justifiably their state's decision to secede and, then, he continued.

> Now any of these positions is perfectly consistent with Catholic morality—& with the highest patriotism. And as you seem to speak in the name of the Catholics of the South —it is important that you do not appear to commit them to one or the other of these views.—If you think proper to advocate one of these yourself in the Propagateur,—although I do not advise your doing so,—yet you must use your own judgment:—but when you write as a representative of *all* of *us*, & declare what *our* opinions are—you must have the largest liberty.—I, therefore, as one of the "Catholiques du Sud"—beg you to make your statement of our opinions more clear to all.[123]

When Father Perché did not reply to Bishop Elder's letter and when the desired clarification failed to appear in the New Orleans paper, Elder still thought seriously enough of the matter to look for outside help. Thus, he approached the Bishop of Chicago. The letter to Bishop Duggan, dated February 19, 1861, is especially interesting, because it reveals Elder's attitude toward "Diocesan Organs," an expression which he never admired or used for Catholic papers. "It occurs to me," wrote Elder to Duggan,

> that it would be well for you to publish an article not over your name—but in a tone which will make it be accepted as a sound Catholic statement—explaining that Bishops are not to be considered as endorsing all the opinions of Catholic papers (?)—& that they do not recognize newspapers as the mediums for giving authoritative decisions in morals.—If you choose to refer to Mr. Perché—you can explain that even if he thinks proper to publish his views of morals in the paper —it is still his view—that he is not acting as an authorized teacher. He may decide as a theologian but his decision has only the authority that each individual chooses to give to it—or rather—say no authority—only weight, according to each one's estimate of his theological accuracy.[124]

The suggested article Elder thought would do much good, but he was convinced that such a statement should originate in the

---

[123] Elder to Perché, Natchez, Feb. 4, 1861; in ADNJ, Elder Letter Book —#6, 37.

[124] Elder to Duggan, Natchez, Feb. 19, 1861; in ADNJ, Elder Letter Book —#6, 65.

North. Were it to come from the South, the Bishop felt that it would be misunderstood and, for that matter, even "disaffect some Catholics from their political duty." [125] A month later Elder was still annoyed by the trend among Southern Catholic papers which he apparently failed to check. How much better it would have been, so Elder thought, if Southern Catholic editors had left the Church to "proceed in her own way, enlightening (individual) consciences—& leaving judgments free." [126]

---

[125] *Ibid.*

[126] Elder to Keogh, Natchez, March 14, 1861; in ADNJ, Elder Letter Book —#6, 132.

Chapter VIII

THE FIRST YEAR OF THE WAR

Catholic response to the formation of the Confederacy and later to the outbreak of war would appear to have been no more and no less enthusiastic than that of the State's Protestant majority. In other words, Catholic Mississippians acted no differently from their fellow citizens.

Ecclesiastical Recognition

In the wake of the news from Jackson that the State had seceded from the Union, Bishop Elder urged quick adjustment of church services to the fait accompli. Thus, on January 10, he addressed the following circular letter to his clergy:

> Revd. & dear Sir
>
> If you are in the practice of reciting in public the prayers for the Ruling Powers—continue to do so.—But as we have heard that our connection with the Federal Government has been dissolved—if the information be confirmed—you will make the following alterations.
>
> In the third paragraph—instead of *'President of these United States'*—read *'Governor of this State.'* Instead of *'Congress'*—read—*'our Legislature.'*—During the sitting of the Convention—read—*'our Convention & Legislature.'*
>
> In the fourth paragraph omit—*'for his Excellency'*—down to *'Assembly'* inclusive: & read thus: *'we pray for all judges ———'* &c.
>
> In the fifth paragraph omit———*'throughout the United States.'*
>
> Urge the faithful to continue praying for God's guidance and protection:—& resume the prayer at Mass Pro quacumque necessitate—until March 4th.
>
> † William Henry
> Bp. Natchez.[1]

---

[1] Elder to Leray, Natchez, Jan. 10, 1861; in AUND: New Orleans Papers. Also in Gerow, *Cradle Days of St. Mary's*, 146.

A month later an opportunity, not of his own making, presented itself to the Bishop for demonstrating publicly his support of the Confederacy. On Washington's Birthday a city-wide celebration was to be held in Natchez in honor of the formation of the new government at Montgomery. Elder was invited to officiate as chaplain at the celebration. Although his priests who at the time were assembled in the city for their retreat advised him to accept, Elder declined the invitation on account of religious scruples. Assuring the Grand Marshal that his refusal did not stem "from a want of appreciating the compliment paid him or from a want of cordial rejoicing in the happy event of the formation of our new Confederacy, & our Provisional Government," Elder went on to excuse himself on the grounds that he would feel "greatly embarrassed to appear for a Public act of Religious Worship or to so honor the occasion without the exterior attendence and forms which are of use for a Bishop in our Church." [2] The "attendance and forms," demanded by the Bishop of Natchez, could not be furnished, because his clergy were making a religious retreat.

Such was the reason assigned by Elder in his reply to the Grand Marshal. However, in a letter to Archbishop Kenrick of Baltimore, Elder acknowledged another reason for his refusal of the invitation:

> The occasion led me to consider further whether it is exactly well for either Bishops or Priests to officiate—by offering prayers &c., before mixed bodies—& in circumstances in which they have to *avoid* what is *distinctively* Catholic . . . Does not the practice strongly favor the prevailing spirit of indifferentism or community in religion—the great heresy of our day? [3]

The excuse offered to the Grand Marshal would seem to indicate a lack of wholesome flexibility and adaptability on the part of Bishop Elder. The other reason, which Elder advanced in his letter to Kenrick, seems to betray a conservative attitude, almost over-cautious even for his day, in the field of Catholic-Protestant relations. Regardless of his motives, Elder's refusal of the invitation could well have provoked bad-feeling and even the suspicion of disloyalty. Probably with this in mind, the Bishop di-

[2] Elder to Metcalfe, Natchez, Feb. 21, 1861; in ADNJ, Elder Letter Book—#6, 69.

[3] Elder to Kenrick (?), undated; in AAB, 29-D-12.

rected that the Cathedral rectory and the girls' orphanage be illuminated and the front windows of the Cathedral be lighted up on the night of the celebration.[4]

Catholic Volunteers

In the early days of the Confederacy no one knew whether to prepare for war or not; the prevailing view in the South was that secession had been peacefully established. Nevertheless early in February Governor Pettus of Mississippi received an order to furnish seven regiments for the Confederate army by March 15. The response to the Governor's call for enlistments was enthusiastic.[5] Thousands of volunteers poured into local camps. On March 26, the first troops left the State; twenty-five companies, recruited mainly from the northeastern and southwestern counties, were sent to Pensacola, Florida. During the spring and summer, volunteering, sparked by the actual outbreak of hostilities, went on at a rapid pace. Few Mississippians at the time envisioned the war as being other than brief and victorious for the South. By July 25, about 125 companies had been mustered into service and nearly fifty more were still waiting to be accepted.[6] Without too much exaggeration, Governor Pettus could report to President Davis that the entire State was "in a fever to get into the field." [7]

Catholic Mississippians appeared to be just as eager as the rest of the young men in the State to get into the field. Sometimes they were organized into distinctively Catholic companies, such as, the "Sarsfield Southrons," commanded by Captain Felix Hughes,[8] or the "Jeff Davis Guards," both from the Vicksburg area.[9] Most of the time, however, they joined units which made no attempt to organize on a denominational basis. Thus, the fact that there were about 350 Catholics in the 16th Mississippi Regiment was purely accidental.[10] Almost every Catholic congregation in the State had

---

[4] Elder to Layton, Natchez, Feb. 25, 1861; in ADNJ, Elder Letter Book –#6, 75.

[5] Bettersworth, *Confederate Mississippi* (Baton Rouge, 1943), 17-18, 25-27.

[6] *Ibid.,* 30.

[7] Pettus to Davis, May 3, 1861, in *Official Records: Army,* Ser. IV, Vol. I, 277.

[8] "M.J. Mulvihill Sketches Work of Priests of Past Years, Tells of Rockwood Family," in *Vicksburg Evening Post,* July 2, 1934.

[9] Walker, *Vicksburg, A People at War, 1860-1865,* 50, 58.

[10] Boheme to Elder, Paulding, March 9, 1862; in ADNJ, File: Elder–B.

members in the army before long. Some were young men like Samuel and Edward Perrault of Natchez who interrupted their studies at Spring Hill College in Mobile to join the army.[11] Others like Dr. Richard O'Leary of Sharon and Martin Hughes of Vicksburg who had just finished their professional training postponed embarking on a career to go off to war.[12] Many others were like William Hamel and his brother of Yazoo City who, though in the country less than two years, decided to throw their lot in with the South.[13] Some were heads of families whose pride would not let them stay behind. Father Boheme of Paulding reported to Bishop Elder that from his small congregation twelve married men with families enlisted in Captain J. J. Shannon's newly recruited company before it left for Virginia.[14] And, finally, there were a few runaway boys like thirteen-year old Baldasero Genasci of Grand Gulf who talked himself into the army [15] and Dennis Mulvihill of Natchez who at the age of fourteen stole away on a steamboat to join the Natchez Fencibles.[16]

As men volunteered and companies were formed during the spring and summer of 1861, Bishop Elder and his priests kept busy preparing the Catholics in these units spiritually and materially. Happily Elder could report to Dr. McCaffrey of Emmitsburg after the first rush to war subsided: "Almost all our Catholic soldiers approach the Sacraments and carry with them their prayer book, crucifix and medal." [17] Sometimes special religious ceremonies were conducted by Elder and his priests for the various units just prior to their departure for the front. Thus, at Sulphur Springs Father Guillou celebrated a special Mass for the volunteers from his congregation who assisted at the service in the company of their friends and neighbors. At the Mass they were all invested

---

[11] Interviews with Miss Isabell Perrault and Mrs. Mary Foggo, Natchez, Oct. 6, 1961.

[12] *Biographical and Historical Memoirs of Mississippi* (Chicago, 1891), vol. II, 531; vol. I, 977-978.

[13] Interview with Miss Maggie Hamel Schaffer, Vicksburg, Oct. 8, 1961. Also *Biographical and Historical Memoirs,* vol. I, 845.

[14] Boheme to Elder, Paulding, March 20, 1862; in ADNJ, File: Elder–B.

[15] Interview by telephone with Mr. Louis Theobald, Sr., Vicksburg, Oct. 8, 1961.

[16] Autobiographical Notes of Michael J. Mulvihill (1855-1935); in private library of Mulvihill family, Vicksburg, Miss.

[17] Elder to McCaffrey, Natchez, July, 1861; in Meline & McSweeney, *The Story of the Mountain,* II, 8.

with the medal of the Immaculate Conception.[18] In May, 1861, the "Jeff Davis Guards," just before they left Vicksburg, attended a special Mass in St. Paul's Church during which their flag was blessed by Father Leray.[19] Bishop Elder performed a similar ceremony for the "Tom Weldon Rebels" on Christmas Day, 1861. After the sheriff presented them with their flag, the Bishop blessed it, and then the whole company with arms, attended the celebration of high Mass in the Cathedral—a "novel spectacle" for the Protestants of Natchez.[20]

Early Impact

Although for many people in Mississippi war was a very distant thing during the summer and fall of 1861———dispatches printed in newspapers and letters from soldiers, for Bishop Elder the War made itself felt from the start. First of all, building programs had to be postponed or curtailed. As early as January, 1861, the Bishop advised Father Leduc at Bay St. Louis to modify his plans to enlarge the Sisters' academy "because of the disturbed state of Public Affairs" at the time.[21] A few days after the bombardment of Fort Sumter, Elder wrote to Father Leray, who was preparing to build an extension for the Sisters of Mercy at Vicksburg, and cautioned the priest not to make any contracts based on previous offers of assistance from himself. "The news of real, formidable war," the Bishop confessed,

> interferes essentially with my engagements.—For the advance which I promised towards the Sisters' building—I relied on my allocation from the Propagation. But war—especially on sea—will so interrupt communication that I cannot tell when it can be received—nor whether it may not be lost. —I relied also on a loan promised to me. But just now I understand the person, who promised it will probably join the army:—if he does so, he will want to leave his money available for his family.[22]

This project, even though the Bishop was later able to make a loan of $2,000 to the Sisters, was postponed until after the War.

[18] Parish Record, Sulphur Springs, (1841-1926); in parish archives, Camden; copy in ADNJ, 25.

[19] Walker, *op. cit.*, 58.

[20] Bettersworth, *Confederate Mississippi,* 287.

[21] Elder to Leduc, Natchez, Jan. 25, 1861; in ADNJ, Elder Letter Book —#6, 5.

[22] Elder to Leray, Natchez, April 16, 1861; in AUND: New Orleans Papers.

At the end of April, Elder wrote a similar letter to Father Mouton, who was planning to build a number of churches in the long-neglected northeastern part of the State:

> In any ordinary circumstances I would certainly authorize you to purchase the lot in Columbus on my security —& I would contribute something to the building of all the churches you propose.—But in the present lamentable condition of affairs, it is out of my power to contribute; & it would be very imprudent for me to take on myself any new obligations.—I can only therefore recommend you to go on to do all that you can accomplish at present—& meanwhile urge the people to pray for peace, that we may undertake something more.[23]

And, finally, for many of the same reasons, Elder also decided to abandon his pet project—the founding of a preparatory seminary at Sulphur Springs—in early December, 1861.[24]

While his fellow citizens were rejoicing over the news of the South's apparently smashing victory at Bull Run—the first major battle of the War, Bishop Elder received information that was less heartening and for which he could blame the War. The Sisters of St. Joseph at Sulphur Springs would be leaving the Diocese for good on August 2. One can well imagine what a reversal this was for the Bishop. As early as 1859, the Sisters had drawn high praise from Elder:

> Your Academy has been but a few years in existence. If I am rightly informed, it has not only paid its current expenses, but discharged a considerable amount of debt. It has given instruction & edification to many Catholics around; it has taught an esteem for our holy religion to many who were filled with prejudice. It has formed part of the centre for one of the most consoling Congregations in the diocese; it has had a large share in the magnificent work of changing a woody wilderness into a happy settlement of true worshippers of God.[25]

---

[23] Elder to Mouton, Natchez, April 30, 1861; in ADNJ, Elder Letter Book—#6, 203.

[24] Elder to Finucane, Natchez, Dec. 4, 1861; in ADNJ, Elder Letter Book—#7, 221.

[25] Elder to Mother Leonie, Natchez, Feb. 3, 1859; in ADNJ, Elder Letter Book—#3, 193.

During the past school year the Sisters had had 108 boarders and day scholars.[26] Surely their school was one of the best in the fledgling diocesan school system.

Admittedly there had been difficulty from the start. The boarders were never numerous enough to provide the Sisters with a sufficient income. The academy's isolation and, for awhile, charges which were thought to be too high accounted for the school's failure to attract many boarders.[27] As early as 1859, the Sisters thought of withdrawing; Father Guillou, their chaplain, suggested instead that they transfer the academy to Vicksburg; but Bishop Elder disapproved of any change on the grounds that insufficient time had been allowed for the project to develop. In a postscript to his letter to the Superior at Sulphur Springs he added what he considered a "very strong consideration" for opposing any immediate change:

> It is the heavy expense that the generous Catholics of the neighbourhood have undergone, to establish your house. They have a right in common justice that every effort be made & every method tried to obtain success.[28]

So matters rested until 1861. A few weeks after Mississippi seceded from the Union, Mother Leonie, the superior at the Springs, again informed the Bishop of her intention to obtain leave to close down the academy and withdraw from the Diocese. The news took Elder by surprise:

> I do not know yet what to say.—It would be a sorrowful thing in our Diocese—so desolate of good religious establishments—to take a step backward—& abandon one of the few.—It would be doubly sorrowful—because I have had so much reason to admire the zeal & good will of yourself & your good Sisters—& I feel so much indebted to you for all you have done.[29]

---

[26] Meador, "Sulphur Springs Parish," in *Catholic Action of the South* (Natchez Centennial Edition), Oct. 14, 1937, 48.

[27] Elder to Mother Leonie, Natchez, Feb. 3, 1859; in ADNJ, Elder Letter Book—#3, 193.

[28] *Ibid.*

[29] Elder to Mother Leonie, Natchez, Feb. 27, 1861; in ADNJ, Elder Letter Book—#6, 80.

This time, however, he could not speak of the Sisters acting precipitously. He was faced with the fact that the school was simply not succeeding as well as the Sisters had a right to expect.[30]

Rather than lose the Sisters completely, Elder suggested that they consider the possibility of establishing their academy elsewhere in the Diocese, in keeping with an earlier suggestion. Apparently the Superior was amenable to the idea. Four different sites were proposed to the Sisters, namely, Canton, Columbus, Holly Springs and Biloxi.[31] Eventually, the Bishop himself ruled out all of them, except Biloxi.[32] Beyond this nothing else was done in the spring of 1861, to prepare for a transfer. In the meanwhile war broke out, and the boarders were called home by their parents.[33] Growing a little impatient and perhaps a little nervous in view of the political events, Mother Leonie announced her intention of visiting the motherhouse at Carondelet, Missouri, to explain the situation personally to her major superior. Understandably apprehensive, Elder quickly wrote to the nun, asking her to defer her visit to the motherhouse, although at the same time he admitted he could give her no definite assurances about altering their situation at the Springs. "Our political affairs are now in such a condition," the Bishop pointed out, "that it is impossible to form projects with any confidence of carrying them out." Consequently, he said: "I cannot give you any definite views of mine at present. If a great war should be carried on, it will be impossible for me to obtain money to accomplish any changes."[34] A week later the Bishop decided to take a definite stand and suffer the consequences. It would be totally unwise, Elder wrote to Father Guillou, for the Sisters to close down their academy at the Springs with the hope of establishing themselves elsewhere in the Diocese if they expected help from him and the people. Elder felt he was in no position to share the expense which such a transfer would entail at a time when the political conditions of the country were so

---

[30] Parish Record, Sulphur Springs (1841-1926); in parish archives, Camden; copy in ADNJ, 27.

[31] Elder to Mother Leonie, Natchez, Feb. 27, 1861, March 12, 1861; in ADNJ, Elder Letter Book—#6, 80, 115.

[32] Elder to Guillou, Natchez, April 23, 1861; in ADNJ, Elder Letter Book—#6, 181.

[33] Memoir of Sister Louis Lynch, May 15, 1891; dictated account (typewritten manuscript) in ASSJC.

[34] Elder to Mother Leonie, Natchez, April 16, 1861; in ADNJ, Elder Letter Book—#6, 161.

unsettled.[35] Informed of the Bishop's decision, Mother Leonie no longer saw any reason for postponing her trip to the motherhouse. After the facts were presented to Mother St. John, the superior at Carondelet, she decided to close the mission in Mississippi. Mother Leonie was told to remain at home—travel through the lines had already become difficult—and the other Sisters at the Springs were recalled.[36]

Although the Sisters' school at Sulphur Springs had been failing long before April, 1861, and most probably would have eventually closed down regardless of the turn of political events, there is every reason to believe that the Sisters, as educators, would have been saved for the Diocese had there been no war. Had the times been normal, they could have opened an academy in another part of the Diocese and continued to contribute to the Catholic educational system of the State.

Besides the postponement or curtailment of building programs and the loss of the Sisters of St. Joseph to the Diocese, the War, as it ran its course the first year, meant still other distressing things to Bishop Elder. It could be spelled out in terms of irregular and uncertain opportunities for communicating with ecclesiastical authorities and benefactors within the Union lines and especially overseas; [37] of difficulty involved in obtaining religious books for distribution among the soldiers; [38] of the mounting number of poor people in the State; [39] of the necessity of postponing visitations in order to economize; [40] and of increasing requests for military chaplains which it was impossible to fill without depriving some portion of the flock of regular spiritual service.[41]

---

[35] Elder to Guillou, Natchez, April 23, 1861; in ADNJ, Elder Letter Book—#6, 181.

[36] Memoir of Sister Louis Lynch, May 15, 1891; dictated account (typewritten manuscript) in ASSJC. The Parish Record speaks of "some difficulties" which arose between the Sisters and "some members" of the congregation as an added reason for the Sisters' departure. Neither Elder nor the memoirs of the two surviving members of the Sisters' community mention these. Parish Record, Sulphur Springs (1841-1926); in parish archives, Camden; copy in ADNJ, 27.

[37] Elder to McCaffrey, Natchez, July, 1861; quoted by Meline & McSweeney, *op. cit.*, II, 8.

[38] Elder to Elliott, Natchez, Dec. 10, 1861; in ADNJ, Elder Letter Book—#7, 237.

[39] Walker, *op. cit.*, 60-61. Georget to Elder, Biloxi, Sept. 5, 1861; in ADNJ, File: Elder—G.

[40] Elder to Mother De Sales, Natchez, Oct. 19, 1861; in ADNJ, Elder Letter Book—#7, 131.

[41] Elder to Odin, Natchez, Nov. 4, 1861; in AUND: New Orleans Papers. Elder to Odin, Natchez, Dec. 20, 1861; *ibid.*

And yet life in Mississippi's Catholic congregations during the first year of the War was far from topsy-turvy. To all external appearances the Church was operating normally. Catholic services continued to be held quite regularly everywhere, even though one priest had already gone off with the army to serve as a chaplain.[42] Clerical conferences were held on schedule.[43] As late as December, 1861, arrangements were made to have Bishop Verot of Savannah preach the annual clergy retreat at Sulphur Springs in January.[44] One could even note signs of progress in the Diocese. At Holly Springs the congregation built a rectory and by the end of the year had paid for all of it, except fifty dollars.[45] And at Jackson, the location of the church at President and Court Streets proving unsuitable, the congregation in late December concluded the purchase of Mr. J. T. Owen's house and lot for $2,400, as the site for a new church.[46]

As the new year opened, the armies were still along the lines of the previous summer. But in a matter of weeks the balance would suddenly be tipped. By April the clash of arms would be heard on the prairies and in the hill-country of northern Mississippi and by the end of May the roar of guns would reverberate off the bluffs of Vicksburg. War in earnest would have finally come to Mississippi to disrupt the life of its people and shatter the complacency of many.

---

42 This priest was Fr. Pont, pastor of Jackson. Elder to Holton, May 22, 1861; in ADNJ, Elder Letter Book—#6, 250.

43 Elder to Huber, Natchez, July 31, 1861; in ADNJ, Elder Letter Book—#7, 11.

44 Grignon to Guillou, Natchez, Dec. 20, 1861; in ADNJ, File: Elder—G.

45 Elia to Elder, Holly Springs, Jan. 12, 1862; in ADNJ, File: Elder—E.

46 Henne, "Capital Parish Among Pioneers in Diocese," in *Catholic Action of the South* (Natchez Centennial Edition), Oct. 14, 1937, 29.

Chapter IX

THE CONFEDERATE CHAPLAIN

One of the earliest demands made upon the Catholic Diocese of Natchez by the War was in the form of repeated requests for military chaplains. From the start of the War it was the biggest problem facing Bishop Elder, who had only eighteen priests to serve fifteen churches and twenty-eight mission stations. His response and that of his priests demonstrate in a splendid manner their loyalty to the new Government and the sincerity of their religious vocation. Elder's efforts and those of his priests to provide spiritually for the men in the army, in camp and in the field, form some of the brightest and most inspiring pages in the history of Catholicity in Mississippi.

In the Confederate States at the beginning of the War there were about 278 Catholic priests.[1] Of this number at least twenty-eight served as chaplains attached to the Confederate army.[2] Besides these who appeared on the official rolls, there were many other priests who ministered to the soldiers in their vicinity—sometimes over 200 miles away!—on an unofficial basis. It would seem that there was only one casualty on the field of battle among these Catholic Confederate chaplains; he was Father Bliemel, O.S.B., attached to the 10th Tennessee Regiment, who was killed at the Battle of Jonesboro while hearing the confession of a dying soldier. After the War three of these Confederate Catholic chaplains, it is interesting to note, were raised to the episcopate.[3]

---

[1] *The Metropolitan Catholic Almanac and Laity's Directory,* 1861 (Baltimore, 1861).

[2] Norton, "The Organization and Function of the Confederate Chaplaincy, 1861-1865," (Ph. D. dissertation,, Vanderbilt Library, 1956) 96-98, gives the following approximate figures for the chief Protestant bodies: Methodists—200; Presbyterians—100; Baptists—100; and Protestant Episcopalians—65.

[3] Germain, "Catholic Military and Naval Chaplains 1776-1917," in CHR, XV (July 1929), 174-175. The future bishops were: Francis X. Leray (Archbishop of New Orleans), Dominic Manucy (Bishop of Mobile), and Anthony D. Pellicier (Bishop of San Antonio).

Government Provision

As early as April 27, 1861, L.P. Walker, Secretary of War, urged the Confederate Congress to pass a law empowering his department to appoint chaplains for the service. "Military experience," the Secretary said,

> demonstrates the importance of religious habitudes to the morality, good order, and general discipline of an army in the camp or in the field. If we expect God to bless us in our struggle in defense of our rights—to terminate, in all probability, only after a protracted and bloody war—we must recognize Him in our actions.[4]

A week later the Confederate Congress gave to President Davis the broad power of appointing chaplains "to such regiments, brigades, or posts as he may deem necessary."[5] Such appointments were to expire whenever the existing war should terminate. At the same time, the Congress ordered that the monthly pay of such chaplains be set at eighty-five dollars. Two weeks later their pay was reduced to fifty dollars.[6] The next year, however, it was raised to eighty dollars where it remained for the rest of the War.[7] Although the chaplain in the North was officially approximated to a captain in the cavalry,[8] in the South he had no special rank. He was allowed to draw the same rations as a private, and toward the end of the War he was also entitled to draw forage for one horse, provided he had a horse![9] In selecting clergymen to fill the office of chaplain, it would seem that the old Federal system was generally followed.[10] The officers of each regiment voted for a clergyman whose name was then forwarded to the War Department, irrespective of the desires or needs of the enlisted men.[11] Although Richmond had been commissioning chaplains for hospital work

---

[4] *Official Records: Army,* Ser. IV, Vol. I, 252. For general treatment see Romero, "The Confederate Chaplain," in *Civil War History,* I (June 1955), 127-140. For part played by Catholic Chaplains in Civil War see Blied, "Catholic Charity in the Army, 1861-1865," in *Social Justice Review,* XXXIX (Sept. 1940), 166-168.

[5] *Official Records: Army,* Ser. IV, Vol. I, 275.

[6] *Ibid.,* Ser. IV, Vol. I, 327.

[7] *Ibid.,* Ser. IV, Vol. I, 1076.

[8] *Ibid.,* Ser. III, Vol. IV, 1207.

[9] *Ibid.,* Ser. IV, Vol. I, 595; Ser. IV, Vol. III, 194.

[10] McGill to Elder, Richmond, Dec. 12, 1861; in AUND: N.O. Papers. Also Wight, "The Bishop of Natchez and the Confederate Chaplaincy," in *Mid-America,* XXXIX (April 1957), 71.

[11] *Official Records: Army,* Ser. III, Vol. I, 57.

since as early as 1862, specific authorization from the Confederate Congress came only at the end of May, 1864.[12]

Faculties for Catholic Chaplains

There was one problem which only the Catholic chaplain had to face and which was not ironed out immediately by the competent authorities. It concerned the spiritual jurisdiction needed by every priest for hearing confessions. A problem arose in the matter just as soon as the Catholic chaplain left the limits of his respective diocese, for his jurisdiction, granted to him by his own bishop, did not extend any further. Before receiving word of other provisions which had been made to cover the situation, Bishop Elder directed his priests, ministering to soldiers outside Mississippi, to obtain jurisdiction from the local bishop, even though, as he pointed out to Father Guillou, without it a pastor has jurisdiction over his subjects everywhere and over all who may be in danger of death.[13] Early in 1862, however, the Holy See took steps to simplify matters. On February 15, Cardinal Barnabò, prefect of Propaganda, sent to each metropolitan of the North and South a list of special faculties which the Pope had granted to all chaplains serving in the War between the States.[14] Archbishop Odin of New Orleans received the list in due time and, as instructed by the accompanying letter, forwarded copies to his suffragans.[15]

On the important question of jurisdiction required to administer the sacrament of Penance, the list stated that this was granted to the chaplains in question by apostolic authority. They enjoyed it, whether engaged with the army in the field or assigned to a post, for a period of two months from the time of entry into a given diocese. Within that time the chaplains were to apply for faculties from the local bishop, but if this should prove impossible, they continued to act validly until the impossibility no longer existed. Among other provisions, chaplains were allowed to dispense troops and

---

[12] *Ibid.*, Ser. IV, Vol. III, 496. For an evaluation of the Confederate government's role in establishing the office of military chaplain see Daniel, "An Aspect of Church and State Relations in the Confederacy: Southern Protestantism and the Office of Army Chaplain," in NCHR, XX (Jan. 1959), 47-71.

[13] Elder to Guillou, Natchez, March 26, 1862; in ADNJ, File: Elder–G.

[14] Barnabò to Odin, Rome, Feb. 15, 1862; copy in the Archives of the Diocese of Mobile-Birmingham, Quinlan Papers, Roman Documents, 1862. Barnabò to Purcell, Rome, Feb. 15, 1862; in Archives of the Sisters of Charity of Cincinnati, published in CHR, I (July, 1915), 199-201.

[15] No copy of these faculties was found in the ADNJ.

others from the laws of fast and abstinence and to impart a plenary indulgence "in articulo mortis" to those who were not able to confess or receive the last sacraments. The priests themselves were given permission to substitute a rosary for recitation of the breviary when a reasonable cause appeared, and the privilege of a portable altar was granted them if no other accomodations were available.[16]

Quality

Not all of the chaplains, especially in the beginning of the War, were of the highest caliber. A good number received "calls" to retire from blacksmithing or woodchopping to preach the gospel. Others with little ability and remuneration at home "patriotically" offered their services to the military.[17] Of the Catholic chaplains, however, it can be safely said that they were men of ability and sincerity. Before they could join the service as a chaplain, they had to have the permission of their bishop or religious superior. Generally, it was he who asked for volunteers. Before going into the service all of them were fully employed in the ministry. All of them were well educated, namely, beyond the college level. As for their conduct and utility while in service they measured up to and in some instances, according to certain Protestant authorities, surpassed their Protestant brethren.[18] Though small in number they formed a group of devoted and sometimes heroic men.

Bishop Elder's Policy

From the time that the first troops left the State, Bishop Elder was concerned with the problem of supplying the Catholics in these units with the services of a chaplain. As he saw it, these soldiers,

[16] Barnabò to Odin, Rome, Feb. 15, 1862; copy in the Archives of the Diocese of Mobile-Birmingham, Quinlan Papers, Roman Documents, 1862.

[17] Norton, "Revivalism in the Confederate Armies," *Civil War History*, IV (Dec. 1960), 411-412.

[18] *Annals of the Propagation of the Faith* (London, 1864), XXV, 393-399. Also Parton, "Our Roman Catholic Brethren," in *Atlantic Monthly*, XXI (May 1868), 572. And Murphy, *The Catholic Church in the United States during the Civil War Period*, in RACHS, XXXIX (Dec. 1928), 311, quoting Dr. T. H. Mann. General Bragg is reported to have paid this high compliment to the Catholic priests working among the Confederate troops: "My observation convinces me no denomination is more zealous or more useful in our service." According to the same source he is supposed to have expressly stated that Catholic priests were the only chaplains that could or would undergo the privation necessary to enable them to attend well to the soldiers. He admired other clergymen for other quaities, but this was one which Catholic priests seemed (to) possess above others. Their training seemed to fit them for works of self-devotion and privation. Newspaper clipping, undated; in ADNJ, File: 1, Folder: Natchez—History of Diocese in Clippings.

even though they might be outside of the territorial limits of his diocese, remained "an important part" of his flock whom he intended to follow with all solicitude.[19] For this reason, even though he had so few priests, Elder gave Father Pont, pastor of Jackson, permission to join the State troops at Pensacola in May, 1861.[20]

In the beginning of the War Bishop Elder because of a very limited number of priests in his diocese was reluctant to allow any one of them to accompany troops outside of the State. It was presumed that wherever Catholic troops were stationed the local Catholic clergy in that area would be able to take care of them. Furthermore, the Natchez prelate was aware that several priests had already been released by their respective bishops to serve as chaplains among the Confederate troops in the field. In the event that the Catholic soldiers in the Mississippi units should be neglected, it was agreed that the same would notify the Bishop or their pastors.[21] When no requests were made to Elder or his priests during the summer and early autumn of 1861, it was taken for granted that all was well, that the Catholics in the Mississippi units were receiving adequate spiritual assistance.[22]

But, then, in late November, Elder received a disturbing letter from a Catholic soldier who was attached to the 18th Mississippi Regiment stationed in Virginia. The soldier lamented the fact that his unit had not seen a Catholic priest for months and, therefore, he asked the Bishop to send one as soon as possible.[23] Still Elder hesitated to dispatch anyone to Virginia. With one of his priests already in the army [24] and with so few priests at home, not all of whom would even be suitable for military life,[25] the Bishop did not feel justified in releasing another man from his post in the Diocese at this time. Without calling into question the accuracy of the report from Virginia, Elder, hoping to correct the situation there without

---

[19] Elder to Quinlan, Natchez, Feb. 26, 1862; in ADNJ, Elder Letter Book—#8, 326. On this subject see Wight, "Bishop Elder and the Civil War," in CHR, XLIV (Oct. 1958), 298-301.

[20] Elder to Pont, Natchez, May 17, 1861; in ADNJ, Elder Letter Book—#6, 236. Elder did not view Pont's departure as anything but a temporary absence from his post in Jackson and therefore he urged him not to seek a Commission.

[21] Boheme to Elder, Paulding, Dec. 16, 1861; in ADNJ, File: Elder—B.

[22] *Ibid.*

[23] Elder to Elliott, Natchez, Dec. 10, 1861; in ADNJ, Elder Letter Book —#7, 237.

[24] Father Pont was commissioned May 21, 1861.

[25] Elder to Odin, Natchez, Nov. 4, 1861; in AUND: N.O. Papers.

losing one of his own clergymen, wrote to Bishop McGill of Richmond.

He asked McGill to have one of his priests visit the Mississippi regiments stationed in Virginia and, if he had no priest to spare, to inform him and he would send one immediately.[26] Back came a reply from the Bishop of Richmond which must have been very disturbing to Elder. McGill wrote:

> I am sorry not to be in a condition to answer your request to send a priest to attend to the Catholics in the Mississippi Regts. at Centreville (Va.) One of my priests is already with the army in that neighborhood & one of Abp. Odin's, Rev. Mr. Smulders (sic), is with the army, especially I think with the 8th Louisiana, which is of the same brigade in which Col. Wheat's Regt. is. I have no priest that I could spare at present. Besides, they tell me that scarcely 25 men attend Rev. Mr. Smulder's mass on sundays, and that he thinks of withdrawing unless he can be appointed to the *Brigade* instead of one Regt. Both Rev. Mr. Smulders and Rev. Mr. Sheeran (?) have been at Centreville, and could have been seen by the men of the 16th Miss. Regt. had they cared to see them. The fact is most of the men care very little about assisting at Mass and, unless a few, care not to see the priest, if not in danger of death from sickness or wounds. So that chaplains visiting the hospitals, are even more necessary than Chaplains in Regiments. I have conversed with others of the Chaplains from Mobile and New Orleans, who seem discouraged at the little disposition shown by Catholic soldiers to avail themselves of their ministry. Father Smulders said Mass in Col. Wheat's Regt., and offered to hear confessions, but I understand very few availed themselves of his offer. However I do not seek to discourage you from sending a priest as you propose.[27]

The reported religious indifference of the Catholics in the Mississippi regiments in Virginia is not altogether surprising. Present-day historians point out that many Johnny Rebs spent a good deal of their time, when not actually fighting, in "kicking over the traces."[28] Understandably, then, these men would not be par-

---

[26] Elder to Odin, Natchez, Dec. 20, 1861; in AUND: N.O. Papers. Also Elder to Elliott, Natchez, Dec. 10, 1861; in ADNJ, Elder Letter Book —#7, 237.

[27] McGill to Elder, Richmond, Dec. 12, 1861; in AUND: N.O. Papers. Fathers James Sheeran and Giles Schmulders were two Redemptorist priests from New Orleans, who were official chaplains, CSA.

[28] Wiley, *Johnny Reb*, 36-59. Partin, "An Alabama Confederate Soldier's Report to His Wife," *The Alabama Review*, III (1950), 22-36.

ticularly interested in the services of a clergyman, in attending a prayer-meeting or assisting at Mass, in going to a revival or making a good confession.

Elder's reaction to McGill's report was to keep what few priests he had at home. A week before the Bishop of Richmond wrote, Elder had written to Father Boheme at Paulding, requesting his services in the event that Bishop McGill could not spare a priest to visit the Mississippi regiments at Centreville, Virginia.[29] Now he directed the pastor of Paulding to remain at his post. However, as the winter months rolled by and alarming reports about life in camp reached him, Bishop Elder changed his mind. Writing to John Quinlan, Bishop of Mobile, Elder raised a number of questions which had been disturbing him and which finally prompted him to reappraise his "do-nothing" policy.

> My conscience has been uneasy lately about our Soldiers. In December I wrote as I promised to Bishop McGill to make some inquiries about Chaplains. From his answer I concluded that a Chaplain would have little to do because he told me the Soldiers has (sic) no care to make use of his services. Consequently I took no further steps. But after all it seems to me, that the soldiers of our respective Dioceses being an important part of our flocks we ought to follow them with our solicitude & make at least all reasonable exertions to bring them to the practice of their religion. Are we obliged to wait till they ask for Chaplains? Is it not better for us to enquire into their needs? If they are indifferent that very indifference is a thing that ought to awake our compassion & call forth our exertions to remove it. It is frightening to read some of the letters from camp & see how wickedness, godlessness & immorality must be prevailing. Besides the number of souls lost in battle & sickness what will be the situation of the country after the war if the great body of our young men come home hardened & demoralized? [30]

Bishop McGill's statement to the effect that a Catholic chaplain would find little to do because of the soldiers' indifference was now viewed differently. The indifference encountered should not serve as a check but as a challenge to any zealous priest. Judging from the fact that two of his priests, working among the troops

---

[29] Elder to Boheme, Natchez, Dec. 5, 1861; in ADNJ, Elder Letter Book—#7, 227.

[30] Elder to Quinlan, Natchez, Feb. 26, 1862; in ADNJ, Elder Letter Book—#7, 326.

at Columbus, Mississippi, were completely occupied,[31] Elder concluded that much depended upon the individual priest's conduct. "If the Priest waited to be called for," he wrote to Bishop Lynch of Charleston, "indifference & human respect will keep men away. But if he be a zealous shepherd he will look on this indifference as the very matter to be remedied & he will be diligent in going to hunt up Catholics & bring them to their duty & thus he will have work enough." [32]

For these reasons Bishop Elder, in the early part of 1862, adopted a more positive policy with regard to the spiritual needs of those members of his flock who were in the army. His new course of action was taken even though he knew that the home missions would be provided with only half the service they enjoyed before and that his priests, already overloaded, would have to shoulder more work.[33] Thus, in the course of the War Elder released for full-time service among the soldiers, besides Father Pont, five other priests—Fathers Boheme, Guillou, Leray, Huber and Mouton. Others, like Fathers Picherit, Elia, Georget and Heuzé, divided their time between their congregations and the soldiers in the area. When Mississippi itself became a battle ground in the spring of 1862, Elder maneuvered his priests about the Diocese as a general his troops, ordering one to the scene of a new battle,[34] directing another to be ready to move at a moment's notice,[35] telling still another priest to move forward and cover a post left vacant because of a recent maneuver,[36] telegraphing for reinforcements when the going got tough,[37] sending a man to the rear when his health showed signs of cracking [38] and, finally, appearing on the scene personally to help lighten the burden.[39] To achieve all this was

---

31 Wight, "Bishop Elder and the Civil War," in CHR, XLIV (Oct. 1958), 299-300.

32 Elder to Lynch, Natchez, March 1, 1862; in ADNJ, Elder Letter Book—#7, 340.

33 *Ibid.*, and Elder to Heuzé, Natchez, March 7, 1862; in ADNJ, Elder Letter Book—#7, 347.

34 Elder to Elia, Natchez, April 5, 1862; in ADNJ, File: Elder—E.

35 Elder to Leray, Natchez, March 15, 1862; in ADNJ, Elder Letter Book—#7, 377.

36 Elder to Huber, Natchez, April 16, 1862, Elder to Holton, Natchez, May 22, 1861; in ADNJ, Elder Letter Book—#7, 472, #6, 250.

37 Elder to Odin, Natchez, April 8, 1862, in AUND: N.O. Papers. Elder to Leray, Natchez, April 23, 1862; in ADNJ, Elder Letter Book—#7, 466.

38 Elder to Huber, Natchez, Oct. 23, 1862, Elder to Elia, Natchez, March 28, 1863; in ADNJ, Elder Letter Book—#8, 126, #8, 332.

39 Elder to Odin, Corinth, May 13, 1862; in AUND: N.O. Papers.

not an easy task for the Mississippi prelate. Between April, 1862, and April, 1863, when the need for Catholic chaplains in the State was great, four of Elder's priests died—three of them from hardships endured or disease contracted while working among the soldiers.[40]

Suggested Improvements

Elder attacked the problem of providing chaplains for the armed forces at all levels. Not content with furnishing manpower from his very limited numbers, the Bishop of Natchez also sought for an improvement in the system of appointing chaplains in the Confederacy.[41] As early as May, 1861, he objected to the method being proposed for use in the appointment of chaplains to the Confederate Navy. It was the old Federal system. Under this system a chaplain was appointed without regard for the beliefs or wishes of the men he was to serve. Elder deplored this method, because "perhaps not one man in fifty believed in his teachings or cared for his prayers—& not a few of them found his service a burden to their conscience." [42] In order that the Catholic seamen would not be ignored or subjected to what was offensive to their beliefs in the matter of religious service, Elder felt that if the old system of appointing one chaplain to a ship was retained "then they ought certainly to take one who is most agreeable—not to the President—not to the officers—but to the majority of souls on board." [43] The Bishop of Natchez was not particularly worried about the officers' opportunities for religious service, because he felt "the officers can better provide for themselves" than the seamen.[44]

As an improvement on this system Elder advanced a plan which involved an even more radical departure from the system in vogue. He suggested that the appointment of chaplains be "made dependent on the *voluntary* system with the government doing something for their encouragement." [45] In a letter to the Bishop of Charleston Elder outlined his plan.

---

[40] Fathers Hearns (April 23, 1862), Boheme (June 23, 1862), Guillou (Feb. 7, 1863), and Elia (April 2, 1863).

[41] Wight, "The Bishop of Natchez and the Confederate Chaplaincy," *Mid-America*, XXXIX (April 1957), 67-72.

[42] Elder to Lynch, Natchez, May 9, 1861; in ADC, Envelope 126.

[43] Elder to Perché, Natchez, May 9, 1861; in ADNJ, Elder Letter Book —#6, 211.

[44] Elder to Lynch, Natchez, May 9, 1861; in ADC, Envelope 126.

[45] Elder to Perché, Natchez, May 9, 1861; in ADNJ, Elder Letter Book —#6, 211.

> Let Government assign a certain portion which (it) would pay to the Chaplain—say one half or one fourth of what he should reasonably expect & let the men if they choose make up the complement for one agreeable to themselves. If they have not religion enough to do this—the govt. will be saved the expense of providing religious service which is not wanted by those interested.—And if the men on one ship are divided in sentiments—each body has religion enough to furnish the complement for a separate clergyman pleasing to themselves—let them have the advantage of two or even three Clergymen. It is a novelty but that is no objection. All progress is novelty. If inconveniences are anticipated a little foresight followed by a little experience will easily devise arrangements & regulations which will remedy all serious inconveniences. And as to lesser ones—they belong to human affairs.[46]

For that matter, the Bishop continued, "it is precisely the duty of govt. to take pains & put themselves to inconvenience—for the welfare of those under their care," whether this entailed supplying men with food and clothing, paying salaries or providing equitable religious opportunities for all. Thus, any objection that this system of providing chaplains would involve additional expense to the government should have no weight. Furthermore, "men who give themselves wholly to the defense of their country—& are willing to give a portion of their pay—the price of their blood—to obtain the help of religion—are certainly entitled to have their wants supplied." This system, as Elder saw it, could be applied not only to the navy, but also to the army and perhaps there with even greater facility.[47]

Bishop Elder was not the only Southern religious leader to find fault with the system followed by the Confederate government in appointing military chaplains. The Southern Baptists voiced an official protest on more than one occasion against the appointment and paying of chaplains by the government. They preferred to see the men of a regiment vote for a clergyman who visited and worked among them and to have the chaplain's salary paid by the men of the regiment and by the missionary board of the denomination of which he was a member. The system in vogue during the War, especially the paying of chaplains by the government, seemed contrary to the emphasis which Baptists had tradi-

46 Elder to Lynch, Natchez, May 9, 1861; in ADC, Envelope 126.
47 *Ibid.*

tionally placed on the complete separation of church and state.[48] At the suggestion of W. P. Miles, Chairman of the Congressional Committee of Military Affairs, the Reverend Moses D. Hoge, a Presbyterian minister, furnished the government in Richmond with an outline of a plan for 'increasing the number and efficiency of the chaplains in the Confederate service."[49] Without intending to interfere in any way with the plan already in operation for the appointment and pay of chaplains, Hoge's proposal is an indirect criticism of the government's method. It highlights the weaknesses of the system in vogue, namely, inadequate pay, appointment of unqualified men to military chaplaincies and lack of specific rank. Writing to Chairman Miles in May, 1862, Hoge proposed:

> Let the different denominations unite in each state . . . in raising whatever amount of money they wish to devote to the support of chaplains. Let the salary of each chaplain be at least $1000 (a year) and let the number of chaplains representing any one denomination . . . be directly in proportion to the amount contributed by such denomination . . . In order to secure the appointment of qualified men, I would have a central committee having charge of the matter at the capital of each state. This committee would be composed of resident ministers representing the denominations contributing to the general fund . . . It should be the business of this committee to nominate to the government men whom they know to be suitable for the office of chaplain, and not only to present the names of approved ministers making applications for the post of chaplain, but to seek clergymen as they know to be qualified for . . . such work and nominate them for appointment.

Hoge concluded by saying:

> All we ask Congress to do is to agree to commission such chaplains as we may select and (may) be willing to support, and that Congress will give to such chaplains, as well as those already in the field, such a rank as will enable them to mess with officers, and secure for them the respect which is always paid to their rank, as well as to ministerial character in the army.[50]

---

[48] Daniel, "An Aspect of Church and State Relations in the Confederacy: Southern Protestantism and the Office of Army Chaplain," in NCHR, XXXVI (Jan. 1959), 58.

[49] Hoge to Miles, May 7, 1862, Moses D. Hoge Papers (microfilm copy in the University of Virginia Library), Charlottesville, Virginia; quoted by Daniel, *op. cit.*, in NCHR, XXXVI (Jan. 1959), 55-56.

[50] *Ibid.*

Neither of these plans was ever adopted by the Confederate government.

Bishop Elder was apparently thoroughly convinced of the practicality of his or a similar plan—he admitted his proposal as outlined for Bishop Lynch was somewhat "crude"—for he wrote to several bishops, to the editor of the *Propagateur catholique* in New Orleans, and to the Natchez newspaper, urging a change from the old Federal system of appointment.[51] To Father Perché, editor of the New Orleans *Propagateur*, Elder recommended the use of every effort speedily. "Do not have any delicacy," the prelate advised, "in writing to Bishops on the matter. The interests are too important & the matter too urgent to suffer scruples of delicacy."[52] Although Elder did not always agree with the views of the priest-editor from New Orleans, he recognized Perché's influence, not only in religious but also in political circles, and he hoped to make use of it. In spite of such measures, nothing ever came of Elder's plan either.

The Missisipi prelate first encountered difficulty with the system in vogue when he contemplated sending Father Boheme to Virginia in December, 1861. On this occasion, Elder had asked Bishop McGill of Richmond to obtain a commission for the priest. The Virginia prelate replied that he was in no position to apply for such an appointment at that time. He had just obtained a commission for the Reverend L. J. O'Connell of Bishop Lynch's diocese, and this only with great difficulty. "Your request with that of the officers of the Mississippi regiments," he informed Elder, "would meet with better success than mine," for, as he explained to the Bishop of Natchez, the authorities in Richmond "do not like to appoint Chaplains *except as asked for by the Regiments.*"[53] Undoubtedly Elder knew the general rule being followed by the War Department, but he had also heard of exceptions being made. It must have irked him to be a victim of the system's discriminatory features.

In the summer of 1862, the method as it stood came under fire of Bishop Elder again.[54] His experience and that of his priests

[51] Wight, "The Bishop of Natchez and the Confederate Chaplaincy," *Mid-America*, XXXIX (April 1957), 71.

[52] Elder to Perché, Natchez, May 9, 1861; in ADNJ, Elder Letter Book —#6, 211.

[53] McGill to Elder, Richmond, Dec. 12, 1861; in AUND: N.O. Papers.

[54] Wight, "The Bishop of Natchez and the Confederate Chaplaincy," *Mid-America*, XXXIX (April 1957), 71-72.

had convinced him that one regiment was not enough to keep a priest occupied full time. On the other hand, he knew that there were many units whose Catholic members were woefully in need of a priest's service. One Catholic chaplain could easily and profitably take care of the needs of the Catholics in several regiments. Elder, therefore, made inquiry of Generals P. G. T. Beauregard and Braxton Bragg as to their power to assign chaplains to a brigade or a division. This power of assignment was not theirs, they informed him; the appointment came from the War Department and the nomination was made by the officers of the regiment. Nevertheless, the two Generals, one Catholic and the other Protestant, saw the Bishop's point and encouraged him to make an application for a change. Meeting with Bishop Quinlan in Mobile, Elder and his fellow-suffragan drew up a memorial to the Confederate Congress requesting that one Catholic priest always be appointed as chaplain to each division of the army. Such a change would guarantee to each Catholic chaplain the freedom of movement which Elder and others thought to be necessary. Their memorial was then sent to the Bishop of Richmond on August 4, who signed it and presented it to the Government.[55] When a favorable response was not forthcoming, Elder in October suggested to McGill that it might be well for him to press the matter of the memorial personally. "With such an amount of multifarious business as the officials of Richmond have on hand, it is very natural for them to forget or to lay aside anything which they are not especially urged to attend to."[56] In spite of the joint efforts of the Bishops of Natchez, Mobile and Richmond to increase the efficiency of their clergy in the Confederate service, no progress was made in the matter once the memorial had been presented. This should come as no surprise, for as the weaknesses in the system became more evident the efforts of the Government remained static. Indeed, one historian does not hesitate to indict the Confederate government with never having made "a sincere attempt to provide for the establishment of an adequate and competent chaplaincy."[57] Its actions in this matter

[55] Elder to McGill, Natchez, Aug. 4, 1862; in ADNJ, Elder Letter Book—#8, 10.

[56] Elder to McGill, Natchez, Oct. 17, 1862; in ADNJ, Elder Letter Book—#8, 94.

[57] Daniel, *op. cit.,* 71.

exhibit "some not uncommon characteristics of the Confederacy—lack of planning, organization and leadership." For that matter,

> had the churches not assumed the responsibility of caring for the spiritual needs of the soldiers by supplementing salaries of chaplains, and more especially by sending civilian missionaries and evangelists to the camps, the army would have been virtually destitute of religious influences.[58]

Surely it can be said of Bishop Elder that he carried his share of the burden created by government neglect.

---

58 *Ibid.*

Father Henry Picherit, a native of France, was pastor of Brookhaven at the outbreak of the Civil War. Tradition links him with the 22nd. Miss. Regt. as its chaplain.

Father Henry Leduc, pastor of Bay St. Louis from 1859-1897, often ran the Union blockade with a small schooner to bring in badly needed food and supplies.

Father Rene Pont, a Breton, served in Vicksburg, Pascagoula and Jackson before going off to war as a Confederate chaplain.

Father Mathurin F. Grignon came to the Diocese from Brittany in 1849. Pastor of the Cathedral from 1852 until his death in 1887, he also served as vicar-general from 1858 onward.

Father John B. Mouton, founder of the Church in northeastern Mississippi, was commissioned as a Confederate hospital chaplain.

Father Francis X. Leray, pastor of Vicksburg, also served as a Confederate chaplain. He accompanied the Sisters of Mercy as they moved about Mississippi & Alabama nursing the wounded & sick soldiers.

Chapter X

SOLDIERS OF THE CROSS

Father Pont

It would seem that the first priest from the Diocese of Natchez to join the army as a chaplain was Father Pont, pastor of Jackson. A good number of his parishioners had enlisted in the 10th Mississippi Regiment which was assigned to the defense of Pensacola. In April, 1861, Pont asked Bishop Elder for permission to join the troops stationed there.[1] With some reluctance the Bishop granted the permission, but he advised the priest: "I will be much better pleased if no Commission is sent to you. Do not let anyone make any further effort."[2] Elder's reluctance stemmed from the fact that he had so few priests. One of these, Father Holton, was away from his parish on sick leave in New Orleans.[3] To another, Father Elia, he had just given permission to leave the Diocese to join a religious community.[4] Among other reasons, Elder was prompted to make the sacrifice, because he thought Pont's absence from his post in Jackson would be only temporary. To his surprise, however, a request previously made for Pont's commission went through, and the priest informed the Bishop that he had been appointed chaplain with General Braxton Bragg's army on May 22, 1861.[5] How much Pont had to do with obtaining this appointment it is difficult to say, but it would seem that the Bishop was not entirely without his suspicions. In September, when Pont wrote to the Bishop about possibly remaining with the army for the duration of the War, Elder was quick to let the young priest know what his status was as far as he was concerned.

---

[1] Elder to Pont, Natchez, April 22, 1861; in ADNJ, Elder Letter Book —#6, 177.

[2] Elder to Pont, Natchez, May 17, 1861; in ADNJ, Elder Letter Book —#6, 236.

[3] *Ibid.*

[4] *Ibid.* Also Elder to Elia, Natchez, May 2, 1861; in ADNJ, Elder Letter Book—#6, 205. If Elia did leave to join the Vincentian Fathers, he did not persevere, for he was appointed pastor of Holly Springs by Bishop Elder on July 16, 1861.

[5] Note in ADNJ, File: Elder—P, stating that Pont sent Elder a memo in 1861, announcing his appointment on May 22, 1861.

> You speak about looking on the camp as *your home*—& say that you told me before leaving there that *Jackson* was not *your home* any longer.—You are under some strange mistake in that respect.—I never once thought of depriving the Diocese permanently of a Missionary. I authorized you to go for a while on account of the urgent needs of the Soldiers: the more willingly, because many of them belong to the Diocese, & some, I believe, to your congregation.—You continue always to be a Priest of the Diocese of Natchez, & I continue to be under the obligation of recalling you to its service, whenever I find that the interests of religion require it.—I believe you remarked to me that if you should be absent very long, you would not expect me to keep the Pastorship of Jackson for you. If you had any other intention in what you said, you did not express it to me:—if you have any other views now, I am glad to correct them at once—rather than have you under a mistake.[6]

After this letter the matter of Pont's status was never taken up again by either the Bishop or the chaplain.

While at Pensacola, Father Pont served as chaplain in the General Hospital.[7] When the city was evacuated in February, 1862, the priest followed the troops which were ordered to Corinth, Mississippi, where Generals Albert Sidney Johnston and Pierre G. T. Beauregard were organizing the Army of Mississippi. A few days before the Battle of Shiloh, Elder received a letter from Pont at Corinth, who reported that there were between six and 10,000 Catholic soldiers in the area. The need for priests, he continued, was critical, because they were expecting a great battle near Corinth and the only other priests in the area were two Frenchmen at Grand Junction, Tennessee, who spoke no English. Father Elia was not available, because he was busy in the hospital at Holly Springs where the Sisters of Charity were nursing the sick and wounded.[8] As Pont and others expected, the "great battle" came, but at Shiloh. For two days, April 6-7, the battle raged back and forth across the Mississippi-Tennessee line. The outcome was a Federal half-victory, for the Union soldiers were driven back by the Confederates the first day, only to rally reinforcements to

---

[6] Elder to Pont, Natchez, Sept. 5, 1861; in ADNJ, Elder Letter Book—#7, 46.

[7] Pont to Odin, near Pensacola, Fla., Jan. 14, 1862; in AUND: New Orleans Papers.

[8] Elder to Mouton, Natchez, April 4, 1862; in ADNJ, Elder Letter Book—#7, 442.

their side and overwhelm the Confederates by force of numbers the next day. Under Beauregard the Confederates retreated to Corinth. Joint casualties on this occasion amounted to 24,000. After ministering to the wounded on the battlefield and behind the ramparts at Corinth, Pont accompanied a number of casualties to Vicksburg.[9] It was here that he most probably received the news from France which made his return home imperative. Returning to Natchez from Europe a year later on May 16, 1863,[10] he was appointed pastor of Pass Christian. Early in July he traveled as far as Brookhaven with the Bishop and then went on to Monticello, where he took a skiff and went down the Pearl River to the Gulf Coast.[11] For the duration of the War Father Pont remained at the Pass.

Father Guillou

Sometime in February, 1862, Archbishop Odin of New Orleans asked Bishop Elder if he could spare a priest to serve as chaplain to the 18th Louisiana Regiment. The whole Regiment, the Archbishop reported, was composed of French Creoles, most of whom were practical Catholics. Before leaving the State the men had asked for a chaplain to accompany them. Odin was able to secure the services of a New Orleans' Jesuit Father, but the priest, because of the press of duties at home, could promise to remain with the regiment for only a few weeks. "These poor men," the Archbishop continued, "seem most anxious not to be deprived of the benefits of religion during the perilous campaign they are going to undertake. They promised to go to their Confession as soon as they reached their first stopping place," and he added, "they will procure a commission for the Priest who shall be sent to them." [12] The appeal had its desired effect. Bishop Elder relayed the request to Father Guillou, pastor of Sulphur Springs.[13] After receiving a favorable reply, Elder gave the priest official authorization in writing "to join the 5th Company, Washington Artillery, of Louisiana, under Capt. Hodgson, and to render to the men of that Company

---

[9] Telegram of Elder to Leray, Natchez, April 23, 1862; copy in ADNJ, Elder Letter Book—#7, 466.

[10] Elder Diary, 35.

[11] *Ibid.*, 41.

[12] Odin to Elder, Feb., 1862, quoted by Elder in a letter to Guillou, Natchez, Feb. 20, 1862; in ADNJ, File: Elder—G.

[13] Elder to Guillou, Natchez, Feb. 20, 1862; in ADNJ, File: Elder—G.

all the spiritual assistance in your power, until otherwise directed by Us." [14]

For Father Guillou Bishop Elder had no immediate replacement. Accordingly, he asked the pastor, before he left, to assure the Sulphur Springs congregation that every attempt would be made to supply them as much as possible with the means of practicing their religion. "They will understand no doubt that in this time of war, we must suffer somewhat at home, in order to save those multitudes of good soldiers who are gone to risk their lives for our defence." [15]

On April 7, while the Battle of Shiloh was going on, Father Guillou left Sulphur Springs to join the Louisiana troops in the vicinity of Corinth. Because of the confusion following the battle the priest was not able to reach Corinth until the 12th. After spending some time in attending the wounded soldiers in the Tishomingo Hotel, Guillou obtained an interview with General Beauregard, who cordially gave him a general pass for all the camps and hospitals in his army. Leaving the General's headquarters, Guillou repaired to the camp of the 5th Company, Washington Artillery. Here he found about fifteen Catholic soldiers, some of whom told him that they were not in need of a priest, since there was another company in their immediate neighborhood whose priest-chaplain could attend to their needs.[16]

Making further inquiries among the Louisiana troops, Guillou encountered, as he later reported to his bishop, not only indifference but even positive opposition to the services of a chaplain. He singled out in particular the 20th Louisiana Regiment as exhibiting such an attitude.[17] About this time Guillou met Bishop Quinlan, who had hurried to the scene by special train when the first news about the battle at Shiloh had reached Mobile.[18] In view of the situation Quinlan advised the priest to return home. The report of Guillou's experience among the Louisiana soldiers must have been received by both Quinlan and Elder with disap-

---

[14] Elder to Guillou, Natchez, March 28, 1862; in ADNJ, File: Elder—G.

[15] Elder to Guillou, Natchez, March 31, 1862; in ADNJ, File: Elder—G.

[16] Parochial Record, Sulphur Springs (1841-1926); in parish archives, Camden; copy in ADNJ, 29.

[17] Elder to Guillou, Natchez, April 30, 1862; in ADNJ, File: Elder—G.

[18] Lipscomb, "The Administration of John Quinlan, Second Bishop of Mobile, 1859-1883," 71.

pointment, if not disillusionment, for shortly before Guillou left for the front Elder had written to him encouragingly:

> You will see from the Archbp's (Odin) letter, that the dispositions of the men (to whom Guillou was being sent) are such as to give you a prospect of more satisfaction in your labors, than you would expect, from the accounts given by the men on furlough from Virginia. Yesterday I received a letter from the Bishop of Mobile, on this very subject of Chaplaincies; and he thinks the indifference in Virginia is in great measure owing to the idleness of winter quarters, & the absence of apprehension of death in battle. He thinks the Chaplains will find plenty to do during an active campaign.[19]

When the "gloomy" news reached him, Elder made the simple comment: "It bodes no good to the Army nor the country." [20] Unexpressed were the fears which must have been his about conditions in Virginia among his own men in uniform. Before Guillou had left for Corinth, Elder had counselled the priest:

> I suspect from the Archbp.'s letter that there is already a chaplain in the Regimt. to which your company belongs. If so it is not improbable you will find you have not enough to do:—that there is not much good to be accomplished there, as there would be at home.—If that should be the case, I do not wish you to remain—Let me know of it,—& I will give you some other directions. But if you can find employment for your sacred powers, either in your *own company* or in *others* around, continue to do all the good you can.[21]

Accordingly, finding no employment with the 5th Company, the priest returned to town and for two weeks attended the sick and wounded soldiers of nine different hospitals.[22] While working among the soldiers, Father Guillou made no attempt to secure a commission. Elder had advised him before going to the army:

> Although it is generally better to have a Commission, yet if your sustenance is well provided for other-wise, & if you have free access to the soldiers without a commission, there is some advantage in being more free to move about, & also in being able to leave at any time, if you should find that the

---

[19] Elder to Guillou, Natchez, March 26, 1862; in ADNJ, File: Elder—G.

[20] Elder to Guillou, Natchez, April 30, 1862; in ADNJ, File: Elder—G.

[21] Elder to Guillou, Natchez, March 31, 1862; in ADNJ, File: Elder—G.

[22] Parochial Record, Sulphur Springs (1841-1926); in parish archives, Camden; copy in ADNJ, 29.

good you do is not as great as you would accomplish at home.[23]

This counsel reveals somewhat more clearly what Bishop Elder's attitude was toward commissions for his priests whom he allowed to work among the soldiers. He was not opposed to them, but he did see two important advantages in not having a commission. Instead of being tied down to one military unit, usually a regiment, a civilian chaplain could move about more freely, making greater use of his priestly powers. Secondly, without a commission a priest, once he realized that he was not being employed with as much profit as he might be elsewhere, could leave the army without difficulty. Bishop Elder saw no sense in limiting the effectiveness of one of his priests when he was so badly needed on the home-front. This would seem to be the key to an understanding of Elder's reluctance to have his priests seek or accept commissions as official Confederate chaplains.

When nearly all of the sick and wounded had been evacuated from Corinth by the first week of May, Father Guillou returned to his congregation at Sulphur Springs.[24] But he was not the same man. His health, never very good since a near-fatal attack of yellow fever in 1854, suffered severely from the privations and exposure endured at Corinth.[25] When he reached the Springs, he was obviously a very sick man. For several weeks the missionary was confined to his bed. What was later diagnosed as consumption had already set in.[26] In June, when he had apparently recovered, Elder cautioned the priest: "I beg you not to expose yourself to the danger of a relapse. Better let the people suffer for a while now—than get another bad spell & deprive them of your assistance for a long time." [27] But Guillou was sicker than he was at first willing to admit. That summer, however, he was finally forced to ask for a leave of absence. In the hope of recovering his health the priest travelled to the Gulf Coast, ending up in Mobile, but by September he was forced to retire to Natchez. From that time on

[23] Elder to Guillou, Natchez, March 26, 1862; in ADNJ, File: Elder—G.

[24] Parochial Record, Sulphur Springs (1841-1926); in parish archives, Camden; copy in ADNJ, 29.

[25] Formal death announcement to clergy by Elder, dated Feb. 11, 1863; in ADNJ, Elder Letter Book—#8, 277.

[26] Cathedral Announcement Book—#2, Sept. 14, 1862; in cathedral archives, Natchez.

[27] Elder to Guillou, Natchez, June 18, 1862; in ADNJ, File: Elder—G.

his constitution deteriorated rapidly. After the New Year he grew considerably weaker. Elder described the priest's death which took place on February 7, to Father Huber:

> He began to be sensibly worse on Friday (Feb. 6). His chief suffering was a very oppressive shortness of breath, which would last for a quarter of an hour at a time. We still expected him to last some days—until only a few minutes before he died . . . He did not talk much. He was too weak—but when he did speak with me, he several times expressed his regret that he had not done still more for God's glory & especially for his own perfection. You know how good he was. How conscientious & pious—and yet he trembled—& sometimes wept to think that he had let opportunities pass of improving his own soul, & doing good among others.[28]

On the day of the funeral, February 9, 1863, Bishop Elder made the following entry in his diary which gives the reader some idea of the great loss sustained by all in Guillou's passing:

> Fr. Guillou's death is a sad calamity for the Diocese. Without injury to any one—I can truly say he was the best missionary in the Diocese—so active, so zealous, so discreet—so disinterested. He was also a favorite with all the other Priests—& a true friend & wise counsellor for them—zealous also for his own perfection & for that of his Brother Priests. I feel as if his death was a judgment upon myself. God grant I may do better hereafter.[29]

Father Boheme

One of the first priests in the Diocese whom Bishop Elder had asked to serve as military chaplain was the veteran missionary, Father Ghislain Boheme, pastor of Paulding in Jasper County. Early in the summer of 1861, when the 13th Mississippi Regiment was being organized at Corinth, Boheme had visited the Catholic soldiers in the unit. They asked the priest to accompany them to Virginia, but he expressed the opinion that they would most probably find a chaplain there. However, if they should be deprived of the comforts of religion at their camp in Virginia, Boheme instructed the men to write to him and he would see what could be done.[30] When the soldiers' long silence was finally broken at

---

[28] Elder to Huber, Natchez, Feb. 10, 1863; in ADNJ, Elder Letter Book—#8, 266.

[29] Elder Diary, 16.

[30] Boheme to Elder, Paulding, Dec. 16, 1861; in ADNJ, File: Elder—B.

the end of November by a letter to Bishop Elder, begging for a priest, the prelate wrote to the pastor of Paulding:

> The Regiment 13th. Miss. which you visited at Corinth, has not been visited by a Priest since it left there.—They are now stationed at Centreville, Virginia. (. . . .) I believe that you would do as much good there as any other Priest in the Diocese—& probably more. (. . . .) Are you willing to go on such a service, if you are needed? [31]

Boheme agreed,[32] but Elder pursued the matter no further. McGill's letter had arrived, correcting the impression given by Elder's correspondent that the Catholics in the Mississippi regiments in Virginia were being neglected spiritually.[33]

In March, 1862, when Elder had definitely decided to abandon his "let's-wait-and-see" policy with regard to providing spiritual assistance for the Mississippi regiments in Virginia, he again turned to Father Boheme.[34] Strangely enough about the same time as the Bishop's letter arrived in Paulding, Elder himself received a communication from Boheme asking for permission to go to the front as a chaplain.[35] Captain James J. Shannon of the 16th Mississippi Regiment, Boheme reported, had just returned from Manasses to recruit for his company. The Catholic officer's description of the soldiers' lack of opportunities for receiving the Sacraments was distressing. Only rarely, and then by accident, did the Catholics in his regiment get to see a priest. In view of the situation the officer begged his pastor to accompany himself and the new recruits to the front. Boheme found it difficult to refuse. In the Regiment there were about 350 Catholics; twenty of them were his own parishioners and some of these were his altar boys. On the other hand, he could not escape the fact that many people, not only in Paulding but throughout eastern Mississippi, would be left without the services of a priest were he to leave for Virginia. When the Bishop's request arrived, Boheme must have felt somewhat re-

---

[31] Elder to Boheme, Natchez, Dec. 5, 1861; in ADNJ, Elder Letter Book—#7, 227.

[32] Boheme to Elder, Paulding, Dec. 16, 1861; in ADNJ, File: Elder—B.

[33] McGill to Elder, Dec. 12, 1861, Richmond; in AUND: N.O. Papers.

[34] Elder to Boheme, Natchez, March 13, 1862; in ADNJ, Elder Letter Book—#7, 374.

[35] Boheme to Elder, Paulding, March 9, 1862; in ADNJ, File: Elder—B. Necrology for Boheme and other priests of the Diocese, covering the years April 5, 1864 to Jan. 10, 1866; in ADNJ, Elder Letter Book—#10, 410.

lieved; at least now the responsibility for his decision rested with someone else.

It may seem somewhat strange that Bishop Elder should have asked Father Boheme to go to Virginia and face the hardships of camp life. At the time the priest was almost sixty years old [36] and he apparently suffered a great deal from rheumatism. Indeed, Elder took cognizance of the latter fact when he wrote to the priest, asking him to volunteer: "Now that the winter is so nearly gone, I suppose you would not be afraid of the rheumatism, if you were to go to Virginia." [37] On the other hand, the choice was not so strange. The pastor of Paulding "showed so much energy and fire of spirit, and . . . boasted so much vigor of body that he seemed well adapted" for the life of an army chaplain.[38] Furthermore, one could hardly ignore the endurance he exhibited for the past nineteen years in riding perhaps the largest circuit in the Diocese. He had every reason to boast. Perhaps, it was to this little bit of pride that Elder appealed when he wrote to the priest in March: "I hope then that . . . you will prove yourself the veteran soldier of our Lord, & teach our younger Missionaries how to fight His battles in camp, as you have done in the country." [39] Both Elder and Boheme decided that it would be best to secure a commission. The priest asked his Bishop to seek the official appointment either through Bishop McGill of Richmond or through President Davis or through the colonel of the 16th Regiment.[40] After his experience in trying to obtain a commission for Boheme in December, Elder made quick reply to this suggestion:

> As you are acquainted with President Davis—which I am not—you had better write to him yourself. But no doubt he will be most influenced by representation, coming from the Regiment, showing him that the soldiers want the services of a Priest. This you can tell him in your letter & you ought to get Capt. Shannon to speak with the other officers, so as to make the proper representations to the President.[41]

---

[36] Obituary of Boheme; in ADNJ, Elder Letter Book—#10, 410.

[37] Elder to Boheme, Natchez, March 13, 1862; in ADNJ, Elder Letter Book—#7, 374.

[38] Obituary of Boheme; in ADNJ, Elder Letter Book—#10, 410.

[39] Elder to Boheme, Natchez, March 13, 1862; in ADNJ, Elder Letter Book—#7, 374.

[40] Boheme to Elder, Paulding, March 9, 1862; in ADNJ, File: Elder—B.

[41] Elder to Boheme, Natchez, March 17, 1862; in ADNJ, Elder Letter Book—#7, 391.

Acting on this advice, Boheme wrote immediately to John J. McRae and Ethelbert Barksdale, representatives from Mississippi in the Confederate Congress. The veteran missionary from Jasper County must have been on fairly intimate terms, not only with these two congressmen, but also with President Davis, for the priest referred to McRae and Barksdale as "personal friends" who would consider it a "pleasant duty" to procure a commission from President Davis "who I am sure will grant it with pleasure."[42] Captain Shannon also agreed to secure Boheme's nomination by the officers of the Regiment. Although he would have preferred to have a commission, Boheme was determined to go to Virginia with or without the appointment. The substance of his petition to the congressmen was "that if no special commission as Chaplain to the 16th Regt.—or the charge of the Miss. Hospital in Virginia can be granted" he might at least receive his "Transport Ticket and be recognized as having the right to act as chaplain to the said 16th Regt."[43] If Father Boheme received anything from the Government, it was this minimum, for there is no record of his ever having been officially commissioned as a Confederate chaplain. Shortly after Easter, about April 25, Father Boheme left for Virginia.[44] He travelled lightly with a new suit of clothes, paid for with money loaned to him by his Bishop,[45] and a Mass kit, made up for him by the Sisters of Mercy at Vicksburg.[46] When he finally made contact with the 16th Regiment, the unit was a part of General "Stonewall" Jackson's army.[47]

In the early part of May, with Union General McClellan's pickets thrust forward to within five miles of Richmond, the Confederate capitol, and with General McDowell on his way south with 40,000 men to reinforce him, Jackson was ordered by Lee to create a diversion. It was Jackson's strategy "not to fight a major battle nor to win and hold this or that place, but to fall consecutively upon the Union commanders before they could unite, and create a

---

[42] Boheme to Elder, Paulding, March 16, 1862; in ADNJ, File: Elder—B.

[43] Boheme to Elder, Paulding, March 26, 1862; in ADNJ, File: Elder—B.

[44] Obituary of Boheme; in ADNJ, Elder Letter Book—#10, 410.

[45] Boheme to Elder, Paulding, March 20, 1862; in ADNJ, File: Elder —B.

[46] Boheme to Elder, Paulding, March 9, 1862, March 20, 1862; in ADNJ, File: Elder—B.

[47] Obituary of Boheme; in ADNJ, Elder Letter Book—#10, 410.

panic as to the safety of Washington."[48] Thus, by successive blows upon Shields, Milroy, Banks and Fremont at different points in the Shenandoah Valley, Jackson "had the Union authorities mystified as to his movements, caused Northern newspapers to shriek 'Washington is in danger' and brought about the detachment of McDowell's corps from McClellan's army"[49]—the one thing that saved Richmond and Lee's army for the time being. To achieve this, Jackson moved up and down the Valley fast and furiously, on one occasion covering sixty miles in three days of incredible marching.

For fear of being separated from the men during these rapid marches, Boheme always stayed with the encampment, refusing to accept more comfortable quarters at houses a little outside camp. It was soon seen, however, that the priest had overrated his strength. The rapid marches and the hardships of camp life were evidently too much for the elderly man. The soldiers themselves begged him to return home and preserve his life for their friends at Paulding. Firm of character but not stubborn, he at first brushed aside their pleadings. Then, toward the end of June, he yielded and agreed to return home.[50] A few days before setting out for Paulding, the priest, though apparently suffering from dysentery himself, went to nurse Captain Shannon, who had taken sick with something like cholera morbus and had bedded down in a farm house near Ashland, Virginia. There, on the morning of June 27, Boheme suffered a stroke and died in a matter of a few minutes. Shannon had the priest's body put into a decent coffin and sent by rail to Bishop McGill in Richmond for burial.[51] The news of Boheme's death must have been especially distressing to Bishop Elder, for within a matter of two months he had lost Father John Hearns, one of his youngest and most promising priests,[52] and now Father Boheme, one of the oldest and most devoted missionaries in the Diocese.

---

[48] Randall, *The Civil War and Reconstruction,* 292.

[49] *Ibid.,* 292-295.

[50] Obituary of Boheme; in ADNJ, Elder Letter Book—#10, 410.

[51] J. J. Shannon to his mother, near Charles City, Va., July 5, 1862; in *A Historical Sketch of the Catholic Church in Laurel and Jones County* by Thomas Hayes (Ellisville, Miss., 1937), 43.

[52] "1862—April 23d. Died Revd. Jno Hearns, at Natchez of Consumption. A young priest remarkable for a rare combination of maturity of judgment and gaiety of disposition." Necrology of the Diocese of Natchez, drawn up by Bishop Elder; in ADNJ, File: Elder—N.

Father Elia

Before Grant's army and Foote's gunboats had battered the center of the Tennessee line into submission in February, 1862, and thus opened the way for the Union advance into the heart of the Confederacy, another of Elder's priests, Father Basilio Elia, was ministering to the spiritual needs of Confederate soldiers as far north as Jackson, Tennessee.[53] Since August, 1861, the young pastor of Holly Springs, at the request of the Bishop of Nashville, had been serving the Catholic congregation of Grand Junction, Tennessee, just across the state line.[54] In November he also assumed responsibility for the congregation at Jackson.[55] When an army camp was established at the latter place, Elia extended his services to the Catholic soliders there. It was easily accessible, connected by rail with both Holly Springs and Corinth.

Early in the spring of 1862, two military hospitals were established in northern Mississippi—one at Holly Springs, the other at Oxford. The hospital at Holly Springs was fortunate in obtaining the services of the Daughters of Charity from New Orleans. At the beginning of April it was reported that there were 600 patients in the hospital at the Springs and 700 at Oxford.[56] As a result, Father Elia was unable to devote himself to the increasing number of soldiers along the northern border of the State. Here Confederate General Albert Sidney Johnston was anxiously trying to reorganize his army as the Union army under Grant began to press down from the north. It was obvious to all that a big battle was in the making. Concerned about these soldiers, thousands of whom were Catholic, Elia wrote to Bishop Elder, asking for permission to abandon his work at the hospitals where there were few Catholics and go to the aid of these men. On April 5, the Bishop sent the reassuring news that Father Mouton was on his way to the Confederate headquarters at Corinth. Pont was already there. As for abandoning his work in the hospitals because of the fewness of Catholics there, Elia received a mild scolding from his Bishop:

---

[53] Elder to Leray, Natchez, March 20, 1862; in ADNJ, Elder Letter Book—#7, 396.

[54] Whelan to Elia, Nashville, Aug. 27, 1861; in ADNJ, File: Elder—E.

[55] Elder to Elia, Natchez, Nov. 4, 1861; in ADNJ, Elder Letter Book—#7, 179.

[56] Elder to Mouton, Natchez, April 4, 1862; in ADNJ, Elder Letter Book—#7, 442.

> Can you not do some good among the sick soldiers even when they are not Catholics? The sick bed is the very place for conversions—& the time of suffering is always a time of grace.—I have heard old missionaries say that they brought a great many into the Church in time of general sickness. There are great numbers of men, who have no religion—& yet wish to have some before they die—& who will welcome the instructions & consolations of a zealous priest.[57]

Elder admitted another reason for wanting Elia to remain at his post in Holly Springs. He had promised Sister Regina, New Orleans superior of the Daughters of Charity, that if the Sisters came to any hospital in his diocese they should have a priest staying near them.

Having finally pulled together the remains of his Tennessee army and organized them in a weird formation, on the morning of April 6, Johnston sent them crashing into unsuspecting Grant at Shiloh. When the battle was over, Johnston was dead, Beauregard had withdrawn to Corinth and Grant had managed to salvage his army and a victory from the tangled battle. Two days later, seventy-five miles to the southwest, train loads of wounded started arriving in Holly Springs, some going on to Oxford, thirty miles further down the Mississippi Central Railroad, swamping the already crowded hospitals. In response to appeals for help from Elia, the Bishop sent Father Huber from Port Gibson and a few days later Father Leray from Vicksburg.[58] At the beginning of May, Elder himself visited the area.[59] On this occasion he reported meeting Father P. F. Dicharry from the Archdiocese of New Orleans who was serving the 3rd Louisiana Infantry and Father Patrick F. Coyle from the Mobile Diocese who was ministering to the wounded and sick at a hospital in Corinth.[60] In the days and weeks immediately following the Battle of Shiloh at least nine priests and two bishops from among the Southern Catholic clergy had moved into northeastern Mississippi to give spiritual assistance and consolation to the wounded in that area.

---

[57] Elder to Elia, Natchez, April 5, 1862; in ADNJ, File: Elder—E.

[58] Elder to Huber, Natchez, April 16, 1862; in ADNJ, Elder Letter Book—#7, 472. Elder to Leray (telegram), Natchez, April 23, 1862; in ADNJ, Elder Letter Book—#7, 466.

[59] Elder to Odin, Corinth, May 13, 1862; in AUND: N.O. Papers.

[60] Father Coyle had been an officially commissioned chaplain up until Jan. 1862, when it is reported he resigned. Germain, *Catholic Military and Naval Chaplains, 1776-1917* (Washington, 1929), 113-114.

Holly Springs unfortunately stood squarely in the path of Union attempts to get into Mississippi from the north. For this reason the town suffered some sixty-one raids by Union and Confederate forces as first one and then the other held the town.[61] The most famous and most destructive of these was the capture of the town by Confederate General Van Dorn and his men on December 20, 1862. The Confederate cavalry sacked the town, destroying property valued at from two to four million dollars. By this time the Confederate wounded had been evacuated and the Sisters had returned to New Orleans. Father Elia's congregation, for the most part, had dispersed, since the iron foundry and the railroad shops which had employed most of his people had for some time been out of operation. Unable to reach Natchez, because both armies lay between him and the episcopal city, the priest retired to Memphis were he lived with the Dominican Fathers.[62] From time to time he visited the few Catholics who had remained in Holly Springs. In the spring of 1863, the priest extended his labors in another direction.

In late December, 1862, General Sherman tried to attack the city of Vicksburg via the impossible approach of Chickasaw Bayou.

> It was a difficult position to attack—low, swampy, dank ground overwatched by bluffs on which the Confederates sat with rifles and artillery. The Northerners wallowed through the muck and tried to climb the bluffs while the Confederates swatted them back like flies. When it was over the defenders counted two hundred casualties and the attackers had lost almost ten times that number.[63]

But the irrepressible Sherman was not finished yet. At the end of January, 1863, after Grant had joined him, he started his troops digging at Williams' abandoned canal across the peninsula opposite Vicksburg in an effort to divert the Mississippi River and enable his troops to make a frontal assault upon the "Gibraltar of the West." When spring came, the task was not finished, but many of Sherman's soldiers were. Fever and dysentery had struck down hundreds of his men who for the past three months had been living, fighting and working in swampy areas along the river. Though

---

[61] *Mississippi in the War Between the States* (Jackson: The Mississippi Commission on the War Between the States, 1960), 13.

[62] Elder to Supr. of Seminary College of Brignole-Sale, Genoa, Natchez, Jan. 20, 1864; in ADNJ, Elder Letter Book—#9, 114.

[63] Walker, *Vicksburg, A People at War, 1860-1865,* 131.

nursed by the Sisters of the Holy Cross,[64] many of the sick men were dying. To add to the tragedy of the situation, no priest was on hand to administer the Last Rites.[65]

When Father Elia learned about the situation among the Union soldiers opposite Vicksburg, he got word through to Bishop Elder, requesting permission to attend these sick and dying men. He also pointed out that the Sisters themselves were without a chaplain. The Bishop gave his consent. Once among them, Elia found so much to do that he worked day and night. Unfortunately, the priest forgot to take care of himself. Before long he himself was attacked by dysentery. He returned to Memphis in a dying state. Six days later, on April 3, 1863, the young Italian missionary passed away, not before having edified his friends by his patience and meekness during his painful sickness.[66]

Father Leray

The priest with perhaps the longest tour of service as a Confederate chaplain was Father Francis X. Leray, pastor of Vicksburg. In the early part of the War he acted as civilian chaplain. In April, 1862, he assisted Father Elia at the military hospital in Holly Springs.[67] During the May-June bombardment of Vicksburg, when a military hospital was established outside of town at Mississippi Springs, he visited the sick and wounded there regularly while he continued to carry out his duties as pastor of the second largest Catholic parish in the State.[68] In the early part of November Leray requested and received permission from his Bishop to assume the post of chaplain at the military hospital in Oxford.[69] Through his influence the services of the Sisters of Mercy from

---

[64] These Sisters from Notre Dame, Indiana were most probably attached to the "Red Rover," a floating hospital that plied up and down the Mississippi River.

[65] Elder to Supr. of Seminary College of Brignole-Sale, Genoa, Natchez, Jan. 20, 1864; in ADNJ, Elder Letter Book—#9, 114.

[66] *Ibid.;* also *Freeman's Journal,* New York, April 18, 1863.

[67] Elder to Leray (telegram), Natchez, April 23, 1862; in ADNJ, Elder Letter Book—#7, 466.

[68] Heuzé to Grignon, Mississippi Springs Hospital, August 21, 1862; in ADNJ, File: Elder—H.

[69] Elder to Leray, Natchez, Nov. 13, 1862; in ADNJ, Elder Letter Book—#8, 156. Bishop Elder wrote to Colonel L. Northrop, Commissary-General in Richmond, requesting a chaplain's commission for Father Leray. Apparently the same was granted. Elder to Northrop, Natchez, Nov. 12, 1862; in ADNJ, Elder Letter Book—#8, 152. Elder to Leray, Natchez, April 4, 1863; in ADNJ, Elder Letter Book—#8, 344.

Vicksburg were obtained for the sick and wounded here in the buildings of the fledgling University of Mississippi.[70]

In December General Grant started to move down the Mississippi Central Railroad from Holly Springs. Hastily the hospital was closed, the Sisters and chaplain evacuating with the wounded to Jackson.[71] With the Sisters installed in another hospital and Father Orlandi, pastor of Jackson, on hand to care for the hospitalized soldiers, Leray returned to Vicksburg temporarily to lighten the burden of his hard-pressed curate, Father Heuzé.[72] Most probably some time after Easter, 1863, Father Leray rejoined the army. At the end of April, General Grant launched the arduous campaign which stands as his greatest achievement during the War.[73] With the assistance of Foote's gunboats and transports he crossed the Mississippi River at Bruinsburg with 20,000 men. When Gregg's brigade came out of Jackson to clash with part of the Union army on May 12, at the Battle of Raymond, Leray was on the scene.[74] Two days later when Grant swept into Jackson, the priest remained behind with the Sisters and the wounded soldiers.[75] After the fall of Vicksburg in July, when the enemy again laid seige to Jackson, Leray chaperoned the Sisters to their new assignment in Shelby Springs, Alabama. Here he remained with the Sisters to act as their guardian and as the hospital's chaplain.[76]

At the begining of 1864, Leray reported to Bishop Elder on his position at Shelby Springs and asked for further instructions.[77] The priest apparently presented the Bishop with three possibilities. He could join the troops in the field as a chaplain, stay with hospital work or return to Vicksburg. The third course of action, in Leray's estimation was the least wise, for he had received reports that the military authorities in Vicksburg intended to deal harshly with all those clergymen of the city who had actively supported the "re-

---

[70] Memoirs of Sister M. Ignatius Sumner, 8; in ASMV.

[71] *Ibid.*, 9-10.

[72] Elder to Leray, Natchez, Feb. 2, 1863, April 1, 1863; in ADNJ, Elder Letter Book—#8, 247, 344.

[73] Randall, *op. cit.*, 529-531.

[74] *The Morning Star*, New Orleans, Oct. 1, 1887.

[75] Memoirs of Sister M. Ignatius Sumner, 14-15; in ASMV. Elder to Leray, Natchez, June 18, 1863; in ADNJ, Elder Letter Book—#8, 424.

[76] Memoirs of Sister M. Ignatius Sumner, 16-20; in ASMV.

[77] Elder to Leray, Natchez, Jan. 16, 1864; in ADNJ, Elder Letter Book—#9, 105.

bellion." The Bishop replied on January 16: "I believe you can do a great deal more good in the Army or the Hospitals at present, than elsewhere." If Leray felt that his services were not being fully utilized in either place, then the next place where he would be most needed would be at home in Vicksburg. As for any threats which may have been made, Elder dismissed them as the rantings of "irresponsible persons." [78] Leray decided to stay on as chaplain in the hospital at Shelby Springs.[79]

When several Sisters, at the request of Bishop Elder, returned to Vicksburg from Alabama in May, 1864, Father Leray accompanied the women as their chaperon.[80] Traveling under a flag of truce with a military escort, they were stopped at the Union lines just outside Vicksburg. Word of their arrival was conveyed to the commanding officer. Leave was given for the Sisters to enter the city, but not Father Leray. The adjutant, Col. Rogers, seemed willing to grant the same permission to the priest, but when General Slocum, the officer in charge, heard of it he fumed at the idea of letting in a Confederate chaplain. At the mention of the priest's name, Slocum is reported to have exclaimed: "What! Let Father Leray enter? I would as soon let in one of Forrest's brigades!" [81] Apparently Leray's flag-blessing and the encouragement he gave to enlistment in the Confederate army had not gone unreported to the Union authorities. The officer showed further petulance by refusing the Sisters permission to take lunch out to the priest or to send anything back to the Sisters who had remained at Shelby Springs.[82] When no word was received from the Sisters, Father Leray and party retired to Major Cook's plantation [83] near Vicksburg to rest before making the return trip. The next day the Sisters were able to pass out through the lines and visit the Cook

[78] *Ibid.*

[79] Memoirs of Sister M. Ignatius Sumner, 19; in ASMV.

[80] *Ibid.*, 22-25.

[81] Newspaper clipping, unidentified, with date pencilled in at the top—"1885"; in ADNJ, File: Elder—L.

[82] After Leray's departure, General Slocum relented and allowed the Sisters to send some things back to the Sisters at Shelby Springs. Memoirs of Sister M. Ignatius Sumner, 26.

[83] Major J. Reese Cook, owner of "Hardtimes," whose wife and children were Catholic, was himself received into the Church during the War (Sept. 10, 1863) by a Federal chaplain, Fr. J. C. Carrier, C.S.C. Baptismal Register (1852-1870), St. Paul's Church, Vicksburg, 109; in parish archives, Vicksburg.

plantation where they apprised Leray of their situation in the city. That same day the priest and the military escort headed east. For the remainder of the War, Father Leray acted as chaplain at the hospital in Shelby Springs.[84]

Father Picherit

Another priest of the Natchez Diocese who is reported to have served as chaplain in the Confederate army was Father Henry Picherit, pastor of Brookhaven.[85] Tradition places him with the 22nd Mississippi Regiment, in particular with the "Sarsfield Southrons," later Company C of that regiment. He is supposed to have been on hand at the Battle of Baton Rouge (August 5, 1862), to have assisted at the retreat from Corinth in the early part of October, 1862, and at the seige of Vicksburg, and to have visited various military hospitals in the State. All of these things the priest is reported to have done without neglecting his parish at Brookhaven. However, dividing his time between the soldiers and the Catholics at Brookhaven would have presented little difficulty, since Picherit's congregation at this time numbered only five or six families.[86]

From the manner in which Bishop Elder was able to direct the movements of Father Picherit during the War[87] and in view of the personal freedom which the priest apparently enjoyed in working with the army, more than likely the pastor of Brookhaven served only as a civilian chaplain. Even though he may have been chosen chaplain of the all-Catholic "Sarsfield Southrons," the action, it would seem, never produced an official commission from the War Department for him.[88]

---

84 Memoirs of Sister M. Ignatius Sumner, 22-26; in ASMV. Also Heuzé to Odin, Vicksburg, June 23, 1864; in AUND: N. O. Papers.

85 Undated French newspaper clipping; in ADNJ, File: 1, Folder: Picherit. *Vicksburg Evening Post,* Vicksburg, July 2, 1934. *In and About Vicksburg* (Vicksburg, 1890), 148.

86 Elder Diary, 42.

87 Elder to Picherit, Natchez, Oct. 17, 1861, Nov. 12, 1861, May 18, 1863, June 20, 1863, April 8, 1864; in ADNJ, Elder Letter Book—#7, 125, #7, 209, #8, 383, #8, 434, #10, 8.

88 Germain, *op. cit.,* does not mention Father Picherit in his list of official Confederate chaplains, nor is any reference made to the priest's chaplaincy in the Elder Letter Books or diary.

Father Huber

Shortly after the famous Battle of Shiloh the pastor of Port Gibson, Father Philip Huber, had gone to the aid of Father Elia at the military hospitals set up at Holly Springs and Oxford.[89] This assignment, however, was only temporary. He was soon back at Port Gibson where he had to face the unpleasant situation of trying to pay the debt on an unfinished church with the help of a congregation that had shrunk to half a dozen persons.[90] In the autumn of 1862, Bishop Elder authorized Huber to visit the army camps and military hospitals in the Brookhaven area for the purpose of attending to the spiritual needs of the soldiers in these places. At the same time the Bishop gave the priest permission to collect funds for his church.[91] About a month later he received word from Huber that he had joined the army after having been chosen by the 10th Tennessee Regiment as its chaplain.[92] The news came as a surprise to Elder, for Huber's health had never been too good. "I had no idea," Elder wrote to the priest, "of your attaching yourself to a Regiment–because I did not think it possible for you . . . to endure the exposure and privations connected with such a life." [93] To satisfy himself that the priest was not foolishly risking his health in order to avoid the difficulties at Port Gibson, Elder added: "If you find your health cannot stand that method of life, you must leave it . . . I think I can find a place for you without your returning to Port Gibson." [94] In spite of this opening, Huber stayed with the Regiment.

During the second week of November Father Huber paid a visit to Port Gibson to settle some debts. From there he went down to Natchez to pick up some warm clothing and to report to the Bishop. The visit dispelled any anxiousness that may have existed on either side. The Bishop was pleased to learn that the priest's health had been excellent. Even now, Elder was happy to note, the priest appeared "fat" and "healthy." For Huber there was the reassuring decision of the Bishop that he need not worry about

[89] Elder to Huber, Natchez, April 16, 1862; in ADNJ, Elder Letter Book –#7, 472.
[90] Elder Diary, 1.
[91] *Ibid.*, 1.
[92] *Ibid.*, 3-4.
[93] Elder to Huber, Natchez, Oct. 23, 1862; in ADNJ, Elder Letter Book –#8, 126.
[94] *Ibid.*

having to return to Port Gibson, the Bishop going so far as to relieve him of all pastoral responsibilities toward that congregation and the missions attached to Port Gibson.[95]

Although the men of the 10th Regiment had requested a commission for their chaplain, Huber was still without it when he returned to his unit on November 12th. For little over a month the priest remained with the army. Then, just before Christmas, "for fear of winter rains," Huber left the regiment. After spending Christmas at Port Gibson, he reported in at Natchez.[96]

When heavy fighting—the Battle of Chickasaw Bayou—was reported to have taken place near Vicksburg shortly after Christmas, the Bishop asked Huber to hurry to the area and do what he could for the soldiers.[97] While the priest was up at Vicksburg, through a mistaken notion that his old unit had called for him, he rejoined the 10th Tennessee Regiment. Even after the matter had been cleared up, probably to the delight of the men, Huber stayed on with the Regiment, travelling south with it to Port Hudson, Louisiana, on the Mississippi River.[98] At Port Hudson Huber became quite sick with a sore throat and a fever and had to bed down.[99] When it became evident that he was also suffering from dysentery, the priest left the army and retired to Woodville, Mississippi.[100] After the priest had partially recuperated, Elder, true to his promise, gave the priest a new assignment in the Diocese, appointing him pastor of Sulphur Springs and Canton.[101]

How pure Father Huber's motives were for attaching himself to the 10th Tennessee Regiment as its chaplain is a debatable matter. Was the army chaplaincy a way of escape for him, for the priest admitted to Elder that he did not want to return to Port Gibson?[102] On the other hand, what kept him in the army when he had the Bishop's assurance that he would be given another post once he left the service? To say the least, his motives, then,

---

95 Elder Diary, 3-4.
96 *Ibid.*, 10.
97 *Ibid.*, 10.
98 *Ibid.*, 12.
99 *Ibid.*, 12.
100 *Ibid.*, 14. Elder to Huber, Natchez, Feb. 10, 1863; in ADNJ, Elder Letter Book—#8, 266-267.
101 Elder Diary, 49-50; Meador, *op. cit.*, in *Catholic Action of the South,* (Natchez Centennial Edition), Oct. 14, 1937, 48. Milot, *ibid.*, 52.
102 Elder Diary, 4.

would seem to have been a mixture of the noble and the purely human—a sense of duty to the men in the army and a need to escape from what seemed to be an impossible situation.

Father Mouton

When Father Pont from Corinth requested help just before the Battle of Shiloh, one of the first men the Bishop sent was Father John Mouton, who was operating in eastern and northeastern Mississippi.[103] The basis for the Bishop's choice was not simply geographical. As early as December, 1861, Mouton had expressed a willingness to serve as a military chaplain.[104] After the Battle of Shiloh the priest remained fully occupied with the soldiers until the end of the War. His specific field of labor was the military hospitals and camps located along the Mobile and Ohio Railroad which ran north and south through the eastern part of the State.

At first it was not thought necessary to apply for a commission. However, when it was seen that the priest's time was completely taken up in ministering to the needs of the soldiers, Elder took it upon himself to apply for a commission for the priest. In August, 1862, Elder wrote directly to the Secretary of War, George W. Randolph.[105] After two months of waiting the Bishop at the suggestion of General Albert Blanchard[106] directed another request to Richmond, this time to Colonel Lucius B. Northrop, Commissary-General.[107] Finally, on November 24, Elder received Mouton's commission.[108] Perhaps, by way of compensating for the long delay the authorities in Richmond had back-dated the appointment to August 4. Mouton was officially commissioned as a

---

[103] Elder to Mouton, Natchez, April 30, 1861, Oct. 10, 1861; in ADNJ, Elder Letter Book—#6, 203, #7, 116.

[104] Boheme to Elder, Paulding, Dec. 16, 1861; in ADNJ, File: Elder —B.

[105] Elder to Mouton, Natchez, August 7, 1862; in ADNJ, Elder Letter Book—#8, 15.

[106] Albert Gallatin Blanchard, a New Orleans Catholic, graduate of West Point and brigadier-general in the Confederate army, was the father-in-law of Bishop Elder's brother, Charles.

[107] Elder to Northrop, Natchez, October 21, 1862; in ADNJ, Elder Letter Book—#8, 120. Northrop, a Catholic West Point graduate from Charleston, had accepted the position of commissary-general at the urging of President Davis. A controversial figure, Northrop was removed from office in February, 1865.

[108] Elder to Mouton, Natchez, Nov. 24, 1862; in ADNJ, Elder Letter Book—#8, 176.

hospital chaplain and directed to "report to the Hospitals on the Mobile & Ohio Rail Road."

Although Elder had made his mind clear to Mouton several months earlier about giving top priority to the spiritual needs of the soldiers,[109] the Bishop had to re-state his position for the priest shortly after Christmas. Apparently while serving as chaplain Mouton was at the same time trying to meet the needs of his civilian congregations along the railroad and as far west as Sulphur Springs. Without mincing words Elder stated firmly:

> With regards to the Hospitals—you know a Priest is bound to leave every thing else if necessary, to attend to the dying; so that even if congregations must be neglected, the sick soldiers must be cared for. I have left several congregations without any Priest at all, for the sake of helping the soldiers: —and I must urge you to look after them, though other labors should be postponed, or even omitted altogether.[110]

Therefore, the Bishop ordered the chaplain to discontinue specifically his regular visits to Sulphur Springs, for as Elder saw it the priest had "too much other work to do." Perhaps it was just as well. One day, while travelling through the interior of the State, Mouton, dressed as he was in gray, was taken for a Confederate officer by an enemy raiding party. The Federal soldiers gave chase, firing as they rode. The priest, being a small man, dropped down behind the dash-board of his buggy and gave his horse free rein. The animal, very temperamental by nature, hearing the balls whistling between his ears, went across the bridges and through the swamps with such lightening speed that the enemy soon gave up the chase. In the run the chaplain lost only his hat.[111]

Fathers Heuzé, Georget & Finucane

Three other priests of the Diocese worked among the soldiers during the War without ever receiving commissions or attaching themselves to any particular military unit. Father Heuzé, who was left in charge of the parish in Vicksburg while Leray was away

---

[109] Elder to Mouton, Natchez, April 4, 1862; in ADNJ, Elder Letter Book—#7, 442.

[110] Elder to Mouton, Natchez, Dec. 28, 1862; in ADNJ, Elder Letter Book—#8, 210.

[111] Vally, "An East Mississippi Pastor," *The Messenger of the Sacred Heart,* III (n.s. xxiii, Jan. 1888), 17-22. Father Louis Vally was a personal friend of Father Mouton.

in the army,[112] was particularly busy between November, 1862, and July, 1863. He was faced with the almost impossible task of ministering to the sick and wounded in the military hospitals in and around Vicksburg and of taking care of the troops in the trenches during the seige. The latter, though not all of them were Catholic, numbered about 32,000. Once the seige began, Heuzé was assisted in his work by at least one Confederate Catholic chaplain, Father John Bannon.[113] While the presence of this priest surely lightened the load, it must be kept in mind that Heuzé was also trying to take care of the spiritual needs of the Catholic civilian population.

In January, 1863, at the request of Bishop Elder, Father Georget, pastor of Biloxi, left his parish and missions on the Gulf Coast and came north to help with the task of ministering to the spiritual needs of the soldiers.[114] On January 20, the Bishop sent him to Port Hudson, Louisiana, where there was a large number of Creole troops who were greatly dependent upon a French-speaking priest.[115] Georget remained with the soldiers until the beginning of March when he wrote to Elder from Jackson, Louisiana, saying he was on his way back to Biloxi. He was too sick, he explained to the Bishop, to stay in camp any longer.[116] The priest, though only in his thirties, must have been bothered with bad health even before coming north, since Elder had raised the question of it in an earlier letter to him.[117] For this same reason, shortly after he had sent

---

[112] Elder to Heuzé, Natchez, Nov. 12, 1862; in ADNJ, Elder Letter Book—#8, 154.

[113] Diary of Father J. C. Carrier, C.S.C., quoted in unpublished Conyngham Manuscript; in AUND. Father John Bannon left Ireland around 1853, for St. Louis, where he labored at the Cathedral, the church of the Immaculate Conception and at St. John's. When the War broke out, the priest sided with the South and went within the lines of the Confederacy. He served as chaplain to the Missouri forces under General Price, in which command there were 1800 Catholics. While serving as Confederate chaplain, he was considered seriously for the vacant see of Little Rock. In the fall of 1863, he was sent to Ireland by the Confederate government to check the flow of Irish immigrants to New York, so many of whom found themselves in the Union army shortly after arriving in the country. Bannon never returned to the United States. He later became a Jesuit and died at Dublin in 1900. Stock, *op. cit.*, in CHR, XVI (July 1930), 7. Elder to Odin, Natchez, May 21, 1863, July 6, 1863; in AUND: New Orleans Papers.

[114] Elder Diary, 6, 14.

[115] *Ibid.*, 14. Elder to Georget, Natchez, Jan. 24, 1863; in ADNJ, Elder Letter Book—#8, 227.

[116] Elder Diary, 19.

[117] *Ibid.*, 6.

the priest to Port Hudson, Elder began to have doubts about the wisdom of his action.[118] Therefore, the news of Georget's return to Biloxi must have come as sort of a relief to the anxious Bishop.

Still another priest of the Diocese who did part-time service among the soldiers was Father John Finucane. In a certain sense, this priest was not as expendable as other priests of the Diocese. He was the Benjamin of Elder's clergy, having been ordained only after the War had started.[119] Consequently, the young priest would have lacked the experience needed to work among the soldiers in camp. Furthermore, it would seem that the priest's health was delicate. During the first part of April, 1863, for example, he suffered a hemorrhage of the lungs with a temporary relapse again in August.[120] Nevertheless, when the needs of the soldiers became pressing, Elder did not hesitate to put Finucane into the field. In December, 1862, the Bishop sent the young priest to visit the induction and training center at Brookhaven, with further orders to visit the hospitals along the railroad south of that town.[121] Afterward he was to report to Father Orlandi at Jackson, who was begging for a priest to assist him in ministering to a great many soldiers who were dying in and around Jackson.[122] When Father Leray and the Sisters of Mercy arrived in Jackson just before Christmas, Elder felt justified in recalling the priest to Natchez soon afterward.[123] These few weeks were apparently the only stint which Finucane did with the military as a civilian chaplain.

Bishop Elder

Not content to be merely a director of operations at headquarters, Bishop Elder got into the field himself on a number of occasions, visiting camps, battlefields and hospitals. In May, 1862, Elder travelled to the northeastern part of the State where some of the first fighting on the soil of Mississippi took place.[124] His untiring devotion to the sick and wounded is revealed in a letter he sent

118 Elder to Georget, Natchez, Jan. 24, 1863; in ADNJ, Elder Letter Book—#8, 227.

119 June 30, 1861.

120 Elder Diary, 27, 28, 61.

121 *Ibid.*, 7.

122 *Ibid.*, 6.

123 Elder to Finucane, Natchez, Dec. 30, 1862; in ADNJ, Elder Letter Book—#8, 217.

124 Elder to Odin, Corinth, May 13, 1862; in AUND: N.O. Papers.

to his vicar-general after having been in the area for almost a month. Writing from Corinth just before General Beauregard retreated south to Tupelo, the Bishop reported:

> Travelling is slow. I started May the 14th, for Okolona. Spent a whole day in the hospitals there—1300 sick. At Rienzi, I stopped for several hours—300 sick. I only reached Columbus, Saturday, and found 2300 sick there.
>
> At Mass, Sunday, we had sixty persons, and twelve men at Holy Communion. Coming back from Mobile, where I had gone to look for Chaplains, I remained two days at Macon; there were one thousand sick soldiers. I baptized many at all these places.
>
> Yesterday, while in camp with Capt. Felix Hughes, his regiment received orders to go to the field. Fr. Picherit and I followed in an ambulance; but thank God, there was no fight at all. We are now going back to camp to hear confessions. If possible, I will start for Natchez to-morrow, but I must stop on my way at Holly Springs. Health excellent, clothes scarce, and some stolen.[125]

In December, 1862, 7,000 Confederate troops under General Gardner were stationed at Port Hudson, Louisiana. Their winter quarters were of the poorest. When it was reported to Elder just after Christmas that a good many of these soldiers were Catholic and had been without the services of a priest for a long time, he hurried down to the camp, travelling by buggy and train via Woodville and Bayou Sara.[126] Arriving at noon on New Year's Day, the Bishop was given a cheering welcome by the soldiers.[127] The officers were no less cordial in receiving him. General Miles offered the Bishop a bed in his own quarters, while a Lieutenant James O'Neil turned over his tent to him for the hearing of confessions. For the next eight days Elder celebrated Mass each morning in front of O'Neil's tent, gave out Holy Communion and heard confessions in the morning and afternoon. One evening out on the parade grounds the Bishop led the soldiers in the public recitation of the rosary and then delivered a sermon to the assembled

---

125 Elder to Grignon, Corinth, May 26, 1862; quoted by Elder, *Character-Glimpses of Most Reverend William Henry Elder, D.D.* (Cincinnati, 1911), 41.

126 Elder Diary, 10-11.

127 Newspaper clipping, Cincinnati, Nov. 1904; in possession of Mrs. Isabel Elder Merrick, Pass Christian-New Orleans.

men.[128] Returning to Natchez on January 9, Elder stopped off at Jackson, Louisiana, where he visited a military hospital and heard the confessions of some Creole soldiers with whom the local pastor, Father Scollard, was unable to converse.[129]

When the Battle of Port Gibson took place on May 1, 1863, the Bishop of Natchez was again on the scene soon afterward to visit the wounded soldiers scattered through several make-shift hospitals and a number of private homes. Although on this occasion Elder found few Catholics, he noted with satisfaction in his diary: "Everywhere I was very well received both by patients & by the families with which they were staying." [130] Faithful to the advice he gave his own priests, the Bishop did not hesitate on this occasion to extend his ministry to the non-Catholic patients. In his diary Elder revealed the routine he followed at such times. Introducing himself as a Catholic bishop, he quite naturally began to talk about the Church. If his exposition brought no immediate response or if it was evident that the patient listened merely out of idle curiosity, Elder would conclude by exhorting the soldier to promise God that he would search for the truth and, once found, embrace it. Finally, before moving on, the Bishop would teach the man how to make an act of contrition.[131]

When Bishop Elder visited the camps or field hospitals, he fared no better than the ordinary soldier—sleeping in a tent or under the stars and eating the same grub. Besides undergoing the privations associated with camp life, the Bishop experienced other hardships while making these visits: being tossed from his buggy in the middle of a stream; falling through a bridge; having to beg for a night's lodging at the houses of strangers; spending a restless night on a flea-ridden bed; tramping along the road while he let a sick soldier ride his horse; and having his clothes stolen. Admittedly none of these things was heroic, but all of them surely helped to identify Elder with and win the confidence of the man in uniform. Furthermore, to his own priests it was encouraging to note that, while their bishop made demands upon them, he was no less willing to make the same sacrifices himself.

---

128 Elder Diary, 11.
129 *Ibid.*, 13.
130 *Ibid.*, 33.
131 *Ibid.*, 34.

In the course of the Civil War Bishop Elder, pressed though he was for clergymen on the home-front, made the gesture of releasing six, perhaps seven, priests to full-time military service as official chaplains.[132] Four others served part-time as civilian chaplains, but even these were directed to give top priority to the spiritual needs of the soldiers. Of these eleven priests three died as a result of sickness contracted or aggravated while serving the troops.[133]

---

[132] The seventh priest about whose official status there is some doubt was Father Picherit. Despite the silence of most of the primary sources on hand, there is one letter written by Elder which implies that Picherit at the time was working among the troops and in particular with the 22nd Mississippi Regiment to which tradition links him as its chaplain. Elder to Grignon, Corinth, May 26, 1862; quoted by Blanchard-Elder, *op. cit.*, 41.—Germain, "Catholic Military and Naval Chaplains, 1776-1917," in CHR, XV (July 1929), 174, lists Rev. James T. Cunningham as the chaplain of the 3rd Miss. Infantry. This priest was not from the Natchez Diocese, but belonged to the Wheeling Diocese; *Metropolitan Catholic Almanac*, 1861, 77.

[133] At least four Catholic chaplains in the Union army served in Mississippi during the course of the War. They were Fathers John (Thomas M. ?) Brady, 15th Michigan Infantry; J. C. Carrier, C.S.C., 6th Missouri Infantry; John Ireland, 5th Minnesota Infantry; and Napoleon Mignault, 17th Wisconsin Infantry.

The first convent of the Sisters of St. Joseph of Bourg at Bay St. Louis, Mississippi, dating back to 1855. Affectionately referred to as "Citeaux" because of the poverty associated with this, the first, foundation of the Sisters in the United States.

The "old Cobb house" in Vicksburg, Mississippi which became the first convent of the Sisters of Mercy in the State. During the Civil War the convent served as a hospital for Confederate soldiers and later as billets for Union officers.

Chapter XI

ANGELS OF MERCY

The strain of war taxed the limited personnel of the Diocese of Natchez even further when two groups of its Sisters went off to war as volunteer nurses. Three Daughters of Charity from Natchez had a tour of duty which lasted a little less than a year, while the Sisters of Mercy from Vicksburg served throughout the War. In the course of the great conflict two other Sisters' communities from out of state served for short periods at military hospitals in Mississippi. Their lives at this time were a mixture of hardship, hazard and heartache, made bearable by unpredictable dashes of humor and miracles of grace.

Daughters of Charity: New Orleans and Mobile

In the spring of 1862, the white cornette of the Daughters of Charity was to be seen fluttering through the wards of the military hospitals of northeastern Mississippi. It was most probably the first time, for that matter, that Catholic nuns had ever been seen in that part of the State.

When the Confederate troops from Pensacola moved north to join General Albert S. Johnston's army organizing along the Mississippi-Tennessee line, these Sisters who had been serving in the military hospitals opposite Fort Pickens followed the soldiers at the request of the military authorities.[1] At least a week before the Battle of Shiloh these Sisters were working in the military hospitals at Corinth and Holly Springs.[2] It would seem that the Sisters who were originally from New Orleans took over the hospital in Holly Springs while those who had been stationed in Mobile prior to the War were installed at the hospital in Corinth. In the latter place the hospital was located in the Corona Female College, a large brick building situated on a hill overlooking a railroad cross-

[1] *Memorial to "The Nuns of the Battlefield,"* speech delivered by Hon. Ambrose Kennedy in the House of Representatives, March 18, 1918 (Washington, D.C.: U.S. Government Printing Office, 1918), 31; Baudier, *Catholic Church in Louisiana,* 430.

[2] Elder to Mouton, Natchez, April 4, 1862; in ADNJ, Elder Letter Book—#7, 442.

ing, for the town of Corinth at that time was little more.[3] After the Battle of Shiloh the Sisters here were assisted by a number of ladies from Mobile, one of whom paid tribute to the Sisters' efficiency and kindness. In her diary under the date April 18, 1862, Kate Cumming wrote: "When we arrived at the hospital, we were charmed with the cleanliness and neatness visible on every side. The Sisters of Charity have charge of the domestic part, and, as usual with them, everything is Parfait. We were received very kindly by them."[4] At Holly Springs the Sisters were most probably employed in the general hospital located on the main square. The Sisters at Corinth returned to Mobile at the end of May, 1862, when the hospital was closed down and Beauregard with his troops withdrew to Tupelo. Not until the autumn did the hospital at Holly Springs cease operation. Exhausted and in tatters, the Sisters dragged themselves back to New Orleans.[5] For their devoted service to the Confederate sick and wounded these Daughters of Charity were presented with a medal of honor "by the request of the commanding General, Braxton Bragg."[6]

Sisters of Charity: Cincinnati

The second group of non-resident Sisters to serve as volunteer nurses in Mississippi was associated with the Union army. They were Sisters of Charity from Cincinnati. Founded by Mother Elizabeth Ann Seton,[7] they were to be distinguished at the time by their black crepe bonnet. From their hospital in Cincinnati, Sister Anthony, the "Angel of the Battlefield," Sister Theodosia and Sister Camilla made several trips to the battlefields of Shiloh in April, 1862, to nurse the wounded on the spot and to help bring others back to Cincinnati by boat.[8] In her memoirs Sister Anthony, then, adds: "After our work at Shiloh was finished, we followed the army to Corinth . . ."[9]

---

[3] Barton, *Angels of the Battlefield: A History of the Labors of the Catholic Sisterhoods in the Late Civil War* (Philadelphia, 1898), 52-53.

[4] Cumming, *Journal of Hospital Life* (Louisville, 1866).

[5] Baudier, *op. cit.,* 430.

[6] Charity Hospital Book, p. 114; in Marillac Seminary Archives, Normandy, Mo.

[7] American convert to Catholicism, Mother Seton died a saintly death in 1821. Her cause of beatification is now being examined in Rome. (1962)

[8] Barton, *op. cit.,* 72-75.

[9] Memoirs of Sister Anthony, S.C., p. 6; in the ASCC.

When the Union army occupied Corinth at the end of May, these Sisters were installed in a hospital—perhaps the one just evacuated by the Confederates—to nurse the boys in blue. The chief cause of sickness at the time was typhoid fever. For a good many of the soldiers it proved fatal. Encountering at first some opposition from the soldiers and civilians, the Sisters quickly won them over by their patience and kindness. Antagonism soon gave way to respect and even friendliness. After a few months the need for the Sisters was found to be more pressing elsewhere and they, accordingly, left the State.[10]

Daughters of Charity: Natchez

In September, 1862, General Albert G. Blanchard asked the Daughters of Charity stationed in Natchez to take charge of a military hospital under his command at Monroe, Louisiana.[11] At the time the Sisters and their orphans were refugees on a plantation outside Natchez which had just been shelled by the Federal gunboat "Essex."[12] The invitation was accepted. Three nuns from the hard-pressed community were sent: Sisters Geraldine Murphy, Emerita Quinlan and Vincentia Leddy.[13] When a dispatch was received announcing the approach of the "Essex," the Sisters together with Bishop Elder crossed the Mississippi River in a skiff in the dead of night.[14] Safely across, they signaled back to their anxious friends on the opposite bank by means of a small night lamp that all was well. The party was met by an ambulance sent by General Blanchard. At this point the Bishop bade farewell to the Sisters and recrossed the river. For the remainder of that night and the following two days the Sisters and escort travelled over rough and dangerous roads. They finally arrived at Monroe on September 8th.[15] At the hospital in Monroe the Sisters found a few cases of typhoid fever and malaria, but nothing like an epidemic

---

[10] Gallagher, "A Study of the Nursing of Sister Anthony O'Connell, Sister of Charity of Cincinnati," unpublished master's thesis presented to the Catholic University of America, Washington, D.C., 1957; copy in ASCC, p. 26.

[11] Annals of the Daughters of Charity, 1929, p. 159 ff.; in the Archives of the Daughters of Charity, Emmitsburg, Md. Kennedy, *op. cit.*, 31-32.

[12] Annals of the Daughters of Charity, 1929, 159; in the Archives of the Daughters of Charity, Emmitsburg, Md.

[13] Kennedy, *op. cit.*, 32.

[14] "Les Filles de la Charité pendant la guerre civile," *Les Missions Catholiques,* LXV (Sept. 17, 1863), 304.

[15] *Ibid.*

prevailed. Most of the patients were wounded men.[16] Their number was fairly small, so the Sisters had no difficulty in nursing them. In June, 1863, after the Battle of Milliken's Bend the picture suddenly changed. The facilities of the hospital were taxed to the straining point. When Sister Mary Thomas, the Sisters' superior at Natchez, visited her subjects on June 11, she found the nuns well but extremely busy, trying to care for over a thousand sick and wounded.[17] Most of the patients, it was discovered, were woefully ignorant of religion, many never having been exposed to any religious instruction. Here as elsewhere the charity and the lives of the Sisters prompted many of the patients to give serious thought to their own salvation. Through the gentle proddings of the Sisters more than fifty soldiers were received into the Church on their deathbeds. In many other cases the example of the Sisters at least dispelled a good deal of prejudice toward the Church and the Catholic Sisterhood.[18]

From the start the soldiers were delighted to have the Sisters and manifested the greatest respect for them. However, through the carelessness of one of the men the Sisters' presence almost ended in tragedy. In a fit of anger an officer fired a gun at a private and hit Sister Emerita, tearing off part of her cornette without hurting her.[19]

Just before the Confederates evacuated Monroe in August, 1863, arrangements were made to transfer the hospital to Mt. Lebanon, Louisiana, a point still farther west. Although General Blanchard asked the Sisters to take charge of the hospital at its new location, it was decided that it would be better for the Sisters to return to Natchez where the growing number of orphans had made it increasingly more difficult for the limited staff to carry

[16] Kennedy, *op. cit.*, 32.
[17] Elder Diary, 39.
[18] Baudier, *op. cit.*, 429.
[19] A Natchez newspaper article of 1896, presents a different account of the episode: "A convalescing officer in one of the wards gave vent to some profanity in the presence of one of the Sisters. The gentle lady kindly and mildly rebuked him. He profusely apologized. When she had passed on a few feet a pistol was fired, and the ball passed through the Sister's cornette, close to her head. The man declared the shot was accidental. He was arrested, and would have been severely dealt with, had not the Sister interceded for him." *The Weekly Democrat*, Natchez, Dec. 2, 1896. It would seem that popular imagination had enlarged upon the facts, since the primary source makes no mention of the rebuke and describes the action as an accident rather than as an intended assault upon the Sister.

on alone. Respecting the Sisters' wishes, the General sent them back to the river under a flag of truce with a military escort of eight men. At Vidalia they crossed over to Natchez, rejoining their religious community after an absence of eleven months.[20]

Sisters of Mercy: Vicksburg

On April 24, 1862, Admiral Farragut smashed by Forts Jackson and St. Philip, the guardians of the approaches to New Orleans. The next day news that the Crescent City had fallen was telegraphed up the river to shake the towns and cities from their sense of safety.

> When the message clicked out in Vicksburg it stunned the people. Forts Jackson and St. Philip were the strongest fortifications on the river; there was nothing left between New Orleans and Vicksburg to hold back the gunboats, and New Orleans was less than five days steaming away. The boats, with gunports yawning black in their hulls, would soon be up the river to anchor off the city.[21]

As soon as the thought of being under Federal guns registered in their minds, many people of Vicksburg began a frantic rush to leave the city. A good many, however, refused to be stampeded by fear and remained behind. Among these more courageous souls were the Sisters of Mercy. They stayed on to continue classes for those children whose parents had not evacuated to the country. Nevertheless, realizing the danger, the Sisters formally brought the school year to a close during the second week of May.[22] And none too soon. On Sunday, May 18, the Federal gunboats, so long expected, finally steamed into view. After futile negotiations between the opposing authorities the guns opened fire on the afternoon of May 22. Vicksburg shuddered under the bombardment. The shelling was not heavy or concentrated, but is was enough to start a new exodus from the city.

Strangely enough the Sisters stayed on in the city for at least a week after the shelling began. But, then, on May 29, Ascension Thursday, urged on by Father Leray who had become anxious for their safety, the Sisters accepted Major Cook's invitation to stay with his family on their plantation outside Vicksburg. However, a few days later Mother De Sales and two other Sisters re-

20 Kennedy, *op. cit.*, 32. Baudier, *op. cit.*, 429.
21 Walker, *Vicksburg, A People at War, 1860-1865*, 72.
22 Memoirs of Sister M. Ignatius Sumner, 6; in ASMV.

turned to the city to nurse the sick and wounded soldiers in their own convent which had been converted into an emergency hospital.[23] Some of the regiments had been hard hit by measles and typhoid fever. As a result, the city's hospital facilities were soon over-taxed. Some of the stricken soldiers were fortunate enough to be taken into private homes and cared for. Many others were left without shelter or made to lie on bare floors in unfurnished buildings requisitioned by the government.[24] After an inexcusable delay the authorities, finally, decided to establish a temporary hospital outside Vicksburg at Mississippi Springs. The services of the Sisters were requested and Mother De Sales quickly agreed to help. She immediately sent two Sisters and a postulant to the Springs to prepare for the arrival of the first patients. What the Sisters found was a dirty, run-down, unfurnished house. Undaunted the trio, soon joined by the rest of the Sisters, set to work cleaning up the building. Before they could get the place in satisfactory condition, the sick began to arrive. One of the first questions the Sisters asked, as the sick were carried in, was: Where are the beds? Oh! you mean the mattresses. They caught fire in transit and burned. During the first week four hundred patients were brought from Vicksburg to the makeshift hospital. By the end of the second week there were over seven hundred. Through the hot summer the Sisters worked day and night at a feverish pace, but, as Sister Ignatius noted in her memoirs, the fatigue felt by the Sisters was much easier to bear than the distress they experienced in being able to do so little to relieve the suffering of their patients, the facilities being so primitive and so limited.[25]

At the end of October the government decided to close the hospital at Mississippi Springs since it was too far removed from the railroad. The surgeon in charge chose to open a hospital in Jackson in the buildings of the Deaf and Dumb Institute and he asked the Sisters to assist him. Mother De Sales agreed. However, the Sisters remained for only a week at the new hospital, for it was soon evident that the doctor could easily manage without them. On the other hand, according to reports from Father Leray,

---

23 *Ibid.*, 7.

24 Hall, *The Story of the 26th Louisiana Infantry, in the Service of the Confederate States,* (no publisher, no place, 1890), 14-15, quoted by Walker, *op. cit.*, 102.

25 Memoirs of Sister M. Ignatius Sumner, 7; in ASMV.

Mother de Sales, Superior of the Sisters of Mercy.

Lyceum building at Ole Miss., Sisters of Mercy nursed Confederate soldiers here after the battle of Shiloh.

post chaplain at Oxford, their services were badly needed at the military hospital set up on the campus of the University of Mississippi. The twelve buildings which made up the University contained about a thousand sick soldiers. Many were extremely ill and neglected. The whole place seemed to be in disorder. With typical energy the Sisters soon had the hospital in fair condition and operating efficiently. With some humor one of the Sisters noted that even "the invariable collegiate tobacco juice was disappearing from the walls." [26] One of the most difficult tasks facing the Sisters was that of providing a suitable diet for the sick soldiers. The Sisters themselves regularly had nothing to eat but corn bread without salt together with a cup of sage tea or sweet potato coffee. On only two occasions were they able to obtain such "precious-as-gold" items as eggs, butter and apples for their patients.[27]

On November 29, 1862, the Union Army of the Tennesse began to advance down the Mississippi Central Railroad from Holly Springs in the direction of Water Valley. In the path of the march was Oxford. The Sisters were alerted. Except for about sixty patients who were too ill to be moved, the sick were hastily evacuated. Two hours before the Federal cavalry swept into Oxford, the Sisters themselves were put on the last train which hurried out of town. They travelled on a flat car over which a canvass had been spread for a covering by day. In vain did the Sisters try to get some rest. One of the Sisters had a broom handle stuck in her ribs for one portion of the trip; another was nearly smothered by a mattress thrown on top of her; still another Sister found herself disputing with some fleas for the possession of a quilt. When a number of soldiers who were crowded on top of the railroad cars tried to join the Sisters on their car where there was more room, a stewart who had accompanied the Sisters from Oxford put them to flight by asking very gravely "if they had had the small pox, as there was a case among the Sisters." [28] At nightfall the train halted. The Sisters laid some mattresses on the floor of the car and thus passed the night. The next day toward evening the refugees arrived in Canton where it was decided to spend the night.[29]

---

[26] *Ibid.*, 9.
[27] *Ibid.*, 9.
[28] *Ibid.*, 11.
[29] *Ibid.*, 9.

In Canton the Sisters were obviously a novelty and, as a result, they enjoyed a few chuckles over the treatment given them. At the train depot the guard on duty, catching a glimpse of the Sisters' coifs and thinking they were Union prisoners with head wounds, hurried over to take charge. He was understandably abashed when he discovered that his "Yankee prisoners" were only meek ladies. Still somewhat mystified, the guard turned to Father Leray who was near at hand and inquired if the ladies were his daughters. Before the priest could explain, the soldier, noting the black habits of the Sisters, added: "Poor things! I suppose their Mother is dead." [30] It was decided to check in at the local hotel. Still unidentified, the Sisters approached the registration desk to make inquiries about accommodations for the night. Cheerily but somewhat informally the owner exclaimed: "You're welcome, my girls, to the parlor. All the rest of the house is full." [31] Obtaining a few quilts, the Sisters spread them on the floor of the parlor and there, in the company of four servant girls who had accompanied them from Oxford, they spent the night. The next morning the refugee train continued on its way to Jackson where it arrived a few hours later.[32]

In Jackson the Sisters enjoyed the hospitality of the pastor, Father Orlandi. Although the Sisters never received any compensation in the way of a salary from the government, they were always permitted to draw army rations. Fortunately they were allowed to draw this minimum even now when they were "unemployed." Shortly before Christmas, 1862, Dr. Warren Brickell of New Orleans took over a large building in Jackson, called the Dixon House, and converted it into a hospital. He invited the Sisters to assist him. The offer was accepted. Into a small four-room cottage adjacent to the main building the Sisters moved. Here they were able to lead a semblance of normal religious life while they assisted in the running of the hospital.[33]

In the beginning the Sisters encountered some opposition from the officers associated with the hospital. The latter would have preferred to manage the hospital alone, for the Sisters' presence made it more difficult for these men to aggrandize themselves at

[30] *Ibid.*, 9.
[31] *Ibid.*, 9.
[32] *Ibid.*, 10.
[33] *Ibid.*, 10.

the expense of the sick, a situation not infrequently denounced by hospital critics during the War.[34] Unfortunately Doctor Brickell was influenced by these unscrupulous men for a time. However, he soon discovered the true state of affairs and stood by the Sisters.[35]

On May 14, 1863, Union General Sherman and his forces occupied Jackson and laid waste to the city, the supply depot for the Vicksburg garrison. Although a good deal of property, civilian and military, was destroyed at this time, the hospital was left intact and the Sisters unmolested, a military guard having been posted outside the hospital buildings during the occupation.[36] Having accomplished his purpose, Sherman withdrew, marched west and joined in the siege of Vicksburg. Once this Confederate stronghold on the Mississippi capitulated, the Union armies returned to Jackson and laid siege to the city from July 10 to 16. During the bombardment the hospital was hit, a shell passing through the ward where the wounded were but fortunately exploding outside. While the city was being evacuated, the Sisters with Father Leray took refuge in the State House. Then, they too were given orders to join the army on the other side of the Pearl River. The order was given so quickly that they were able to pack very little before leaving. On July 16, the day the Union army reoccupied Jackson, the Sisters boarded the last train leaving the area. Travelling in box cars, they continued their odyssey of mercy which took them this time out of the State to Shelby Springs, Alabama, a "watering place" about sixty miles north of Selma.[37]

Apparently Shelby Springs was a health resort. The main building, consisting of two parts, had a large ball room which was conveniently converted into a surgical ward. There was also a long line of cottages which may have provided comfort for those trying to escape the summer's heat but which were too airy for hospital patients. As usual, Sister Ignatius noted, dirt was "in melancholy ascendancy." Consequently, the Sisters had to spend many long hours scrubbing floors, walls and hearths in getting the place ready to receive the sick and wounded. The task was not particularly easy, since one of the Sisters was herself recuperating from a bout

---

34 Coulter, *The Confederate States of America, 1861-1865,* 436.
35 Memoirs of Sister M. Ignatius Sumner, 10-11; in ASMV.
36 *Ibid.,* 16.
37 *Ibid.,* 16-17.

with jaundice and all were put on half rations until the sick should arrive to save on their limited food stores.[38]

During their stay at Shelby Springs the Sisters experienced the hardships and privations which were common to other refugees in Alabama from Louisiana and Mississippi. They had to mend their black habits with white thread. From their limited resources they were forced to pay $113 for enough material to make a calico dress for a postulant who had joined their community at the Springs. Shoes made by Father Leray from rabbit skins eventually were the only footwear available. For six months they received no mail. On the other hand, they were quite fortunate in being able to lead a fairly normal religious life, enjoying daily Mass, time for most of their religious exercises, recreation taken together, and an annual retreat preached by Father Usannaz, S.J. of Mobile. One of the Sisters was even able to make her profession.[39]

Not long after the hospital was established at Shelby Springs, Dr. Brickell was transferred. The Sisters soon came to regret his departure, for he was followed by several other doctors who neglected their duties and capitalized on their position to supplement their salary at the expense of the sick soldiers. Their example in turn was copied by the lower ranking officers. Unfortunately through some subtle influence the patients were made to believe that they suffered through the Sisters' fault. Either personally or through another the Sisters filed an official complaint with the Medical Director and a full investigation followed. The Sisters were exonerated and to their delight Dr. Brickell was returned. From that time on until the end of the War, although provisions continued to be scarce, it was the policy at Shelby Springs to sacrifice everything in favor of the sick, and, consequently, they were better fed than they had been at any previous time.[40]

Here as at Mississippi Springs, Oxford and Jackson, the Sisters through their charity led a number of patients to embrace the Catholic faith and at the same time broke down a good deal of prejudice. In some patients prejudice against the Church and the Catholic Sisterhood was so great that they turned away in indignation when the Sisters tried to nurse them. One soldier who needed

[38] *Ibid.*, 18.
[39] *Ibid.*, 19; Sister M. Teresa Newman made her profession on Jan. 6, 1864.
[40] *Ibid.*, 19.

attention badly resisted every effort on the part of one of the Sisters to dress a sore on his side. No amount of patient pleading on her part could win him over to accept her services. When she approached him a third time, the sick man burst into tears and asked her forgiveness, admitting that he had been taught to believe the worst about Catholic nuns. A Tennessee soldier with a serious neck wound whose life was slowly ebbing away refused to have a Sister even sit beside him to hold a compress in place. When he finally relented, he confessed that his prejudice sprang, not from any personal experience, but from bad reading and bad preaching.[41] In one of the hospitals a naive stewart, convinced that the Sisters had been entrapped and were living in ignorance of the dangers to which their souls were exposed, kindly lent one of the nuns a copy of *The Scarlet Lady,* a book describing the "horrors" of convent life. To offset the good impression the Sisters were making upon the soldiers with whom they came in contact, copies of Maria Monk's *Awful Disclosures* [42] were circulated through the hospitals. However, by degrees the Sisters through their indiscriminant and self-sacrificing service dispelled such prejudice and ignorance, their actions speaking far louder than the printed word.[43]

On August 11, 1863, Bishop Elder wrote to Mother De Sales about conditions in Vicksburg since the city's occupation by the Union army. The convent, he reported, was damaged very little by the shelling. The commanding officer, General McPherson, had given the assurance that the Sisters, once they returned, would have no difficulty in reoccupying their convent, but in the meanwhile it would be used if needed. For this reason the Bishop judged it wise for the Sisters to return as soon as possible. There was another important reason. The parents of the congregation were very concerned about their children who had now been without school for fifteen months. Realizing at the same time the importance of their work at the Springs, how difficult it would be to leave the sick, Elder ended his letter on this note: "I leave you and Fr. Leray to exercise your discretion in the circum-

---

[41] *Ibid.,* 13-14.

[42] Monk, Maria, *Awful Disclosures of the Hotel Dieu Nunnery of Montreal,* 1st edit. (New York, 1836)—a vile attack upon the life of the Sisters in Catholic convents.

[43] Annals of the Sisters of Mercy, St. Francis Xavier Academy, Vicksburg, Mississippi; in ASMV.

stances."[44] Nevertheless, he suggested that it might be well if at least one or two of the Sisters returned. In November Elder paid a personal visit to the Sisters at the Springs. After surveying the situation, he still recommended that they make such arrangements as would facilitate their prompt return to Vicksburg.[45]

Toward the end of January, 1864, Father Grignon arrived at Shelby Springs to escort the Sisters home. Not understanding the difficulties involved in travelling across the State, much of which was still no-man's-land, the Vicar-General had failed to secure the necessary military passes for the Sisters. When two of the Sisters applied at the office of Confederate General Polk in Meridian, Mississippi for the necessary passes, the Bishop-turned-General[46] refused to grant them for military reasons. Apparently there was still a good deal of military movement going on between Meridian and Vicksburg. After waiting around for two or three weeks, hoping that conditions might change, Father Grignon finally returned to Natchez via New Orleans without the Sisters.[47]

When his Vicar-General arrived in Natchez on March 5, Elder was understandably disappointed to see him arrive alone, but he did not give up. Two days later when he again wrote to the Superior of the Sisters at Shelby Springs, the Bishop made it clear that there was to be no change in plans and urged the nun to continue to press the Sisters' case.

> It was quite a disappointment to me, & it will be a much greater one to the people of Vicksburgh, that you are not able to return.—I hope however, that it will not be long before you can succeed. (. . . .) Nothing is more important for the welfare of the South than the good Christian education of its children. (. . . .) Please to say to Fr. Leray that I desire him to do all in his power to effect your return—& either to accompany you, or to get some one who will do so.—I think that after all your faithful services to the soldiers, & having followed them so far away from home,—you ought to have yourselves and your baggage carried back by the government conveyances or at government expense—& to have also a flag of truce to accompany you if needful. I have no doubt

---

44 Elder to Mother De Sales, Natchez, Aug. 11, 1863; in ADNJ, Elder Letter Book—#8, 460.

45 Memoirs of Sister M. Ignatius Sumner, 20; in ASMV.

46 Major General Leonidas Polk of the Army of Tennessee was Bishop of the Episcopal Diocese of Louisiana when he entered the Confederate army.

47 Memoirs of Sister M. Ignatius Sumner, 20-21; in ASMV.

that Genl. Polk—or the authorities at Richmond will direct that this be done, if proper representations are made.[48]

Just as soon as it was reported that it was relatively safe to travel, Father Leray made application again to General Polk on behalf of the Sisters. The General this time granted the necessary passes but would not or could not provide any other facilities for the Sisters' return trip. Not long afterward Polk was ordered to the field. He was replaced by General Johnson who not only granted the requested passes, but also provided transportation and permitted Father Leray to take a leave of absence so that he might accompany the Sisters. It was decided that four of the Sisters would remain behind to continue nursing the sick, while Mother De Sales, Sister Ignatius, Sister Philomena and Sister Antonia, a novice, would return to Vicksburg.[49]

On May 23, 1864, Father Leray and the Sisters set out. Travelling by rail, they had a nearly fatal accident about three miles east of Meridian. The car in which they were traveling ran off the track, turned over and was barely saved from plunging into a deep pond by the trunk of a tree. The remainder of the trip to Meridian was made in mud cars, a promiscuous jumble of men and women nurses, trunks, soldiers and Sisters. At Meridian the Sisters spent the night in a railroad car. The next morning they continued on their way to Jackson, which was again in Confederate hands. Here they were met by Bishop Elder.[50] It was through the Bishop's efforts that an army ambulance was provided as a conveyance for the Sisters for the rest of the trip. The party was also given a military escort—a provost marshal and a private bearing a flag of truce. This last lap of their journey made a deep impression upon the Sisters. Working in the hospitals, they had seen what war could do to human bodies. Now they saw more graphically than before what it could do to the countryside and to property. "Desolate" Sister Ignatius described the region through which they passed,

---

[48] Elder to Mother De Sales, Vicksburg, March 7, 1864; in ADNJ, Elder Letter Book—#9, 198. From the persistence with which Elder urged the Sisters to return to Vicksburg it is quite obvious that he was very interested in restoring as much normalcy to Catholic life in Vicksburg as possible. However, it also prompts one to raise the intriguing question: did Elder at this time consider the South's cause doomed?

[49] Memoirs of Sister M. Ignatius Sumner, 22; in ASMV; also Elder Diary, 111.

[50] Elder Diary, 81.

marked as it was by what seemed to be a "relentless and savage destruction."[51] The nun's description was not exaggerated, for even Sherman himself, who had already begun his scorched-earth policy, had reported to Grant on July 18, 1863: "Jackson will no longer be a point of danger. The land is devasted for 30 miles around."[52] After spending the night in a private home just on the other side of the Big Black River, the refugees and escort continued on their way early the next morning. The country on this side of the river showed the same signs of desolation and destruction, growing worse as they drew closer to Vicksburg—deserted encampments, carcasses of dead animals, craters in the road, torn up fences. At three o'clock in the afternoon of May 28 the party reached the Federal lines just outside the city. As has been noted, only the Sisters were permitted to enter the city. They were conducted under guard to headquarters, where after being informed that they could not reoccupy their convent they were released, accepting the hospitality of Mr. and Mrs. A. Genella.[53]

The other half of Mother De Sales' community remained on at Shelby Springs for the rest of the War. Eager to relieve the needs of these Sisters as soon as possible, the Superior applied to General Slocum for permission to send a few badly needed articles back to her Sisters in Alabama. After an initial rebuff from the General the nun finally obtained permission to send a few items back to the Sisters at Shelby Springs via the man who brought in their baggage from Jackson. In July Mother De Sales received permission to take a trunk with clothing through the lines to Meridian. The trip was only a partial success. Through a mix-up the telegram she sent to Father Leray and the Sisters arrived at the Springs too late for them to rendezvous with her at Meridian. A second trip made in March, 1865, was more successful. This time she could deliver a load of supplies personally to Sister Vincent, who had come from Alabama to Jackson with Father Leray. They brought along a New Orleans' postulant who had joined the community at Shelby Springs. The young lady, Miss Amanaide Poursine,[54] returned to Vicksburg with Mother De Sales. Although the Confed-

[51] Memoirs of Sister M. Ignatius Sumner, 23; in ASMV.
[52] *Official Records: Army,* Ser. I, Vol. XXIV, II, 530.
[53] Memoirs of Sister M. Ignatius Sumner, 22-25; in ASMV.
[54] On May 30, 1865, Miss Amanaide Poursine received the habit of the Sisters of Mercy and was given the name of Sister Mary Xavier. Bernard, *The Sisters of Mercy in Mississippi,* 26.

erate forces operating in Mississippi had surrendered to Union Major General Edward R.S. Canby on May 4, 1865, it was not until the end of May that Father Leray and the four Sisters who had stayed on at the Springs were able to return home, traveling via Mobile and New Orleans. During the second week of June, 1865, they finally arrived in Vicksburg. Thus came to an end an odyssey of mercy begun three years before.[55]

In the course of the War Catholic Sisters from New Orleans, Mobile, Cincinnati and Vicksburg served in the military hospitals of Mississippi. Another group from Natchez as well as the Sisters from Vicksburg served outside the State. Through their nursing these nuns accomplished two things: seeing neither gray nor blue, they performed efficient and heroic service in the cause of charity, and they did much to better understanding of the Catholic Church and all it stands for.

---

55 Memoirs of Sister M. Ignatius Sumner, 26-28; Annals of the Sisters of Mercy, St. Francis Xavier Academy, Vicksburg, Miss.; in ASMV.

Old State Capitol, Jackson, Mississippi.

Senate Chamber in the old Capitol. Mass was celebrated here by a Union Catholic chaplain during the occupation of Jackson.

Chapter XII

IN THE FACE OF THE WIND

Until April, 1862, the War for most people in Mississippi had been a distant thing, touched with a kind of glory. It had created few problems which disturbed the normal life of Mississippians and their institutions. While it is true the Catholic Church in the State had felt the effects of the War from the very outset, the early problems that the War created were hardly more than inconveniences and did little to upset the smooth functioning and even the growth of this institution. Now, however, in the spring of 1862, the storm which had hung for so long on the horizon rolled in over the State and unleashed all its devastating and disruptive power. Indeed, for the next three years war would deluge the land, making it nigh impossible for any one person or institution in the State to escape being affected by the military operations. It will be interesting, therefore, to observe how the Catholic Church in Mississippi reacted to the military tempest as it raged around her.

Property Damage

War inevitably brings destruction of property and lives. From the viewpoint of property damage, hardest hit was the Catholic congregation at Jackson. On the morning of May 16, 1863, as the Union forces were evacuating Jackson, orders were given to burn some tar stored in an old shed just beyond the Catholic church. Because of the shed's proximity to the church, Father Orlandi, the pastor, begged to be allowed to roll the barrels into the street where there would be less danger to the church. The officer in charge of the detail refused on the score that the transfer would take too much time. Even a Federal army surgeon, Dr. H. Hewit,[1] intervened but to no avail. So thoroughly did the detail do its work that the only water hose available was cut. With tears streaming down his face Father Leray, a former pastor of Jackson, removed the Blessed Sacrament to the makeshift chapel in the Sisters' cot-

---

[1] Dr. H. S. Hewit, a Catholic convert, was a brother of Rev. Augustine Hewitt who was one of Fr. Isaac Hecker's associates in founding the Paulist Fathers.

tage near the hospital. Fortunately all the ornaments and furniture from the church were carried to safety by volunteers, Catholic Union soldiers and citizens. As was expected, the fire spread and in the conflagration that followed the church, rectory, schoolhouse and outbuildings were completely destroyed.[2] While the enemy was laying siege to Vicksburg, the Catholic congregation in Jackson with great trouble and expense fixed up the largest hall remaining in town for their church. A week after Mass was celebrated here for the first time, the enemy was back in Jackson. This time the building which served as a church for the Catholic congregation was deliberately set fire to. In the fire all the church ornaments as well as the church records were destroyed. Before setting fire to the building, the soldiers ransacked it, breaking the altar crucifix and making off with the chalice used at Mass. Fortunately a Catholic soldier redeemed the cup from his companions who were using it for drinking purposes and, though broken now, returned it to the pastor. Five days later Bishop Elder arrived in Jackson. The conditions he found on the occasion of this visit he described in his diary.

> The sight of Jackson is indeed saddening. Perhaps one fourth of the town is in ashes.—Some entire blocks & many single houses. All the stores are broken open & sacked. (The soldiers) were carrying off boxes that seem to contain books of the State House Library. Some of the people of Jackson are still in the woods where they took refuge during the bombardment. Many have gone away—Strong Southerners toward Alabama—others to Vicksburg & Memphis &c. Others intend going. . . . probably most of the people are living on rations from the Federal army. The Army is going back to the Big Black (River) tomorrow. There is nothing in town to eat: all the neighborhood is desolated:—from a distance nothing can be brought. There are no teams & no roads—no bridges. The policy seems to make Jackson untenable, for soldiers or civilians.[3]

After making inquiry, the Bishop found Father Orlandi at the home of one of his parishioners, Mrs. O'Connor. The meeting was understandably sad. To add to his distress the Bishop learned that the pastor's quarters had been broken into and all his clothes and what provisions he had stored up had been stolen. At present the

---

[2] Memoirs of Sister M. Ignatius Sumner, 14-15; in ASMV. Elder Diary, 35.

[3] Elder Diary, 40.

priest was living on army rations but even with these he had no place to cook them. That day he had eaten only some crackers. Deciding to stay over night in Jackson, Elder left his horse and buggy for safe-keeping at General Ewing's quarters. Presenting himself to the Union General, a Catholic from Ohio, the Bishop limited himself to the elementary courtesies, for as he noted in his diary: "I could not talk much. I felt myself choaked with sadness and indignation." [4] After the army departed, the congregation fixed up a little chapel in a room over the engine house, "supplying it with such ornaments as they had saved and filling deficiencies by begging and borrowing from their neighbors." [5] In January, 1864, Father Orlandi filed damage claims with the United States authorities for the church property destroyed in Jackson, but no compensation was awarded.[6] That February the city was reoccupied for the third time by the enemy. On this occasion the Catholics saw their makeshift chapel ransacked, two large statues smashed to pieces and the altar used as a butcher's block. This last setback broke Father Orlandi's spirit, and the missionary obtained leave from Bishop Elder to return to his native Italy.[7] After Father Huber took charge at Jackson, the congregation was deprived of even the little room over the engine house, the building being taken over by the military authorities for a powder magazine. Undaunted the congregation rented a fairly large room over a saloon. As late as November, 1865, six months after the War, the Holy Sacrifice of the Mass was still being celebrated there, no other suitable place being available.[8]

In spite of the long bombardment of Vicksburg the Catholic church there did not fare so badly. After the siege Bishop Elder visited the city and then drew up the following notes in his diary:

---

[4] *Ibid.*, 48.

[5] Elder to Huber, Natchez, Nov. 14, 1865; in ADNJ, Elder Letter Book —#10, 451.

[6] Elder to Orlandi, Natchez, Nov. 14, 1864; in ADNJ, Elder Letter Book —#9, 86. After the War the incumbent pastor filed damage claims again, but these were dismissed on the score that the property was never officially used or occupied by the army.

[7] Elder to Orlandi, Natchez, March 16, 1864; in ADNJ, Elder Letter Book —#9, 217. Elder Diary, 76, 78. Given a leave of absence for nine months, Orlandi went back to Italy where he decided to remain. He was given an exeat by Elder on March 30, 1870.

[8] Elder to Huber, Natchez, Nov. 14, 1865; in ADNJ, Elder Letter Book —#10, 451.

> The Church has some nine holes through the walls & windows—all small—except the big one over the sacristy window, made in May 1862.—One Parrot shell burst over the altar of the B. Virgin while the people were waiting for 6 o'clock Mass Sunday morning. (. . . .) The same day I believe Mr. (Michael) Donovan lost his arm at the Church door:—a shot passed thro the Presbytery cutting off the leg of the chair on wh. a soldier was sitting talking to Fr. Heuze tearing his coattail to ribbons.[9]

The rectory next to the church was "very much shattered," while the barn and stable were completely destroyed.[10] Examining the convent, the Bishop found that two of the columns supporting the front portico had been knocked down. He also noted: "The front room upstairs west side has been damaged by a shell that came thro' the window passed through the partition wall into the hall, & there up into the ceiling." [11] A number of household items had been carried off by the servants of a General Dennis who had lived in the building for a short time. At the time of Elder's visit, however, the convent was unoccupied.[12]

Considering the devastation to which Holly Springs was subjected during the War, one is almost tempted to see something miraculous in the fact that the church and rectory there escaped destruction. However, the church was subjected to some vandalism. A Union soldier of the 15th Iowa Infantry, Cyrus F. Boyd, whose unit entered Holly Springs on December 22, 1862, recorded in his diary that that day and the next "soldiers could be seen (pillaging) everywhere . . . in every house and garret and cellar, store and church, and nook and corner." Wandering through the town, he came upon

> . . . a fine large Roman Catholic Church. A lot of soldiers were in the building some were taking the organ to pieces and had the pipes out blowing on them and throwing them away. Up in the pulpit was a squad playing *cards* and another lot were scattering the library over the floor. One daring and reckless soldier climbed to the pinnacle of the temple and took off the little silver image of "Jesus" that stood there.

---

[9] Elder Diary, 57.

[10] Diary of Fr. Carrier, C.S.C., quoted by Conyngham in *Soldiers of the Cross* (unpublished); in AUND: Conyngham Ms.

[11] Elder Diary, 57.

[12] *Ibid.*, 57. Elder to Mother De Sales, Natchez, Aug. 11, 1863; in ADNJ, Elder Letter Book—#8, 460.

> It was at a giddy height but he got it—said to be worth several hundred dollars.[13]

Notwithstanding this vandalism Father Elia could report to his bishop at the beginning of March, 1863, that the church and the rectory were safe.[14]

Another Catholic church in the State to suffer war damage was the one in Yazoo City. When the Bishop visited the town in the spring of 1864, he noted in his diary:

> The Federals were here this week (May, 1864), and burned fourteen houses, including the Court House.—They were here in March & had a street fight. One cannon ball passed entirely through the Church—breaking the stove & cutting one of the posts.—A great number of Minnie Balls penetrated the Church—especially the tower, both below & above.[15]

In the spring of 1863, Bishop Elder blessed the recently completed church at Port Gibson. Five days later the Battle of Port Gibson took place. After the fighting Confederate General Bowen and his troops withdrew, and the town was occupied by the Federals. Fortunately the church silver had been hidden before hand. After the enemy had departed, it was discovered that, though the church had been opened, no damage had been done. The only thing missing was the chain off the thurible.[16]

In July, 1863, the Federal army occupied Natchez. One of the regiments camped on Rose Hill, a piece of property owned by the Diocese just within the city limits. While the army was occupying the site, the picket fence surrounding the property was damaged. The brick house built by the Bishop for the caretaker was taken down to make room for fortifications. One of the barns on the property was torn to pieces by the freed Negroes, while the hay stored in it by the Sisters from the orphanage was taken away by the soldiers. Finally, an impressive grove of oak trees on the prop-

---

13 Throne (ed.), *The Civil War Diary of Cyrus F. Boyd*, 98; in Bettersworth (ed.), *Mississippi in the Confederacy*, 208. The Church about which Boyd speaks may well have been the new Episcopal church in Holly Springs, for it is somewhat difficult to accept his "fine large Roman Catholic Church" as applying to the small white frame bldg. used by the Catholics for worship.

14 Elder Diary, 19.

15 *Ibid.*, 81.

16 *Ibid.*, 32. Elder to Picherit, Natchez, May 18, 1863; in ADNJ, Elder Letter Book—#8, 383.

erty was completely demolished.[17] Although the Bishop filed a claim for damages with the United States government, there is no evidence one way or another that compensation was ever made.[18] Some time in October of the same year the fence surrounding the graveyard [19] was torn down either by freed Negroes who were building shanties for themselves under-the-hill or by lawless soldiers. Elder filed a complaint with the military authorities. After surveying the situation personally, General Crocker assured the Bishop that the fence would be repaired as soon as the lumber could be sawed.[20] This was done, but about a year later Elder noted that the fence was again being ripped apart by people looking for wood to build with or to burn.[21] The fences on the property of the boys' asylum met the same fate. Here too a large number of peach trees were cut down for fire-wood.[22]

One other piece of church property may have been damaged during the War. Local tradition maintains that Bay St. Louis was shelled by the Federal navy and that during this bombardment the steeple of the Catholic church was hit.[23]

Demands By The Military

The Catholic Church in Mississippi had little that might be coveted by the armies of either side. Nevertheless some demands were made upon her. Along with a number of Protestant churches in the State the Catholic church in Jackson donated its bell in response to an appeal made by General Beauregard. The bells were to be melted down and the metal used for military purposes. However, when a civic committee in March, 1862, called on Bishop Elder and asked for one of the two cathedral bells, the prelate stalled. When he explained that "articles used in the immediate service of God, ought not to be turned to other purposes—still less to those of warfare except in the very last necessity," the committee

[17] *Ibid.*, 65. Undated claim for damages on Rose Hill property drawn up by Bishop Elder; in ADNJ, Elder Letter Book—#9, 38.

[18] Gerow, *Cradle Days of St. Mary's*, 155.

[19] A plot of ground adjoining the far side of the city cemetery was purchased and blessed shortly before the War.

[20] Elder Diary, 66, 69.

[21] *Ibid.*, 110.

[22] (Janssens), *Sketch of the Catholic Church in the City of Natchez, Miss.* (Natchez, 1886), 43.

[23] *The Daily Herald*, Biloxi and Gulfport, July 29, 1958, 23 A.

agreed "that if any should be spared, Church bells should be reserved for the last:—but they thought from Genl. Beauregard's appeal, that all would be needed."[24] In the face of this judgment Elder replied that he would have to consult other religious authorities in the matter. Writing to his metropolitan, Archbishop Odin of New Orleans, Elder revealed his reasons for being reluctant to give up any of the cathedral bells. Although he had correctly stated the moral principle involved to the committee men, he was apparently not sure of himself, for he asked Odin: "Is it lawful to use Church bells for such purposes, unless compelled?" Secondly, Elder was not convinced that the need for the bell metal was that critical, that Beauregard was really calling upon the churches to give up their bells. It was Elder's opinion that

> (Beauregard) gives the example of Churchmen—in a time when there were no fire bells except in Churches. Now—the Church bells—unless in New Orleans & Mobile—are but a trifling portion of the bell metal scattered over the country. —I will recommend them to take first, *what the General calls for—planters' bells.* Afterward if he calls for Church bells, it will be time enough to send them.[25]

By this decision Elder apparently stuck, for we read no more about the matter in his correspondence or diary.

Finding suitable quarters is always a problem for an army away from its home base. When this army happens to be an occupying force, it has little scruple in taking over whatever building in the area appears to be suitable. This happened to the convent of the Sisters of Mercy in Vicksburg after the capitulation of that city to the Union army.[26] Upon the Sisters' return to Vicksburg from Shelby Springs, as they were being escorted to military headquarters located across the street from their old home, the Sisters were startled to see a United States flag flying from it. One can well imagine their dismay when they were informed that the building had been taken over just a few days before by the army for staff officers' quarters. A few days later, Mother De Sales, falling back upon General McPherson's promise to Bishop Elder that the convent

[24] Elder to Odin, Natchez, March 16, 1862; in ADNJ, Elder Letter Book —#7, 383. Original in AUND: New Orleans Papers.

[25] *Ibid.*

[26] Memoirs of Sister M. Ignatius Sumner, 25-27; in ASMV. Annals of the Sisters of Mercy, St. Francis Xavier Academy, Vicksburg; in ASMV. Heuzé to Odin, Vicksburg, June 23, 1864; in AUND: New Orleans Papers.

would be restored to the Sisters just as soon as they returned, made application to the authorities for permission to reoccupy the property. In command of the district at this time was Major-General Henry W. Slocum.[27] The General objected strongly to the Sisters' request since the convent was so conveniently located for him and his staff. However, he left the Sisters with some hope when he said he would think the matter over. At the next interview the General informed the Sisters that he did not intend to give up the convent but that he would provide them with another house in the city. Not wanting to deprive other citizens of their property, the Sisters refused the offer. With this the General closed the interview abruptly, remarking somewhat sternly that neither he nor the United States government recognized their claim to any more rights than any other citizen.[28] When the Sisters asked to be allowed to occupy the quarters of the woman caretaker, this request met with a refusal, too. Informed of the Sisters' predicament, Bishop Elder advised Mother De Sales:

> I cannot believe that the President will sanction your being deprived of your convent. By all means write to *him* directly—*yourself* & state the case.
>
> And to Fr. Ignatius's Brother (Hon. Francis Kernan?)—write to your own Sisters in the *Hospitals* at Washington & elsewhere. They can do vastly more than any one else can. Tell them to write directly to the Presidt. to claim justice for their Sisters.—If they date their letters from the side of the deathbeds of the soldiers Mr. Lincoln will certainly not refuse them simple justice.—If he should let their letters be published—& the voice of the whole people will persuade him to reconsider it.[29]

Acting on the Bishop's advice, Mother De Sales wrote to Francis Kernan,[30] a member of the United States Congress from New York,

---

[27] Henry W. Slocum, of New York, Colonel 27th New York Vols. from Aug. 9, 1861; promoted Major-General July 4, 1862; resigned Sept. 28, 1865. *Personnel of the Civil War*, edited by William Frayne Amann (New York, 1961), II, 8, 25.

[28] In her memoirs Sister Ignatius accused General Slocum of prejudice and explained it by the fact that the General was a nephew of the man who was the protector of the infamous Maria Monk; Memoirs, 26.

[29] Elder to Mother De Sales, Natchez, July 7, 1864; in ADNJ, Elder Letter Book—#10, 12.

[30] Francis Kernan (1816-1892), a Georgetown graduate and a Catholic lawyer from Utica, N.Y., was elected to the House of Representatives in 1862. In 1874, he was elected U.S. Senator from New York, the first Democrat from that State in 24 years.

describing their situation in Vicksburg and asking him to seek redress on their behalf. In the meanwhile the Sisters stayed on as the guests of the Genellas. At the same time the Sisters were given some hope again when General Slocum, before whom Mr. Genella pleaded the Sisters' case, promised to let the Sisters move into the convent just as soon as he received transfer orders.

Although he did not despair that the Sisters would receive a favorable hearing in Washington, Elder thought it wise to consider what other courses of action the Sisters might follow should they fail to obtain redress. Writing to the Superior on July 21, 1864, the Bishop presented three possibilities and asked the nun for her views on them. One possibility, as Elder saw it, would be to take another house in Vicksburg and try to carry on a school as best they could. Another course open to them lay in returning to the hospital at Shelby Springs. Elder admitted, however, that this plan had its difficulties. It would be hard to find a conveyance for the Sisters and the trip would involve an expense which neither the Bishop nor the Sisters were in a position to bear. As a third alternative Elder suggested that the Sisters take refuge for a while with the nearest community of their order, in this case, the Convent of Mercy at Helena, Arkansas.[31] As matters turned out, none of these alternatives had to be adopted. The delay experienced in obtaining redress was occasioned by the fact that the Sisters' letter to Representative Kernan, which was to be presented to him by Father Early, S.J. of Georgetown University, arrived in Washington after Congress had adjourned for the summer. Luckily, when the letter reached Father Early at Georgetown, a friend of Mother De Sales was in the area, namely, Bishop Michael O'Connor, S.J.[32] At one time the Bishop had been the nun's confessor and later, as ordinary of the Diocese of Pittsburgh, he had received her profession. Once he learned of the Sisters' predicament, he went to Mr. Stanton, Secretary of War, and pleaded their case. The Secretary promised to take the matter into hand. As a result, on August 15, 1864, General Slocum sent the Sisters in Vicksburg a formal resignation of

[31] Elder to Mother De Sales, Natchez, July 21, 1864; in ADNJ, Elder Letter Book—#10, 83.

[32] Irish-born Michael O'Connor was appointed first Bishop of Pittsburgh in August, 1843. In 1860, he resigned his see and entered the Jesuit Novitiate in Germany. A brilliant man, he later taught at Boston College and at Loyola of Baltimore. He died October 18, 1872, and is buried at Woodstock, Md. *The Catholic Encyclopedia,* XII, 121-126.

the property with the accompanying permission to reoccupy the convent immediately.[33]

Church Discipline

Church discipline after 1861 was also affected by the War. At first President Lincoln's blockade of the southern ports, proclaimed on April 19, 1861, was only a paper one, but gradually it was strengthened. By the spring of 1862, this limitation on trade with foreign countries was felt within the Confederacy. This action, coupled with the system of impressment of supplies and the gradual breakdown of the railroads as a means of distribution, soon brought a scarcity of foodstuffs in many parts of the new nation. Passage of the armies through the various states of the South also served to bring the people almost to the point of starvation. These scarcities forced the Bishop of Natchez to exercise his discretionary powers in the matter of the observance of Lent by his people.[34]

Thus, just before the beginning of Lent, 1862, Elder had the following announcement made from the pulpit to the various congregations of his diocese:

> In consideration of the extraordinary difficulty of obtaining food suitable for days of abstinence, there will be no extra abstinence required during Lent. Flesh meat is allowed every day except Friday.—On Ash Wednesday, we recommend that abstinence be observed, by all who can observe it.[35]

The food situation in Mississippi became worse after the State was invaded. It was not simply a case of abstinence foods being scarce and costly, but it was also a matter of being able to obtain meat rarely and then only by chance. Accordingly, Bishop Elder fearing that consciences might become perplexed and at the same time wanting to lighten the burdens of his people insofar as he could, advised all pastors in the Diocese to dispense their people from the law of abstinence on all Fridays and other prescribed days of the year.[36]

---

[33] Memoirs of Sister M. Ignatius Sumner, 27. Annals of the Sisters of Mercy, St. Francis Xavier Academy, Vicksburg; in ASMV.

[34] Wight, "Bishop Elder and the Civil War," in CHR, XLIV (Oct. 1958), 295-296.

[35] Announcement Book—#1, of the Natchez Cathedral, under the date March 2, 1862; in the Cathedral archives, Natchez, Miss.

[36] Elder to Heuzé, Natchez, June 2, 1863, Elder to Leduc, Natchez, June 8, 1863; in ADNJ, Elder Letter Book—#8, 406, 411.

In 1862, at the recommendation of President Davis the Confederate Congress passed the first national law in American history providing for the conscription of troops. After the passage of the act, amendments to it were proposed at every session of Congress. The law read that "ministers of religion in the regular discharge of ministerial duties . . . shall be and are hereby exempted from military service in the Armies of the Confederate States." [37] To administer the draft, a Bureau of Conscription was set up which used state officers as far as governors would permit. At first Elder's clergy experienced no difficulty in establishing their exempt status. Even after claims to exemption came under closer scrutiny because of abuses connected with the system, Major Clark, a conscription officer in Mississippi, informed the Bishop of Natchez that it would be sufficient for any of his priests to present or to send the Bureau of Conscription "an affidavit that he is regularly authorized to preach according to the laws of the Catholic Church,—having the seal of the court attached to the affidavit—& then his certificate of exemption will be forwarded to him." [38] This information Elder passed on to his clergy. As simple as it sounded, the directive was apparently misunderstood by one of his priests. Father Orlandi felt that meeting the demands of the conscription bureau involved a renunciation of the dignity and sacred rights of the priesthood and the acknowledgment of a non-existent right in Congress. Elder patiently explained to the Italian priest:

> . . . in this case there is no renunciation, neither expressed nor implied. The Congress has passed a law calling on the citizens to do duty as soldiers—& exempting some from the call—Priests among others.
>
> Major Clark calls on all, either to come & serve, or to satisfy him that they are not bound to serve, that they are exempt. If I go & show to him that I am a Priest, & therefore entitled to exemption, I make no acknowledgment of any right in him nor in Congress to oblige me to serve.[39]

Whether Father Orlandi accepted this line of reasoning and submitted an affidavit or invoked his Italian citizenship instead is not known. Elder was personally against the idea of his priests

---

[37] *Official Records: Army,* Ser. IV, Vol. I, 1081.

[38] Elder to Le Corre, Natchez, Feb. 14, 1863; in ADNJ, Elder Letter Book #8, 279.

[39] Elder to Orlandi, Natchez, March 12, 1863; in ADNJ, Elder Letter Book —#8, 309.

invoking their foreign citizenship as a means of remaining free to exercise their ministry during the War. In a letter to Father Le Corre of Yazoo City the Bishop explained why:

> You may perhaps count on claiming French citizenship —but so many persons have claimed foreign protection as an excuse there is a good deal of odium attached to that practice (?) which will probably injure the influence of a Priest. And it may be that the government will place some restriction on such persons, or burdens of extra taxes and forbid them to leave a particular district (?).[40]

How Le Corre proceeded is not known. In any case, there is no record of either priest ever coming into conflict with the conscription officers of the State.

While the Bishop of Natchez recommended cooperation to his priests on the subject of claiming exemption from military service, he was not indifferent to the idea of priests taking up arms. Indeed, he had very definite ideas on the subject. He did not believe, as he told the Bishop of Richmond, that there was room to question that it would be "positively sinful for any Priest actually to engage in the soldier's life; & it seems to me that no grave reason like compulsion, imprisonment, or other punishment would be sufficient (reason to) justify him in entering on it." [41] Furthermore, envisioning the possibility that some officials might be allowed discretionary powers to exempt or to detail some of the clergy who were needed at home for ministerial duty, Elder was of the opinion that, if the exemption took the form of a gratuitous favor, then the bishops should not allow applications to be made by their priests. If necessary, this prohibition could be strengthened by attaching to it an ecclesiastical censure.[42] Apparently, then, the Bishop of Natchez did not believe the exemption granted by the government to clergymen in 1862 to be in the nature of a gratuitous favor.

---

[40] Elder to Le Corre, Natchez, Feb. 14, 1863; in ADNJ, Elder Letter Book —#8, 279.

[41] The Bishop of Richmond differed with Elder on this matter. McGill could discover "no law direct and positive forbidding priests to bear arms under all possible circumstances" but found that "writers on Canon law say that a priest who carries arms and fights a *just defensive* war *pro ecclesia vel pro patria* does not therefore become irregular." McGill to Lynch, Dec. 17, 1863; in ADC, Envelope 149.

[42] Elder to McGill, Natchez, Sept. 25, 1862; in ADNJ, Elder Letter Book —#8, 94.

In the early part of 1864, Elder became alarmed over what appeared to be mounting evidence that in the near future his priests might be drafted into the army. In January he heard from a member of the Louisiana legislature that a new militia law, passed in the neighboring state, exempted clergymen only if they had been ordained or licensed for at least seven years.[43] In February the Mississippi legislature, meeting at Macon, had given serious thought to a measure withdrawing clergymen from the list of citizens exempt from military service.[44] About the same time Elder received a surprise visit from Father O'Connor, who had been substituting for Father Orlandi in Jackson. O'Connor, a priest for less than a year, had been told by the enrolling officer at Jackson to report at the conscript camp at Enterprise, because the law exempted only those who had been "licensed to preach" before the law was passed in 1862.[45] Opposed as he was to priests serving in the army, Elder wrote to Archbishop Odin, explaining the O'Connor case and asking for his cooperation.

> He (O'Connor) cannot go out again without danger of being seized for a deserter.—I have no place for him here—& I am afraid there is none at Vicksburg—the only congregations in the Federal lines.—Would you perhaps have occasion for his services in New Orleans or elsewhere, until circumstances allow me to provide for him? [46]

We do not know what the Archbishop's reply was, but it would seem that O'Connor stayed within the Federal lines at Natchez. Perhaps it was at the suggestion of Odin that Elder sent in an application to Colonel Lucius B. Northrop, Commissary-General, asking for exemption from conscription for priests not ordained before the passage of the first law. Sometime in June the Bishop received a favorable reply from Richmond.[47] Although his fears concerning the conscription of priests were never realized, Bishop Elder worried over the matter throughout the War.[48]

---

43 Elder Diary, 13.

44 Taylor, "When the Ministry Was Ordered to the Front," *Harper's Weekly*, LI (Jan. 26, 1907), 120, 139. Bettersworth, *Confederate Mississippi*, 298-299.

45 Elder to Odin, Natchez, Feb. 6, 1864; in AUND: New Orleans Papers.

46 *Ibid.*

47 Elder Diary, 80.

48 Elder to Odin, Natchez, Sept. 2, 1864; in ADNJ, Elder Letter Book —#10, 124.

The Emancipated Negro

Wars, usually begun to settle differences, almost always create problems as great as the ones they had hoped to settle. Ostensibly the Civil War, at least as far as the North was concerned, was being fought to free the slaves of the South. Unfortunately it was a short-sighted program, for it included no provision for helping the Negroes to make the difficult transition from slavery to freedom. As a result, their release from bondage was accompanied by unexpected hardship. "Those Negroes who were assembled in contraband [49] camps died by the thousands; those who were employed on plantations received treatment little better than that which they had received under the old regime; those who entered military pursuits were dealt with in a manner more becoming slaves than freedmen." [50] Thus, their first experience as free men left the Negroes discouraged and disillusioned.[51]

In Mississippi, during the summer of 1862, Negroes of the coast and river districts began to leave their owners in considerable numbers. In the northern border counties the majority of the slaves seem to have run away by the end of the year. In some cases planters sought to retain their slaves by removing them to the swamps or even into neighboring states. During the last two years of the War the tide of runaways seems to have been practically uninterrupted.[52] If some would like to think that the treatment given the slaves by Catholic owners was superior to that meted out by Protestants, it is interesting to note at this point that it won for the Catholic planter no greater loyalty. For instance, in the middle of June 1863, it was reported to Bishop Elder that Mr. Moore of Port Gibson had lost all the Negroes off one of his plantations and twenty off another.[53] By July 1863, Dr. Michael O'Reilly of Madison County had been deserted by all his Negroes.[54] When the Bishop passed by Mrs. Norton's plantation in Wilkinson County, there was only one Negro left on the place.[55] Although Mr. Ben Roach who lived north of Vicksburg did not lose any of his slaves,

---

[49] The term "contraband" was applied to slaves, viewed as a species of enemy property, when they were captured by Union military forces.

[50] Wiley, *Southern Negroes,* 344.

[51] *Ibid.,* 175-344.

[52] Bettersworth, *Confederate Mississippi,* 163-164.

[53] Elder Diary, 38.

[54] *Ibid.,* 50.

[55] *Ibid.,* 86.

he found himself in a worse predicament than many planters who had. Elder described conditions as he found them on the Roach plantation in his diary under the date July 31, 1863.

> The Negroes are not gone—but worse they are on the place doing no work, & eating up what the soldiers have left —the corn & fruit & cattle. They kill the cattle wh. they find in the woods—eat what they want, & sell the rest to the soldiers. Occasionally a good natured servant will send a piece to the white family, as a compliment.[56]

One group of slaves, not content with running away, returned and murdered their Catholic mistress. The woman, Mrs. Reese Cook, mistress of "Hardtimes" Plantation near Vicksburg, had played hostess to the Sisters of Mercy during the first bombardment of Vicksburg.[57]

In 1863, when Vicksburg and Natchez were occupied by the Union army, the two cities became refuges for Negro runaways. Here problems began to multiply, leaving the Negroes bewildered, the military authorities embarrassed and the native population angry. Bishop Elder was away from Natchez when the city was occupied by the Federals and did not arrive back in his see city until some three weeks later. As a result, his first experience with the Negro problem came with his stopover in Vicksburg on his way home. During this visit Elder noted how rapidly difficulties multiplied with the influx of freed Negroes and how totally unprepared the Federal government was for coping with the situation.

> The negroes are dying in the streets of Vicksburg. The Federal Army expresses a willingness to feed all of them—but there is such a multiplicity of offices in the town that some of the Negroes can hardly find out who to apply to. But those who have plenty are exposed to sickness from change of place, & diet—& water & from want of some one to look after them. No exercise—no occupation—separated from old associations—naturally wanting in energy—no cleanliness—no foresight—no comforts—no medicine.—Dr. Hewit says they suffer from home sickness, depression of spirits—& just give themselves up to sink.—I have asked several Federal Officers what are the intentions or what is the policy of the govt. in regard to the negroes. Everyone whom I have

[56] *Ibid.*, 53.

[57] Mrs. Hamilton Fox to writer, Vicksburg, Nov. 29, 1961. *In and About Vicksburg* (Vicksburg, 1890), 172-175.

> asked has lamented that he thinks there is no policy in their regard, except to deprive the masters of their services & their belief is that as far as the Fed. Govt. & army prevail the race will die out like that of the Indians.—They throw the blame on the South.[58]

So desperate was the situation among the liberated Negroes in Vicksburg that many parents were abandoning their children; mothers were throwing away even helpless infants.[59] On his trip down the river from Vicksburg the Bishop had another experience which acquainted him still better with the freedman and his problems. He met a disillusioned Negro man who had been "employed" by the government. The poor man had worked for the government for three weeks but at the end of that time he could find no one who was supposed to pay him. After a fruitless search he left the area without having collected a cent.[60] Thus, as Elder stepped off the steamboat at the Natchez landing, he was in some measure prepared for what he was about to face in his own cathedral city.

After the occupation of Natchez in July, 1863, thousands of runaway Negroes—men, women and children—flowed into the city.[61] One report put their number at 20,000. Most of them were hungry and bewildered, many of them having left their plantations with nothing but the clothes on their backs. Understandably, when they reached Natchez, they camped as close as possible to Union headquarters, for the Federals were their liberators, their benefactors. The situation soon got out of hand, as hordes of Negroes crowded around the stately mansions which had been requisitioned for headquarters and officers' billets. In an effort to cope with the embarrassing situation, the army built a stockade on the old cotton press grounds below the bluffs of the city, down along the river. Thousands were herded into this "corral" as it came to be called. With no provision for proper sewerage, no drinking water except from the polluted river, scant protection from the weather, an inadequate diet, and tormented by hordes of hungry mosquitoes and sand flies, hundreds were struck down by one of the many sicknesses which soon prevailed—scarlet fever, small pox, measles and

[58] Elder Diary, 56-57.

[59] Elder to Odin, Natchez, July (August) 9, 1863; in AUND: New Orleans Papers.

[60] Elder Diary, 58.

[61] Moore, *Natchez Under-The-Hill* (Natchez, 1958), 102-103.

Natchez Under-the-Hill. Site of Negro Stockade. *(Miss. Dept. of Archives & History)*

Frank Leslie's Illustrated Newspaper, Aug. 8, 1863.

Arrival at Chickasaw Bayou of the Negro Slaves of Jefferson Davis, from his Plantation on the Mississippi.

dysentery. Given almost no medical attention, they died rapidly, sometimes as many as twenty a day. Every morning a detail would go around with the dead wagon, pick up the corpses and then bury them in pits, one on top of the other.[62]

Only after he had been in town for some ten days did Bishop Elder instruct one of his priests to check on conditions at the corral.[63] The plight of the Negroes there, as described by Father Finucane, prompted the Bishop to accompany the priest to the stockade the next day. He recorded his experiences that day in his diary.

> Went down with Fr. Finucane to the Negro camp on the old Cotton Press grounds, back to the hills. Met three or four gangs of Negro men marching under white officers—probably going to work. Negro sentinels at the gate.—There seem to be some thousands. They have made shelters of boards—forming rows of rough cabins, with plank roofs. The roof generally very low. Sometimes high enough: generally floored. For window, one plank is left out on one side of the cabin. Rough & dirty enough. Most of the men are gone out to drill or to work. Only the sick & feeble left—but crowds of women & children.—Great numbers of the children sick, & they say of those that sicken seriously very few get well. The cabins are in rows of some regularity. They seem to have enough of meat & flour furnished by the Fed. army but no vegetables nor fruit. Diarrhea & Dysentery prevailing. Some say they saw a Doctor this morning—I suspect it was Fr. Finucane—for we separated, to do more work. No medicine. I baptized twenty four infants. Found two or three Catholics,—Celestine Craig from Point Coupée & her mother, both baptized—but they never went to confession, & Frank Evans who lived at Calvary, Kentucky till he was 22 years old, & went to the Sacraments frequently. Since he came South he was not permitted to go. He promised to come to the house for confession.[64]

For the next ten months or so Bishop Elder and the priests attached to the Cathedral devoted themselves wholeheartedly to the spiritual needs of these unfortunate Negroes. "We have been occupied," Elder reported to a European correspondent,"—some times one & some times three of us—a part of almost every day preparing

---

[62] *Ibid.*, 103.

[63] Elder Diary, 59.

[64] *Ibid.*, 59-60.

them for death."[65] When a young Belgian priest, Father Charles Van Queckelberge, arrived in the Diocese in December, 1863, he was allowed to devote himself almost exclusively to this work until his own health broke down.[66] Terse entries in his diary give us some idea of the long hours the Bishop himself put in at the corral and at the hospital of a Negro regiment[67] at the Forks-of-the-Road on the outskirts of the city. Thumbing through his diary one comes across such entries as "spent the morning with colored soldiers"—"went to the corral about midday, & remained till sun set"—"spent the afternoon at the colored camp." In the autumn of 1863, he personally had the happiness of baptizing more than five hundred Negroes.[68] Generally these colored people "were well disposed to receive the teachings of the Church" and were "glad to be baptized."[69] Typical was the case of an old man of ninety-two whom Elder found lying on a bundle of rags in the corner of a room in the "hospital" belonging to the corral. As the Bishop moved about the room, the old Negro called to him to come and pray for him. Accordingly, Elder reported:

> I instructed him briefly—& had no hesitation about baptizing him. He accepted explicitly the Catholic Church, & promised to follow it if he shd. recover. The next day I gave him Extreme Unction & the Scapular wh. he received with sensible devotion.[70]

In many cases, however, there was little time for instruction. In the same room mentioned above Elder found a dying boy—he was breathing very hard—lying in the middle of the room on the floor. "He had no covering but a shirt—nothing to lie on but some coats & rags, under his head & a part of his body.—I talked with him. He seemed to understand & answer affirmatively. At a risk I baptized him & gave him absolution."[71] Many of the sick in the

---

[65] Elder to Society for the Propagation of the Faith, Natchez, March 22, 1864; in ADNJ, Elder Letter Book—#9, 230.

[66] *Ibid.* An alumnus of the American College at Louvain, Father Van Queckelberge was ordained in 1861, for the Diocese of Natchez. Coming to America that same year, he was unable to reach Natchez because of the War until the end of 1863. He died in 1878, of yellow fever at Ocean Springs and was buried there.

[67] 6th Mississippi colored Regiment of the U.S. army. Elder Diary, 67.

[68] Elder to Society for the Propagation of the Faith, Natchez, March 22, 1864; in ADNJ, Elder Letter Book—#9, 230.

[69] *Ibid.*

[70] Elder Diary, 63.

[71] *Ibid.*, 62-63.

corral whom the Bishop and his priests baptized were dying infants. This fact may account for the relatively large number of baptisms reported.

While Bishop Elder was chiefly concerned about the spiritual welfare of the emancipated Negroes, he was not insensible to their material wretchedness. Though he felt somewhat uncomfortable doing so, on three different occasions the Bishop of Natchez brought to the attention of the Federal military authorities the wretched conditions in the Negro "hospital" just outside the corral.[72]

It may sound strange to hear that a Catholic bishop would feel "somewhat uncomfortable" about pleading for the alleviation of human misery, but one must bear in mind the social and political situation which prevailed in the Natchez area at this time. To assume the role of champion of the freed Negroes who only a few months before represented the wealth of so many of his flock would have left Elder open to the charge that he was insensible to the Catholic planter's present economic distress, perhaps even to the charge that he had been a secret abolitionist all the while. This danger will explain Elder's reaction to a proposal made to him in the summer of 1863, by Dr. Hewit, a Catholic surgeon attached to Grant's staff. In view of the many abandoned Negro children in Vicksburg, the doctor had proposed that a religious community be invited to open an asylum in that city.[73] "I told him," Elder wrote in his diary, "I should put no obstacle to it, but from the very nature of the case, it was necessary that it should be conducted entirely by the people of the North, & connected with the Army, without any positive co-operation on my part."[74] Although Dr. Hewit wrote to the Fathers of the Holy Cross at Notre Dame in Indiana in an attempt to interest them in the project, nothing ever came of it.[75] It is also true that the Bishop of Natchez, in spite of his initial reluctance to become involved, made a half-hearted attempt to obtain help for the colored people crowding into Natchez and Vicksburg by addressing himself to Archbishop Purcell of Cincinnati, one of the "friends of the oppressed race." That nothing came of this offer either did not particularly distress Elder, since, as he later con-

---

72 *Ibid.*, 64, 66.

73 Elder to Odin, Natchez, July (Aug.) 9, 1863; in AUND: New Orleans Papers. Elder Diary, 59.

74 Elder Diary, 59.

75 *Ibid.*

fessed to Bishop Spalding of Louisville, "there was some little Christian malice in my anticipation of what would be the results of offering the opportunity." [76]

At the end of the War the Negro problem was still on hand, but it was apparently not as acute as it had been in 1863 and 1864. Many of the Negroes had died. Others disillusioned had returned to their former masters. Still others who had crowded into Natchez were forced to leave the city as a result of a military order issued in March, 1864, stating that "no contraband shall be allowed to remain in this city of Natchez who is not employed by some responsible white person, in some legitimate business, and who does not reside at the domicile of his or her employer." [77] Now, the Negroes in Natchez and Vicksburg constituted not so much a problem as they did a challenge.[78] Elder saw them, especially the youngsters, as potential converts. In the spring of 1865 a great number of colored children were going to school and this for the first time in their lives. It was unfortunate, however, in the eyes of Bishop Elder, that so many of them were going to "New England Teachers" who were circulating among their pupils "all sorts of puritan papers & tracts." [79] For this reason the Bishop of Natchez tried, even before the Confederate forces in Mississippi had surrendered, to obtain the services of the colored Oblate Sisters of

---

[76] Elder to Spalding, Natchez, Dec. 30, 1863; in ADNJ, Elder Letter Book —#9, 58.

[77] Order from the Health Office, Natchez, Miss., March 19, 1864; quoted in *Freeman's Journal*, May 28, 1864.

[78] As far as the white man in the South was concerned, not until the Reconstruction Period was there any such thing as a "race problem" in the South. However, during the second half of the War various incidents took place in almost every Southern community occupied by the Federals which indicated how relations between the two races would develop. One such episode took place in Vicksburg between Fr. Heuzé and several Negroes. On Pentecost Sunday, 1864, an hour before Mass, a number of Negro officers recently recruited by the Union army entered the Catholic church. Ignoring the back pews generally occupied by the colored Catholics, they marched up front and occupied the first seats in the church. Convinced that the Negroes acted out of arrogance rather than devotion, Fr. Heuzé admonished them from the pulpit by preaching a sermon on the Scribes and Pharisees who always sought the first places at suppers and the front seats in the synagogues. At the end of the sermon the Negroes stormed out of the church. After Mass they beseiged the rectory, calling for the priest and demanding an apology. When they could draw no retraction from him, they withdrew, hurling insult at him and promising to get even. Two days later three of them actually tried to surprise the priest and assault him, but their plot was foiled. With this the incident closed, and Fr. Heuzé apparently had no further trouble. *Freeman's Journal*, Aug. 20, 1864.

[79] Elder to Spalding, Vicksburg, April 27, 1865; in AAB, 33-U-8.

Providence for both Natchez and Vicksburg where a "brown harvest" was waiting to be reaped.[80] That Elder was unable to secure their services or those of any other religious community does not come as a surprise to modern historians of the Catholic Church in the United States. It fits into the pattern of circumstances which caused the Church to lose an opportunity for large scale conversion of the Negroes to Catholicism after the Civil War.[81]

Orphans

Maintaining the diocesan institutions of charity—the orphanages at Natchez—became extremely difficult from 1862 on through the rest of the War. In February, 1862, Elder wrote to Father Le Corre, pastor of Yazoo City, asking him to send in his oprhans' collection taken up at Christmas just as soon as possible, because St. Mary's Asylum was more than $800 in debt for food and clothing.[82] In the same letter he added significantly: "Any presents of provisions will (also) be very serviceable to them." [83] As the War progressed, it became more difficult to operate the asylums, because just as the number of orphans increased so too did the prices for the necessities of life. For instance, in Mississippi in 1861, a barrel of flour sold for $10; in 1862, for $30; in 1863, anywhere from $75 to $105. For a sack of salt in 1861, one could expect to pay anywhere from $1.50 to $1.75; in a year's time the price skyrocketed to $12; while in the spring of 1863, those who had salt to sell were demanding $100 a sack.[84] In November, 1862 the orphans at D'Evereux Hall were so badly in need of clothing that carpets from the cathedral rectory were used as blankets and the asylum's blankets turned into jackets and pants for the boys.[85] So hard pressed was this institution during the first six months of 1864, that Father Muller

---

[80] *Ibid.* Also Elder to Odin, Natchez, May 6, 1865; in AUND: New Orleans Papers.—The Oblate Sisters of Providence were founded by Father James Joubert, S.S. in Baltimore in 1829. The growth of the community has been slow. Today (1960) they number 295.

[81] The Church in the U.S. lost the opportunity to convert the Negroes on a large scale after the War "through a combination of racial prejudice, timidity, and scarcity of manpower and resources." Ellis, *American Catholicism,* 99-100.

[82] Elder to Le Corre, Natchez, Feb. 27, 1862; in ADNJ, Elder Letter Book —#7, 331.

[83] *Ibid.*

[84] Bettersworth, *Confederate Mississippi,* 107. "Diary of a Mississippi Planter, Dr. Martin W. Philips of Hinds Co., Miss." edited by Frank L. Riley, in PMHS, Vol. X, p. 481.

[85] Elder Diary, 5.

could serve meat to his boys only twice a week.[86] At the end of the year he found the institution $873 in debt.[87] St. Mary's Asylum fared no better. In the middle of the summer of 1864, Sister Mary Thomas reported that the girls' orphanage was in debt for the sum of $1,200, with the need for fall and winter clothing still pressing.[88]

The situation at both orphanages might have been even worse had it not been for the generosity of the Catholics of the Diocese, the United States army and individual Union officers and men. Hardpressed as they were themselves, the Catholics of Mississippi obviously made an heroic effort to support the orphans at Natchez. As late as the spring of 1863, when wartime austerity was being felt by everyone in the State, the Cathedral parishioners gave $200 toward the support of the orphans while the congregations at Vicksburg and Jackson collected $580 and $870 respectively.[89] Once the city of Natchez was occupied by the Union army, the orphans were supplied with many items from the commissary. The first instance of application being made to the army for supplies for the orphans seems to have taken place on September 19, 1863.[90] The commanding officer at the time was General Walter Gresham.[91] When Sister Mary Thomas appeared before him, the General not only graciously endorsed her list for supplies, but he also told her to have Father Muller send in his. During the interview, when Gresham said he could not promise any clothing, a Colonel Schatz of the 30th Missouri Regiment stepped into the breach and said he would see to it that at least each orphan boy was provided with a suit of clothes.[92] From this time on, at regular intervals, stores from the commissary were obtained for the orphans. For the duration of the War the orphans were also the objects of the charity of a number of military units stationed at Natchez whose contributions, ranging from $46

---

86 Annual Financial Report for D'Evereux Hall, Jan. 1, 1865, drawn up by Rev. F. Muller; in ADNJ, File: Orphans–D.

87 *Ibid.*

88 Sister Mary Thomas to Headquarters, U.S. Forces in Natchez, Aug. 19, 1864; in ACHS: Brayman Papers.

89 Elder to Leray, Natchez, April 1, 1863; in ADNJ, Elder Letter Book #8, 344. Financial Statement of St. Paul's Church, Vicksburg, for the year 1863, drawn up by Fr. Heuzé, dated Jan. 6, 1864; in ADNJ, File: Elder–H.

90 Elder Diary, 65.

91 Walter Q. Gresham, Colonel 53d Indiana Vols.; Brigadier-General from Aug. 11, 1863; mustered out April 30, 1866. *Personnel of the Civil War,* edited by W. F. Amann, II, 41.

92 Elder Diary, 65.

to $223, were acknowledged from the Cathedral pulpit.[93] Sometimes the needs of the orphans, especially for clothing, made it necessary for the Sisters to travel down the river to New Orleans. However, even when this called for the crossing of military lines, they apparently had no difficulty. On her visits to the Crescent City Sister Thomas was given every possible assistance by the commanding general, N. P. Banks.[94]

The privilege of drawing stores for the orphans at the commissary was renewed by each succeeding commander at Natchez until August, 1864. Sister Thomas describes what happened at this time.

> When we applied for rations as usual at the beginning of this month—the Adjutant of the new commander required us to get a declaration from the Capt. of Commissary. We did so: and on presenting it—it was returned to us with the answer we must get an order from higher authority.[95]

The new commander at Natchez was Brigadier-General Mason Brayman.[96] After denying the Sisters permission to draw supplies at the commissary, he forwarded a report of his action to district headquarters in Vicksburg. The district commander at this time was Major-General Slocum, who was being pressed by the Sisters of Mercy to vacate their convent. Three days after he was ordered to return the convent to the Sisters, Slocum upheld Brayman's action [97] and, when Sister Thomas appealed to him directly, the district commander had his assistant adjutant send the following reply:

> I am directed by the Maj. Gen. Comg. to acknowledge the receipt of your communication of the 19th inst. and say in reply that he is not authorized to distribute charities for his Government—neither could he take credit to himself as an almoner in the dispensation of unauthorized bounties.

---

93 Announcement Books—#1, #2, of the Natchez Cathedral; in the Cathedral archives, Natchez, Miss. Also Gerow, *op. cit.,* 216-217.

94 Sister Mary Thomas to Headquarters, U.S. Forces in Natchez, Natchez, Aug. 19, 1864; in ACHS: Brayman Papers.—General N.P. Banks replaced the controversial B.F. Butler as commander at New Orleans on December 17, 1862.

95 *Ibid.*

96 Mason Brayman, of Illinois, Colonel 29th Ill. Vols.; Brig.-Gen. from Sept. 24, 1862; mustered out Aug. 24, 1865. *Personnel of the Civil War,* edited by W. P. Amann, II, 34.

97 Rodgers to Brayman, Vicksburg, Aug. 18, 1864; in ACHS: Brayman Papers.

> Such charities belong properly to the people of Natchez, and it is well if the talents of Bishop Elder are partly devoted toward the convincing of those people, of the necessity of thier (sic) attention to that duty.
>
> The comg. General knows no authority for the issue of rations refered (sic) to—but if it is done he hoped it is with proper authority.[98]

The tone of the letter is hardly sympathetic. The reference to Bishop Elder's "talents" is made with sarcasm. During the summer Elder and Brayman had clashed, with the Bishop winning out with help from Washington.[99] But Sister Thomas was not to be checked by the pettiness of the two Union generals. At the same time that she sent in her appeal to General Slocum, the nun laid her case before the military commander of the whole western theater at New Orleans, Major-General E. S. R. Canby. In a matter of a few days her written appeal was returned to her. On the back side of the letter, however, was this important note, dated August 22, 1864: "This issue of rations for the orphans of the asylum is authorized conforming in this issue to Executive (?) Order No. 30, War Dept., Adj. Gen's. Office, Jan. 25th, 1864.—By order of Maj. Gen. E. R. S. Canby."[100] Armed with this authorization, Sister Thomas presented herself at military headquarters in Natchez and received the badly needed supplies. It was the second defeat off the field of battle handed General Brayman within a month and this time by a determined woman in a white cornette.

Concern for the orphans of the Diocese was not limited during the War to their material support. From the spring of 1862, when New Orleans surrendered, until the day that Natchez was herself occupied by the enemy in July, 1863, the Bishop and Sisters were in dread for the children's personal safety should military action occur in the area. In this event handling over a hundred small children would be no easy task. In anticipation of military action at Natchez—a possibility which could not be considered remote since Federal gunboats were prowling up and down the river—Bishop Elder made arrangements to evacuate the orphans to an

---

[98] Rodgers to Sister Mary Thomas, Vicksburg, Aug. 21, 1864; copy in ADNJ, File: Orphans—O.

[99] Cf. Chapter XIII.

[100] Sister Mary Thomas to Headquarters Mil. Div. W. Miss., Natchez, Aug. 19, 1864; in ACHS: Brayman Papers.

old plantation home about five miles from town, if this should prove necessary. The arrangement was made none too soon. A few days later, on September 2, 1862, because of a misunderstanding, the city was shelled by the Federal gunboat "Essex." [101]

As the shells began raining in on the town, Bishop Elder and Father Grignon hurried to the girls' orphanage. Unfortunately many people panicked and invaded the asylum, feeling somehow that they would be safe there. Their presence only added to the confusion. One of the Sisters later described how the Bishop and his Vicar-General upon their arrival

> . . . were soon surrounded by the children, some, non-Catholics, begging to be baptized, and others, Catholics, asking to go to confession. All hurried into the Chapel, where the Bishop wished to give general absolution. On our way thither we thought our house would be blown to pieces from the noise of the shells. Reaching the Chapel, we found it crowded with people of all denominations from the city, who there sought protection. We crowded the children in as best we could, then the Bishop requested all to say the Act of Contrition aloud, after which he gave absolution, blessed all with the holy Ciborium, and consumed the Sacred Species. When all were quiet, His Lordship exhorted us to confidence in Our Lord and His Immaculate Mother, telling us Our Lord understood our wishes, but that it was not possible to baptize and hear confessions then, as all must leave the Orphanage and seek a place of safety.[102]

Immediately afterward the orphans were hurried to the dormitory to gather up their belongings. "It was amusing," one eye-witness said, "to see the dear Bishop, in his endeavor to hasten matters, handing dresses to a large girl that only a small girl could wear, and consoling them with 'never mind, put it on, you all must carry on your backs what you cannot carry in your hands.'" [103] When everyone was finally ready, they started out on foot, following behind a horse and wagon which carried twenty of the smallest children and two sick girls. With shells exploding overhead and

---

[101] Moore, *Natchez Under-The-Hill*, 99. A boatload of bluejackets, coming ashore to buy some ice for a sick seaman, was mistaken for a landing party coming to occupy the city, and accordingly, it was fired upon. Only then did the Essex open fire.

[102] Memoirs of Sister Mary Rose Brady, quoted in Annals of the Daughters of Charity, 1929, 159; in Archives of the Daughters of Charity, Emmitsburg, Md.

[103] *Ibid.*

the little children in tears, one of the nuns, Sister Mary Rose, had the piety as well as the good sense to begin the Litany of the Blessed Virgin, which drew a loud response and had a calming effect. Out of the city and into the country the procession of children and nuns wound its way. Without a mishap they reached the old cotton plantation and the abandoned house which the Bishop had obtained earlier. Fortunately their stay at the plantation was not long, for the house was a "veritable rat-den." In two weeks time they were able to return to the city, the enemy having withdrawn. Located in the upper town, the asylum buildings suffered no damage, although a few shells fell in the yard.[104] When the city was permanently occupied by the Union army in July, 1863, the move must have come, in a certain sense, as a relief to the Bishop and Sisters. At least now the suspense was over and there would be less to worry about.

Schools

Although only one school—the parochial school at Jackson—was destroyed during the War, all of the Catholic institutions of learning in the State were affected adversely by the War to a greater or lesser degree. The school conducted at Vicksburg by the Sisters of Mercy was closed down in May, 1862, and remained so until the autumn of 1864, while the Sisters went off to nurse the sick and wounded soldiers.[105] The school at Holly Springs closed down in 1862, when the town became subject to alternate raids by the Federals and Confederates and the congregation as a result broke up.[106] It never re-opened. Although a parochial school was in operation at Paulding when the War broke out, the available records for the war years make no mention of it. One sketch of the parish makes the claim, however, that a school was attached to the parish from 1859 to 1878.[107] The boys' school conducted in the basement of the Cathedral in Natchez apparently continued operating through the War just as the girls' school conducted by the Sisters

---

[104] Annals of the Daughters of Charity, 1929, 159 ff. in Archives of the Daughters of Charity, Emmitsburg, Md. "Les Filles de la Charite pendant la guerre civile," *Les Missions Catholiques,* LXV (Sept. 17, 1863), 303.

[105] Memoirs of Sister Mary Ignatius Sumner, 6; in ASMV. Annals of the Sisters of Mercy, St. Francis Xavier Academy, Vicksburg; in ASMV.

[106] Elder to Mrs. Thomas Semmes, Natchez, Aug. 21, 1862; in ADNJ, Elder Letter Book—#8, 38.

[107] Dogny, "St. Michael's—Paulding," in *Catholic Action of the South* (Natchez Centennial Edition), Oct. 14, 1937, 27.

of the orphanage. Only once did the War interfere with the normal running of the school for girls at Natchez. This occurred in September, 1862, when because of the shelling of the city the opening of the school was deferred for about two weeks.[108] The schools in Natchez, as did most of the schools in the State, experienced a shortage of text books during the War. At least such is implied in the announcement made from the pulpit of the Cathedral on September 6, 1863: "If there should be any difficulty about procuring a full supply of school books the first will be allotted to those who are first enrolled." [109]

The War was also indirectly responsible for delaying badly needed improvement of the boys' school in Natchez. Never operating to the complete satisfaction of either the Bishop or parents before the outbreak of hostilities, the school even lost further ground during the War, except for a temporary change for the better under Father Hearns' brief administration.[110] The man whom the Bishop employed to assist and at times actually run the school was evidently a good instructor but a poor disciplinarian.[111] Nevertheless, because of the shortage of teachers during the War, Elder retained the man as long as he could.[112] By February, 1865, the school had come to a sorry state. In a letter to the Archbishop of Baltimore, Elder reported:

> They (the boys) are taught now by two ladies. The number of scholars is small—the spirit is poor—no ambition & little piety. The ladies are well disposed: but there has always been a lethargy over both boys & parents:—which I see no way of shaking off, without a thorough change.[113]

The change which Bishop Elder had in mind was to have some community of teaching Brothers take over the school.

> I have long been trying to get them. Before the war Bro. Facile of Montreal—now I believe visitator & living in France—promised to send them soon. Since the opening of the Mississippi, he wrote to me that they had very few novices

[108] Announcement Book—#2, of Natchez Cathedral, under the date Sept. 7, 1862; in the Cathedral archives, Natchez, Miss.

[109] Announcement Book—#2, of the Natchez Cathedral; in the Cathedral archives, Natchez, Mississippi.

[110] Elder to Spalding, Natchez, Feb. 20, 1865; in AAB, 33-U-5.

[111] Elder Diary, 20, 28.

[112] *Ibid.*, 22, 28, 63.

[113] Elder to Spalding, Natchez, Feb. 20, 1865; in AAB, 33-U-5.

> & the most of them were very young.—Some years ago Fr. Sorin of the Holy Cross answered me favorably—but two letters that I wrote there last year have brought no answer at all.[114]

Accordingly, Elder begged Spalding to use his influence to help him obtain a few Brothers to take charge of the school in Natchez. A month later, when the situation at the school had deteriorated still further, Elder directed a plea to the refugee Brothers of Christian Instruction in New Orleans, asking his metropolitan to support his request.[115] Unfortunately, Elder's efforts to obtain Brothers for the school in Natchez did not materialize until after the War. There were two reasons among others for not succeeding earlier: difficulties in travel and communication, and fear on the part of the Brothers that they might not be able to support themselves in a city the size of Natchez which was at the same time going through the throes of military occupation.

Hardest hit were the schools at Bay St. Louis, conducted by the Brothers of Christian Instruction and the Sisters of St. Joseph of Bourg. Soon after Ship Island, commanding the Mississippi Sound, was occupied by the Federals on December 3, 1861, the Sisters and Brothers raised the French flag over their schools.[116] As a consequence, they were never molested by raiding parties from either side. However, the blockade soon made itself felt. As it became more and more difficult to obtain food and as travel for the Louisiana boarders, after the fall of New Orleans, became equally difficult, ten of the Brothers withdrew to New Orleans in December, 1863.[117] Here, near the church of the Annunciation, they opened a temporary boarding school to serve about twenty-five boys, former pupils from the plantations of Louisiana.[118] In this way they found both work and support which they had not

---

114 *Ibid.*

115 Elder to Odin, Natchez, March 17, 1865; in AUND: New Orleans Papers.

116 At the outbreak of the War the French consul in New Orleans had presented the flags to the Brothers and Sisters since they were French citizens. Eugenie, "Sisters of St. Joseph of Bourg—New Orleans Province," unpublished thesis, New Orleans: University of Loyola, 1953, 57.

117 Brother Athanasius to Brother Alphonse, New Orleans, Dec. 27, 1863; quoted in original manuscript of *A Century of Service for the Sacred Heart* by Brother Macarius, 125; in archives of the Brothers of the Sacred Heart, Rome.

118 Macarius, *op. cit.*, 124.

been able to obtain at the Bay. Four of the Brothers remained behind at the Bay when the others departed for New Orleans, and continued operating the school for the sake of students from the area.[119]

The girls' academy remained open through the war years, too, but this was due largely to the stamina and ingenuity of Mother Esperance, superior of the Sisters at the Bay. To keep her community of nuns and students alive, time and again she had to go through the blockade to New Orleans, a trip lasting four or five days in an open boat and often enough made in rough weather. Sometimes the round-trip involved an unexpected delay in New Orleans where the Bay superior would be detained until she could obtain a pass from the military authorities for the return trip.[120] "I have forced myself to get used to this kind of travel," the plucky nun wrote to her major superior in France,

> so as not to let the Community die of starvation. For a long time famine has made itself cruelly felt on this side (of the blockade). The inhabitants are for the most part without clothing. We ourselves have no more dresses or veils. I shall be obliged to go to the city shortly to buy black merino . . . We have made aprons with some petticoats, and little sleeves with neckerchiefs—which does very well, because here, black sleeves fade on our arms . . . In spite of the misery of the times we view it somewhat of a miracle that we have thirteen boarders. . . .[121]

Of invaluable assistance to the Sisters during these trying years was Father Leduc, pastor of Bay St. Louis. Together with a former altar boy, Pierre Prudeaux, the priest ran the blockade with a small schooner, called appropriately "Hard Times," to bring in badly needed food and supplies. However, he made one trip too many and was captured by Federal gunboats, taken to New Orleans and imprisoned. Later he was released and returned to the Bay—without his boat.[122] Equally helpful to the Sisters were the Brothers operating the boys' school. Fortunately the Brothers had won the esteem of the Federal officers at Fort Pike which guarded

---

[119] The four Brothers who remained at the Bay school during the War were: Brothers Florimond, Eusebe, Adalbert and Francois. Macarius, *op. cit.*, 124.

[120] Mother Esperance to Mother St. Claude, Bay St. Louis, July 7, 1863; translation of French original in ASSJB.

[121] *Ibid.*

[122] *The Daily Herald,* Biloxi and Gulfport, July 29, 1958, 4 A.

the lake-approach to New Orleans. On one occasion in a skirmish near the Bay, four Federal soldiers were wounded. They lay untended on the shore some distance from the college. As soon as the Brothers heard of it, they brought the wounded men bedding, medicine and cordials and nursed them till they were out of danger. The men made a glowing report to the Fort and the government at New Orleans.[123] As a consequence, Brother Adalbert had little difficulty in making periodic trips to the city. On these trips, not only did the Brothers carry provisions for the Sisters, but on one occasion they also escorted a number of girls whom the Sisters could no longer feed back to their homes in New Orleans.[124]

With an eye to the overall picture, then, the Catholic schools in the Diocese of Natchez suffered, as a result of the War, to the same degree as did the public schools and other private institutions of learning in the State. Although not so extensive as to paralyze the schooling of children under Catholic auspices, the havoc brought by the War and the hardships it caused disrupted Catholic education in the State. In some places the teaching was halted; in other places it was carried on in the face of great difficulties, succeeding only because of the determination of Bishop Elder, the Brothers and Sisters.

Religious Life

The religious life of Mississippi's Catholics did not escape the War's influence. In this case, the War was responsible not only for disrupting what regularity had been established for the practice of their religion prior to the spring of 1861, but also for creating liturgical and moral problems ordinarily not encountered in peacetime.

At the beginning of the War most Catholics in the State were able to practice their religion with a fair amount of regularity; that is to say they enjoyed the services of a priest either every week or on the average of once a month. This regularity was completely disrupted by the departure of a number of priests who went off to serve the spiritual needs of the soldiers. As a consequence, many congregations, some of them accustomed to the services of a resident pastor, had to be content with only an occasional and, often

123 Macarius, *op. cit.*, 132.
124 *Ibid.*, 133-134.

enough, an unannounced visit from a priest. Thus, after the departure of Father Guillou for the battlefield and his subsequent death in Natchez, the congregation at Sulphur Springs had only a part time resident pastor. Later in the War he was removed, and the congregation had to be content with only a monthly visit from him. Completely neglected were the missions attached to the parish. In this particular case, Bishop Elder gave some idea of the difficulties involved in serving the congregation at Sulphur Springs when he wrote in February, 1865: "The nearest Priest is at a distance of forty four miles—eighteen of them without public conveyance, & the Priest has no horse." [125] Paulding, after the departure of Father Boheme for the army and his death in Virginia, received only an occasional visit from a Jesuit Father from Spring Hill College in Mobile, a visit which could be made only when the boys were away on vacation.[126] Some regularity, however, was restored for about five months when Father Finucane was sent to take charge of the parish and its missions in September, 1863.[127] After the pastor joined the army as a chaplain in the fall of 1862, Port Gibson was left without regular attendance. For the duration the Catholics in that area were accorded only an occasional visit from Father Picherit stationed at Brookhaven or from a priest attached to the Cathedral in Natchez.[128] The parish in Jackson was left without a priest when Father Orlandi returned to Italy in the middle of April 1864.[129] This vacancy was filled almost immediately when Father Huber was appointed the new pastor a month later.[130] This arrangement, however, was made at the expense of the Catholics at Sulphur Springs and Canton. Between these two points Father Huber had been dividing his time since the previous July.[131] Now these two congregations to assure themselves of even a monthly visit would have to provide transportation for the priest.[132] During its greatest distress Vicksburg which ordinarily enjoyed the services of two priests was limited to those of one, and half of this priest's time was taken

125 Elder to Spalding, Natchez, Feb. 23, 1865; in AAB, 33-U-6.
126 *Ibid.*
127 Elder Diary, 63. Elder to Finucane, Natchez, Sept. 9, 1863; in ADNJ, Elder Letter Book—#8, 480.
128 Elder to Picherit, Natchez, June 20, 1863; in ADNJ, Elder Letter Book —#8, 434. Elder Diary, 32, 77.
129 Elder Diary, 76.
130 *Ibid.*, 80.
131 *Ibid.*, 49, 80.
132 *Ibid.*, 80.

up ministering to the needs of the soldiers in the hospitals or rifle pits.[133] If any Catholics remained on at Holly Springs after the congregation there broke up late in 1862, they were most probably deprived of the services of a priest, for the available records make no mention of a replacement being made after the withdrawal of Father Elia to Memphis and his death there in the spring of 1863. In practice, then, the shortage of priests during the War meant fewer opportunities for assisting at Mass and in particular for fulfilling one's Sunday obligation; it also meant less chance for receiving the Sacraments; and, where it was felt most, it meant that some people died without the consoling Last Rites of the Church. This last mentioned consequence caused the Bishop no little distress. On one occasion when he reflected on the matter, he exclaimed: "What account must I render? May God have mercy on me." [134]

To provide even this limited service, priests on the homefront were called upon to exercise a good deal of courage and stamina. Although Bishop Elder left his priests quite free in the matter of staying at their posts or withdrawing in the face of danger, he did make known his preference when he wrote to Father Le Corre. After expressing his surprise and his sorrow upon hearing the news that the enemy was expected at Yazoo City, Elder continued:

> With regard to remaining in town or leaving it, there are so many circumstances to be considered, & it is so entirely impossible to foresee all the circumstances, that I shall not undertake to give you direction.—Exercise your own judgment as to what will be your best course, what it is that God wishes you to do.

But, then, he added:

> I admire most that a Priest keep at the post as long as he can do good there: but as his post is with his congregation, it may happen that if all the congregation go away, it is best for him to go away with them.—On the other hand he may find more good to be done among the Soldiers by staying. And then there is always his Church; which he should endeavor to take care of as well as he can.—Hence I am not sorry that you are remaining there.[135]

---

[133] Heuzé to a friend, Vicksburg, July 7, 1864, quoted by David Conyngham; in AUND: Conyngham MS.

[134] Elder to Spalding, Natchez, Feb. 23, 1865; in AAB, 33-U-6.

[135] Elder to Le Corre, Natchez, March 28, 1863; in ADNJ, Elder Letter Book—#8, 328.

It must have afforded the Bishop a good deal of consolation during these trying times to see how faithful the majority of his priests were.[136] For instance, Father Elia stayed at his post until his congregation broke up and the military hospitals closed down. Not only did Father Leduc face the hazards of running the blockade time and again to bring in supplies for the Sisters and other needy people at Bay St. Louis, but also on one occasion his presence of mind and his courage saved the town from being burned to the ground by the enemy. In the spring of 1864, a company of Federal soldiers from Fort Pike at the entrance to Lake Pontchartrain landed at Bay St. Louis and was met by a company of Sibley's Confederate Cavalry. The Confederates repulsed the Yankees and took a few prisoners. About two weeks later, two hundred Federals landed from the gunboat "Commodore" to rescue the prisoners. This time the enemy seemed determined to burn the town, for they had already set fire to several properties when in their path, in the neighborhood of the church, appeared Father Leduc. Advancing toward them while holding aloft a crucifix, the priest pleaded with the soldiers to stop their burning. Embarrassed by the Cross of Christ and impressed by the authority and courage of the unarmed priest, the Yankees, most of whom were Irish Catholics, doffed their hats and withdrew, sparing the town further destruction.[137]

Outstanding in his devotion to duty was Father Heuzé. During the siege of Vicksburg his church was the only one open in town. Here he celebrated Mass faithfully every morning. During the day he moved about the city, tending to the spiritual needs of the civilian population, visiting the three or four hospitals in the beleaguered city and going among the soldiers in the rifle pits. Moving about the city and along the front lines, the priest was almost continually exposed to danger. A year later he wrote somewhat jokingly to a friend about one particularly hair-raising trip to the front lines.

> I administered the holy Viaticum and Sacred Unction to a dying man in a rifle pit and while so doing two shells en-

---

[136] Only three priests withdrew from the Diocese during the War—Fr. Orlandi with whom it is easy to sympathize, Fr. Finucane who may have done so at the suggestion of Elder himself, (Elder Diary, 74) and Fr. Heuzé who left to join the Marist Fathers.

[137] Fahey, "Our Lady of the Gulf," in *Catholic Action of the South* (Natchez Centennial Edition), Oct. 14, 1937, 39.

> tered (the trench) and on my way home two bullets flew by me, and three or four rifle balls whistled around my ears. I hastened my steps—a ball struck a fence in front of me.—A shell fell some paces in front of me and turned up the earth and covered me with dust.—But that is all! [138]

While deeply appreciated by those whom he served, Heuzé also impressed those who were not of his faith. Having a chance to observe the priest's routine during the siege, a Presbyterian officer, William A. Drennan, admitted that the priest's conduct at this time among other factors prompted him to reconsider his previous attitude toward Catholics. Writing to his wife, the officer reported:

> There is not a church open in the City—except the Catholic.—I see the priest nearly every day as I pass that way—over to the Arsenal—and Mr. Rutherford the Presbyterian Minister that Johny thought so much of—is housed up in a cave.—The Catholic religion may and perhaps does place too much of the hope of heaven of its believers in *Works*—but I tell you that I would rather see Works of charity—the self denial—and courage that is required to go among the sick and wounded, and there attend them as if they were brothers—than all the boasts of that faith that is unseen.—Faith is all well enough—Would to God I had some of it—but "faith without Works" is nothing.—I have been reading for two days past, during my leisure time "Grantley Manor" written by Lady Fullerton a catholic lady of literary celebrity—and in which the heroine is a Catholic—and that together with what I see of Catholics here—has given me a much milder view of the harshness of their creed than many Protestants have.[139]

Well past the halfway mark of the War the Diocese received two new priests, Fathers Charles Van Queckelberge and Patrick McCabe.[140] Their coming to the Diocese, however, did not in-

---

[138] Heuzé to a friend, Vicksburg, July 7, 1864, quoted by David Conyngham in *Soldiers of the Cross* (unpublished); in AUND: Conyngham MS.

[139] Drennan, William A., Diary of the Defense of Vicksburg from May 30 to July 4, 1863 (Vol. II); in Mississippi State Archives. Lady Georgiana Charlotte Fullerton (1812-1885) was an English convert to the Catholic Church. Her book "Grantley Manor," a study of character, was published in 1847. *Catholic Encyclopedia*, Vol. VI, 318.

[140] Van Queckelberge arrived most probably some time in Dec. 1863. Elder Diary, 71. McCabe, an alumnus of All Hallows, was ordained to the priesthood in Ireland on Sept. 10, 1864. He arrived in the Diocese at the beginning of February, 1865. He died at Vicksburg, his first and only assignment, on Oct. 12, 1865, of typhoid fever. Elder Diary, 116. Elder to Very Rev. T. Bennett, D.D., President of All Hallows, Natchez, Oct. 17, 1865; in ADNJ, Elder Letter Book—#10, 401.

crease the religious opportunities of Catholic Mississippians. In February, 1864, Father Finucane left the Diocese and about a month and a half later Father Orlandi did the same.[141] For that matter, less than three months after his arrival Father Van Queckelberge left the Diocese for reasons of health and did not return until March, 1865,[142] and the very week that Father McCabe reported in at Natchez, Father O'Connor transferred to the Archdiocese of Baltimore.[143] McCabe was immediately assigned to Vicksburg where Bishop Elder himself had been filling in since January 10, when he had given Father Heuzé permission to withdraw from the Diocese to join the Marist Fathers.[144]

During the course of the War shortages which occurred in certain fields created liturgical problems for the Bishop and his priests. In April, 1862, Elder asked the Archbishop of New Orleans to consecrate holy oils for him as he found it difficult to secure olive oil.[145] Because of a shortage of altar wine some priests of the Diocese were compelled to cease offering the Holy Sacrifice of the Mass except on Sundays. Even at the Cathedral in Natchez one ordinary bottle of wine had to last for thirty Masses.[146] During the siege of Vicksburg Father Heuzé paid $15 for one bottle of wine which in normal times would have cost about $1.25.[147] Fortunately, at the beginning of April, 1863, Elder was able to announce to his priests that a supply of wine, "sufficient to enable

---

141 Elder Diary, 74, 76.

142 *Ibid.*, 118.

143 *Ibid.*, 116. O'Connor was sent to Baltimore with the understanding that Archbishop Spalding would release three priests belonging to the Natchez Diocese whom he had been allowed to employ temporarily because of conscription difficulties. Apparently Elder succeeded in getting only one of these priests, viz., Fr. Patrick Murtagh. An alumnus of All Hallows, Murtagh arrived at Natchez in the early part of April, 1865. Elder to Van Queckelberge, Natchez, April 9, 1865; in ADNJ, Elder Letter Book—#10, 200.

144 Ever since the seige was over, Heuzé had been begging the Bishop for permission to leave the Diocese and become a religious. Elder Diary, 115. He entered the Marist Fathers' novitiate at Lyon, where he was professed on April 29, 1866. After serving in Dublin and London, he was assigned in 1869, to Australia. He died there on August 26, 1883, while pastor of St. Patrick's Church, Sydney. Necrologie—No. 27; in the archives of the Marist Fathers, Rome.

145 Elder to Odin, Natchez, April 5, 1862; in ADNJ, Elder Letter Book—#7, 449.

146 Elder to the Clergy of the Diocese of Natchez, Natchez, April 1, 1863; in ADNJ, Elder Letter Book—#8, 346.

147 Diary of Fr. Carrier, C.S.C., quoted by Conyngham in *Soldiers of the Cross* (unpublished); in AUND: Conyngham MS.

every Priest in the Diocese to offer Mass every day for more than a year," had been obtained.[148] By the middle of the War Elder reported that it was impossible for him to obtain any church goods. Yet the need for things used in divine worship and articles of devotion was increasing as they wore out, were destroyed or were stolen. Therefore, to a priest who was coming to the Diocese from the North, the Bishop wrote in August, 1863: "Whatever you have, or can conveniently get for Missionary use, I advise you to bring; such as Chalice, Vestments, Pixes, Oil Stocks &c. —also Beads, Medals, small Crucifixes & *small* prayer books &c. —None of these things can be got here." [149]

There does not appear to have been any extraordinary increase of religious fervor among Mississippi's Catholics during the War. Indeed, in February, 1862, Bishop Elder complained to his metropolitan of a spiritual languor among his people which even the military reverses experienced by the Confederate armies in the early part of 1862, did not disturb.

> For my part I have been disheartened for some time past, at the want of religious fervor among them: the continued neglect of religious duties among so many—& the absence of any manifest improvement among the most of them. I apprehended that God sees we need more chastisement.[150]

Although the religious spirit of Catholic Mississippians was not very consoling to their Bishop, there does not seem to have been any decline of religion among them during the disruptive war years. For that matter, on at least two occasions the Bishop was impressed by demonstrations indicative of spiritual renewal among his people. They continued to value very highly the services of their priests and repeatedly called for them when deprived of their ministrations for any great length of time.[151] Before leaving for the army almost all of the Catholic men received the Sacraments and in many cases were invested with the Scapular.[152] While the

148 Elder to the Clergy of the Diocese of Natchez, Natchez, April 1, 1863; in ADNJ, Elder Letter Book—#8, 346.

149 Elder to Van Queckelberge, Natchez, August 23, 1863; in ADNJ, Elder Letter Book—#8, 475.

150 Elder to Odin, Natchez, Feb. 20, 1862; in AUND: New Orleans Papers.

151 Elder Diary, 78. Elder to Picherit, Natchez, June 20, 1863; in ADNJ, Elder Letter Book—#8, 434. Elder to Spalding, Natchez, Feb. 23, 1865; in AAB, 33-U-6.

152 Elder to McCaffrey, Natchez, July, 1861; in Meline & McSweeney, *The Story of The Mountain,* II, 8. Parish Record, Sulphur Springs, (1841-1926); in parish archives, Camden; copy in ADNJ, 25.

men were away at the front, the people at home increased their requests for Masses to be said for their safe return.[153] In response to Pope Pius IX's peace appeal to Archbishop Odin of New Orleans,[154] Bishop Elder urged his priests to carry out the Forty Hours devotion wherever this was practical or to substitute another appropriate devotion on behalf of peace. As it turned out, only at the Cathedral and at the parish church in Bay St. Louis could the Forty Hours devotion be carried out with proper solemnity. "But," Elder was happy to report to the Archbishop of New Orleans, "I invited all to offer up prayers for Peace—& along the Gulf Coast, I assisted at them myself, & everywhere there seems to be an unusual movement of the grace of God." [155] So encouraged was Elder by his experiences on the Gulf Coast that he could not help reporting the same news to Archbishop Purcell of Cincinnati. "There has been for some months past a very promising advancement in the spirit of religion in the little congregations on the Gulf Coast & on this occasion (the holding of devotions for peace) the churches were filled (?); the Confessions & Communions were more numerous than before . . ." [156]

Perhaps, the most unique expression of Catholic piety during the War occurred in Natchez. In September, 1862, shortly after the shelling of the town, Elder arranged to have Forty Hours devotion celebrated in the Cathedral. It was the first time that the devotion had been celebrated in the Diocese. The people of the parish manifested so much fervor and the spiritual fruits were so great during the celebration "that it appeared to be a suitable occasion for establishing something permanent for preserving and always augmenting the devotion of the People towards the Adorable Sacrament of the Holy Eucharist." [157] An added reason for establishing some permanent religious observance at this time was

---

[153] Elder to Huber, Natchez, June 18, 1863; in ADNJ, Elder Letter Book —#8, 425.

[154] On October 18, 1862, Pope Pius IX sent identical letters to Archbishop Odin of New Orleans and Archbishop John Hughes of New York in which the Pontiff implored them to use their influence that the domestic strife might soon come to an end. *Official Records: Navy*, Ser. II, Vol. III, 559-569—a translation.

[155] Elder to Odin, Natchez, Dec. 25, 1863; in ADNJ, Elder Letter Book —#9, 47.

[156] Elder to Purcell, Natchez, Dec. 30, 1863; in ADNJ, Elder Letter Book —#9, 60.

[157] Barnabò to Elder, Rome, Feb. 25, 1864; in ADNJ, "Vow, Corpus Christi." A translation of the original Latin letter appears in *Cradle Days of St. Mary's* by Gerow, 152-153.

the desire on the part of the people to thank God for the protection He had extended to their city during the recent bombardment [158] and to secure it for the future. Accordingly, at the suggestion of Bishop Elder, "The Clergy and Faithful of the City of Natchez offered to God a public vow, that they should every year thenceforth sanctify the Festival of Corpus Christi . . . by assisting at the Holy Sacrifice of the Mass." [159] This vow was publicly read at the closing of the Forty Hours devotion in the Cathedral on September 18, 1862. It did not enjoin the obligation to abstain from servile work on the feast of Corpus Christi, and it affected only the Catholics of the Cathedral city.[160]

Moral Problems

By the autumn of 1861, prices became disturbed in a few commodities, but by the middle of 1862 almost everything had been caught up into the whirlwind. Chief factors in the rise of prices were the scarcity of commodities as the blockade became more and more effective and the oversupply of Confederate money. Prices skyrocketed still further as fear of defeat led to a lack of faith in Confederate money. Near the end of the War prices became fantastic and meant nothing. Such a situation was an invitation to speculators whose operations were not always consonant with the moral law.

Before making any public statement on the matter, as the moral guide of his people, Bishop Elder sought the advice of his fellow-suffragan, Bishop Quinlan of Mobile.[161] "Where is the line to be drawn between lawful gains and exortiant (sic) ones?" he asked. "Theologians have granted," Elder noted, "that a man may buy at the lowest market price and sell at the highest for the market price is kept from growing exorbitant by the competition

[158] The bombardment lasted for one hour. Damage in the upper town, the residential district, was negligible. Some buildings Under-the-Hill were damaged and others burned. There were only two casualties. Moore, *Natchez Under-The-Hill,* 100.

[159] Barnabò to Elder, Rome, Feb. 25, 1864; in ADNJ, "Vow, Corpus Christi." Translation in Gerow, *op. cit.,* 152-153.

[160] This vow remained in force until 1913, when Bishop Gunn, sixth ordinary of the Diocese, considering the change of conditions warranted a release from the obligation, petitioned the Holy See for a dispensation from the vow. This was granted through the Sacred Congregation of the Council, August 22, 1913. Gerow, *op. cit.,* 153.

[161] Cf. Wight, "Bishop Elder and the Civil War," in CHR, XLIV (Oct. 1958), 297-298.

of the sellers."[162] As Elder saw it, there was no check to the rise of prices unless the purchasers could not get money or unless they preferred suffering privations to paying a large price. The problem, therefore, could be stated thus: "Are men at liberty then to raise the price as high as they feel people (are) willing to give? If not how high can they go?"[163] At the same time, the Bishop of Natchez was not unaware that the vendors had a case, for he wrote:

> On the side of these exorbitant sellers, it is said that all prices are conventional, there is no *intrinsic* relation between an article & a certain amount of money. Values always rise in proportion to scarcity & demand & if the price is twenty times greater than it was, the simple reason is that the scarcity is greater. That only if there were enough to supply the wants of all, the prices would fall, & since there are not enough for all; it is fair that those should have the article who feel the need of it so much as to give the highest price for it. At the same time, the seller says he is doing no business except in those few articles—he is paying rent & other expenses & he in turn is obliged to give enormous prices for everything he uses for himself and family.[164]

After presenting arguments both pro and con in the case, the Bishop of Natchez concluded by asking Quinlan whether it would be advisable to give any instructions on the subject from the pulpit or otherwise. As far as the internal forum was concerned, Elder had already determined as a practical principle to allow net profits of 100% over the cost of an article to the seller, but he was still anxious to know what was being followed elsewhere and whether any public statement should be made by a person in his position.[165] We do not know what Bishop Quinlan's advice was, but it would seem that the Bishop of Mississippi refrained from making any pronouncement. While Elder appears to have judged himself strictly in his personal life, to have been a man with a delicate conscience, inclining to be somewhat scrupulous, this same tendency kept him from making public pronouncements not only on the delicate and difficult issues of secession and slavery, but also on the complicated subject of wartime profit making.

---

[162] Elder to Quinlan, Natchez, Nov. 17, 1862, in ADNJ, Elder Letter Book—#8, 161.

[163] *Ibid.*

[164] *Ibid.*

[165] *Ibid.*

The War or more precisely Federal occupation created another moral problem for Bishop Elder and his flock. It concerned the oath of allegiance to the United States government and Constitution which the occupying military authorities were asking the inhabitants to take. In New Orleans, for instance, General Butler on June 19, 1862, required the oath from all who exercised public authority of any kind, or asked any favors of the government beyond police protection.[166] In St. Louis, Louisville and Memphis similar policies were being followed. After the fall of New Orleans which gave the Union navy access to the Mississippi River and made the occupation of Natchez all but inevitable, Bishop Elder wrote to the Bishop of Mobile on the subject of the oath, because, as he said, "if possible we ought to try to act uniformly." The Mississippi prelate stated his views in considerable detail for Quinlan:

> It is not all impossible that the Federals may take possession of Natchez this winter, & may demand an oath of allegiance. My opinion is that whoever takes it is bound by conscience to observe it. He cannot claim absolution from it under the Confederate govt. because the very import of the oath is to exclude the Confederate govt. unless it be otherwise explained. But how long is it binding? Does it cease, if the Federalists are driven away from the place? It seems to me that unless otherwise explained, it continues in force until released by the consent of the Federal Govt. which will only be given I suppose on making peace. Otherwise it is nothing but an agreement to submit for the present.
>
> Regarded in its rigorous sense is it lawful for a citizen to take it to save his property & his family? Had we better leave it to each one to judge for himself—weighing his own circumstances?[167]

In the same letter Bishop Elder took issue with "Genl. Butler's reasoning, that all who are not with the Federal govt. are against it, & are to be treated as enemies.—It seems to me," Elder continued,

> that the very fact of their recognizing our soldiers as belligerents, giving titles to our Generals & exchanging prisoners—is a confession that the Confd govt. whether lawful or unlawful in their eyes, has sufficient authority to justify its

---

166 Dabney, *One Hundred Great Years* (Baton Rouge, 1944), 159.

167 Elder to Quinlan, Natchez, Nov. 17, 1862; in ADNJ, Elder Letter Book —#8, 161.

> citizens in their conscience for adhering to it & consequently refusing to renounce it. . . .[168]

In substance, then, Elder was asking: Should a Southerner take the oath of allegiance to the United States government once his home fell within the Federal lines? and What was the binding force of such an oath once taken?

The problem became real enough for Elder and his flock when both Vicksburg and Natchez were permanently occupied by the Federals in the summer of 1863. Just as he left the consciences of his people free during the heated debate on secession, so too now the Bishop of Natchez left it to the individual to decide whether he wanted to take the oath and thus renounce his allegiance to the Confederacy or not. In the next chapter we shall see what course of action the Bishop himself chose to follow. However, to the question: what was the binding force of such an oath once taken, a purely moral issue, Elder felt not only competent but also obligated to make a public statement. Thus, on Sunday, July 3, 1864, almost a year after the city's occupation by the Union army, the following announcement was made from the Cathedral pulpit of Natchez:

> I must remind you of the Instruction which was given to you some time ago, on the nature of Oaths, & the obligations begotten by them.
>
> An Oath is a solemn calling on God to bear witness to the truth of what you say, & to your fidelity in keeping your promise.
>
> An Oath does not need one form of words, nor any one outward sign. Whatever words, or whatever sign expresses a calling of God as witness, is sufficient for an oath;—& it is not necessary that you utter those words yourself;—but if any one else utters them, and you give any sign that you assent, you take an oath:—whether that sign be laying your hand on the Gospel, or signing your name, or lifting up your hand, or bowing your head, or saying 'yes,'—or saying or doing anything else, which in the circumstances expresses your assent.
>
> The meaning of an Oath administered by a Public Officer in the discharge of his office must be drawn from the

[168] *Ibid.*

> true & obvious meaning of the words, as they are commonly & fairly understood in those circumstances; & no one has a right to put on them a private & contrary interpretation of his own.
>
> To take an Oath which a person does not intend to keep in its fair & honest sense, is a mortal sin of perjury,—& no excuse of inconvenience nor of compulsion can authorize a person to insult Almighty God by calling on His divine Majesty to bear witness that he intends to do, what in truth he does not intend to do.
>
> And to violate an oath, by doing that which a person has sworn that he will not do, is likewise a mortal sin,—being equally an insult to Almighty God, since by your oath you have pledged God's own honor for the fulfillment of your promise.[169]

Although an earlier instruction on the subject had apparently been given, Elder felt it was necessary to repeat it, because recently a number of people had been scandalized "in the arrest of some Catholics charged with smuggling out goods &c in violation of the oath of allegiance which they had taken to the U.S." It had also been reported to the Bishop "that several Catholics have spoken very lightly of the obligation of that oath."[170] The members of his flock were free to take the oath or not, but, once they had taken it, Elder insisted that they keep it.

Not until the spring of 1862, did the Catholic Church in Mississippi begin to feel the full impact of the War. From that time on, however, she had her share of problems. Her property was damaged or sequestered. Interrupted or curtailed were her religious life, her charitable activities and her efforts in the field of education. New problems were created by the emancipation of the Negro, by the requested oath of allegiance and by the shortage of commodities, problems which further tested her patience, her prudence and her purpose. But through those turbulent years she held her ground. At the end of the War, unlike so many other institutions of the South, the Catholic Church in Mississippi was still on hand, determined to carry on her mission; she had not, like so many others, "Gone With The Wind."

---

169 Announcement Book—#4, of the Natchez Cathedral; in the Cathedral archives, Natchez, Mississippi. This entry is in Bishop Elder's handwriting.

170 Elder Diary, 90.

Chapter XIII

THE BISHOP AND THE ENEMY

The effectiveness of any minister of religion depends to a very great extent on his ability to gain and retain the confidence of the people whom he serves. To an equal extent it depends on his ability to move about freely among these same people, that is to say, on the degree of civil freedom he enjoys. After the Union army invaded the state of Mississippi, but especially after his cathedral city was occupied by the enemy, Bishop Elder found it increasingly difficult to secure the one condition without endangering the other. To avoid any action which could be construed by the occupying authorities as hostile to them and at the same time to encourage and support his people in the pursuit of their legitimate political ambitions—this was the problem facing Bishop Elder during the last two years of the War. Unfortunately, in the summer of 1864 the balance he tried so hard to maintain was destroyed, and the Bishop of Natchez clashed with the military authorities occupying his see city. "Incidit in Scyllam qui vult vitare Charybdim."

Policy

With the enemy massing for battle on the northern border of Mississippi, Bishop Elder wrote to Father Mouton who was preparing to leave for the battle front. This letter contains the first known statement of policy on how the Bishop expected his priests to conduct themselves when dealing with the enemy.

> If the *Federalists* should come down so far as to bring you into contact with them—I shall be glad that you do all you can for their souls—but do not do any thing that would have an appearance of making them welcome; such as visiting them for pleasure, taking dinners of pleasure with the Officers &c. They will be likely to try to draw you into such things for the sake of pleasing Catholics. Treat them as a Christian ought to treat enemies—with Charity—but not intimacy. I do not wish you to go to their camps to offer Mass. You can administer Communion there to those, who are dangerously sick—& you may *hear Confessions* for all:

because these are cases of necessity. But if those who are in good health wish to receive Holy Communion or to hear Mass, let them come to your usual place of saying Mass.— Be zealous and prudent.[1]

It is obvious that Elder had no intention of alienating his flock by excessive zeal on the part of himself or his priests.[2] To this policy the Bishop would adhere fairly closely for the remainder of the War.

Early Contacts

At the time that Natchez itself was occupied by the enemy, Bishop Elder was visiting Brookhaven with the intention of going on to Jackson from there. A few days before he reached the state capital, the Confederates withdrew and the Federals took over for the second time within three months. It was here, consequently, that the Bishop made personal contact with the enemy for the first time. According to his diary, Elder had no difficulty crossing the picket line.[3] Once inside the city, he presented himself before Brigadier-General Hugh Ewing,[4] a Catholic from Ohio. This he did, not from any desire to strike up a friendship with the officer, but merely to find a safe place for his horse and buggy. On this occasion the meeting was limited to an exchange of formalities.[5] When the Catholic chaplain attached to Ewing's brigade, Father J. C. Carrier, C.S.C.,[6] extended to the Bishop what hospitality the army had to offer, Elder declined. Not from any lack of appreciation did Elder refuse, as his diary reveals.

---

[1] Elder to Mouton, Natchez, April 2, 1862; in ADNJ, Elder Letter Book —#7, 442.

[2] A Southern prelate with far less discretion than Elder was the Bishop of Nashville, James Whelan, O.P. This prelate saw no harm in openly fraternizing with enemy officers at a time when a number of his priests were serving as chaplains in the Confederate army; the costly foundation of the church in Chattanooga had been torn down; his own cathedral had been converted into a military hospital; and the sympathies of the majority of his flock were with the South. O'Daniel, *The Father of the Church in Tennessee,* 573.

[3] Elder Diary, 46.

[4] Hugh Ewing, of Ohio, Colonel 13th Ohio Vols.; Brigadier-General from Nov. 29, 1862; mustered out Jan. 15, 1866. *Personnel of the Civil War,* edited by W. F. Amann, II, 38.

[5] Elder Diary, 48.

[6] Father J. C. Carrier, C.S.C., from Notre Dame, Ind.; chaplain to the 6th Mo. Inf. Germain, "Catholic Military and Naval Chaplains, 1776-1917," in CHR, XV (July 1929), 173.

> Saw . . . Rev. Mr. Carrier, C.Ss.Cr. Chaplain of Genl Ewing's Brigade. He was kind—& wished to do all that he could to make me comfortable. (. . . .) Fr. Carrier invited me to lodge & eat at Genl. Ewing's quarters—but when our poor flock is in such distress I thought it would be unfeeling. I had rather share their fare. Fr. Carrier says Mass in the Senate Chamber. Tho' I have not said Mass for a week —yet I did not like to say it there in the present circumstances.[7]

Elder ran into difficulty with the Federal military authorities for the first time on the occasion of this visit. He apparently annoyed Brigadier-General Blair [8] a great deal by sending for a pass to Canton rather than making application for it personally. It was only after Elder appeared before the General with Father Carrier that the officer granted the pass, displaying at the same time what in Elder's estimation were ill manners.

On his way back to Natchez the Bishop decided to visit Vicksburg to survey the conditions there after the siege. Toward evening he reached the Federal camp outside the city where he had to apply for a pass. Here he spent the night, enjoying the hospitality of one of the officers. While in camp, Elder learned that there were a good many sick men in the army hospitals in the immediate area. The next morning, therefore, he presented himself before the commanding officer and offered to visit the sick. The offer was quickly accepted by the Union general. Present on this occasion was a Catholic lieutenant colonel who prevailed upon the Bishop to stay on in camp for another day to allow the men of his regiment to make use of Elder's services. After visiting the hospitals, Elder heard confessions that afternoon and again the next morning. During his stay in the Federal camp Elder got along well enough with the officers. "The officers here are very pleasant in conversation," the Bishop noted. "Strong for the Union, but gentlemanly in expressing themselves." [9]

Arriving in Vicksburg, the Bishop went with Father Heuzé to see General Grant. Stating his business in a note hastily scribbled while sitting under a tree outside the General's office Elder was

---

[7] Elder Diary, 48.

[8] Frank Blair, of Missouri, Colonel 1st Mo. Artillery, from Aug. 7, 1862; promoted Brigadier-General Nov. 29, 1862; resigned Nov. 1, 1865. *Personnel of the Civil War,* edited by W. F. Amann, II, 10.

[9] Elder Diary, 54.

received by Grant. Although the conversation between the two men was brief, the General attended to the business at once and favorably. To obtain the requested protection for the Sisters' convent the Bishop was directed to General McPherson. Since Father Heuzé was attending the Union soldiers without pay, Grant directed that the priest be given provisions as well as a horse and buggy and forage. He also gave Elder a travel permit and free transportation by boat to Natchez for himself, his servant and his horse and buggy. When the Bishop called an General McPherson [10] about the Sisters' convent, the prelate was received pleasantly and given the assurance he was looking for.[11] Returning to Natchez in the early part of August, 1863, Bishop Elder must have felt that his future relations with the military authorities occupying his cathedral city would be amicable enough.

And so they were for the next nine months. As we have seen, the orphans were supplied from the military commissary; the cemetery fence which had been destroyed by the Federal soldiers was repaired when the Bishop lodged a complaint; and whenever Elder came in contact with the authorities, he was always treated respectfully. On an unofficial basis the officers and men gave a helping hand to the Sisters whenever they could; they took up collections for the orphans; Colonel Schatz arranged to supply each orphan boy with a suit of clothes; General Gresham sent the Bishop and his priests a load of forage, bearing the expense personally when he could not authorize them to draw it from government stores;[12] and a Colonel Shaw promised to supply an oil painting for the Cathedral.[13] Bishop Elder and his priests on their part tended to the spiritual needs of the Union soldiers in the area as conscientiously as they did those of their own flock. This in itself was no small task, for it meant visiting a number of military hospitals at a time when they were also trying to care for the horde of Negroes who had flocked to Natchez. So heavy was this

---

[10] James B. McPherson, U.S. Vols., Brigadier-General from Oct. 8, 1862; killed July 22, 1864. He was in command of the District of Vicksburg from July 4, 1863 until March, 1864. *Dictionary of American Biography,* Vol. XII, 160-161.

[11] Elder Diary, 55-56.

[12] *Ibid.,* 66. Walter Q. Gresham, Colonel 53d Indiana Vols.; from Aug. 11, 1863, a Brigadier-General; mustered out April 30, 1866. From August, 1863, until the spring of 1864, he was in command of the Natchez district. *Dictionary of American Biography,* Vol. VII, 608.

[13] Elder Diary, 65.

extra work that for eight months or more it was the chief occupation of two of the priests attached to the Cathedral.[14]

As smoothly as things ran during this early period of the occupation of Natchez, Bishop Elder had cause for growing apprehensive on two occasions. Before going off to war, a number of individuals had deposited sums of money with the Bishop for safekeeping. When a military order was published in October, 1863, directing the people of Natchez to pay all rents to the U.S. government, Elder became alarmed. He felt the next step would be an order calling for all deposits. However, during an interview with the military commander at Natchez the Bishop was told not to be uneasy. It was the General's opinion that nothing would be done to molest him in the matter.[15]

Oath of Allegiance

Another thing that caused Elder a good deal of worry was the growing emphasis being placed upon taking the oath of allegiance as a way of demonstrating one's loyalty to the occupying power. Eight months before the arrival of the enemy in Natchez, Bishop Elder considered the problem of the oath which he knew he would most probably have to face in the not too distant future. Writing to the Bishop of Mobile on this subject, Elder posed two relevant questions: "Shall they (his priests) be left to follow their own judgment with regard to the oath or ought I to lay down a rule, & forbid them to violate it under censure? And ought a Bishop himself to take it under any circumstances?" The first question Elder left unanswered in this letter.[16] On the second point, however, he gave it as his opinion that a bishop should not take the oath, for

> . . . a man, whose character & position make him a non-combatant, is entitled to be unmolested. Such is the case with the Catholic clergy; & it seems to me that a Bishop ought to stand upon this ground. Whether he yields or refuses there is danger of injury to religion: but I think that in refus-

[14] Elder to Odin, Natchez, Feb. 6, 1864; in ADNJ, Elder Letter Book—#9, 139.

[15] Elder Diary, 69-70.

[16] There is no evidence that Bishop Elder ever made any ruling for his priests on the matter of the oath at any time during the War. However, we do know his personal feelings on the subject and that he was always interested in seeing the Catholic clergy of the South act uniformly in such delicate matters.

> ing he maintains the right & throws the odium upon those who chose to violate it.[17]

Shortly before the occupation of Natchez, Elder asked his metropolitan to obtain permission for him to visit New Orleans, already in Federal hands, without having to take the oath. In the letter the Mississippi prelate explains his unwillingness to submit to this military regulation.

> Being devoted to spiritual interests I have no hostility to any government that may be established de facto: but to bind myself by permanent obligation opposed to the sentiments of the majority of my flock, would deprive me of all power of usefulness. And while the contest is still undecided, it seems to me it would not be right to make a promise which I might not be able to fulfil.[18]

Of the same mind in this matter as the Bishop of Natchez, Quinlan of Mobile also steadfastly refused to take the oath even though this meant a severe curtailment of his activities outside the Diocese and, in time, even within. Indeed, Father Oscar Lipscomb suggests that the Alabama prelate was influenced in part by Elder's attitude.[19]

After the occupation of Natchez the oath, as elsewhere, was employed for determining the loyalty of the people to their new government. A number of Natchez's citizens, Catholics included, took the oath. Some took it sincerely; others as a subterfuge. Apparently Elder was not called upon to take the oath. However, in the weeks that followed rumors must have reached the Bishop that his loyalty to the military authorities was being questioned, that he was suspected of advocating, if not by word, at least by example, passive resistance. It was most probably for these reasons that in the course of an interview with General Gresham in October, 1863, Elder introduced the subject of the oath. The substance of his remarks to the commanding officer at Natchez the Bishop recorded in his diary.

> I explained our general position: viz. that we did nothing to bring about the war. When it was begun, we like many in the North wished our own side to win, especially when we

[17] Elder to Quinlan, Natchez, Nov. 17, 1862; in ADNJ, Elder Letter Book—#8, 161.

[18] Elder to Odin, Natchez, July 9, 1863; in AUND: New Orleans Papers.

[19] Lipscomb, "*The Administration of John Quinlan, Second Bishop of Mobile, 1859-1883*," 82-85.

> saw what evils the South wd. suffer from being subdued. But we had never preached war sermons—nor urged people to go to war. Our desire was to do good to souls—we labored for all souls in our reach from North or South. Personally I was willing to bear true allegiance to any govt. Russian or Kamschatkan—but I did not wish to do anything wh. wd. injure my usefulness among my flock—as taking the oath of allegiance wd. do.[20]

Although the Bishop explained his position to General Gresham satisfactorily so that the latter saw no reason for obliging him to take the obnoxious oath, the Bishop remained in the eyes of some people, even his own, a symbol of passive resistance to the "Yankees" by not taking the oath. It was an image which unfortunately would create difficulty for him later on.

The Bishop and General Tuttle

Trouble really came only in the spring of 1864, with the change of commanders at Natchez. Replacing General Gresham was General James M. Tuttle.[21] Less than a month after his arrival the new commander, while interviewing Bishop Elder, inquired of the prelate whether a prayer for the President and the authorities of the United States was a part of his church service. Elder explained, as he later reported,

> that the said Prayer[22] is not at all a part of our regular Church service, & is not found in the book which contains our Service, the Missal:—that it has indeed been recited sometimes during the Divine Service, but only at the free choice of the Priest or the Bishop, & even with some stretch of his discretionary powers; since the canonical usage of the Church excludes the public recital during Mass, of any prayer not contained in the Missal:—& that in a great many Churches in the United States—I believe, in the great majority of them,—it has never been recited publicly.[23]

Apparently satisfied with this explanation, the General dropped the matter. Five days later, however, on March 16, Elder received

---

[20] Elder Diary, 70.

[21] James M. Tuttle, of Iowa, Colonel 2d Iowa Vols.; promoted Brigadier-General June 9, 1862; resigned June 14, 1864. *Personnel of the Civil War,* edited by W. F. Amann, II, 32.

[22] Prayer for Civil Authorities, composed by Bishop John Carroll in 1791.

[23] Elder to Abraham Lincoln, Natchez, April 7, 1864; in NAW, Records of the Office of the Secretary of War, Letters Received, K 400 (128). Published in *Catholic Telegraph,* Cincinnati, Nov. 3, 1904; also in Gerow, *Cradle Days of St. Mary's,* 161-165.

a curt summons from the General, who wanted to know why he had not complied with his request that the prayer for civil authorities be said at services in the Cathedral. Elder replied that he did not believe such an order had been given. Tuttle answered that he had indeed given no order, but he had made a request. Even now he refused to give an order, and only requested that the prayer be read as a favor to himself. "But he immediately nullified his own distinction," Elder reported,

> by declaring that if I did not comply with his request, he should regard it as a proof of disloyalty, which would be subject to punishment. He further explained his meaning by these words: "You are free to read it or not, as you choose: but if you do not choose (to read it), you must take the consequences." And in reply to my inquiry whether he would not, before passing a sentence against me, make a specific charge, & allow me a hearing on the matter, he said that I might have a trial, or I might not.[24]

Without explicitly refusing to comply, Elder tried to explain that to the Church alone belongs the right to regulate her worship and that, therefore, the General's "request" was tantamount to unwarranted interference in purely ecclesiastical affairs. Tuttle brushed aside this appeal to principle. Since their previous interview Tuttle had come into possession of a Catholic prayer book published with the approbation of Archbishop Hughes of New York. It contained a number of private prayers, among them Bishop Carroll's prayer for civil authorities. Tuttle brought this to Elder's attention, implying that the latter had tried to hoodwink him during their previous meeting. The Bishop tried to explain that his neglect to read the prayer was no sudden "about-face" move on his part.

> I have told him that in Natchez, during the time that I have been here, (about seven years,) we sometimes read it, sometimes omitted it, & sometimes read some other prayer in its place:—that for a while I read a similar prayer for the Confederate Authorities, but afterwards I laid aside all these prayers of a local character, & conformed more closely to the approved usages of the Church, by adopting a prayer belonging to the authorized Liturgy, the Litany of the Saints. This change was made in November 1862, long before the United States forces occupied Natchez, & while the Confederate Military were in quiet possession of the place.[25]

---

24 *Ibid.*
25 *Ibid.*

The explanation made no impression on the General. When it was pointed out to Tuttle by one of his own officers how incongruous it would be to recite the prayer in question at the present time, since it recommends to the favor of God both the United States government, and the Governor, Legislature and Civil Officers of Mississippi, the declared enemies of the United States, the General still insisted that the prayer be read "just as it is in the book." [26]

Elder continued to remonstrate with the General, pointing out what repercussions his demand might have in other quarters.

> I remarked to Genl. Tuttle that such an attempt to compel a Bishop to alter the form of Divine Service in his Cathedral, would necessarily give pain & alarm to all Catholics throughout the whole country. (. . . .) I told him that the Catholic Officers & Soldiers of his command, & of all portions of the United States Army & Navy, would feel themselves injured in this attempt—the first that I have heard of,—to dictate to a Bishop with regard to his ecclesiastical administration, & that certainly those Soldiers did not deserve such an offence at his hands.[27]

Finally, the General revealed what was really bothering him. "Of all things, I hate most a traitor. I believe there are many traitors in this community, and I believe you are one!" [28] Elder was stunned as well as filled with indignation at the charge. There was nothing in his conduct, as he saw it, that could have prompted Tuttle to offer him such a "gross indignity." Suppressing his indignation as best he could, Elder replied: "General, I thank you for your compliment. That is an exceedingly harsh term that you have applied to me. I request you to state the facts on which you ground your charge(s); & the evidence that you have for them." [29] Tuttle's only answer was that his resistance to saying the prayer was fact enough.

In all there were three meetings between the Bishop and the General. On all three occasions Elder was accompanied by his Vicar-General, Father Grignon. At the third and last interview, during which the whole matter was rehashed, the Bishop also re-

---

[26] *Ibid.*
[27] *Ibid.*
[28] *Ibid.* Also *The Freeman's Journal*, Aug. 27, 1864; another newspaper clipping, undated, in ADNJ, File 1: Folder—N.
[29] *Ibid.*

quested the presence of two Union officers, friends of his, one Catholic and the other Protestant.[30] After each meeting Elder was free to go. No effort was made to detain him or to interfere with the exercise of his ministry. How long he would continue to enjoy such freedom Elder did not know.

News of the pressure being brought upon Bishop Elder spread quickly about the city and caused a good deal of uneasiness, not only among the members of his congregation, but also among other Catholics in the city, military and civilian. Strangely enough the warmest friends of the Union in Natchez were the first to recommend that Elder refer the case immediately and directly to President Lincoln. However, the Bishop thought it best to submit the matter to the commander of the department at Vicksburg.

Before dispatching his letter of protest to the Vicksburg commander, Bishop Elder, in a spirit of fair dealing, submitted the document to General Tuttle for his perusal. The gesture so impressed the officer that he paid Elder the following compliment: "Bishop, I must give you credit for being the most candid man I ever met." [31] To Tuttle's credit it must be said that, while awaiting a decision from higher authority, he did not press the matter of the prayer any further. In the meanwhile, Elder learned that the commander at Vicksburg could not be easily reached just then. Moved by the urgency and importance of the case, Elder decided to follow the advice given to him earlier and have immediate recourse to President Lincoln. Accordingly, he re-wrote his letter for the President.[32]

Appeal to Lincoln

In the first half of the seven-page letter, composed and written by himself, the Bishop related in detail all that had transpired between himself and General Tuttle from the very beginning. He insisted that his resistance to the General's "request" was not prompted by political reasons. He pointed out that he had

[30] *Ibid.* The two Union officers were Major James A. Farrish and Major O. T. Turney. The latter was the Catholic. Major Farrish was received into the Church a few days after he accompanied the Bishop to his third interview with General Tuttle. Baptismal Register—#2, of St. Mary's Cathedral, Natchez, p. 305-306; in Cathedral archives, Natchez.

[31] *Freeman's Journal*, Aug. 27, 1864.

[32] Elder to Odin, Vicksburg, April 14, 1864; in AUND: New Orleans Papers.

stopped saying the prayer in question while the Confederate authorities were still in peaceful possession of Natchez. Should these have insisted that he reintroduce the prayer, which they did not, Elder assured the President: "I should have resisted then as I resist now."[33] Going to the very heart of the problem, as he saw it, Elder continued: "My resistance is based simply on the broad ground that our Church Service is a matter to be regulated exclusively by the authorities of the Church."

In the second half of the letter Elder made his appeal and, in making it, gave the President ample reason for considering his petition favorably.

> Accordingly I most respectfully pray Your Excellency to give such directions as will secure us from this and all similar interference.—The preceding Commanders at Natchez, Genl. Ransom, Genl. Crocker, Genl. Gresham, & Col. Johnson, found no reason to molest us. They left us to attend to our spiritual ministrations in peace, and even favored us with such facilities as were in their power. And no one of them had reason to complain of any evil consequences to their authority & respect.—I have never attempted to influence the political opinions or conduct of the people under my care. And the Clergy of this Diocese, to the best of my knowledge, have abstained from any such attempts: or rather I believe they have never felt disposed to teach politics: but they have devoted themselves to rendering spiritual services to all who desired them at their hands, without distinction of politics of section or of color.
>
> One among them whom I most esteemed and loved, Revd. Basil Elia, lost his life a year ago, from having volunteered with my approval, to go to the assistance of the dying Soldiers of the United States Army opposite to Vicksburgh, who had no Catholic Chaplain at that time to give them those consolations of their Religion, which they valued vastly more than their lives. His own congregation had been dispersed by the events of the war: & when I wrote to him to come into another portion of the Diocese, he asked me to allow him to go rather to those Soldiers, because they had more need of his labors. After three weeks of fatigue & exposure he contracted the prevailing sickness, & died at Memphis, April 2d. 1863.
>
> At this moment a Priest of our Cathedral is lying sick for three weeks, in consequence of four months of incessant

[33] Elder to Abraham Lincoln, Natchez, April 7, 1864.

labor among the Soldiers & others connected with the United States service,—a large number of them being Negroes dying of the Small Pox.—And this present letter has been delayed many days, & I am now compelled to send it without as careful a revision as I should wish to give it,—because I have been personally attending to some of his labors in his place.

We have not received any temporal remuneration, nor applied for any,—but the least we can expect is your protection.

In concluding his letter Elder reminded the President that an important principle was involved in the case being referred to him.

This is not merely a question concerning personal annoyance to ourselves. It is one that involves the religious liberties of the thousands of Catholic Soldiers, & the millions of Catholics not Soldiers, who are subject to the laws & government of the United States.—For all, as well as for myself, I ask protection, & in calling on Your Excellency, I am sure I shall not ask in vain.

I have the honor to remain, with profound respect,

Your Excellency's
most humble servant

†*William Henry Elder,* Bishop of Natchez.[34]

Natchez, Mississippi
April 7th. 1864.

On April 11, 1864, Bishop Elder forwarded the memorial he had drawn up for President Lincoln to Father J. Early, S. J., President of Georgetown University in Washington, D.C. He asked the Jesuit "to provide the best means of bringing it to the favorable consideration of the President." [35] If the Bishop was acquainted with the famous McPheeters case of St. Louis [36] into which Presi-

[34] *Ibid.*

[35] Elder to Early, Vicksburg, April 11, 1864; in Georgetown University Archives. Fr. Early was an alumnus of Mount St. Mary's, Emmitsburg. Probably he and Elder had been classmates there. This may explain why the Bishop sent his memorial to the Jesuit.

[36] Dr. Samuel McPheeters was the minister of an important Presbyterian church in St. Louis. In December, 1862, the commanding general of the Department of the Missouri deposed McPheeters from his pulpit and ordered both him and his wife to leave the state within ten days. This action was taken because of McPheeters' refusal to declare his loyalty to the United States, and also on the ground that his influence greatly encouraged the enemies of the government, while his wife had openly avowed that she was a rebel. Sweet, *The Story of Religion in America* (New York, 1950), 322.

dent Lincoln had been drawn at the beginning of 1863, then the prelate, in sending his memorial to Washington, must have felt somewhat confident that it would produce the desired effect. In January, 1863, the Chief Executive brought the long and drawn-out McPheeters case to a close when he wrote to the military commander of the department of Missouri:

> I add that the United States Government must not, as by this order undertake to run the Churches. When an individual, in a Church or out of it, becomes dangerous to the public, he must be checked; but let the Churches, as such, take care of themselves.[37]

This clear-sighted policy Lincoln maintained throughout the War, even though his military commanders, on more than one occasion, would act otherwise, much to his embarrassment and annoyance.[38]

Decision From Washington

When Father Early received Bishop Elder's memorial, he placed the document in the hands of a Catholic congressman from New York and an alumnus of Georgetown, Francis Kernan. On April 27, Kernan called on Lincoln's Secretary of State, William H. Seward, who advised the Congressman to lay the matter before the Secretary of War, Edwin C. Stanton. Seward was kind enough, however, to volunteer a letter to the Secretary of War, favoring the Bishop's appeal. As Kernan later reported to Father Early, Stanton "received the application in a proper spirit & promptly told me that he would *this very day* cause the proper letter of instruction to be written to Gen. Tuttle to remedy the difficulty." [39] True to his word, the Secretary had the following restraining order sent from the War Department to the General at Natchez:

> The President has referred to this Department a complaint from the Catholic Bishop of Natchez, Miss., of an interference on your part with his duties and with the form of worship prescribed for the churches in the diocess (sic) of which he is the bishop, and the Secretary of War directs me to say that you will abstain from all interference in ecclesiastical

[37] Quoted without reference in Sweet, *op cit.*, 322.

[38] Sweet, *op. cit.*, 322-323. Shea, *History of the Catholic Church in the United States*, IV, 611.

[39] Kernan to Early, Washington, April 27, 1864; in Georgetown University Archives.

> matters; that you will not proscribe any form of prayer or of service or in any other way interfere in matters of church administration except in cases of disloyalty when you will report the facts to this Department and take its orders.[40]

The order, signed by Brigadier-General Ed. R. S. Canby, A. A. G., was dated April 27, 1864.

Not until the first week of June did Bishop Elder hear of the results of his appeal to the President. Details were furnished by Father Early and Mr. Kernan. In his letter Mr. Kernan took the liberty of suggesting to the Bishop that he "say nothing and do nothing which indicates any triumph over the Military Commander. —This would only cause him to seek occasion to annoy you, while it would embarrass the Secretary who desires in a quiet way to relieve you from improper interference." [41] While waiting for news from Washington, Elder had written to Archbishop Odin, informing him of his clash with General Tuttle. At the same time, he enclosed a copy of his memorial. In this letter Elder revealed that he was toying with the idea of making the document public.

> I have been strongly advised to have it published—because it concerns the Church thro' the whole country. Of course I cannot do that till I get the answer, or ascertain the result. Whether I shd. publish it then I do not know.—
>
> I will be glad to have your opinion about it.[42]

After receiving the good news from Washington, Elder decided that the memorial ought to be made public "for the guidance of others," at least so he informed Mr. Kernan.[43] It would seem, however, that Elder never carried out his plan. Most probably the Congressman convinced the Bishop that such a move would be unwise, but, as we shall see, Elder showed more foresight than his adviser in Washington in wanting to make the document public.

---

[40] Canby to Tuttle, Washington, April 27, 1864; in NAW, Records of the Office of the Secretary of War, Military Book, Vol. 55B; also in Gerow, *op. cit.*, 166-167.

[41] Kernan to Elder, Washington, April 27, 1864; in AADC: Elder Papers. Published in Gerow, *op. cit.*, 166 (imperfect).

[42] Elder to Odin, Vicksburg, April 14, 1864; in AUND: New Orleans Papers.

[43] Elder to Early, Fair Oaks near Natchez, June 11, 1864; in Georgetown University Archives.

The Bishop and Colonel Farrar

The same week that Bishop Elder learned about the successful outcome of his appeal to Washington, a new military regulation was issued by the military commander in Natchez which posed another difficulty for the Bishop in the exercise of his ministry. During the course of a visitation of the western part of his diocese Elder was informed that no one was being allowed to leave the city of Natchez without taking the oath of allegiance to the United States government.[44] It should be noted that the Union army's control extended at this time no farther than two miles beyond the city's limits. Writing to his metropolitan from a plantation nine miles outside Natchez, Elder informed Odin of his new predicament.

> Your favor of the 28th. reached me last evening.—Since April 8th. I was at home only once for a few hours.—Now on my approach to Natchez I learn that no egress is allowed but to those who take the oath of allegiance. Fr. Grignon is in town. He had applied for an exception in my favor.— I go to Woodville tomorrow, & visit my Brother John above Baton Rouge. When I return here if they will not grant me an exception, I shall probably visit the eastern part of the Diocese. After that if there is no change, I must choose I suppose (on) which side of the line to remain.[45]

After visiting his brother in Louisiana, Elder returned to the Diocese, stopping off at Woodville in the southwestern corner of the State. Here he found several letters waiting for him. Among them was a copy of a military order issued by the new commander at Natchez. Dated June 18, 1864, the special order read:

> The Col. Comdg this District having been officially notified that the pastors of many churches in this city neglect to make any public recognition of allegiance to the Government under which they live—and to which they are indebted for protection and further—that the regular form of prayer for "the President of the U. S. and all others in authority" prescribed by the ritual in some churches and by established custom in others—has been omitted in the stated services of churches of all denominations—it is hereby "ORDERED" —that hereafter, the Ministers of such churches as may have the prescribed form of prayer for the President of the United States shall . . . read (it) at each and every service in which

[44] Elder Diary, 83.

[45] Elder to Odin, Fair Oaks near Natchez, June 9, 1864; in AUND: New Orleans Papers.

it is required by the rubrics—and that those of other denominations which have no such form—shall on like occasions pronounce a prayer appropriate to the time and expressive of a proper spirit towards the chief magistrate of the U. S. Any Minister failing to comply with these orders will be immediately prohibited from exercising the functions of his office in this city—and renders himself liable to be sent beyond the lines of the U S Forces—at the discretion of the colonel Comdg.[46]

The order was given at the command of Colonel B. G. Farrar.[47] Apparently, the previous commander, General Tuttle, had left no record in headquarters' files of the War Department's communiqué, ordering him to desist from interfering in ecclesiastical affairs at Natchez.

The very same day that the order was delivered at the Cathedral rectory, Father Grignon requested an interview with Colonel Farrar.[48] The commander granted it. During the interview the Vicar General reviewed for the officer all that had taken place between the Bishop and the previous commander on the question of prescribing prayers for the President of the United States. As a result, the Colonel agreed to postpone taking any action until the priest could produce Mr. Kernan's letter to Elder or until the Bishop should himself return to Natchez.[49]

Perhaps, sensing that a showdown between himself and the military authorities at Natchez was in the offing, Elder decided to conclude as much business in Wilkinson County as he could before going up to Natchez. Consequently, as late as June 30, Elder was still south of the Homochitto River.[50] After waiting for almost two weeks for the Bishop to put in an appearance in Natchez, Colonel Farrar finally let the Vicar-General know that he expected the Bishop to present himself at headquarters within the next two days.

---

46 Special Orders, No. 31, III, Headquarters US Forces, Natchez, Miss., June 18, 1864; in NAW, Records of U.S. Army Commands, Department of Mississippi, Vol 42. Also in Gerow, *op. cit.*, 167-168.

47 Bernard G. Farrar, of 30th Missouri Regt.; promoted Brigadier-General of 6th Regt. U.S. Col. Artillery, March 9, 1865. *Personnel of the Civil War*, edited by W. F. Amann, II, 71. This officer had been a lay student at Mount St. Mary's at Emmitsburg at the same time that Elder was enrolled there as a seminarian. Elder Diary, 64.

48 Grignon to Farrar, Natchez, June 18, 1864; in ACHS: Brayman Papers.

49 Elder Diary, 88.

50 *Ibid.*, 89.

Father Van Queckelberge delivered the ultimatum to Elder at Mrs. Norton's plantation near Kingston. The Bishop decided to go in at once.[51] Elder reached Natchez late in the afternoon of July 1, only to find the commander absent on an expedition. The following week, when Farrar had returned, the Bishop and his Vicar General called on the military commander. The exchange which took place on this occasion Elder recorded in his diary.

> When I would show him the unreasonableness of his Special Order requiring prayers for the President,—& remove all his defences of it, he always fell back to the position that the other Churches had done it, & he must therefore require us to do it:—as if the doing of injustice to one person justified the doing of the same injustice to another. —I proposed to him in conclusion that I should write to him a letter explaining my position & the reasons for it: & that he should suffer the letter to be published in my justification. It would at the same time serve him for a justification in revoking the Order. —He said he would consider the proposition—& that I should send for his answer at 2 PM.[52]

At the specified hour the Bishop went himself for the Colonel's answer. Farrar agreed to accept a letter of explanation from the Bishop which the officer said he would submit to the district commander in Vicksburg, General Slocum. In the meanwhile, however, he would expect the Bishop to read the prescribed prayer. Elder's reaction to this directive was a flat refusal. "I then told him definitely—what I had not said before—that I positively declined doing it:—& I would thank him to let me know what the consequences were to be so as to avoid collision." [53] Elder was of the opinion that the Colonel regretted having ever published the order, that "he wd. not have done it—if he had known how seriously we viewed it." [54] Apparently, wanting to avoid an open clash as much as the Bishop did, Farrar finally consented to let the matter rest, until the prelate should give him the letter and he should hear from the district commander at Vicksburg.[55]

Elder took a week to prepare his letter to Colonel Farrar. The document, sixteen pages long, is a masterpiece of logic, theology

[51] *Ibid.*
[52] *Ibid.*, 90.
[53] *Ibid.*
[54] Elder to Rev. William McCloskey, Natchez, March 23, 1865; in ASCC: Elder Papers (unsigned letter in Elder's script).
[55] Elder Diary, 90.

and diplomacy. After expressing his appreciation of the politeness shown him by the Colonel in their recent interview and his gratitude for past favors, especially to the orphans, the Bishop went to the heart of the matter, namely, his reasons for refusing to comply with Special Order No. 31. First of all, Elder rejected reasons attributed by others to his non-compliance in the past.

> And I now expressly declare that my declining to submit to this "order" is not intended as an expression of disregard, or dislike, towards any Civil, or Military, authority; nor towards any person exercicing (sic) such authority. It is not intended as a manifestation of "Disloyalty" or of "Loyalty." It has no political signification.

Then, the Bishop went on to state positively:

> The chief reasons for resistance may be reduced to these two. One is that Religious Worship ought to be directed exclusively by Religious Authorities. I speak not of the negative right of other powers to suppress acts of intended and unmerited insult, of which there is no question here;—but of the positive ordering of prayers, sermons, etc.
>
> The other reason, special to the present case, is that Divine Worship, being directed to God, it is not proper to introduce anything into it for the purpose of exhibiting our sentiments in temporal things. This appears to be addressing our devotions to "men" in stead of "God."

Further ahead in the document, Elder returns to the question of loyalty and throws down the following challenge:

> If it should ever be charged that I, or any Priest of the Diocese—had in his conduct departed from his office, and done anything injurious to the Government, let the charge be stated and examined; let the individual be held responsible for his own conduct: like any other Citizen, and let not God's solemn Worship be altered nor interfered with on a man's account.

There then follows a long exposition on the subject of religious liberty wherein Elder appeals to reason, to the Constitution of the United States and to his own conduct and that of his priests. Should the preceding arguments prove of no avail, the Bishop ends up with the following ringing declaration:

> But if you demand of Us, in the name of the Civil or Military Government, to alter our Religious Worship—the

care of which is entrusted by God to the church—Our line of conduct is simply and clearly marked out, by the Divine Author of both Church and State, and with the assistance of His grace we hope to adhere to it:

"Render to Caesar the things that are Caesar's and to God, the things that are God's."[56]

General Brayman

On July 13, when Bishop Elder delivered his letter at military headquarters in Natchez, he found that Colonel Farrar had been replaced by Brigadier-General Mason Brayman.[57] The new commander spoke civilly enough to the Bishop and Father Grignon, who had accompanied the prelate, but it was soon evident to both clergymen that the officer had the idea that anyone who opposed him must be a rebel. When discussing the subject of the prayer prescribed by Special Orders No. 31, Brayman declared that he did not approve of men being compelled to read prayers against their conscience, but, as Elder reported, "if he found that we (Fr. Grignon & I) were rebels he would treat us as such."[58] As for the letter of explanation, the new commander set it aside, saying he would consider it later. The General terminated the interview by asking to see the official books used at Catholic services. Elder promised to send the Roman Missal in English.

Three days later, while the Bishop and his household were having lunch, the following communiqué was delivered at the rectory.

Headquarters United States Forces,
Natchez, July 16th, 1864.

Rev. William H. Elder
Bishop of Natchez

Sir:

I have to acknowledge the receipt personally of your communication to Col. B. G. Farrar, my predecessor, in command, in which you are understood to refuse obedience to Special Order No. 31, issued June 18th ultimo concerning prayer for the President &c, with your reasons for such refusal.

---

56 Elder to Col. B. G. Farrar, Natchez, July 13, 1864; copy in AUND: New Orleans Papers.

57 Mason Brayman, of Illinois, Colonel 29th Ill. Vols.; Brigadier-General from Sept. 24, 1862; mustered out Aug. 24, 1865. *Personnel of the Civil War*, edited by W. F. Amann, II, 34.

58 Elder Diary, 91.

> I have to advise you that military orders are to be obeyed, not discussed. Waiving therefore a formal reply, or an examination of your claim to exemption from that duty of love and loyalty which rests upon all eclisious (sic) teachers,
>
> I commend the matter to your careful reconsideration, leaving you to the responsibility which may attend your action.
>
> Very Respectfully
>
> Your Obt. Servant
> M. Brayman
> Brigd. Genl., Command[59]

As he read the General's letter, Elder saw that the contest had come to a point which he had always hoped to avoid. "But it was not of my seeking," he wrote in his diary,

> —nor did it concern my private interest—but the interest of religion, the liberty of the Church, & the general liberty of conscience for the whole country. It was clear that I had nothing else to do but oppose a passive resistance,—& I leave the consequence to God.[60]

This decision, however, was not suddenly arrived at, as is evident from the rest of the diary entry.

> It had appeared to me from the beginning that I ought not to consent. The more I had studied the matter over in the light of calm reason, the more I was confirmed in the conviction. I had also made it an especial object of prayer, of my intentions in the Holy Sacrifice: & had . . . both consulted the judgment & begged the prayers of those in whom I could best confide. Every light that I could obtain from every quarter had strengthened my conviction of the duty that I owed to God, & to the Church.[61]

Although Elder was determined to fulfill his duty as he saw it, the prospect of a guard seizing the Cathedral the next day or the day after, having it turned into a hospital or barracks with everything beautiful and holy about it defaced and desecrated, seeing the most sacred vessels carried off, having all the priests driven from the rectory and the people left without the Sacraments and religious consolation—all of these awful consequences, Elder admitted, unnerved him. "For a few minutes a severe pain shot across

---

[59] Brayman to Elder, Natchez, July 16, 1864; in AADC: Elder Papers.
[60] Elder Diary, 91.
[61] *Ibid.*, 92.

the top of my head—& I feared I was going to have a sharp attack of sickness.—Thanks to God however it passed away." [62] In the end, he came to the same conclusion: "to yield would be for me to do a grievous injury to religion." As for the consequences of his refusing, these were in God's hands. "He would not hold me accountable." [63]

The Bishop of Natchez was not only apprehensive after reading the General's reply, but he was also apparently annoyed by the almost flippant way in which Brayman had dismissed his well-thought out, well-phrased and beautifully written letter. Perhaps, it was just what was needed to provoke the Bishop to answer the General that very afternoon as follows:

Natchez, July 16, 1864

Brig. Genl. Brayman
Commanding

Sir:

I do not know whether in military usage your communication of this day would admit of a reply. But we are both Christians & Gentlemen, & in this character, I beg your attention to the following points:

The Order in question cannot in fairness be reckoned as a Military Order:—because it commands an act which is not in any sense a military act, nor connected with military affairs, nor under the control of the military authority. It is in every sense a Religious Order, only issued by the direction of a Military Commander.—The highest Military Authority in the Country, under the President, the Secretary of War, has sanctioned that view of it—& I claim his protection.—

I must correct your misapprehension in supposing that I claim in this case an exemption from any duty of any kind —I decline complying because it is not a duty—but on the contrary, it is opposed to a conscientious duty of religion.—

You have been considerate enough to declare that you did not approve of forcing a person to utter prayers contrary to his conscience:—"but if you found us to be rebels you would treat us as such."—On this word, I rely with confidence, that you will leave our Divine Services unmolested. —If you understand that I am guilty of rebellion or of any other act deserving your punishment, I trust that you will

62 *Ibid.*, 91.
63 *Ibid.*, 92.

hold me alone personally responsible and give me the opportunity of an Examination & a trial.

If possibly I have misunderstood you, and it is your determination to inflict any of the penalties intimated in your Special Order—then, as I sincerely desire to avoid giving you unnecessary offence, I beg you to let me know what we shall be suffered to do—as we have a great variety of ecclesiastical functions.—

At least be good enough to let me know this afternoon whether we shall be suffered to hold our Public Services tomorrow in our usual manner unmolested,—that we may avoid the indecency & sacrilege of a public disturbance during Divine Worship—which would be of no benefit to anyone.

We have also Catechism taught to the children at 9 A.M., and to the colored people at 4 P.M.:—likewise a less solemn service at 6 A.M. both Sundays and week days: at which in our usage there would be no room for such a prayer.—Shall we be suffered to hold these?

Very respectfully

Your Obt. Servant in Christ
William Henry Elder
Bishop of Natchez.[64]

One of the Catholic gentlemen of the Cathedral parish, Mr. James O'Cavanagh, delivered the Bishop's letter to military headquarters. At first the General did not want to give a reply, but after O'Cavanagh pressed for one, Brayman promised to give an answer by 8 o'clock that evening. In the meanwhile, he drew up another letter which he asked the gentleman to deliver to Elder, along with the original letter of Mr. Kernan and the copy of the Roman Missal which Elder had sent to the General upon request.[65] Without saying so Brayman refused to accept the letter of Congressman Kernan as proof that General Tuttle's order had been countermanded by the War Department. "No action on the part of the Secretary having, so far as I am advised, been taken, I am without instructions on the subject."[66] As for the Roman Missal sent for his inspection, Brayman had this to say:

---

[64] Elder to Brayman, Natchez, July 16, 1864; in ADNJ, Elder Letter Book—#10, 50. Rough copy also in AADC: Elder Papers.

[65] Elder Diary, 93.

[66] Brayman to Elder, Natchez, July 16, 1864; in AADC: Elder Papers.

> I . . . return with thanks, the copy of the *Roman Missal* sent for my inspection. Upon urgent enquiry I had your assurance that no other books published by your Church were of authority with respect to the prayer for the President, etc. that such prayer was not enjoined, but left to the discretion of the officiating priest, the Missal being the only authority, and in response to my request for any bearing on the point of enquiry, you sent me this one.
>
> In this book I find no form of prayer for the President, etc. Six other books no(w) lie before me, published for use of the Catholic Church, under the authority (of) and approved by its highest dignitaries in America. One of these is republished as late as the year 1863, bearing the approval of at least twenty seven Bishops, and among them the *Bishop of Natchez.* All these contain in full the usual prayer for the President of the United States.
>
> It must have been from some of these books that yourself and others officiating in like offices, recited the prayer for the President of the "Confederate" States.
>
> I cannot compliment your cander (sic) in sending me almost the only book of Service which does not contain the prayer in question.[67]

As is evident from this letter, General Brayman was unable to appreciate the distinction between a liturgical book and a book of private prayers which enjoyed episcopal approval. In view of this confusion one can readily understand why the commanding officer would have charged Bishop Elder with a lack of candor. Elder sent a letter of further explanation on Monday, July 18,[68] but it did little to clear up the misunderstanding, because two days later Brayman wrote again on the subject:

> You will recollect that in our personal interview you informed me that previous to the war you read the usual prayer for the President of the United States, and afterwards changed it to the prayer for the president of the "Confederate" States.
>
> I am yet unadvised what books were used on those occasions. Please enlighten me.[69]

In a certain sense, one can appreciate the General's line of thought. If the Bishop and his priests at the Cathedral could pray

---

[67] *Ibid.*

[68] Elder to Brayman, Natchez, July 18, 1864; copy in AADC: Elder Papers.

[69] Brayman to Elder, Natchez, July 20, 1864; in AADC: Elder Papers.

for the President of the United States and later for the President of the Confederate States at a public and official service from a non-liturgical book, why could they not do so again? To the General's way of thinking, Elder's stressing of the distinction between the books was pure casuistry and a subterfuge for his real political preference. Certainly, by belaboring this distinction and neglecting to present for the General's examination the prayer books containing the prayer for civil authorities, Elder did not help his case. On the contrary, it only distracted from the more important reason for resisting Special Order No. 31, namely, to the Church alone belongs the right to regulate her worship. Thus, to many people the clash between the Bishop and the General must have appeared, not as a noble defense of principle, but as a petty squabble with political overtones.

Saturday evening, true to his word, General Brayman had a reply ready in answer to the Bishop's query whether he and his priests would be allowed to conduct services in the Cathedral Sunday morning without a public interruption. Mr. O'Cavanagh called for the letter at military headquarters and delivered it to the Bishop.[70] Beginning his letter by belittling the Bishop's anxiety, the commander wrote:

> There is no need of embarrassment. The Order of Col. Farrar only requires that the usual Service of the Church be performed in its appropriate manner, time, and place. You of course, as a learned, Bishop know how and where the prayer was used by you before the rebellion, and while praying for the President of the "*Confederate*" States. To do the same thing, in good faith, is not a difficult duty.
>
> I cannot say that I value, or count upon the efficacy of a prayer, reluctantly read, from a book, upon compulsion of a Military Order.
>
> But *here is the point.* If you are a patriotic and loyal man, attached to the Government of the United States, and opposed to this rebellion, and desire your people to be of that mind, you will read the prayer for the President with pleasure, and have no difficulty in knowing how to do it. But if you approve this treason, that has drenched the land in blood—if you would overthrow this good and benefical Government—the guardian of Liberty and Christian civilization—if you would rather still pray for the President of the

[70] Elder Diary, 93.

"Confederate" States, and wish to make traitors of your flock, then you will not, and *ought* not to mock *God*, or offend against public decency by pronouncing the prayer.

The action you take will be accepted as a declaration on which side you choose to stand.

I cannot of course indicate to you the measures I shall take in either event.

Very Respectfully

Your Obedient Servant
M. Brayman
Brig. Genl. Comd'g.[71]

It is quite evident from this letter that the General viewed the contest between himself and the Bishop as a political one. In wanting to use divine worship as a means of finding out a man's true political leanings and of fostering public support of a political regime, Brayman saw no wrong. Furthermore, there does not appear to be any doubt that the General suspected Bishop Elder of being a dyed-in-the-wool rebel. After all, there was Elder's record of consistently refusing to pray for the President of the United States and of neglecting to take the oath of allegiance. This last point in itself was enough to make a man suspect in Brayman's eyes.[72] Finally, the General could point to the public image which Elder unwillingly but de facto presented, namely, that of an ardent supporter of the Confederacy.[73]

After discussing the letter with his vicar-general and two laymen of the parish, Mr. O'Cavanagh and Mr. Quegles, the Bishop was persuaded that the General would not create a public disturbance at Sunday Mass. Services, therefore, would be held as usual.[74] The next day passed without any disturbance.

Monday morning at 9 o'clock, several prominent gentlemen, Catholic and Protestant, of the city gathered in the Bishop's library at his invitation. The purpose of the meeting was not to stir up any feeling for himself, but merely to explain his past conduct

---

71 Brayman to Elder, Natchez, July 16, 1864; in AADC: Elder Papers.

72 Found among Brayman's papers, was a list, drawn up on headquarter's stationery, of "citizens who are suspected." Almost all of them it was noted had not taken the oath of allegiance. Elder's name, however, was not among them; in ACHS: Brayman Papers.

73 Elder Diary, 94.

74 *Ibid.*, 93.

and his motives for acting as he did. In the face of recent developments Elder felt that such an explanation was in order.

> Some Catholics & many more Protestants, were under the impression that my refusal to read the Prayer arises from a preference which I give to the Southern Confederacy.— I wanted them to understand that it was not so—but simply from an unwillingness to acknowledge the right in any secular power to direct our religious worship:—& my own especial unwillingness to use my sacred ministry in maintaining either power, or in support of any political views.[75]

After explaining his position, the Bishop disbanded the meeting. He sought no advice; he asked for no opinions. Thus, no one would ever be able to accuse him of organizing sedition.

That same day, at 1:30 p. m., Elder received a note from the General, inquiring if Special Order No. 31, had been complied with at Sunday's services in the Cathedral.[76] Before answering the General's inquiry, Bishop Elder reported this second case of military interference in ecclesiastical affairs at Natchez to the Secretary of War in Washington. Noting that "the present Commander says he does not find any instructions from you on the subject recorded in his office," Elder begged the Secretary "to give permanent effect to your promise, by sending instructions which may be recorded for the guidance of the present and future Commanders." [77]

Then, Elder drew up the following reply to Brayman's inquiry as to the observance or non-observance of Special Order No. 31.

> St. Mary's Cathedral
> Natchez, July 19th, 1864.
>
> Brig. Genl. M. Brayman
> Commanding
>
> Sir
>
> I have already made a sincere profession of respect for all authority—& of course for yours, in all matters to which it extends.

---

[75] *Ibid.*, 94.

[76] *Ibid.*, 94. Brayman to Elder, Natchez, July 18, 1864; copy in AADC: Elder Papers.

[77] Elder to Stanton, Natchez, July 19, 1864; in ADNJ, Elder Letter Book—#10, 72. Copy in AADC: Elder Papers. Published in Gerow, *op. cit.*, 175-176.

In regard to my religious devotions offered to God, in public or in private, I cannot see that I am bound to render an account of them to anyone but God, and those whom He has appointed to teach me religious worship.

As an act of courtesy however, I am willing to reply to your polite note of yesterday asking information.

On Sunday last we offered our Divine Service "in the usual manner": & in the course of it as we have been accustomed to do, we recited prayers which the ecclesiastical authority judges to be—"appropriate to the times, & expressive of a proper spirit toward the Government under which we live and to which we are indebted for protection"—(words taken from Special Order No. 31). The Prayers that I refer to are mentioned more particularly in the communication which I had the honor to hand you on the 13th inst.

If perhaps you should think differently, & should desire to compel me to depart from our usual mode of conducting Divine Service—I take the occasion with all respect to say to you again directly and explicitly that I have given you satisfactory evidence of an assurance from the Secretary of War that we should not be molested in this matter—that I have already applied for an official instruction from the Secretary,—and that I this day communicate to him what has recently passed between us—and appeal to him for the fulfillment of his assurance.

It is not for me to advise, but you will not be offended at my expressing my opinion, that in a matter affecting the religious liberty of all persons in the United States, and consequently their attachment to the Government, and the fair name of that Government throughout the Christian world as a protector of the liberty of worship, there can be no harm done, by waiting until the administration at Washington makes known definitely its policy in this respect. The Commander in New Orleans has not enforced it.

And if substantial services cheerfully rendered form any ground for asking a favor, I request you not to molest me in my religious ministrations—me—who have done no injury to the United States, & who intend not to injure it, nor any other Government—but who have labored without pay for the United States Soldiers during several months of the past year—have many times risked my life for them by continuous hours spent over them in the Small Pox Hospitals—& have sent other Priests to labor for them, one of whom lost his life in their service, and another has shortened his by destroying his constitution through exposure among them.

Pardon the foolishness of speaking thus about ourselves. It is right that you should understand the case. The surgeon who attended the Hospitals last fall and winter can I hope give you more satisfactory information if you desire it—and the preceding Commanders of Natchez can testify whether we have ever given any just cause of offense. (. . . . .)

Very respectfully

Your Obt. servant in Christ
†*William Henry Elder*
Bishop of Natchez [78]

To this letter General Brayman made no immediate reply.

In his difficulties with the military commanders at Natchez Bishop Elder suffered a great deal. By nature he was not argumentative. Gentleman that he was, he disliked hurting anyone, even when his personal integrity was impugned. Always conscious of his episcopal office, he was greatly afraid of giving scandal to his flock as well as to non-Catholics. As the contest grew sharper, he became quite upset by the thought that his action might eventually lead to "irreparable damage . . . to Church property" and "great injury to souls." [79] Especially distressing to the Bishop of Natchez was his inability in the circumstances to consult any of his fellow bishops in the matter. Writing to his friend, Archbishop Spalding, several days after he had reached the point-of-no-return in his clash with General Brayman, the Mississippi prelate complained: "I have had no opportunity to consult with any Brother Bishop. I have mentioned the case to the Archbp. of N. O.—but he has to be very cautious." [80]

Distasteful as the whole affair was, Bishop Elder was not one to avoid unpleasant situations at all costs. From the start he discerned that an important principle was at stake in his contest with the military commanders. Furthermore, it was a principle which he as a Catholic bishop had an obligation to uphold. "I think the question is one of deepest consequences," Elder wrote to his metropolitan on July 12, "—& it would be best for both religion &

---

[78] Elder to Brayman, Natchez, July 19, 1864; in ADNJ, Elder Letter Book—#10, 65. Published in Gerow, *op. cit.,* 174-175. Copy in AADC: Elder Papers.

[79] Elder to Spalding, Natchez, July 22, 1864; in AAB, 33-T-5. Also in ADNJ, Elder Letter Book—#10, 90.

[80] *Ibid.*

government, to have it brought plainly before the administration & before the public—and have it settled conclusively."[81] To his close friend, the new Archbishop of Baltimore, Elder confided:

> I attach a great practical importance to the question: because I am persuaded that the principle once admitted . . . will be greatly extended in application. They will require us to publish proclamations—to preach in favor of the govt. & of govt. measures,—& in various ways bring the Church into the services, not only of the State, but of the administration which happens to be in power: & even local rulers of cities & country districts, may after a while require the Priests to enter into their views & promulgate them in the congregations. (. . . .) In my own judgment, it has seemed to me an occasion on which fidelity to the interests of Religion required me to be firm—& of which I could with safe conscience leave all the consequences to the Providence of our Lord.[82]

Four days after he had requested General Brayman to suspend the penalties of Special Order No. 31, until Washington could be heard from, Elder in a letter to Archbishop Spalding expressed the belief that the "awful consequences" of his non-compliance would not be as great as he had expected. "The Commander appears to be better disposed,—& to intend not doing more than he may judge essential for vindicating his military authority."[83] Another Sunday went by with services held in the usual manner. Still there was no word from military headquarters.

Exile

Unknown to the Bishop a Special Order had been drawn up on Friday, July 22, at the command of General Brayman which would leave little room for optimism of any sort. Delivered to the Bishop at his residence on Monday, July 25, the order charged Elder with being "in rebellion against the United States," with "repudiating and denying the authority of the Government, and its officers," and by "utterly refusing obedience to said order (No. 31)," with "encouraging the people under his authority in treasonable practices, and impairing the force of discipline." In view of such conduct,

---

[81] Elder to Odin, Natchez, July 12, 1864; in AUND: New Orleans Papers.

[82] Elder to Spalding, Natchez, July 22, 1864; in AAB, 33-T-5.

[83] *Ibid.*

It is therefore,

ORDERED:

First. That the said *William Henry Elder,* Bishop of Natchez, be expelled from the lines of the Army of the United States, not to return without permission, on pain of imprisonment during the continuance of the rebellion.

Second. That the Provost Marshal close, and hold military possession of *St. Mary's Cathedral,* situate in the city of Natchez, and all other houses or places of worship within his command, and under the ecclesiastical jurisdiction of said Bishop William H. Elder, in which the prayer for the President of the United States has heretofore been, but is not now, read.

Inasmuch, however, as the said Bishop William H. Elder, has requested in a respectful manner, that any action under said order No. 31, be suspended "until communication can be had with the authorities at Washington:" *It is further,*

ORDERED:

That action under said order No. 31, and the paragraph "*First*" and "*Second*" of this order be accordingly suspended until further orders; and that, in the meanwhile, the Provost Marshal of Natchez, cause the said *William H. Elder,* Bishop of Natchez, to report in person, within Twenty-four (24) hours after receiving a copy of this order, to the Officer commanding the U. S. Forces at Vidalia, and remain within his military lines under penalty of the immediate execution of the before named orders.

The Provost Marshals at Natchez and Vidalia, respectively, will see to the strict observance of this order.

By order of Brig. Gen. M. BRAYMAN
J. H. Odlin, Capt. and Ass't Adjt. Gen jy 29 [84]

During the next twenty-four hours Elder made preparations for his departure. He was informed by the provost marshal that he would be allowed to take some wearing apparel and a few books. Through the evening and the next morning the Bishop received visits from sympathizing friends, Catholic and Protes-

[84] Newspaper clipping of Special Orders No. 11, Headquarters United States Forces, Natchez, Miss., July 22d, 1864, published July 29, 1864; found in Bishop Elder's diary, Archives of Woodstock College, Woodstock, Md. See also a printed copy of the order, signed by Odlin, in ADNJ, and published in Gerow, *op. cit.,* 176-178; also a handwritten copy in AADC: Elder Papers. The text of all three documents is identical.

tant. Of the latter, some had never been in the episcopal residence before. Especially touching was the farewell visit made by the Sisters and all the orphans. "Their sobs," Elder confessed, "unmanned me more than anything else." [85]

At the actual hour of departure Elder found many people waiting Under-the-Hill at the ferry landing to bid him farewell. In his diary the Bishop described the final scene and his personal reactions. "As I was about stepping on the boat they all fell on their knees—in the sand & dust, to crave a parting blessing.—God forgive me for not doing my duty better by such a people!" [86]

Several Catholic gentlemen accompanied the Bishop across the river to Vidalia, La., a very small courthouse town. When Elder presented himself to the post commander there, the officer, Colonel McCaleb, received the Bishop civilly, and placed no other restrictions upon him than to remain on that side of the river and within the lines, and not to hold any written communication with anyone without his permission. He then referred the Bishop to the provost marshal for quarters. This officer claimed that he had no instructions on the matter. Accordingly, he took the Bishop to the only hotel in town until he could make further arrangements. In the afternoon, when the provost marshal returned to say that, if Elder stayed at the hotel, he must pay for his own expenses, adding somewhat threateningly that he had better do so, the Bishop balked and asked what would be the alternative if he refused. There, then, followed a brisk exchange which Elder recorded in his diary.

> He said he wd. find a room for me some where, & give me soldier's rations. I asked him to state that in writing. He refused. He said I might be lodged in jail if they thought proper—I told him I was in Genl. Brayman's hands, & I wanted to know what treatment Genl. B. thought suitable to me.—If he ordered me to be sent to jail—he could do so,—I would be glad to have it authenticated in writing—so that it might hereafter be known beyond cavil.—He said he had no idea of confining me in jail—but he could only do for me as much as he had said.—I told him that in the circumstances, I believed it was the General's duty to provide for me what treatment he thought I ought to have.[87]

---

85 Elder Diary, 96.
86 *Ibid.*, 96-97.
87 *Ibid.*, 97.

Realizing that the provost marshal could do no more than he said he could, that the fault lie with General Brayman for not providing adequate instructions on the matter, Elder, then, asked the officer if he might be allowed to provide for himself at the home of a Catholic family in town, the McDowells. Apparently, there was some difficulty involved in granting this permission, for the marshal said he would see about it. In the meanwhile, the Bishop took a room in the hotel.[88]

The following afternoon the provost marshal called on Elder to show him the instructions he had received from General Brayman. They said in substance that the Bishop must provide for himself. At the bottom of the letter was the terse note: "No quarters, no rations." [89] At the same time, the marshal informed the Bishop that the post commander did not want him to take up residence at the McDowell's. As Elder later learned, there was a charge against Mr. McDowell which had not yet been investigated. Accordingly, the Bishop stayed on at the hotel.

During his stay at the hotel Bishop Elder drew up another appeal to the Secretary of War in Washington, the second since his difficulties with General Brayman arose. Submitting a copy of the order which called for his removal from Natchez, Elder went on in his letter to the Secretary to deny the charges made against him in the order.[90] The Bishop, then, enclosed the appeal in a letter to General Brayman. Typical of his sense of fairness, Elder asked the Natchez commander to check the accuracy of his report to the Secretary of War. He, then, continued:

> I add now a request.—In three years of war, an active instigator must have shown his activity in many strong & unequivocal acts: & these must be known to the public, or at least to many.

---

[88] *Ibid.*, 97. Elder was not the only Catholic bishop of the South to have been arrested and confined during the Civil War. Some time in January, 1863, Bishop John Quinlan of Mobile was placed under arrest in Columbus, Mississippi, where he had gone to lay the cornerstone of a new church. He was detained over night in jail by a Confederate assistant provost marshal until his passport could be verified. Lipscomb, "The Administration of John Quinlan, Second Bishop of Mobile, 1859-1883," 78-81.

[89] *Ibid.*, 98.

[90] Elder to Stanton, Vidalia, July 30, 1864; in ADNJ, Elder Letter Book —#10, 320. Copy drawn up by Elder; in AADC: Elder Papers. Published in (Blanchard-Elder), *Character-Glimpses of Most Reverend William Henry Elder*, 53-57.

I respectfully ask you to take evidence in my conduct in this regard.

I think you will find the practical members of the Cathedral Congregation well instructed & impressed with regard to the solemnity of an oath. Examine the best of them under oath.

Take testimony from others who have known me, persons of responsibility.

If you should have reasons not to let me know the names of the witnesses, allow me at least to know the testimony, if any should appear unfavorable.

If you do not find unequivocal proof that I have been active in bringing or keeping my flock in opposition to the United States Government, there can surely be no injury to discipline, in your publishing that I am not the dangerous person I was taken for, & restoring me to my Cathedral.[91]

It is obvious from these two letters and earlier exchanges between the Bishop and General Brayman that Elder found the charge of being an instigator of treason far more difficult to bear than the strain of the contest or even exile from his diocese.

With the permission of the post commander in Vidalia, Elder moved in with the McDowell family on the last day of the month. Here the Bishop was given the family parlor as his room. "During my whole stay," Elder recorded in his diary,

they did everything they could think of to make me comfortable. (. . .) The room was airy:—most of the time there was a pleasant breeze blowing.—The front gallery was very pleasant. The table was such as to create a relish.—Friends from Natchez brought every day various little comforts in quantity to supply the family, & sometimes the visitors.

But more than bodily comforts, was the kindness of the sympathy shown by the many who came to visit me; & the many others who could not come, but who sent kind messages:—& the many others still who did all in their power for me by their fervent prayers; in Natchez, Vicksburg, New Orleans & every where.[92]

---

[91] Elder to Brayman, Vidalia, July 30, 1864; copy in Elder's script, in AADC: Elder Papers.

[92] Elder Diary, 99.

Thus, during his exile Bishop Elder suffered very little physical discomfort. As for the psychological distress which he experienced, this was mitigated by marks of loyalty shown him almost every day by friends, both Catholic and Protestant.

For a while during the Bishop's exile it appeared as though Father Grignon was to be harassed by General Brayman as Elder had been. On Monday, August 1, the Vicar-General received the following communication from the military commander of Natchez:

Sir:

Understanding service to be under your charge during the absence of Bishop Elder, I have to request you to advise me whether Order 31, respecting prayers for the President of the United States, &c. was complied with on yesterday.

Your Ob't Serv't

M. Brayman
Brig. Genl. Com'dg.[93]

Fr. Grignon's reply, delivered by himself in the company of Mr. O'Cavanagh and Mr. Dix, former mayor of the city, read:

Sir:

In answer to your request of yesterday respecting order No. 31., I have to say that in view of order No. 11. in which I read that "until Communication can be heard from the Authorities at Washington," action under said order No. 31 was suspended; I have felt myself justified to hold Divine Service as usual.

I am your Respectfull (sic) Servt
M. H. G.[94]

Although the General was polite in receiving the priest and his companions, he made no reply to Father Grignon's letter. When Mr. Dix inquired whether the priest would be allowed to hold services in the Cathedral in the usual manner next Sunday, Brayman said he would answer later.[95] Thus, from day to day

[93] Brayman to Grignon, Natchez, Aug. 1, 1864; in ADNJ, File: Elder–B. Also in Gerow, *op. cit.,* 180.

[94] Grignon to Brayman, Natchez, Aug. 2, 1864; copy in ADNJ, File: Elder–B. Also in Gerow, *op. cit.,* 180.

[95] Elder Diary, 100.

the Vicar-General never knew whether the military commander would press the matter of the prescribed prayer any further. About this time, too, Father Grignon sent off letters to Father Early, S.J., and Congressman Kernan, informing them of recent developments in Natchez and asking for their help.[96]

In another matter the commander's behavior only increased rather than allayed Father Grignon's fears that a clash between them was imminent. On August 4, a seriously ill Union soldier at the Marine Hospital in Natchez sent for a priest. Father Grignon had a pass for the military hospital, originally granted by Colonel Farrar and renewed by General Brayman, but it had now expired. The priest sent Mr. Joseph Arrighi, one of the men of the parish, to military headquarters to have the pass renewed so he could answer the sick call. After being informed of the urgency of the case, the officer who received the petition took the pass into the General's room. Shortly afterward he returned with the following message: "The General desires me to say to you that he is neither renewing passes nor granting them." [97] With that explanation, the officer tore up the old pass and threw the pieces into the fireplace. The next day the wardmaster from the hospital called at the rectory. The sick soldier, he informed Father Grignon, was almost frantic and had declared that he would jump out of the window if a priest did not come soon. Distressed, the Vicar-General explained that the fault was not his, that his hands were tied. On the third day the surgeon at the hospital wrote to headquarters, requesting a pass for Father Grignon to visit the sick soldier. The General finally relented, but petulant to the end, he granted the pass for only one day and even then did not have it delivered to the priest until 2 o'clock in the afternoon.[98] Such was the atmosphere in Natchez during the absence of Bishop Elder.

Recall

On August 12, the picture suddenly changed. About 4 o'clock in the afternoon, a military orderly brought Bishop Elder a communication from General Brayman. It read:

---

[96] Early, S.J., to Grignon, Georgetown, D.C., Aug. 8, 1864; in *The Catholic Telegraph,* Cincinnati, Nov. 3, 1904. Also in (Blanchard-Elder), *Character-Glimpses of Most Reverend William Henry Elder,* 58.

[97] Elder Diary, 100-101.

[98] *Ibid.,* 101.

Head-Quarters United States Forces
Natchez, Miss, Aug. 12th, 1864.

Special Orders
No. 31 Extract.

I.

Military Authority having been, for the time, vindicated, so much of Special Order No. 11. as requires Rev. *William Henry Elder*, Bishop of Natchez, to remain within the military lines of the Post of Vidalia, La. is suspended, and he may return to his home and duties until the pleasure of the War Department be known in his case.

And as all solemn appeals to the *Supreme Being*, not proceeding from honest hearts and willing minds, are necessarily offensive to *Him*, and subversive of sound morality, so much of Special Order No. 31. June 18. 1864, as requires public prayers to be pronounced in behalf of the *President of the United States*, and the *Union*, is suspended until further orders; leaving all persons conducting Divine Worship, at liberty to manifest such measure of hostility, as they may feel, against the Government and Union of these States, and their sympathy with rebellion, by omitting such supplication, if so minded.

By command of
Brig. Genl. M. Brayman
J. H. Odlin
Asst. Adjt. Genl.[99]

Bishop Elder's comments on this document are both interesting and enlightening. He made them in his diary under the date of August 12, the day of his recall. First of all, as the Bishop saw it, the tone of the order was hardly conciliatory.

> The wording of the Order seems to indicate a person acting somewhat angrily against his will.—There were various opport(unit)ies for the Genl. to recall me with better grace. —Especially when I asked him July 20th. to take sworn testimony as to whether I had instigated hostilities.—

To Elder it seemed that the General became so tangled up that he condemned himself as well as contradicted himself without realizing it.

---

99 Special Orders, No. 31, Extract, I., Head-Quarters United States Forces, Natchez, Miss., Aug. 12th, 1864; in AADC: Elder Papers. This is the copy of the order delivered to Bishop Elder at the McDowell residence in Vidalia, La. See also Gerow, *op. cit.*, 181; also (Blanchard-Elder), *Character-Glimpses of Most Reverend William Henry Elder*, 58-59.

> The reason that he gives for suspending Order 31. is really a severe condemnation both of Col. Farrar for issuing it, & of himself for endeavoring to enforce it, because such prayers would have been offensive to God & subversive of sound morality—on the 16th. July when he wrote me that "Military Orders must be obeyed & not discussed"— & on the 28th July when he banished me for not pronouncing them—just as much as on the 12th. of August.—
>
> It is strange too that while he says these prayers are so bad—he only suspends the Order requiring them "until further orders."—

As for his future relations with the Natchez military commander, Elder felt that the General had removed what little opportunity there was for reconciliation.

> The conclusion about leaving persons free to manifest their hostility, seems more than any other part to betray the petulance of a person doing something against his will. But I am thankful for the change in affairs: & if there were any opening for me to express my thanks I shd. be glad to do so. The wording of the Order (however) effectually precludes it.[100]

Bishop Elder's recall came so quickly and unexpectedly that there was no opportunity to tender him a formal welcome. Nevertheless, the spontaneous demonstrations of joy which took place made his return no less triumphant. One of his parishioners, Mr. Grant, was visiting the Bishop at the time he received word from General Brayman that he was free to return to Natchez. The gentleman accompanied Elder across the river. At the landing they were joined by another Catholic gentleman, Mr. Botto. Bishop Elder provides the rest of the details of his return in his diary.

> Some few observed me as we drove through the streets. Several met me at the gate of the house.—I went immediately to offer my thanks in Church.—Both bells were rung—& before I got thro' my visit to the church—persons were coming in both there & to the house:—& oh! what a greeting those good people gave me. The Sisters came crowding in more noisy than any others—God only knows the happiness of all those hearts—All had been praying fervently. Many had offered their Communion the first Sunday. All were now making the Novena of the Assumption—hearing Mass

---

[100] Elder Diary, 103.

> every morning.—What fervent thanks to God, what joyous congratulations to me.—I gave full scope to my own joy.—Personally I had endured no suffering. But I had seriously feared the dreadful consequences of desecrating the Church, & perhaps banishing all the Priests as the Order had declared. So that there was truly great reason for rejoicing that the cloud had passed & done no harm.[101]

For some time after his recall, it was not clear to Bishop Elder who was really responsible for it. Three days after his return to Natchez, he wrote to his metropolitan, Archbishop Odin: "There are various conjectures about the immediate cause of my recall, but they are only conjectures."[102] In the same letter Elder admitted that at first he himself was under the impression that General Brayman had acted voluntarily in allowing him to return to Natchez. According to the Bishop's way of thinking, the General, expecting Colonel Farrar's order to be revoked at Washington, banished Elder to Vidalia for the purpose of not letting Elder's refusal pass without some penalty. When he felt that his claim to be obeyed had been sufficiently vindicated, he recalled the Bishop. However, a closer reading of the order permitting him to return to his diocese convinced Elder that it was drawn up by a person "acting somewhat angrily against his will."[103]

Seven months after the episode, during which time Elder was able to check various stories, he wrote to the Reverend William McCloskey, rector of the American College in Rome, and stated that his release "was owing to the recommendation of Brig. Gen. Lorenzo Thomas Adjt. Genl. of all the U.S. Army," who was visiting Natchez on business during Elder's absence.[104] Not only did Thomas' own good judgment tell him that the commander had made a mistake, but he was also approached by a number of people, asking him to use his influence with General Brayman to secure the Bishop's release. Elder singled out one person in particular. "Different persons spoke to him," Elder reported,

> but I really think the most efficacious impulse was given him by a good old Irish lady—nurse in the house where he

[101] *Ibid.*, 102.

[102] Elder to Odin, Natchez, Aug. 15, 1864; in AUND: New Orleans Papers.

[103] Elder Diary, 103.

[104] Elder to William McCloskey, Natchez, March 23, 1865; unsigned letter in Elder's script in ASCC: Bishop Elder Papers.

> staid—a plain woman but of remarkable good sense & earnest faith—& who commands the profound respect of the wealthy Protestant family she lives in—& of their whole circle of acquaintances—Nancy Lynch.[105]

The Bishop had heard of General Thomas' intervention the very day of his release, but at the time it was one of many stories, circulating in town, which were attempting to explain the real reasons for the Bishop's release.[106]

In his letter to the rector of the American College in Rome Bishop Elder also acknowledged the efforts of Bishop Michael O'Connor, S.J., to secure his release.[107] When the former Bishop of Pittsburgh approached Mr. Stanton in Washington on the subject, O'Connor learned that Elder was no longer a person in good standing in the United States' capital. Earlier, it is true, the Secretary of War had intervened on Elder's behalf. At that time, however, he was unaware that the Bishop of Natchez had at one time prayed for the President of the Confederate States. Although Elder had volunteered this information in his memorial presented to the Secretary by Mr. Kernan, Stanton had not read the document, being satisfied with a verbal statement of the controversy by the Congressman. When Stanton saw General Brayman's order of July 22, and the fact that Elder had prayed for the Confederate President was brought to his attention, he maintained that this note changed the whole character of the controversy between Elder and the military commander. As O'Connor reported later:

> (Stanton) considered the Bishop's act in reciting that prayer as abetting treason, and in one of his high and Sacred position as involving peculiar guilt. He said he did not wish recital of the prayer to be pressed for its own sake but he considered it a favor offered to the Bishop to allow him to purge himself of his former treasonable act by this means.[108]

---

105 *Ibid.* In his diary Elder called his Irish benefactress "Nancy McGinnis." The woman was employed in the home of Dr. and Mrs. Page. The writer was unable to identify the woman any further. Elder Diary, 102.

106 Elder Diary, 102.

107 Elder to William McCloskey, Natchez, March 23, 1865; unsigned letter in Elder's script in ASCC: Bishop Elder Papers.

108 O'Connor to Stanton, August 16, 1864; signed copy in AADC: Elder Papers. See postscript which most probably was not in the original but intended for a reader ignorant of the details of O'Connor's interview with the Secretary of War.

At the close of O'Connor's interview with the Secretary, the latter assured the Bishop that he would treat the matter as leniently as he could without failing in his own duty. Apparently, the news of Elder's release was slow in reaching Washington, for Bishop O'Connor had the above reported interview with Stanton on August 15, three days after Elder had been permitted to return to Natchez. The day after the interview O'Connor, it would seem, presented a lengthy letter of explanation on Elder's case to the Secretary.[109] In the document the Bishop tried to meet the various objections which Stanton had raised in the course of their interview the day before. It would further seem that in the end O'Conner finally persuaded the Secretary to intervene on Bishop Elder's behalf, for the Bishop of Natchez stated in his letter to the rector of the American College in Rome that O'Connor "succeeded in obtaining an Order from Washington for my release—which however had been anticipated here by the Commander." [110]

There still remain two pieces of evidence which seem to indicate that General Brayman ordered Bishop Elder's release, not only at the suggestion of General Thomas, but also in view of official directives from the War Department. It seems quite clear that Bishop O'Connor sent either Bishop Elder or his vicar-general a copy of his letter to Secretary Stanton, dated August 16. At the bottom of this copy the Jesuit Bishop added a postscript of explanation. It begins with the following significant sentence:

> To understand several allusions in the foregoing letter, it is necessary to state that Mr. Stanton had already twice issued orders requiring the Generals in command of Natchez not to molest Bishop Elder, by requiring from him the recital of any particular prayer.[111]

We already know that the first time an order was issued by command of the Secretary of War, checking a military commander for interfering in the affairs of the Catholic Church at Natchez, was at the end of April, 1864, while General Tuttle was in command there. If a second similar order was sent and this before August 16, as Bishop O'Connor noted, the only other occasion

---

[109] *Ibid.*

[110] Elder to William McCloskey, Natchez, March 23, 1865; unsigned letter in Elder's script in ASCC: Bishop Elder Papers.

[111] O'Connor to Stanton, August 16, 1864; signed copy with postscript in AADC: Elder Papers.

warranting such an order would have been the six weeks period following the publication of Colonel Farrar's Special Order No. 31. Granted that the Secretary of War sent a countermand during this period, it seems that it would have been sent in response either to Bishop Elder's appeal to Secretary Stanton, dated July 19, or to Father Grignon's letter which was sent a few days later and which Father John Early, S.J., was supposed to forward to Congressman Kernan. Most probably it was Grignon's letter which prompted Stanton to come to the aid of Elder a second time, for on August 8, the President of Georgetown University addressed the following communication to Elder's vicar-general:

> Very Reverend and Dear Sir—Your letter and the enclosed reached me long after the departure of Mr. Kernan. I entrusted the matter to my esteemed friend, Col. Hardie, and am glad to inform your reverence that through his influence an order has been sent to Major General Canby, commanding the Department of the Mississippi, to forbid his subordinate to interfere with the rights of Catholics in your diocese. The order was sent on last Saturday by the Assistant Secretary of War.
>
> Yours most truly
>
> John Early, S.J.[112]

Thus, another witness speaks of a second order issued by the War Department, and, what is more, sets the date on which it was issued as August 6. However, one important question remains to be answered: did this order sent by the Assistant Secretary of War reach Natchez soon enough so that it might be said that General Brayman acted in response to this official directive rather than to General Thomas' urging? The only evidence on hand is the text of the order permitting Elder to return to Natchez. While the document offers nothing conclusive, the wording, especially in the second half of the order, as Elder himself remarked, seems to indicate a person acting somewhat angrily against his will. If Brayman were acting only at the urging of General Thomas, he

---

112 Early, S.J., to Grignon, Georgetown, D.C., Aug. 8, 1864; in *The Catholic Telegraph*, Nov. 3, 1904. Also in (Blanchard-Elder), *Character-Glimpses of Most Reverend William Henry Elder*, 58. James A. Hardie, 5th U.S. Artillery, Lieut.-Colonel and Additional Aide-de-camp from Nov. 29, 1862; Inspector-General from March 13, 1865. *Personnel of the Civil War*, edited by W. F. Amann, II, 4, 35.

would have been under no compulsion[113] but would have been acting voluntarily and, therefore, there would have been no reason for manifesting such obvious petulance as he did. Further developments amounting to circumstantial evidence will support this view.

Press Reaction

The reaction in the press, both religious and secular, to Bishop Elder's exile might have been predicted. The *Vicksburg Daily Herald* which was currently run by a pro-Union editor made the following comment on the action:

> The confiscation of the Catholic Cathedral and removal of the disloyal Bishop of Natchez to the other side of the river, Mississippi, on account of the persistence of the Bishop in disloyalty, is one of the most prominent acts of Brig.-Gen. Brayman, since he has taken command of the Post of Natchez. The General is determined not to tolerate disloyalty in rich or poor, high or low. It is a subject of congratulations among loyal men that Natchez has now a commandant, who is no respector of persons, and who cannot be influenced by wealth or beauty.[114]

To the editor's credit, however, it must be pointed out that he printed the complete text of Bishop Elder's letter to Colonel Farrar on two successive days.[115] The letter, lengthy as it was, took up more than a page of the four-page newspaper. It appeared without comment. In the *Catholic Mirror* of Baltimore the complete text of Special Order No. 11, appeared with the following temperate comment by the paper's pro-Southern editor, Courtney Jenkins. Writing under the headline "Arrest of The Right Rev. Dr. Wm. H. Elder, Bishop of Natchez," Jenkins referred to the Mississippi prelate as "the venerable Bishop of Natchez, whose offence appears to consist in the simple fact that he declined to take orders, as to the prayers to be said in his Cathedral, from a military official." He then continued:

> In a country in which it is to be hoped that Church and State will always be kept separate, it is a matter of prime

[113] Although General Thomas was Adjutant General of the U.S. Army at the time of his visit to Natchez, he apparently had no authority to interfere in General Brayman's administration of affairs at Natchez. Elder Diary, 104.

[114] *Vicksburg Daily Herald,* Aug. 6, 1864.

[115] *Ibid.,* Aug. 25, 1864, Aug. 26, 1864.

> importance to prevent the first encroachment on either hand. We sincerely trust that the General Government will promptly restore Bishop Elder to his flock and to his duties.[116]

The Freeman's Journal of New York had a heyday when it received news of Bishop Elder's arrest. Violently opposed to the Lincoln administration, the paper identified the arrest of Elder with an attack on the Catholic Church as such. Under the headline "Like Slavery, Popery Is Doomed!" the paper announced:

> "*Slavery*" not yet disposed of, the *formal* war on "Popery" has begun. One of Abraham Lincoln's satraps has seized, and made a prisoner, of a Catholic Bishop. He has loaded him with insults, outraged his sacred person, and interdicted his holy functions of peace to men of good will!
>
> Bishop Elder, the Catholic Bishop of the See of Natchez, comprising the whole State of Mississippi, is a prisoner in the hands of negro soldiers, under the command of Abraham Lincoln! The crime charged against him, is not anything he has *done*, but it is that he has *not* conformed the religious liturgy of the holy Roman Catholic and Apostolic Church to the ritual prescribed by the satrap of Abraham Lincoln who commands the negro troops at Natchez! Bishop Elder, for *not* interpolating that holy office, which is said alike throughout the world, "from the rising of the sun to the going down of the same," with a *special* prayer for that scourge of the country, Abe Lincoln, has been made a prisoner.

Trying his utmost to discredit the Lincoln administration, the writer charged that Elder was

> . . . one of the *first* Bishops, if not the first, persecuted by the Lincoln-Seward Administration, for being a *Catholic Bishop!* All honor to him! The hands of Catholics who are helping Lincoln and Seward, must be *strengthened* by knowing that the persecution of their Church has already begun, and that they—*Catholics*—are *tools of the persecution!*[117]

Fortunately, an objective presentation of the facts connected with Elder's case appeared the following week in the same paper

---

[116] *Catholic Mirror*, Aug. 20, 1864.

[117] *The Freeman's Journal*, Aug. 20, 1864. The danger that Elder's arrest might be politically unwise was pointed out to President Lincoln by a Union sympathizer of Natchez. A. Wolcott to Lincoln, Natchez, July 27, 1864; in NAW, Records of the Office of the Secretary of War, Letters Received, D 1141/131/. The article in *The Freeman's Journal* shows how quickly the enemies of the Lincoln administration preceived this and tried to capitalize on it.

when a letter to the editor was published.[118] In the *Catholic Telegraph* of Cincinnati no mention was ever made of Bishop Elder's difficulties with the military authorities at Natchez. The paper's silence, however, is understandable. Editor Purcell had no intention of embarrassing the Lincoln administration, which he had backed from the outset of the War.

Later Relations

For the remainder of General Brayman's stay at Natchez, Elder's relations and those of his priests with the commander were far from cordial. Elder on his part had been open to the idea of reconciliation from the start.[119] While the occasion of his recall would have offered Elder an excellent opportunity to make a step in the right direction by expressing his gratitude to the commander, the wording of the order precluded such a move.[120] As the days went by, the atmosphere did not improve. Time and again Brayman showed his pettiness. When Father Grignon sent a written application to the commander, requesting a pass to visit the sick Federal soldiers in the military hospital at Natchez, the messenger was informed that "if the Genl. shd. conclude to give a pass, he would send it." [121] Annoyed by such unreasonableness, Elder called on General Thomas, who was still in town, and asked for his help. The Adjutant General "expressed his surprise & dislike," Elder reported, and said that while he could not directly interfere, he would speak to the commander.[122] When Elder called on Thomas a few days later, the officer explained why the commander was not cooperating with Elder and his priests. According to Thomas, Brayman had interpreted the ringing of the church bells on the occasion of the Bishop's return from Vidalia as an expression of triumph over the military commander. Elder quickly explained to the Adjutant General that "there was joy, but *no triumph.* The bells were rung for joy & to announce the fact (of my return). If the Genl. intended to do a favor," Elder pointed out, "he should feel complimented that we rejoiced & made the

---

118 *Ibid.*, Aug. 27, 1864.

119 Elder Diary, 105.

120 *Ibid.*, 103.

121 Grignon to Brayman, Natchez, Aug. 22, 1864; copy in ADNJ, File: Elder–B. Also in Gerow, *op. cit.*, 183-184. Elder Diary, 104.

122 Elder Diary, 104.

most of it."[123] In any case, Thomas informed the Bishop, General Brayman was now disposed to grant the requested passes. Acting on this information, a few days later Elder applied through Mr. O'Cavanagh for a pass to visit the military hospitals in the city. The messenger was told to come back the next day for an answer. When O'Cavanagh called at headquarters the next afternoon, he was told the pass was not ready. He then asked the officer in charge to send word when the pass would be ready. After three days passed without any word from military headquarters, the Bishop wrote to the district commander at Vicksburg for the necessary passes.[124] Sometime during the last week of September a general order was published, stipulating that a soldier, requesting a visit from a clergyman of his own denomination, may receive the same without interference.[125] Although General Brayman did not appear to be interested in improving his relations with the Catholics of Natchez,[126] the Bishop did his best to smooth things over and eliminate possible areas of friction between himself and the military authorities at Natchez. He continued to serve without distinction the spiritual needs of the Federal troops in the area. Whenever any of the officers called at the episcopal residence, they were received cordially. During purely social calls care was taken to avoid embarrassing or provoking them. When several highly emotional and inaccurate newspaper accounts of the difficulties which Elder and his priests had experienced with the military authorities in Natchez appeared, the Bishop had his vicar-general publish under his own name the following letter in the *Natchez Courier:*

> Mr. Editor
>
> Some newspaper publications have been shown to me which profess to give authentic accounts of the refusal to grant me a pass to see a Soldier in the Hospital.
>
> The articles contain some misstatements, together with language both intemperate & vulgar, & grossly disrespectful.
>
> There have been other publications made lately concerning the Bishop of Natchez, which likewise contained errors of statement & great improprieties of language & sentiment.

[123] *Ibid.*, 105.
[124] *Ibid.*, 106.
[125] Handwritten letter to the Editor of the *Natchez Courier*, St. Mary's Cathedral, Natchez, Oct. 3, 1864, unsigned; in ADNJ, File: Elder–B.
[126] General Brayman was a Baptist.

As some of these writers claim to be particularly well informed, persons not acquainted with our dispositions might be seriously disedified, supposing that we had been applied by the writers & had in some way given at least an indirect sanction or encouragement to such articles.

At the Bishop's desire therefore I express both for him & for me, our great disapprobation both of the language & the spirit of those publications; & our mortification that the writers should have had so little respect for us, as to use our names in such connection.

At the same time in justice to those interested, I correct some of the misstatements which we have noticed in those articles.

No profane language has been used by any Officer to us, nor in our presence, nor in any message to us that we have heard of.

When the pass was refused it was not said that no passes would be granted to Priests.

The Soldier in question did not die without the Sacraments. Two days after the first application, a pass was granted me for that occasion.

Recently a General Order has been published, providing that Soldiers who ask, may be visited by a Clergyman of their own denomination.

The Bishop when in Vidalia was not in (?) close confinement, nor did he receive any insult or disrespect from colored soldiers. He had the freedom of the place within the lines. The first few days he stayed at the village hotel and afterward in a private family.

We are pursuing unmolested the duties of our office, & thankful for the peace & protection that we enjoy, without any desire of further public notice.

Respectfully

(M. F. Grignon) [127]

St. Mary's Cathedral
Natchez
Octr. 3d 1864.

---

[127] Handwritten letter to the Editor of the *Natchez Courier,* St. Mary's Cathedral, Natchez, Oct. 3, 1864, unsigned; most probably a copy of the letter written by Fr. Grignon (Elder Diary, 108); in ADNJ, File: Elder—B.

In February, 1865, General Brayman was transferred.[128] He was replaced by General Davidson.[129] The new commander was a convert to the Catholic Church. From this time on relations between Bishop Elder and the military authorities at Natchez were cordial and uncomplicated.

Determined from the start of the War not to become politically involved, Bishop Elder would not have encountered ordinarily any difficulty in exercising his spiritual ministry during the Federal occupation of Mississippi. Once, however, the United States military authorities overextended themselves by interfering in purely ecclesiastical affairs, the Bishop of Natchez resisted. In so doing he defended not only the rights of the Catholic Church, but also the religious liberty of all Americans.

---

[128] *Dictionary of American Biography,* II, 611.
[129] Elder Diary, 117.

CONCLUSION

On May 4, 1865, the Civil War came to an end for Mississippians with the surrender of all the Confederate forces operating in the State to Major-General Edward R. S. Canby. As far as Bishop Elder was concerned, peace had come none too soon. As early as September, 1864, he had written longingly about peace to his metropolitan:

> It is saddening indeed to see the distress produced by the war—the more sad in some instances because the people are deprived in some parts of my diocese of those comforts of religion which form indeed the only compensation for all their afflictions.—There is so much talk on both sides of a desire of peace that I sometimes hope to see it soon:—but again it appears as if each one wanted peace only on his own terms.[1]

On this occasion Elder expressed a willingness to publish a pastoral letter on peace, instructing his people not to encourage the continuance of the War "through obstinancy," but he did not feel that he could do so "without giving offense to one side or the other."[2] At the end of March, 1865, when many other people were of the opinion that the War would soon be over, the Bishop of Natchez did not share this view.

> There appears to (be) a spirit on each side that defies all accommodation with what the other deems essential: & while the success of war depends greatly though not wholly on means—the continuance of it depends on the spirit of the people.[3]

It was this unaccommodating spirit which Elder felt would prolong the unhappy war. We can well imagine, then, the Bishop's satisfaction when he heard that the Confederate forces operating in Mississippi had finally laid down their arms.

Elder's eagerness for peace is understandable. Having never become personally involved in the politics which led to secession

---

[1] Elder to Odin, Natchez, Sept. 13, 1864; in ADNJ, Elder Letter Book —#10, 150.

[2] *Ibid.*

[3] Elder to William McCloskey, Natchez, March 23, 1865; unsigned copy in Elder's script in ASCC: Bishop Elder Papers.

and the formation of the Confederacy, but rather having always devoted himself to purely spiritual interests, he felt with the coming of peace that once again he would be able to advance the kingdom of God in Mississippi without the vicissitudes of war to check his efforts and those of his priests. Indeed, the War had not only checked, but in some areas even reversed what gains had been made prior to the outbreak of hostilities. Surveying conditions in his diocese toward the end of the War, Elder became so discouraged that at one point he considered the feasibility of resigning his see.[4]

From twelve priests which he had at the beginning of the War Elder was reduced to eight and of these, three or four were in poor health. As a consequence, at least three parishes were left without pastors and many missions deprived of regular priestly attendance. The church-rectory-school unit of one of the most promising parishes in the Diocese suffered a total loss when the three buildings burned to the ground. The convent-school at Sulphur Springs, having stood empty for most of the War, was falling into ruin. The two boarding schools on the Gulf Coast were struggling along with only a token enrollment. Several parish schools had closed down, thus dealing a severe blow to the new-born parochial school system. The finances of the Diocese presented an equally discouraging picture. Toward the end of the War, the Bishop of Natchez reported that the Diocese was several thousand dollars in debt.[5] While there was hope of paying off this debt upon the reception of a legacy, the legal difficulties connected with the case prevented Elder from being too optimistic.[6] For that matter, six months after the War he had still not gotten his hands on the promised money.[7] So poor were the finances of the Diocese that Elder, eager though he was to replace as soon as possible the clergy he lost during the War, found himself unable to make any new engagements for the education of seminarians. At the same time, he could do little to relieve the poverty of his priests, one of whom did not even have enough money with which

[4] Elder to Spalding, Natchez, Feb. 23, 1865; in AAB, 33-U-6.

[5] Elder to Spalding, Natchez, Dec. 13, 1864; in AAB, 33-T-11. Elder to Odin, Natchez, Feb. 2, 1865; in AUND: N.O. Papers.

[6] *Ibid.*

[7] Elder to Bennett, Natchez, Oct. 17, 1865; copy in ADNJ, File: Elder—A.

to buy a pair of pants.[8] As bleak as the future looked, Bishop Elder did not remain discouraged. Besides the encouragement he received from his friend, the Archbishop of Baltimore,[9] his own deep sense of faith buoyed him up and gave him the incentive to move ahead. Even before the end of hostilities he began to tackle the problems created or left waiting by the War—looking for colored Sisters to educate the many Negro children in Natchez and Vicksburg, appealing to several communities of teaching Brothers to take charge of the failing boys' school in Natchez, and arranging to have Missions preached throughout the Diocese.

Six months after the War, when in some respects the Diocese was worse off than before, the Bishop of Natchez reported that he was clinging all the more desperately to his trust in God. "In every case I feel more disposed than ever I did before to trust to the mercy of God . . . & to rely on His providence to guide me for the future." [10] Such hoped-for guidance would be badly needed by Bishop Elder and his priests, for they were entering a period in the history of the South which was to be more troubled and tragic than the war years had ever been. In fact, the Reconstruction would come very near to being, among other things, the destruction of the Catholic Church in the South.[11]

Having weathered one storm, would the Catholic Church in Mississippi be able to ride out another?

---

[8] Elder to William McCloskey, Natchez, March 23, 1865; unsigned copy in Elder's script in ASCC: Bishop Elder Papers.

[9] Elder to Spalding, Natchez, Nov. 20, 1865; in AAB, 33-U-11.

[10] *Ibid.*

[11] Maynard, *The Story of American Catholicism,* II, 25.

SOURCES

I. UNPUBLISHED SOURCES

Archives of Annunciation Church, 808 College Street, Columbus, Miss.
Baptismal Register—#1.

Archives of the Archdiocese of Baltimore, 408 N. Charles Street, Baltimore, Md.
Kenrick Papers
Spalding Papers

Archives of the Archdiocese of Cincinnati, Mount St. Mary's Seminary of the West, Norwood, Ohio.
Elder Papers

Archives of the Chicago Historical Society, Chicago, Ill.
Brayman Papers

Archives of the Diocese of Charleston, 114 Broad Street, Charleston, S.C.
Lynch Papers

Archives of the Diocese of Natchez-Jackson, 237 E. Amite Street, Jackson, Miss.
Chanche Papers
Van de Velde Papers
Elder Letter Books—#1—#10 (letter press copies of most of the letters written by Bishop Elder.)
Letters, original and copies, written and received by the clergy of the Diocese between 1841 and 1865.
Miscellaneous materials, such as necrologies, financial statements, newspaper clippings, copies of parish records, etc.

Archives of the Diocese of Mobile-Birmingham, 400 Government Street, Mobile, Ala.
Quinlan Papers

Archives of the Diocese of Pittsburgh, 111 Blvd. of Allies, Pittsburgh, Pa.
Thomas Heyden Correspondence

Archives of the Eudist Fathers, 1 rue Jean-Dolent, Paris.
Annales des Eudistes, Ms.
Dossier G (Natchez, Miss., U.S.A.)

Archives of the Sacred Congregation de Propaganda Fide, Piazza di Spagna, Rome.
Acta della Sacra Congregazione de Propaganda Fide.
Volume 200 (1837)
Volume 203 (1840)

Scritture Riferite nei Congressi, America Centrale, dal Canada all'Istmo di Panama.
Volume XIII (1841-1844)
Volume XIV (1845-1848)
Volume XV (1849-1851)
Volume XVI (1852-1854)
Volume XVII (1855-1857)
Volume XVIII (1858-1860)
Volume XIX (1861-1862)
Volume XX (1863-1865)

Archives of St. Mary's Cathedral, 107 South Union Street, Natchez, Miss.
Announcement Books—#1, #2, #3, #4.
Baptismal Register (1852-1865)
Minutes of the Meetings of the Trustees of the D'Evereux Hall Orphan Asylum (1858-1865)
Minutes of the Meetings of the Roman Catholic Society of Christians of Natchez (1821-1861)

Archives of St. Mary's Seminary, Roland and Belvedere Avenues, Baltimore, Md.
Seminary Registers, Vol. I

Archives of St. Paul's Church, 714 Crawford Street, Vicksburg, Miss.
Baptismal Register (1852-1870)
Marriage Register (1852-1886)

Archives of the Sisters of Charity of Cincinnati, Mount St. Joseph, Ohio.
Memoirs of Civil War Nurses
Bishop Elder Papers

Archives of the Daughters of Charity, St. Joseph's Central House, Emmitsburg, Md.
Civil War Annals

Archives of the Sisters of Mercy, St. Francis Xavier Academy, Vicksburg, Miss.
Memoirs of Sister M. Ignatius Sumner
Annals of the Sisters of Mercy (1860-1865)

Archives of the Sisters of St. Joseph of Bourg, 3 rue du Lycee, Bourg-en-Bresse, Ain, France.
Lettres de Baie St. Louis et Nouvelle-Orleans.

Archives of the Sisters of St. Joseph of Bourg, 1400 Mirabeau Avenue, New Orleans, La.
Bay St. Louis Correspondence, 1854-1865.

Archives of the Sisters of St. Joseph of Carondelet, 2307 South Lindbergh Boulevard, St. Louis, Mo.
Notes on Sulphur Springs, Miss. foundation, 1890, 1891.

Archives of the University of Notre Dame, Notre Dame, Ind.
David Conyngham Ms.
Natchez Papers
New Orleans Papers
Cincinnati Papers

Georgetown University Archives
Bishop O'Connor, S.J. Papers
Bishop Elder Papers

Marillac Seminary Archives, Normandy, Mo.
Charity Hospital Book
Annals of the Daughters of Charity, 1863, 1893.

Mississippi State Archives, Department of Archives and History, Jackson, Miss.
Drennan Diary
Governors' Correspondence

Mulvihill Family Library, 2727 Washington St., Vicksburg, Miss.
Michael J. Mulvihill Ms.

Old Court House Museum, Vicksburg, Miss.
Journal of Mrs. R. J. Cook of Bovina, Miss., (1855-1858).

II. PUBLISHED SOURCES

Annales de la Propagation de la foi, Lyon: L'Oeuvre de la Propagation de la foi, 1850, 1884.

Annals of the Propagation of the Faith, London: Society for the Propagation of the Faith, 1857-1868.

A Tract for the Times: Slavery And Abolitionism, being the substance of a Sermon preached by Rt. Rev. A. Verot, D.D., Vicar Apostolic of Florida in St. Augustine's Church, St. Augustine, Fla. on Jan. 4, 1861. /n.d./ n.p./

Berichte der Leopoldinen-Stiftung im Kaiserthume Oesterreich, Wien: Leopoldinen-Stiftung, XVI (1843), XIX (1846), XXII (1850).

Concilia Provincialia Baltimori habita ab anno 1829 usque ad annum 1849, Baltimore, 1851.

Concilium Neo-Aurelianense Provinciale Primum. Habitum Anno 1856. N.O.: Le Propagateur catholique, 1857.

Ellis (ed.), *Documents of American Catholic History,* Milwaukee: Bruce Publishing Co., 1956.

Gerow (ed.), *Diary of Bishop William Henry Elder,* Jackson: Richard O. Gerow, 1961.

Guilday (ed.), *The National Pastorals of the American Hierarchy, 1792-1919,* Washington: National Catholic Welfare Council, 1923.

(Martin), *Lettre Pastorale de Mgr. L'Evêque de Natchitoches à l'Occasion de La Guerre du Sud pour Son Independence,* 21 août 1861. /n.p.

Metropolitan Catholic Almanac and Laity's Directory for the United States, Canada and British Provinces, (The), Baltimore: Lucas, 1844, 1851, 1852, 1853, 1857; Baltimore: John Murphy & Co., 1861.

Missions Catholiques (Les), LXV, Sept. 17, 1863.

Official Records of the Union and Confederate Navies in the War of the Rebellion, Washington: U.S. Government Printing Office, 1904, Ser. II, Vol. III.

Rietti (ed.), *Military Annals of Mississippi: Military Organizations which entered the service of the Confederate States of America,* Jackson: J. C. Rietti, /n.d./

Sadlier's Catholic Almanac and Ordo, New York: D. & J. Sadlier & Co., 1864, 1865.

Shearer, *Pontificia Americana: A Documentary History of the Catholic Church in the United States (1784-1884),* Washington: Catholic University Press, 1933.

Synodus Diocesana Natchetensis prima, habita ab illmo. et rmo. Gulielmo Henrico Elder, Episcopo Natchetensi, hebdomada secunda post Pascha anno 1858. New Orleans, 1858.

Tourscher (ed.), *The Kenrick-Frenaye Correspondence, 1830-1868,* Lancaster, Pa.: Wickersham Co., 1920.

War of the Rebellion: A Compilation of the Official Records of the Union and Confederate Armies, Washington: U.S. Government Printing Office, 1880-1901, Ser. III, Vol. I, IV, Ser. IV, Vol. I, III.

III. NEWSPAPERS

Baltimore	*Catholic Mirror* (1861-1864)
Cincinnati	*Catholic Telegraph* (1864)
Columbus, Ga.	*Pacificator* (1864)
Natchez	*Daily Courier* (1855)
	Free Trader (1842, 1848)
	Semi-Weekly Courier (1848)
New Orleans	*Catholic Standard* (1861)
	Morning Star (1887)
	Propagateur catholique (1861)
	Times-Democrat (1887, 1893)
New York	*Freeman's Journal* (1858-1864)
	Tablet (1860)
Vicksburg	*Daily Herald* (1864)

BIBLIOGRAPHY

IV. REFERENCE WORKS

Amann (ed.), *Personnel of the Civil War,* New York: Thomas Yoseloff, 1961.

Appleton's Cyclopaedia of American Biography, New York: Appleton and Company, 1888.

Catholic Encyclopedia, New York: Appleton Company, 1907.

Dictionary of American Biography, New York: Charles Scribner & Son, 1929.

Dyer, *A Compendium of the War of the Rebellion,* New York: Thomas Yoseloff, 1959.

O'Donnell, *The Catholic Hierarchy of the United States, 1790-1922,* Washington: Catholic University Press, 1922.

The Revised Code of Laws of Mississippi, Natchez: Francis Baker, 1824.

V. BOOKS AND PERIODICALS

Abell and others, *A History of the United States,* New York: Fordham University Press, 1951.

Audinet, J., "L'Enseignement 'De Ecclesia' A St. Sulpice Sous Le Premier Empire, Et Les Debuts Du Gallicanisme Modere," in *Unam Sanctam,* 34 (1960), 115-139.

Barton, *Angels of the Battlefield: A History of the Labors of the Catholic Sisterhoods in the Late Civil War,* Philadelphia, 1898.

Baudier, Roger, *The Catholic Church in Louisiana,* New Orleans: Roger Baudier, 1939.

Bernard, Mother M., *The Story of the Sisters of Mercy in Mississippi,* New York: P. J. Kenedy and Son, 1931.

Bettersworth, John, *Confederate Mississippi,* Baton Rouge: Louisiana State University Press, 1943.

(ed.), *Mississippi in the Confederacy,* Vol. I, Jackson: The Mississippi Department of Archives and History, 1961.

Mississippi: A History, Austin: The Steck Company, 1959.

Blied, Benjamin, "Catholic Charity in the Army, 1861-1865," in *Social Justice Review,* XXXIII (Sept. 1940), 166-168.

Catholics and the Civil War, Milwaukee: (author), 1945.

Boyd, Jesse L., *A Popular History of the Baptists in Mississippi,* Jackson: The Baptist Press, 1930.

Brokhage, *Francis Patrick Kenrick's Opinion on Slavery,* Washington: Catholic University of America Press, 1955.

Butsch, Joseph, "Negro Catholics in the United States," in *Catholic Historical Review,* III (April 1917), 33-51.

Cain, John B., *Methodism in the Mississippi Conference, 1846-1870,* Jackson: Mississippi Conference Historical Society, 1939.

Cabaniss and Cabaniss, "Religion in Ante-Bellum Mississippi," in the *Journal of Mississippi History,* VI (Oct. 1944), 191-224.

Carter and Ragusin, *Gulf Coast Country,* New York: Duell, Sloan and Pearce, 1951.

Catholic Action of the South, Natchez Centennial Edition, Oct. 14, 1937.

Claiborne, John F., *Mississippi, as a Province, Territory, and State,* Jackson: Power & Barksdale, 1880. Vol. I.

Clarke, Richard H., *Lives of the Deceased Bishops of the Catholic Church in the United States,* 3 Vols., New York: P. O'Shea, Pub., 1872.

Coulter, E. Merton, *The Confederate States of America, 1861-1865,* Baton Rouge: Louisiana State University Press, 1950.

Cumming, Kate, *Journal of Hospital Life,* Louisville, 1866.

Curley, Michael J., C.SS.R., *Church and State in the Spanish Floridas, 1783-1822,* Washington: Catholic University of America Press, 1940.

Venerable John Neumann, C.SS.R., Washington: Catholic University of America Press, 1952.

Dabney, Thomas Ewing, *One Hundred Great Years,* Baton Rouge: Louisiana State University Press, 1944.

"The Butler Regime in Louisiana," in *The Louisiana Historical Quarterly,* XXVII (April 1944), 487-526.

Daniel, W. Harrison, "An Aspect of Church and State Relations in the Confederacy: Southern Protestantism and the Office of Army Chaplain," in *North Carolina Historical Review,* XXXVI (Jan. 1959), 47-71.

Delanglez, Jean, S.J., *The French Jesuits in Lower Louisiana, 1700-1763,* Washington: Catholic University of America Press, 1935.

"Documents from our Archives: Diary of Bishop Rosati; Rosati to Cardinal Consalvi, April 2, 1823," in *St. Louis Catholic Historical Review,* III (1921), n. 313.

Dumond, Dwight L., *Antislavery Origins of the Civil War in the United States,* Ann Arbor: The University of Michigan Press, 1959.

Easterly, Frederick J., C.M., *The Life of the Rt. Rev. Joseph Rosati, First Bishop of St. Louis, 1789-1843,* Washington: Catholic University of America Press, 1942.

Eaton, Clement, *Freedom of Thought in the Old South,* Durham, N.C.: Duke University Press, 1940.

Elder, Susan Blanchard, *Character-Glimpses of Most Reverend William Henry Elder, D.D.*, New York & Cincinnati: Pustet & Co., 1910.

Ellis, John T., *American Catholicism,* Chicago: The University of Chicago Press, 1956.

Eugenie, Sister M., "Sisters of St. Joseph of Bourg—New Orleans Province," unpublished M.A. thesis, New Orleans: University of Loyola, 1953.

Federal Writers Project of the WPA, *Mississippi, A Guide to the Magnolia State,* New York: Hastings House, 1946.

Gallagher, Sister Ann Seton, "A Study of the Nursing Activities of Sister Anthony O'Connell, Sister of Charity of Cincinnati," unpublished M.A. thesis, Washington: The Catholic University of America, 1957.

Garraghan, Gilbert J., S.J., *The Catholic Church in Chicago,* Chicago: Loyola University Press, 1921.

The Jesuits in the Middle United States, 3 vols., New York: America Press, 1938.

(ed.), "Right Reverend James Oliver Van de Velde, D.D.," in *Illinois Catholic Historical Review,* IX (July 1926), 56-70.

General Directory for the City of Vicksburg, Vicksburg: H. C. Clarke, Publisher, 1860.

Germain, Aidan Henry, O.S.B., "Catholic Military and Naval Chaplains, 1776-1917," in *Catholic Historical Review,* XV (n.s. IX) (July 1929), 171-178.

Gerow, Richard O., *Catholicity in Mississippi, Natchez:* (author), 1939.

Cradle Days of St Mary's at Natchez, Natchez: (author), 1941.

Gillard, John T., *Colored Catholics in the United States,* Baltimore: Josephite Press, 1941.

The Catholic Church and the American Negro, Baltimore: St. Joseph's Society Press, 1929.

Goodspeed (ed.), *Biographical and Historical Memoirs of Mississippi,* 2 Vols., Chicago: The Goodspeed Publishing Co., 1891.

Guilday, Peter, *A History of the Council of Baltimore, 1791-1884,* New York: Macmillan Co., 1932.

Hayes, *A Historical Sketch of the Catholic Church in Laurel and Jones County, Miss.,* Ellisville, Miss.: the Progress-Item, 1937.

Herbermann, Charles G., *The Sulpicians in the United States,* New York: The Encyclopedia Press, 1916.

In and About Vicksburg, Vicksburg: The Gibraltar Publishing Co., 1890.

Jackson, Luther P., "Religious Instruction of Negroes, 1830-1860, with Special Reference to South Carolina," in *Journal of Negro History,* XV, 72-114.

Janssens, Francis A., *Sketch of the Catholic Church in the City of Natchez, Miss., on the occasion of the consecration of its Cathedral, Sept. 19, 1886,* /n.p./n.d./

Jolly, Ellen Ryan, *Nuns of the Battlefield,* Providence: The Providence Visitor Press, 1927.

Jones, John G., *A Concise History of the Introduction of Protestantism into Mississippi and the Southwest,* St. Louis: P. M. Pinckard, 1866.

Kennedy, Hon. Ambrose, *Memorial to "The Nuns of the Battlefield,"* Washington: U.S. Government Printing Office, 1918.

Kenny, Michael, *Catholic Culture in Alabama,* New York: The America Press, 1931.

Kenrick, Francis P., *Theologia Moralis,* Vol. I, Baltimore, 1841.

Krieger, Byron J., *Seventy-Five Years of Service,* New Orleans: Redemptorist Fathers, 1923.

Lang, John H., *History of Harrison County, Mississippi,* Gulfport: (author), 1936.

Lebreton, Dagmar Renshaw, *Chahta-Ima, The Life of Adrien-Emmanuel Rouquette,* Baton Rouge: Louisiana State University Press, 1947.

Leflon, Jean, *Monsieur Emery,* Paris, 1944.

Lipscomb, Oscar H., "The Administration of John Quinlan, Second Bishop of Mobile, 1859-1883," unpublished M.A. thesis, Washington: Catholic University of America, 1959.

Lipscomb, Dr. W. L., *A History of Columbus, Mississippi, during the 19th Century,* Columbus, Miss.: S. D. Lee Chapter of the Daughters of the Confederacy, 1909.

Lowry, Robert and McCardle, *A History of Mississippi,* Jackson: R. H. Henry and Co., 1891.

Macarius, Brother, *A Century of Service for the Sacred Heart in the United States,* /n.p./ 1946.

Maynard, Theodore, *The Story of American Catholicism,* New York: The Macmillan Company, 1945.

McCain, William D., "Education in Mississippi in 1860," in *Journal of Mississippi History,* XXII (July 1960), 153-166.

Meline and McSweeney, *The Story of The Mountain,* 2 Vols., Emmitsburg, Md.: Weekly Chronicle, 1911.

Mereness, Newton D., *The Journal of Divon d'Artaguette, 1722-1723, in Travels in the American Colonies,* London: Macmillan Co., 1916.

Messmer et al. (ed.), *The Works of the Right Reverend John England,* 7 Vols., Cleveland: Arthur H. Clark Company, 1908.

Mississippi in the War Between the States, Jackson: Mississippi Commission on the War Between the States, 1961.

Moore, Edith Wyatt, *Natchez Under-the-Hill*, Natchez: Southern Historical Publications, Inc., 1958.

Moore, John Hebron, "Economic Conditions in Mississippi on the Eve of the Civil War," in *Journal of Mississippi History*, XXII (July 1960), 167-178.

Moore, Margaret DesChamps, "Religion in Mississippi in 1860," in *Journal of Mississippi History*, XXII (Oct. 1960), 223-238.

Nicoly and Hay (ed.), *Abraham Lincoln: Complete Works*, 2 Vols., New York, 1920.

Murphy, Robert Joseph, "The Catholic Church in the United States during the Civil War Period (1852-1866)," in *Records of the American Catholic Historical Society*, XXXIX (Dec. 1928), 271-346.

Norton, Herman, "Revivalism in the Confederate Armies," in *Civil War History*, VI (Dec. 1960), 410-424.

The Organization and Function of the Confederate Chaplaincy, 1861-1865, Ph. D. dissertation in Vanderbilt Library, 1956.

O'Daniel, Victor F., O.P., *The Dominican Province of St. Joseph*, New York: National Headquarters of the Holy Name Society, 1942.

The Father of the Church in Tennessee, Washington: The Dominicana, 1926.

Overdyke, *The Know-Nothing Party in the South*, Baton Rouge: Louisiana State University Press, 1950.

Partin, "An Alabama Confederate Soldier's Report to His Wife," in *The Alabama Review*, III (1950), 22-36.

Parton, James, "Our Roman Catholic Brethren," in *Atlantic Monthly*, XXI (April 1868), 432-451; (May 1868), 556-574.

Phillips, Ulrich Bonnell, *Life and Labor in the Old South*, Boston: Little, Brown and Company, 1930.

Pressly, *Americans Interpret Their Civil War*, Princeton: Princeton University Press, 1954.

Price, Beulah M. D'Olive, "The Rev. John Baptist Mouton: Confederate Chaplain," in *Journal of Mississippi History*, XXIV (April 1962), 102-106.

Rainwater, Percy Lee, *Mississippi, Storm Center of Secession 1856-1861*, Baton Rouge: Louisiana State University Press, 1938.

Randall, James G., *The Civil War and Reconstruction*, Boston: D. C. Heath and Company, 1937.

Rice, Madeleine Hooke, *American Catholic Opinion in the Slavery Controversy*, New York: Columbia University Press, 1944.

Roemer, Theodore, O.F.M. Cap., *The Catholic Church in the United States*, St. Louis: B. Herder Book Co., 1950.

Ten Decades of Alms, St. Louis: B. Herder Book Co., 1942.

Romero, Sidney J., "The Confederate Chaplain," in *Civil War History*, (June 1955), 127-140.

Rowland, Dunbar, *Mississippi*, 3 Vols., Atlanta: Southern Historical Publishing Association, 1907.

Mississippi: The Heart of the South, 2 Vols., Chicago-Jackson: The S.J. Clarke Publishing Co., 1925.

Saunders, Dr. P. H., "Col. Felix Labauve," in *Publications of Mississippi Historical Society*, VII (1903), 131-140.

Shea, John G., *History of the Catholic Church in the United States*, Vol. IV, New York: D. H. McBride & Company, 1892.

History of the Catholic Missions Among the Indian Tribes of the United States (1529-1854), New York: Edward Dunigan & Brother, 1885.

Life and Times of Archbishop John Carroll, New York: John G. Shea, 1888.

Silver, James W., *Confederate Morale and Church Propaganda*, Tuscaloosa, Ala.: Confederate Publishing Company, Inc., 1957.

(ed.) *Mississippi in the Confederacy*, Vol. II, Jackson: The Mississippi Department of Archives and History, 1961.

Spalding, John Lancaster, *The Life of the Most Rev. M. J. Spalding, D.D., Archbishop of Baltimore*, Baltimore: John Murphy & Co., 1873.

Stock, Leo Francis, "Catholic Participation in the Diplomacy of the Southern Confederacy," in *Catholic Historical Review*, XVI (April 1930), 1-18.

Sweet, William W., *The Story of Religion in America*, New York: Harper Bros., 1950.

Sydnor, Charles S., *A Gentleman of the Old Natchez Region—Benjamin L. C. Wailes*, Durham, N.C.: Duke University Press, 1938.

Taylor, "When the Ministry Was Ordered to the Front," in *Harper's Weekly*, LI (Jan. 26, 1907), 120-139.

Theobald, Stephen L., "Catholic Missionary Work among the Colored People of the United States (1776-1866)," in *Records of the American Catholic Historical Society of Philadelphia*, XXXV (1924), 325-344.

Thompson, "St. Stanislaus School for Boys," in *The Daily Herald*, Biloxi and Gulfport, Mississippi Coast, July 29, 1958.

Vally, Louis, "An East Mississippi Pastor," in *The Messenger of the Sacred Heart*, III (n.s. xxiii) (Jan. 1888), 17-22.

Walker, Peter F., *Vicksburg, A People at War, 1860-1865*, Chapel Hill, N.C.: The University of North Carolina Press, 1960.

Walmsley, James E., "The Presidential Campaign of 1844 in Mississippi," in *Publications of the Mississippi Historical Society*, IX (1906), 179-197.

Wight, Willard, "Bishop Elder and the Civil War," in *Catholic Historical Review,* XLIV (Oct. 1958), 290-306.

"The Bishop of Natchez and the Confederate Chaplaincy," in *Mid-America,* XXXIX (n.s. xxxviii), No. 2, 67-72.

"The Churches and the Confederate Cause," in *Civil War History,* VI (Dec. 1960), 361-373.

"Some Wartime Letters of Bishop Lynch," in *Catholic Historical Review,* XLIII (Oct. 1957), 20-37.

Wiley, Bell Irvin, *Johnny Reb,* New York: Rinehart & Company, 1943.

Southern Negroes, New York: Rinehart & Company, Inc., 1953 (2nd edition).

INDEX